The Falklands Guns

DEDICATION

I dedicate this book to the Fallen of the 1982 Falklands Campaign, especially those who have no known grave, and to those who carry the painful wounds of conflicts before and since, both visibly and invisibly, to this day.

The Falklands Guns

The Story of the Captured Argentine Artillery that Became Part of the RAF Regiment

Mike Fonfé

AN IMPRINT OF PEN & SWORD BOOKS LTD
YORKSHIRE – PHILADELPHIA

First published in Great Britain in 2023 by
FRONTLINE BOOKS
an imprint of Pen & Sword Books Ltd
Yorkshire – Philadelphia

ISBN 978-1-52677-442-2

A CIP catalogue record for this book is available from the British Library.

Typeset by Concept, Huddersfield, West Yorkshire, HD4 5JL
Printed on paper from a sustainable source by
CPI Group (UK) Ltd, Croydon CR0 4YY

Pen & Sword Books Ltd incorporates the Imprints of Aviation, Atlas, Family History, Fiction, Maritime, Military, Discovery, Politics, History, Archaeology, Select, Wharncliffe Local History, Wharncliffe True Crime, Military Classics, Wharncliffe Transport, Leo Cooper, The Praetorian Press, Remember When, White Owl, Seaforth Publishing and Frontline Books.

For a complete list of Pen & Sword titles please contact
PEN & SWORD BOOKS LTD
47 Church Street, Barnsley, South Yorkshire, S70 2AS, England
E-mail: enquiries@pen-and-sword.co.uk
Website: www.pen-and-sword.co.uk
or
PEN & SWORD BOOKS
1950 Lawrence Rd, Havertown, PA 19083, USA
E-mail: uspen-and-sword@casematepublishers.com
Website: www.penandswordbooks.com

Contents

List of Illustrations and Maps

Illustrations

Maps

Foreword

By Fabian Ochsner

After graduating from the Swiss Air Force Officer School as a 35mm Oerlikon air-defender, I joined the Oerlikon Company in 1984. My first assignment was as an instructor in operations and tactics at the Oerlikon Overseas Customer Gunnery School at Faldingworth in the United Kingdom. I still recall the very special emotion I felt when I first saw the Oerlikons just returned from the Falklands Campaign and witnessed how they were brought back to life to be used by the Royal Air Force. Two years later it was a great privilege to return and visit the newly set up 2729 Squadron of the Royal Auxiliary Air Force Regiment at RAF Waddington and see the young men and women crewing the Oerlikons. I am honour-bound to say we, as a company, used the fact that the Oerlikon 35mm gun and the Skyguard fire-control unit had played a significant role in the 1982 Falklands Campaign; this was an important message that we took to our customers worldwide. I did this proudly throughout my parallel careers in both the Oerlikon Company and in the Swiss Air Force. Eventually I became the commander of the largest Oerlikon Regiment in the Swiss Militia; at the same time I rose to become the Chief Executive Officer of today's direct successor to Oerlikon, Rheinmetall Air Defence AG, a company which continues to design highly sophisticated 35mm calibre-based air defence systems.

The story behind the UK Oerlikons has to be the most unusual one and its charm has not diminished in the four decades that have passed. Many of the exciting details might have been lost for ever had they not been preserved by the original players of that time. What unfolds is a very remarkable and fascinating piece of history brought to life by the main actor of the day: Mike Fonfé. Due to his single-minded initiative as a very junior staff officer in the Ministry of Defence of the United Kingdom and his recognition of the quality and operational effectiveness of what was then the newest and most advanced anti-aircraft gun and radar system of the time, the equipment was recovered from a far-away battlefield, evaluated, refurbished to 'as new' and entered service in the air defence of the UK in the NATO order of battle – an unprecedented event indeed.

What is more extraordinary is that Mike was actually directed to pursue this idea as a side-line to his main staff responsibilities, a task to be carried out in his own time. He became the principal staffer, the project manager and, ultimately, the commanding officer of the new unit. His part-time effort covered every aspect of introducing a complex and valuable piece of equipment into Royal Air Force service, from raising the necessary funds, to carrying out a feasibility study, to staffing it all the way to Air Force Board approval and then commanding the unit of his own creation. Not content with that, he also pioneered the breaking of the gender barrier to employ females alongside males in the full spectrum of combat duties in all ranks operating both the guns and the radars, using reservists forty years before the British opened up the same opportunity to their Regular, full-time armed forces.

The professionalism and motivation of a tiny number of full-time Regulars enabled the unit to recruit and train part-time civilians at breakneck speed to achieve NATO operational declaration in the same timescale as a full-time Regular unit, which demonstrates why the all-volunteer British Armed Forces, based on meritocracy, perform so well in the global arena.

Thanks to Mike's precise recollection of the past details, you will now have the pleasure of diving into a fascinating period in time to read the story of how the Argentine Oerlikons and their Skyguard radars entered operational service in the Royal Air Force at the height of the Cold War. It should come as no surprise that Mike Fonfé became the first Gold Medal recipient and first Life Member of the Oerlikon Alumni. This is his story.

Fabian Ochsner
Former chief executive officer,
Rheinmetall Air Defence AG

Preface

My Contribution to Galtieri's Downfall

Immensely frustratingly for me, my only direct contribution to General Galtieri's downfall in the South Atlantic was to fight him with model aircraft. In my previous but two appointments, I was the RAF Rapier instructor-in-gunnery at the Royal School of Artillery, Larkhill, where I had invented a totally new system of aircraft recognition training for the British Army; I also authored the new Army coded aircraft recognition training manual. The 'Fonfé System' had come about early in my tour at Larkhill when, as the RAF Rapier Instructor, I sat in on my first army aircraft recognition lesson on the IL-18 helicopter, NATO code-named for reporting clarity as the HIP. I clearly remember the army sergeant's opening words: 'Now gentlemen, you can always recognize this 'ere as an 'IP 'cos Russian T-54 tanks is in the foreground.' In that Eureka moment, I realized that there was something seriously wrong with army anti-aircraft training. When I reported this to my colonel chief instructor, his solution was short and simple: 'Well, Mike, it's the Royal Air Force that flies the planes; they are your mates, right? So why don't you sort it out?' And so, I did. In place of randomly accumulated magazine pictures taken at airshows over many years, each and every British Army and RAF anti-aircraft unit received a structured training package of scaled aircraft images at exactly the size that they would be seen in the missile operator's optics. To commit to an opening fire decision, the pass mark was 100 per cent; in the event of not being sure, one had to declare 'Not Recognized', when the decision to open fire would depend on orders in place for friendly aircraft being in the area or not. Each unit pack was around 4,500 35mm slides appropriate to their theatres of operation and I photographed all the master images. In the process I was given a Ministry of Defence Inventor's Award of £1,000 for my efforts and, more frivolously, the Royal School of Artillery's *Golden Film Award* for shooting more rolls of 35mm film than any other British Army photographer. As an additional gift, the School of Artillery gave me a spoof, framed picture of an Army coded aircraft recognition poster of the series I had also designed, with me in place of the aircraft as a cartoon Baldeagle, a moniker that has stuck to me ever since. The final twist of humour, however, came from the RAF personnel management centre, which saw fit to post me from Larkhill, not to my heart's desire of a Rapier squadron, but to command of an RAF Regiment infantry squadron on internal security rotations to Northern Ireland, about as far away from air defence as it was possible to get. Back to the posters, I still had the last laugh. The printing masters for every one came to me for final checking before the print run of thousands. I added a tiny bald eagle's head and so there is a little me smiling an invisible 'Gotcha!' in just about every British Army garrison office. The happy postscript to this was that, eventually, my training material was adopted by virtually every anti-aircraft unit in NATO, in a final production run amounting to about 1.3 million 35mm slides, for which further small royalties came to me. Little was I to know that the measurement of 35mm would figure so large in my later RAF career, which is how I now came to play my part in the downfall of the Argentine president, General Galtieri.

On the Monday immediately following the Falklands invasion, now at my Ministry of Defence desk in London, I organized the scratch production of aircraft recognition training slides of Argentine Pucaras, Skyhawks and Super Etendards for the British Rapier and Blowpipe anti-aircraft units going to war. This involved calling up a retired modelmaker, who I knew had hand-built models for the RAF's Fighter Command. Such was his motivation that, following my phone call, he carved an excellent scaled likeness of the Pucara for me from scratch out of solid balsa wood overnight and it was in my hands the next day. That evening, taking a route diversion on my commute home from the MoD, I visited my favourite London toy and model shop and bought the best possible plastic scale models of the Skyhawk and Super Etendard, neither aircraft being on our NATO aircraft recognition list. At home I assembled them, all bombed-up and painted to match the aircraft paint schemes of the training series I had invented.

Next day, as an alternative to my lunchtime jog around St James's Park, I visited the Soho studio which had previously duplicated the first batch of 120,000 aircraft recognition slides for the Army and RAF. Luckily, they still had the master slide backgrounds and slide-labelling machine from the production run of three years previously. The following day, with all three models in hand, I nipped out for my lunchbreak, set the models up in the studio and photographed them in the same ninety-four standard viewing angle sequences and ranges of all the other slides in the Army programme. The films were developed overnight, with each aircraft flight position married up with the corresponding slide background for that flight attitude and rephotographed as composite pictures of aircraft-plus-background. The end product was that for any random numbered picture of either the Pucara, Skyhawk or Super Etendard, the flight attitude, viewing range and background imagery of that slide number would be identical to every other aircraft in the entire NATO series with the same slide number. Thus the only clue as to the identity of the aircraft would be the aircraft itself, with no visual cues at all coming from the slide background, however interesting it might be. Moreover, by projecting the same numbered slides of opposing aircraft side-by-

Fig. 1. NATO poster showing how to recognize the author Baldeagle at a range of 1km.

side at the same time, an instant, direct, visual comparison of, say the Sea Harrier, or a Harrier GR3, could be made at every possible viewing angle with its look-alike opposite number, the Argentine Skyhawk, at exactly the size they would appear in the weapon optics, typically that of a squashed fruit fly.

Back to the British response to the Argentine invasion, codenamed Operation Corporate. The sets of aircraft recognition training slides of Argentine enemy aircraft were now labelled, boxed-up and ready to go – the only snag was that the slides were still in Soho while the Rapier and Blowpipe crews were already embarking on the next wave of ships about to sail. I aired my problem to a staffer in the Air Force operations room, who told me that the Defence Secretary, John Nott, was flying out by helicopter to the departing Task Force for final briefings to take place at sea. If I could possibly get the slides to the staffer immediately, he would ensure they were included in the Defence Secretary's considerable bundles of last-minute briefing material. And so, I zoomed round to Soho, picked up the slide sets and delivered them to MoD Main Building.

Breathlessly, I got back to my office only to find my air commodore Director demanding an explanation for my absence. As I confessed the nature of my lunch-time expeditions, I could see him becoming quite vexed. 'It's not your job,' he said, pointing out that as his principal Rapier specialist, I should stick to RAF Rapier matters. 'The job should have been done by the Army.' I protested, 'But, but, Sir, I invented the training system. I personally have the closest access to the production assets here in London to do the job and I have done it in less time than it would have taken me even to explain to the Army what was required and, finally, Sir, I can say with absolute certainly, they would have literally missed the boat.' This cut little ice with the Director and was an indication to us junior staff officers that our top-level RAF Regimental masters did not wish to appear too keen to participate in the only all-arms, tri-Service 'proper shooting war' to come our way since the Suez débâcle of twenty-six years before.

Surely, if any Harriers were going to go to war on an airfield in an area carved out of a rear battlefield, in range of the enemy special forces and aircraft, then it was the essence of our Regimental Corps' very existence to be there, in order to secure and protect that forward airfield with our armoured fighting vehicles and the Rapier missiles that we had spent our entire careers training to use to the highest degree of efficiency. Quite simply we, the RAF's organic force protection force, needed to be there. Not so; the dictum from the top came back: 'If we are needed, they will send for us, period.' We squadron leader junior staff officers were stunned. And so, for my only contribution to Operation Corporate and Galtieri's downfall, I basically got a bollocking.

Introduction

This book is about the ex-Argentine Swiss-made Oerlikon twin 35mm anti-aircraft artillery pieces and their Skyguard all-weather fire-control radars deployed around the Falkland Islands in 1982 by the ill-fated Argentine *Malvinas* invasion force. The weapons, worth £30 million and virtually brand new, fell into British hands with the unconditional Argentine surrender. Three years later they entered Royal Air Force service as part of NATO's air defence of the UK at the height of the Cold War. Not since the Nazi submarine U-570[1] fell into the Royal Navy's hands during the Battle of the Atlantic to become HMS *Graph* has such a major prize of war from a battlefield been used to enhance the operational capability of the British Armed Forces as a named and numbered unit.

So successful was the equipment in British service that additional radars were purchased and the original single RAF unit was expanded into a wing of two squadrons: one to defend the Airborne Early Warning and Control System (AWACS) aircraft base at RAF Waddington and the other to defend the nearby Tornado air defence fighter base at RAF Coningsby. Extraordinarily, forty years on from the Falklands Campaign, and long after the end of the Cold War, these very same ex-Argentine Skyguard radars are still in active RAF service in 2022: they are now used to give electronic warfare and flak-avoidance training to NATO aircrews and also to police British low-flying training areas. In the first quarter of the twenty-first century, the Oerlikon-Skyguard combination continues to be one of the most potent anti-aircraft weapon systems in operational service in dozens of countries around the world, including China. Indeed, China has cloned hundreds of Oerlikon twin 35mm guns and Skyguard from an insane small-scale sale by Switzerland, while the Swiss manufacturer Oerlikon-Buhrle has in turn sold out to the German armament group, Rheinmetall Air Defence AG.

The book itself is in four parts. The first part deals with the invasion of the Falklands and introduces the players, British and Argentine, up to the point just before combat begins. The second part covers the retaking of the Islands, with particular focus on the anti-aircraft battles by both sides: the Argentine Army, Navy, Marines and Air Force versus the British Royal Navy, Royal Artillery, Special Air Service Regiment, Royal Air Force and RAF Regiment, to give an overall picture of the air-to-ground attacks and the retaliatory ground-to-air defence aspects of the campaign. The effectiveness of anti-aircraft weapons at sea and on land both shaped and restricted the use of air power on both sides and many lessons can be drawn from the experiences. Interestingly, the two most successful anti-aircraft weapons were Sidewinder missiles and troopers of the Special Air Service, whose success highlighted the vulnerability of aircraft on the ground.

In reverse, the most successful killers of the Argentine 20mm Rheinmetall AA guns were 2 Para's Milan anti-tank, wire-guided missiles at Goose Green. Also at Goose Green, it was small arms ground-fire from 2 Para that disabled the Skyguard radar there; its two associated twin 35mm Oerlikon guns on the isthmus survived completely intact the final cluster bomb and rocket attack on the Goose Green garrison by the Harrier GR3s that prompted the Argentine overnight surrender to the Paras. Indeed, these two Oerlikons were deemed to be in such good condition that, following the full British recovery of the Falklands, they were moved by RAF Chinook from Goose Green directly to Sid's Strip at San Carlos Water, the Harrier forward operating base, on the initiative of a junior RAF Regiment officer, Flying Officer Peter Kaye, who actually test-fired them. However, they were never manned operationally and were abandoned for a second time when Kaye completed his short Falklands tour.

Extraordinarily, the other Skyguard-Oerlikon killer was the Vulcan heavy nuclear bomber, commanded by Squadron Leader Neil McDougal of 44 (Rhodesia) Squadron, who dived his massive bomber in like a ground-attack fighter to destroy a Skyguard fire-control radar and kill its crew with a single Shrike anti-radar missile, for which he was rightly awarded the Distinguished Flying Cross. That Vulcan sortie, however, is better remembered in aviation lore for its emergency landing, with a broken refuelling probe, in neutral Brazil, with the other, misfired but very much secret Shrike still attached under its wing.

The third part of the book covers the recovery of the abandoned Oerlikon guns and radars, which were scattered across a wild and hostile terrain the size of Wales, some 12,800km away from the United Kingdom, together with the staff work required to grasp this unexpected windfall of foreign equipment that was, in many aspects, better than our own. It was an exercise against a tide of conventional wisdom, military and civilian bureaucracy, cultural inertia, vested interest and simply 'not invented here'. In short, it was a Sisyphean undertaking akin to rolling a large lead ball up a steep, greasy hill. However, three years of hard staff work paid off when the Air Force Board approved the introduction of the captured Oerlikons into RAF service on 1 April 1985 as 2729 (City of Lincoln) Squadron, Royal Auxiliary Air Force Regiment; as a reward for my initiative in the process, I was finally let loose, back into air defence, and given command of the new unit.

Later a second Skyguard-Oerlikon Squadron, 2890, would be formed, also under my initiative, with both squadrons coming under command of 1339 Wing, RAuxAF Regiment. All these unit numbers had previous, strong historical associations that pre-date the RAF Regiment: they belonged to founder RAF formations that had previously been raised back in the 1940s, actually at RAF

Waddington, as forerunner numbered RAF airfield defence ground gunner squadrons which were then absorbed into the RAF Regiment when it formally formed in February 1942. In 1985, 2729 Squadron also pioneered the full employment of women in all combat appointments forty years ahead of the major legal changes that, in 2019, would eventually empower women to enter all combat roles in all three full-time Regular Armed Forces. My basis for staffing the employment of women in all combat roles in 2729 Squadron back in 1985 was that it was constituted as a UK Home Defence Unit, and thus initially not liable for overseas contingency operations in peacetime. Nevertheless, at the time, the very thought that women in command were empowered to actually to press a fire button and shoot down an enemy aircraft caused some senior and junior tooth-sucking, mainly in the RAF Regiment and the Royal Artillery.

The fourth part of the book deals with the experiences of raising a highly technically equipped Reserve Forces unit totally from scratch, literally starting with empty, unfurnished buildings and completely blank sheets of paper in virtually every area of administration, engineering, recruiting, training and live firing, in order to reach the final goal of operational declaration to NATO. Creating and then commanding this unique Royal Auxiliary Air Force unit was an unforgettably rich and rewarding experience for me, as it was also for most of its part-time participants who joined. Forty years on, additional and sometimes improbable anecdotes continue to emerge from the very active Oerlikon Alumni Association on 2729 Squadron's Facebook site, and every now and again they serve to remind readers that this is as much a story about people as it is about 'Star Wars' military hardware.

Chapter 1

The 1980s Military Scene

Forty years on, it is necessary to understand the contemporary events of the 1980s, when the Cold War was at the peak of confrontation between the offensive Warsaw Pact and defensive NATO. The Soviets had recently introduced two new swing-wing, deep-penetration bomber aircraft, the SU24 (NATO nickname Fencer) and the TU22 (NATO nickname Backfire), which could reach UK airfields avoiding radar detection by flying at very low level; this forced MoD planners to reappraise the need for short-range, close-in, ground-based air defence for key RAF airfields in the UK. For the first time since the Second World War the RAF faced an air threat capable of attacking its UK bases from any direction at low level.

The first layer of defence for the nuclear-armed Buccaneer and Vulcan UK bomber bases in East Anglia and Lincolnshire involved the reassignment of Bloodhound medium-range surface-to-air missiles from high level to low level defence, plus the introduction into service of the first two of the six planned Rapier short-range air defence (SHORAD) missile squadrons for the UK, both squadrons going to Scotland, one to defend the Atlantic and Arctic Ocean patrol base of the Nimrod maritime patrol aircraft at RAF Lossiemouth, near Elgin, and the other to the Phantom air defence fighter base at RAF Leuchars, near Dundee.

To enable air defence fighters to be directed to deal with these attackers flying low, under the sight of land-based long-range radars, it was also necessary to procure a look-down airborne early warning (AEW) radar-equipped aircraft. At the time the MoD owned a mothballed fleet of Comet 4 airframes which had been converted to an overly large number of Nimrod maritime patrol aircraft. It was decided to place a powerful, long-range, look-down radar in these surplus aircraft, with separate aerials in the nose and tail to give it 360-degree radar coverage, the radar manufacturer Marconi promising to give the Nimrod AEW a better performance at a lower cost than buying the already in-service US Air Force E3D AWACS based on a Boeing 707 airframe. The deployment base for this aircraft was to be RAF Waddington, near Lincoln, home of the retiring Vulcan bomber force that was about to hand over nuclear deterrent duties to the Royal Navy's submarine-launched Trident missiles. With its ability to look down at any aircraft flying low over the UK, the Nimrod AEW's home at RAF Waddington was to be the next most important UK base requiring its own dedicated short-range ground-based air defence protection.

However, while the Secretary of State's Statement on the Defence Estimates of 1982 would continue to place the air defence of the UK as its highest funding priority, the reality was that the requirement for four further Rapier squadrons, each equivalent in cost to a squadron of Harrier jump jets, was quite simply unaffordable, given all the other pressures on the Defence Budget. The Falklands Campaign was also seen as a distraction from the main aim of prosecuting the Cold War; indeed, the prevailing MoD view at the end of the Falklands Campaign was, unbelievably to us junior officers, that it offered absolutely no new military lessons to be learned. In terms of all-out nuclear war this was possibly true, but in lesser conflicts, below the atomic scale, there were lessons to be learned and Her Majesty's Stationery Office, HMSO, eventually published a tome of Lessons Learned. Cost-wise, the Falklands Campaign had already created an additional burden on the Defence Budget to replace sunken ships, lost aircraft, ammunition and equipment drawn permanently out of the NATO area to garrison the Islands. Then there was the cost of building a brand new, modern, militarily survivable, war-fighting RAF airfield in the middle of the boondocks 12,688km away at RAF Mount Pleasant; this airfield included one extra RAF Rapier squadron to replace NATO hardware then deployed at Stanley. My staff appointment task in the MoD was to oversee the current RAF Rapier force of six squadrons and help fight the corner for the purchase of the further four UK Rapier squadrons. The financial and manpower outlook, however, was not good.

Now fast-forward to about eight months after the 'distraction' of the Falklands Campaign. By now, the MoD had finally completed an inventory of all the military hardware surrendered by the Argentinians and circulated it around the staffs. When this list percolated down to my level, I became totally absorbed reading through the enormous range and quantities of war material that the Argentine occupying force of over ten thousand men had had to abandon upon their unconditional surrender. Scattered around in random parts of the inventory were elements of some of the very latest all-weather, radar-directed anti-aircraft artillery in the world. Given my prior multi-gun-and-missile weapon instructional background experience as a graduate instructor-in-gunnery at the Royal School of Artillery, known as an IG in Army parlance, covering everything from shoulder-launched Blowpipe to radar-directed 40mm Bofors guns, the new Rapier short-range missile and the then in-service long-range, high-altitude, massive, medium-range Thunderbird missile system and all its associated radars, first cousin to the RAF's Bloodhound missile system, I suddenly became very interested in this ex-Argentine arms inventory.

By the end of 1982 sizeable quantities of the booty had already been squirrelled away by units that participated in the campaign, taken to the UK from the Islands as trophies to be displayed at home. Then, follow-up units, which subsequently garrisoned the Islands on four-to-six-month rotations, followed suit. Collecting enemy kit had become a bit of a free-for-all and the MoD was, at last, to set about gripping a situation not experienced since the winning of the Second World War. Some equipment was in the hands of Defence Research Establishments for evaluation and some had already been given away informally to military museums, which were actually non-MoD private organizations. However, a fair proportion of equipment still remained on the Islands, locked away in uncharted minefields and possibly even booby-trapped as well, scattered over an area about the size of Wales but considerably wilder. To satisfy my immediate curiosity, I arranged to see physical examples of this most modern piece of the captured equipment: the 6-ton Oerlikon twin 35mm anti-aircraft field gun and its associated 5-ton Skyguard mobile fire-control radar that were already in the UK. Amazingly, both examples I saw were in perfect working order. A quick phone-around and further visits to various other units and museums around the country enabled me to establish the condition and quantities of equipment available: in round figures the value was about £24 million, potentially a nice little windfall to my specialist area of the Defence Budget. Later a further £6 million of additional guns and British-made ammunition would also be recovered from the Falkland Islands. The germ of an idea began to crystalize in my mind: why not put this equipment back into operational use in the Royal Air Force and fill a declared hole in our all-weather ground-based air defence capability?

Aside from the physical dispersion of the equipment, the other difficulties were considerable. First of all, there was already a manpower ceiling in place for the Armed Forces; this completely ruled out the possibility of another Regular RAF unit unless some other unit disbanded to release the necessary personnel. Then there were the training, engineering, maintenance and logistic problems of operating a one-off unit whose entire inventory had by-passed the MoD's seemingly Byzantine procurement and logistic support system.

Normally, introducing a new weapon into service would be directed from the highest level of Defence Planning Staff in the MoD; a Project Manager would be appointed with appropriate staff in the MoD Procurement Executive, MoD (PE), and all the supporting service branches would work together under a stated directive from on high. Critical to all of this would be funding spread over the projected lifetime of the project. In the normal course of events, the appropriate financial, procurement, engineering, logistic, training and manning authorities would all work together and constantly update the master plan. Launching a new squadron with equipment plucked out of thin air on the personal, bottom-up initiative of a junior staff officer, who was not even a project manager of anything, was quite another matter. However, three years of training as an officer cadet at the RAF College 'to prepare officers for the highest rank' and an intense year on the British Army's single most expensive technical and operational course at the Royal School of Artillery, the instructor-in-gunnery course at Larkhill, had generated a much-encouraged level of initiative, enthusiasm and technical knowledge for my first go as a junior staff officer and so, with youthful innocence still untainted by the reality of 'Yes, Minister', old age and treachery, I dived in.

Luckily, I shared my MoD office in London with the staff officer responsible for our part of the RAF's part-time reserve force, the Royal Auxiliary Air Force Regiment. With the financial constraint of a Regular manpower ceiling in place, the growing need to provide a greater level of ground defence security to protect RAF installations against Soviet *Spetznaz* Special Forces was being trialled by the pilot formation of part-time, company-sized infantry squadrons of the RAuxAF Regiment. Enter a development of my original idea: why not raise another Auxiliary-manned unit and let part-timers instead of Regulars man the captured Argentine equipment? My masters were not at all convinced. However, I was allowed to explore the possibilities further on the strict condition that I did this extra 'investigation' entirely in my own time. Thus, in between my main jobs of the day, I put together a first, straw man, formal proposal to raise such a unit, signed it off at my squadron leader rank level and circulated it around every other specialist squadron leader in the MoD who might possibly want to be involved in one way or another, were this kite to fly. Most of the responses were encouraging and some were positively helpful. I think there was a goodly element of 'Falklands Factor' involved from those who, like me, felt that they had missed out on playing a part in winning a war they had wanted to be in; I guess also the novelty of launching a much-needed operational unit with gratis Argentine booty helped. But first, some explanation of my own branch within the Royal Air Force, the Royal Air Force Regiment and its participation in the Falklands Campaign is required.

Chapter 2

The Royal Air Force Regiment and the Royal Auxiliary Air Force Regiment

At this point it would be appropriate to introduce the RAF Regiment. For the military minded, it is not actually a regiment at all; it is a Corps, but is uniquely styled a regiment. 'The Regiment', as it is known within its parent Service, is an integral part of the Royal Air Force. For this reason, its role and *raison d'être* are frequently misunderstood by the other services and nations and even by some members of the Royal Air Force itself, who may only have come into contact with one or two individuals of the Regiment during their service due its small numbers performing a very wide range of duties and sub-specializations within the Corps in small numbers all over the world.

The RAF Regiment was born in the early days of the Second World War out of an urgent need to address the total lack of airfield protection. At home in the UK, in the years between the First and Second World Wars, the Royal Air Force had to scrimp and save in so many areas to maintain any significant numbers of aircraft in the European theatre of 'peace in our time' that, for the ground defence of its installations, there were only a few rifles between hundreds of men and no anti-aircraft weapons worthy of mention with which to meet any threat.

Churchill's 1918 Defence White Paper for the formation of the Royal Air Force had envisaged that a major task for the new Service would be to police Persia (Iran), Mesopotamia (Iraq) and Palestine (later Jordan and Israel) from the air in place of the British Army, as a cost-saving measure. The air bases there were defended by RAF ground gunners equipped with Rolls-Royce armoured cars fitted with ground-to-air-wireless, enabling them to call up direct air support; the effectiveness of this air-armour combination was ignored in a pique of 'not invented here' by much of the British Army in the 1920s and 1930s, which did not go unnoticed in defeated Germany, where the nascent Luftwaffe tested out the concept in Franco's Spain and delivered it as *Blitzkrieg* to Belgium, Holland, France, Poland and the Soviet Union in 1939–40.

During the fall of France and the Low Countries, when the RAF deployed squadrons across the Channel, it was found that when the land battle went badly, the Army not unnaturally pulled their troops out from airfield defence duties in order to attend to tasks which, as a single service, they saw as a higher priority. In many cases Army-defended airfields, which hitherto had provided the Army with aerial top cover, were subsequently easily overrun through lack of airfield defences, thus denying the land forces vital air support at a critical time and exacerbating an already difficult situation on the ground, culminating in the retreat to Dunkirk.

After the extraordinary Royal Navy extraction of the third of a million defeated but trained soldiers from the beaches at Dunkirk, the threat of imminent German invasion rose to its highest ever level, running up to a peak during the Battle of Britain in September 1940; in response, the Army had to deploy thousands of soldiers on airfield defence duties. The operational weakness of this arrangement came to a head with the fall of Crete in 1941, when German forces made a feint at a seaborne landing, which drew most the Army defences off the RAF airfields, whereupon those airfields were then subsequently captured by German airborne parachute assault. Luftwaffe paratroopers landed directly on the inadequately defended British airfields, whose airmen only had a few small arms between them. Within hours, the airfields were taken and were immediately used to air-land literally thousands of troops, forcing an undignified retreat and a perilous evacuation of the Army and RAF from Crete, carried out by the Royal Navy at a cost of many valuable ships lost. Ordered to abandon the evacuation, the on-the-spot Naval commander responded with a retort worthy of Nelson: 'It takes three years to build us a major warship; it has taken three hundred years to build our reputation. We will see this task through.' And so he did, biting on the bullet in much the same way as the Royal Navy would do so again forty years on, under a similarly fierce air onslaught against the warships covering the British landings in the Falklands Campaign.

The loss of Crete was a huge blow to Churchill, who was furious. He angrily described the Royal Air Force as 'a collection of technical airmen, uniformed civilians in the prime of life, being defended by detachments of soldiers'. This was followed by his other, much quoted edict that 'forthwith, every airman is to be a fighting air-ground soldier prepared to die in defence of his airfield'. Driven by high-level committees, this edict percolated down into the issue of a Royal Warrant signed by King George VI authorizing the formation of a new Corps, the RAF Regiment, on 1 February 1942. The Brigade of Guards was assigned to raise and train the new force, which would eventually total some eighty-two thousand all ranks, who served throughout the Second World War in every theatre of operations with great distinction. More importantly, an estimated ninety-two thousand trained soldiers were released from static airfield defence duties and returned to the main body of the British Army to conduct their primary role of field mobile land warfare in all active theatres.

The new RAF Regiment showed itself quick to learn and was given the honour by HM the King to take over the Mounting of the Guard at Buckingham Palace and the Tower of London from the Brigade of Guards, a tradition which continues right up to the present day with the Queen's Colour Squadron of the Royal Air Force, 63 Squadron, RAF Regiment. The demands for the operational services of the new RAF Regiment have never ceased: squadrons battled the Japanese daily in the jungle airfields of Burma to keep them open, one notable action using elephants to transport men and heavy weapons to attack the enemy from their rear; in North Africa they chased the Luftwaffe out of their desert air strips and even ate their abandoned lunch in the officers' mess in one notable, lightning action; in Italy the RAF Regiment took heavy casualties along with the Polish Division participating in the bloody assault of Monte Cassino; and closer to home, the anti-aircraft element of the RAF Regiment formed a very large part of the screen of thousands of anti-aircraft guns deployed to counter the onslaught of V-1 flying bombs, while other squadrons landed on the beaches of Normandy as part of the RAF's Second Tactical Air Force, protecting its forward airfields in France, and some units rushing ahead to capture German airfields for British use, as well as fanning out to capture advanced German radars, jet aircraft and rockets intact on the ground before they could be destroyed. The RAF Regiment also lays claim to being the first Allied unit to get into the centre of Paris and accepting the surrender of huge numbers of Germans cut off in Denmark. Indeed, there has never been a period in its subsequent history when some part of the RAF Regiment has not been on continuous operational service somewhere in the world since 1942, and today is no exception.

At the peak of the Cold War in the 1980s the RAF Regiment had six tracked, lightly armoured squadrons and four Rapier anti-aircraft missile squadrons assigned to forward RAF bases in Germany. A further six Auxiliary Field (Infantry) squadrons provided key defence for airfields in the UK against expected attacks by Russian *Spetsnaz* Special Forces and two Rapier squadrons defended our most northerly airfields in Scotland. The RAF Regiment also provided a decades-long presence of 40mm Bofors AA guns, then Tigercat surface-to-air missiles and finally Rapier anti-aircraft missiles in Belize to deter invasion by Guatemala, and thereafter, similarly, Rapier surface-to-air missiles for over twenty years in the Falkland Islands after its liberation from the Argentinians. An infantry squadron protected airfields in Northern Ireland during the thirty years of Troubles, as well as providing further squadrons, on and off, to assist the Army along the border with the Irish Republic. Overseas, an armoured squadron protected the UK's Sovereign Base airfield in Cyprus. Finally, every single person in the RAF is given their basic military training skills by RAF Regiment instructors at the various RAF training establishments; those skills are then maintained by further RAF Regiment instructors located on every operational base.

The success of this in-house operational capability has been the envy of other air forces and many, including the *Fuerza Aerea Argentina*, saw fit to develop their own RAF Regiment clones. The RAF Regiment's closest foreign bond, however, is with the United States Air Force, where exchange postings take place at senior staff officer and junior officer levels in each other's headquarters, training schools and operational units. Thus, every man in either the American or the British airfield protection force has been trained by an opposite number from the opposite force. Nowhere else in the NATO Alliance is there such a closeness of personnel training and staff. At the peak of the Cold War the US Air Force went a step further and underwrote the defence of American airbases in the United Kingdom with Rapier anti-aircraft missiles, manned by RAF Regiment personnel. In an even more intimate operational relationship, US Air Force nuclear-armed Cruise missiles, of RAF Greenham Common fame, were protected on the ground and in the field by a mixed force of US Air Force Security Force and RAF Regiment personnel. And in a follow-on to this, the RAF Regiment and RAF Police co-guarded the RAF's nuclear weapons in the last days of the Cold War, until Royal Navy submarines took over the nuclear role.

The final accolade came in the late 1990s, when the German Luftwaffe saw fit to send a team of senior staff officers over to the UK to study the RAF Regiment, fifty years after their predecessors had compelled the British to create it in the first place, following their capture of Crete. The Luftwaffe now has its own force protection clone, the *Objeckschutz Gruppe* and, naturally, British and German officers and NCOs are exchanged with this force also.

In addition, the RAF Regiment has another role: as the RAF's training and operational defence specialists in post-attack nuclear, biological and chemical warfare survival and recovery. This latter skill very much came to the fore in peacetime: offering assistance to the Japanese in tracking radioactive fallout from their earthquake and tsunami-based nuclear power station meltdown and, more recently, in evidence gathering and chemical decontamination of the Russian *Novichok* attack in Salisbury. All of this capability is bundled together as a military function called 'Force Protection', so the RAF Regiment is the RAF's Force Protection Force with a One Star Force Protection Force Commander, whilst another officer is currently appointed at Two Star level as Commandant General of the RAF Regiment by the Sovereign. At the operational level in 2022 the RAF Regiment is organized into composite Force Protection Wings located at the bases of each main aircraft operating type, which support Expeditionary Air Wings on deployments abroad. Expeditionary Wings are structures tailored to meet each new operational requirement as it arises. Each Force Protection Wing has a Regular, enhanced-firepower, infantry company-sized RAF Regiment squadron with some armour and a composite RAuxAF Squadron of Regiment Gunners and RAF Police; one of the wings contains a special unit, the Air Land Integration Cell, which provides RAF Regiment Tactical Attack Controllers for directing aircraft to their targets in air-to-ground operations and, separately, Tactical Air Control Parties for setting up temporary landing zones and points anywhere in the world.

The account would not be complete without some mention of the RAF's part-time reserve, the Royal Auxiliary Air Force, RAuxAF, the RAF's lesser-known equivalent of the Territorial Army, of which the RAF Regiment is the largest element. The Auxiliary Air Force was initially provided for in the Air Force Constitution Act of 1919 by Lord Trenchard, the 'Father of the Royal Air Force'.

In 1925 the first squadrons of the Auxiliary Air Force, 600 (City of London) and 601 (County of London) Squadrons, were equipped with the DH-9A, the advanced fighter of the day. Later, the force would be expanded to twenty flying squadrons operating in all roles, plus forty-seven barrage balloon squadrons and the Women's Auxiliary Air Force, whose members manned the early air defence radar stations and operated the fighter control centres. In 1940 the Auxiliary fighter squadrons were equipped with Hurricanes and Spitfires, and Auxiliaries comprised one fifth of all fighter pilots in the Battle of Britain, and, thereafter, they destroyed one-in-every-three German aircraft shot down. Auxiliary pilots were credited with shooting down not only the first German bomber on British soil but also the first V1 flying bomb, and later, an Auxiliary squadron was the very first RAF squadron to be equipped with the new Meteor jet fighter.

In 1947, in recognition of its distinguished war service, the Auxiliary Air Force was granted the prefix 'Royal' by King George VI. After the war Auxiliary flying squadrons were equipped with Spitfires, Meteors and Vampire jets. A transport squadron, five reconnaissance squadrons and twenty-nine fighter control units were also raised, along with twelve Bofors 40mm anti-aircraft gun squadrons of the RAuxAF Regiment. Ten years later, with the advent of the Nuclear Tripwire Policy, Duncan Sandys published his famous 1957 Defence White Paper which predicted that, in future, neither manned bombers nor manned fighters would be required. Under a nuclear umbrella, the whole of the Royal Air Force was to shrink considerably, while the Royal Auxiliary Air Force was virtually disbanded overnight. As the UK Nuclear Tripwire Policy of the 1950s gave way to the concept of Flexible Response, by the early 1970s it had become apparent that airfields in the UK were once again vulnerable to Soviet conventional attack from the air and by special forces on the ground.

Additional Regular manpower to meet these new commitments was out of the question, and so the then Chief of the Air Staff, Air Chief Marshal Sir Michael Beetham, directed the formation, on a trial basis, of three RAuxAF Regiment infantry (Field) squadrons, one each at RAF Scampton, RAF Honington and RAF Lossiemouth. Even before the trial period had expired, it was decided to form a further three units at once. Other branches of the RAF capitalized on the success; soon an RAuxAF Movements Squadron and an RAuxAF Aeromedical Evacuation Squadron were formed. A small trial in early 1981 indicated that the Auxiliaries could also be trained to operate the Rapier surface-to-air missile system, while a number of RAuxAF pilots and navigators were now also flying RAF VC 10 passenger and cargo jets, an aircraft then in common use with British

Airways. With the successful resurrection of the RAuxAF, the scene was set to bring Auxiliaries back into air defence, along with the revival of another Second World War precedent, that of employing women in the full spectrum of anti-aircraft warfare on home ground. Considering that the Argentine booty had the potential to double the number of UK airfields defended with close-in, all-weather, day-and-night anti-aircraft units for only a tenth of the cost of its Regular-manned elements, this certainly had to be a way ahead that Lord Trenchard would certainly have applauded.

On the Falklands front, aside from my aircraft recognition contribution, things went very quiet on the RAF Regiment side once the Royal Navy's 3 Commando Brigade had set sail, with its tailor-made amphibious warfare ships and its fleet of logistic landing ships, named after Knights of the Round Table. It was a self-contained, integrated force going to war to do exactly what it was designed for: to land on a far-away beach and storm the enemy. Since the battle for air supremacy between supersonic Mirages and subsonic Harriers was perceived to be a challenging, close-run thing, the Commando Brigade had already been enhanced by two battalions of the high-readiness Parachute Regiment, the Paras, plus Royal Artillery daylight-only Rapier surface-to-air missiles and Blowpipe man-portable missiles intended to take over protection of the beachhead from Royal Navy warships as soon as possible after the landings. The flip side of this force sailing so stunningly quickly was that the Argentinians now realized they might actually have to fight the British and oppose a landing intended to take the Islands back. Consequently, they poured in reinforcements to the Falklands, now renamed *Islas Malvinas*. In turn, it quickly became clear to the British that a much greater landing force would be needed.

Thus, a second brigade, 5 Brigade, was created, very much on-the-fly, made up of the next high-readiness battalion of Gurkhas, plus two light scales battalions, the Scots Guards and Welsh Guards. As it was becoming clearer that a serious campaign was developing, a badge battle of prestige to participate overruled war preparedness in the selection of units added to the brigade, along with further elements of supporting arms. Additional Harrier GR3s were included as anticipated battle-loss replacements for Sea Harriers. It was obvious that, once ashore, Harrier response time in support of the land forces could be speeded up to a matter of minutes, compared to having to first fly 100 nautical miles (NM) or more from distant aircraft carriers doing their best not to be sunk by Exocet missiles by keeping well out of range of Argentine aircraft. There was thus an imperative to get Harriers and helicopters ashore as soon as possible onto the kind of instant airstrip that the Harriers were specifically designed to operate from. Integral to the Harrier Force in Cold War front-line Germany was their all-weather, day-and-night capable, RAF Regiment Rapier squadron; this was, at last, added to 5 Brigade at the last minute, just in time for its sailing. That unit was 63 Squadron RAF Regiment, which landed with 5 Brigade at San Carlos and would later undertake the first garrison rotation of RAF Stanley Rapier operations.

Also integral to the ground defence of the Harrier Force in the field were two further RAF Regiment light armoured squadrons equipped with the Scorpion family of tracked fighting vehicles, each company-sized unit fielding more fire-power than a light scales infantry battalion. Incomprehensively, only the RAF Rapier squadron was committed to join 5 Brigade's later sailing, which meant that a pair of type-designed, rear-area defence units of RAF Regiment light armoured squadrons, which could easily have freed up a whole Royal Marine battalion-sized Commando from its landing area and Harrier strip rear area force protection duties prior to the battle for Goose Green, never went. Whilst we junior staff officers could see this with blinding clarity and articulated it loudly, we could not get past the 'If we are needed, we will be called for' mindset at the top.

The other rather unsung but equally important task that the RAF Regiment did for the Harrier Force, as well as defence, was to provide the administrative camp commandant to run the domestic side of the Harrier deployment, over-seeing everything from tents to fire-fighting, slit trenches to air raid warnings and post-attack recovery, thus freeing the RAF aircrew to get on and fly and the RAF engineers to keep the aircraft flying. This RAF Regiment Harrier element only deployed after the campaign was over. If there was one thing the Harrier Force did outstandingly well, it was functioning in the field like clockwork, enabling each pilot to fly four, five, six or more hard-hitting sorties a day in support of the Army land battle. Without that armoured RAF Regiment squadron, that was not going to be the case and the frustration of not being allowed to do it for the Falklands Campaign burned into the psyche of a whole generation of junior Regi-ment staff officers, not to be assuaged until years later, when the RAF Regiment properly went to war with great distinction in Kuwait, Iraq and Afghanistan, demonstrating its war-fighting ability internationally on a par with the Paras, Royal Marines and US Marine Corps.

Meanwhile, back in 1982, ad-hoc action was not the exclusive province of the Argentinians. Publicity images of a Vulcan nuclear bomber testing its capa-bility to release a string of twenty-one conventional iron bombs out of its belly prompted the Argentine Army to deploy its considerable anti-aircraft artillery assets, the Argentine Marines and the Air Force having already deployed their more modest organic assets of 20mm, 30mm and 35mm cannon to protect their own single-Service interests. As events in the South Atlantic gradually unfolded, this narrative will weave together the parallel anti-aircraft resources and experi-ences of each side. In order to better understand the respective resources, the characteristics, strengths and weaknesses inherent in each weapon system, partic-ularly where their Falklands deployment and employment took them out of their intended design operational environment, will be discussed in detail. This will enable the reader to better understand the anti-aircraft battles that took place and will hopefully debunk some of the more extravagant claims of some parties. For the record, the two most successful anti-aircraft weapons in the Falklands Campaign were the Aim 9L Sidewinder fire-and-forget infra-red homing missile, and troopers of the Special Air Service Regiment armed with Nobel's 808 explosives. What the other anti-aircraft weapons did, however, in addition to their primary role of shooting down enemy aircraft, was to shape the air-to-ground battlespace in such a way that forced both sides to operate their aircraft far less effectively than they were capable of by design.

The 1990s Balkans break-up of Yugoslavia provided the RAF Regiment with new and very different, testing experiences in operational peace-making. All through the 1990s the Regiment still continued to provide ground-based air defence of the airfields in Belize and the Falkland Islands, as well as close security protection of Aldergrove International Airport and RAF Bishop's Court airfield in Northern Ireland. The RAF Regiment's parachute squadron also performed the first British operational parachute assault since the Suez Crisis of 1956 when it secured an airfield in Sierra Leone in a show of force projection to enable the SAS to rescue British soldiers captured by local insurgents.

Needless to say, having missed out of being thrown together with the other two services in the 1982 Falklands Campaign, when Gulf War I and Gulf War II came along, the RAF committed 80 per cent of the RAF Regiment to the task, where it acquitted itself in some very hot actions, taking its share of fatal casualties along the way. Then came Afghanistan: a situation in many ways similar to Mesopotamia in the 1920s, where air power held sway over ground actions and force protection forces on the ground faced intense enemy action, with the RAF Regiment again being internationally recognized as the leading experts in airfield protection of NATO assets in Afghanistan. For those who might question why RAF Regiment units were not at the forefront of the final RAF air evacuation at Kabul Airport, the irony of the situation was that it was the victorious Taliban who, more or less, successfully guaranteed the external force protection of Kabul airfield against their own other sworn enemy, ISIS.

And now, as the second decade of the twenty-first century develops, the British Armed Forces are the smallest they have ever been. As we enter the age of drones, clones and robotic combat, we are in a situation where intelligence about the location, intent and identity of the enemy is paramount to enable us to deal with them in ways we would have considered science fiction in earlier years. However, for the moment there is still the universal need to protect as well as attack. There will always be a need for boots on the ground in the hazardous, specialist working environment of valuable aircraft, and in this role a future RAF Regiment and its RAuxAF Reserve will surely play their part to enable air power to be deployed effectively.

Chapter 3

Invasion Prelude: Morgan and Drake

In 1982 the military Junta in Argentina was in a political plight. The people of Argentina had taken to the streets in protest at the soaring rate of inflation, a stagnant economy and a legion of 'Disappeared Ones'. Some desperate measures were needed to boost the seriously flagging popularity of the military government. The junta may well have recalled the advice of Machiavelli in 1514 to the Prince of Florence, Lorenzo de Medici: 'Giving away to the people whatever belongs to foreigners is an easy way to increase your standing at home and increase your popularity'; this was absolutely just what the junta needed to do at that very moment.

Fostering the idea of colonial independence from European powers is one of the founding principles of the United Nations. For five hundred years the Portuguese, the Spanish, the Dutch and the English had spread their influence and populations around the globe in an unprecedented age of exploration, discovery, settlement, infrastructure development, education and trade. In time, some of these ex-colonies became major powers in their own right and have established the quintessence of good relations with their neighbours. Of the many other ex-colonies, only a few may be considered to be properly democratic in the true meaning of the word; many have crumbled into poverty-stricken, despotic dictatorships, falsely blaming their colonial past for their current misery. Whilst geography and inherited borders may have something to do with some of the current world problems, the true cause of the misery of poverty has been created by the political aim of those despots presently in power to remain in power at absolutely any cost. Whilst tidying up imagined or actual trespasses of state boundaries is not a new phenomenon in history, since the end of the Second World War the United Nations' internationally agreed post-1945 consent has been that the status quo should remain the order of the day. However, sadly, almost all post-Second World War border and territorial disputes have been settled by force or confrontation. Two examples, on the surface, set models for the 1982 resolution of the Argentine claim to the Falkland Islands by invasion: firstly, the reoccupation of Goa by Indian forces on the direction of a 'non-aligned' President Nehru after five hundred years of Portuguese rule; and, secondly, to a much lesser extent, the occupation and annexation of the three hundred year-long Sultanate of Zanzibar by Tanganyika, under the direction of another 'non-aligned' leader, President Julius Nyerere, the British having long banished Arab slavery in the continent of Africa and tamed the Omani Sultan to rule benignly for a century and a half. Many colonies in the British Empire were protectorates, where the British left the local rulers and structures in place and funded them to keep the peace and not keep slaves. Most of the latter include the current-day successful Gulf States. In Africa ex-protectorates like Bechuanaland, which became Botswana, hold up the bright candle of good governance. Even South Africa, with its eleven ethnic tribes, has managed to replace four Presidents post-Mandela in good order without civil war and bloodshed. But swathes of Africa, South America and Asia, hugely rich in natural resources, have failed their populations due to despotic greed and bad governance. Meanwhile, the Middle East, being at a strategic crossroads of continents, has been criss-crossed by so many bands of conquering civilizations that power games by the twisted ideologies of Russia and Iran continue to blight the area, and even today, it is a place which has never, ever, been at peace for very long in the last five thousand years.

Almost all of the preamble to the Falklands crisis of 1982, however, can be put down to the Peronists who, much influenced by the ideas of Nazi Germany, came to power in Argentina in the 1940s. They began the systematic education of generations of Argentine schoolchildren to believe that the Falkland Islands legitimately belonged to them. Most importantly, in the 1970s several years of pseudo-military, and incidentally unopposed, Argentine occupation of the British South Sandwich Islands were followed by the loss of automatic right of residence in the United Kingdom for members of the former British Empire, particularly from India, Pakistan, Africa and the Caribbean. For the purposes of perceived fairness, the same rules were also applied to the former long-independent Dominions of Canada, Australia, New Zealand and South Africa, and the few remaining Island colonies such as the Falkland Islands. Taken together, the Junta interpreted this as loss of British interest in its former Empire. The final signal was the pre-announced impending withdrawal of HMS *Endurance*, the only physical manifestation of significant British military power in the South Atlantic, the twenty Royal Marines based in the Falkland Islands being seen as a ceremonial dressing simply to serve the Governor. Taken together, in Argentine eyes at least, British interest in the area totally lacked credibility. The blame for this lies firmly in the left-leaning British Foreign Office taking such a weasel-like position on 'What to do with the Falkland Islands?' Contrast this with the robust position that both Labour and Conservative governments were taking against Guatemala and its claim to Belize, to which they responded overnight with Royal Navy Buccaneer jets (which could refuel each other), and later with the permanent deployment of Harrier jets, Tigercat missiles, 40mm Bofors anti-aircraft guns and finally Rapier. An equally robust British diplomatic stand is taken over Spain's claims to Gibraltar, which, if granted, would expose the hypocrisy of

Spain's continued parallel possessions across the Straits of Morocco, in North Africa.

The quest for a diversion from the pressure of internal unrest in Argentina was not a hastily conceived last moment thought. Documents such as the Argentine Army's own publicly released Report on the Malvinas War, *Informe Offiçial Ejerçito Argentino Conflicto Malvinas*, shows that invasion preparations had already been long drawn up for execution by a predetermined date if negotiations failed to deliver the Falklands Islands. The Argentine operation was planned as a Joint-Service effort under a unified command. It is hard to imagine that the Argentine Foreign Ministry, totally subservient to the military Junta, could be negotiating for a transfer of sovereignty of the Falkland Islands without being aware of such invasion plans. Argentine impatience and fake frustration at the justifiable reluctance of the British to hand over their most distant kith and kin to an unpleasant Latin military dictatorship brought forth international diplomatic gaffes on an epic scale on live television, such as the reference by Costa Méndez, the Argentine Foreign Minister, stating that the British Prime Minister's negotiating position was influenced by 'her time of the month'.

Clearly this Latin macho attitude is deeply ingrained in the Argentine psyche, as is the belief that the British Elizabethan heroes such as Drake, Morgan and Raleigh were pirates responsible for the downfall of Spanish world dominance. They were, of course, the licensed agents of Elizabeth I, fighting a proxy war against Spain. Some sense of this popular feeling may be gleaned from some of the documents abandoned by the Argentinians upon their surrender. The sonnet *Morgan y Drake* sent to the Governor of the *Malvinas*, Brigadier Menéndez, by the *Centro de Mererices Unides* (United Merit Centre) is one such example; *Nuestras Malvinas Marcha*, the 'Malvinas March', is another. Both documents, kindly translated by my friend 'Her Majesty's Interrogator', the late Flight Lieutenant Guy Bransby of the RAF Regiment, is reproduced in full in Appendix I; it loosely refers to 'Margaret the Arrogant, descendant of pigs and pirates; a petulant menopausal ruin, believing herself to be of iron instead of tin; an example of new neurotic delusion …' The sonnet ends with a postscript informing *El Grobenador de Las Malvinas* that authenticated copies had been sent to Her Gracious Majesty, the Queen of England, to all her lying subjects, to the cheat Haig (then American Secretary of State), to all Anglican pastors, to all British brothels and to the poor subjects of British colonies. It is interesting to note the reverence given to Her Majesty the Queen: was this the last vestige of unrequited love that the rejected King Philip of Spain supposedly declared for the first Queen Elizabeth? The Malvinas March, of course, forgets that 150 years previously the British were busily assisting the Argentinians in winning their independence from Spain. History, as they say, is the perspective of events by the winners.

We do, however, have to confess that the tiniest bit of English popular prejudice also survives these centuries. We learned in school that the Catholic King was rejected by a greater Queen of England, a virgin queen who, in her own words, declared to her troops that 'though a weak woman, I have the heart and stomach of a king, a King of England, no less'. The outcome of the defeat of the Spanish Armada invasion force is a fact, just as much as the reality that 'Britons never, never shall be slaves.' All this lies deep in the British psyche, a deep-seated grudge against Spain and things Spanish. A tabloid newspaper of 1982 summed it up neatly in a succinct headline: 'King of Spain Still Peeved over Armada', which rather reinforces the perception.

Unlike most other overseas colonies, the Falkland Islands have absolutely no indigenous native population, being historically populated only by the temporary military garrisons of the French and then the Spanish, before the British made their possession permanent. The tiny British population of the Falkland Islands, civilian for over 150 years, was quite happy to cooperate with the descendants of King Philip just so long as pseudo-Spanish rule was not actually imposed upon them. Indeed, they were able to invoke the key United Nations Founding Principle that subjects of any colony should be allowed to determine their own future. The Falkland Islanders voted and determined to be British, spurred on by an instinctive dislike of the Argentine 'Dirty War', the generally foreign militarily-led nature of Spanish-speaking dictatorships on the mainland and the leftist, elitist, weaseling efforts of the British Foreign Office to divest itself of the Islands. It was one thing to go shopping in Buenos Aires but it was quite another to accept being ruled by that place.

Contrary to the popular British view, the men of the officer class of Argentina are highly motivated and well educated. In the main, they set themselves high patriotic standards in military institutions in which most Europeans would find a familiar Western outlook towards the Soviet Union and its proxies of the Cold War. It was fear of the Latin American Left, the threat of communism imported from Cuba, that led the United States to court Argentina as part of its Pan-American foreign policy. Traditionally too, Britain enjoyed excellent historical relations with Argentina: not only did the British assist in their War of Independence from Spain, but Britain virtually built the new nation's national infrastructure of railways, post offices, telephone communications and much of their industry, including their beef-raising agriculture. Parts of Buenos Aires look just like Pretoria, Colombo or New Delhi. Many huge cattle ranches are still either British owned or British managed and a very substantial Anglo-Argentine population remains in the country to this day. Famously, there is a centuries-old proud community of Welsh-speaking loyal Argentinians, whom others might describe as a colony within an ex-colony, living peaceably in Argentina today. Much of the Argentine military equipment, aircraft and warships came from Britain, some even named after the British admirals who helped them to win independence.

The Argentine Air Force Major Prize at the Royal Air Force College Cranwell is a large, wonderful sculpture in solid glass, competed for by officer cadet trainee pilots and was usually presented in person by the uniformed Argentine Air Force Air Attaché in the UK. I well remember, as an officer cadet back in 1965, that during the rehearsal for a Graduation Award of Wings and Prizes, the winner of the Argentine Air Force Trophy played a prank when, after being handed the large glass structure, upon his going off-stage behind the curtains, there was heard the most enormous, gasp-making, shattering of glass. It was, of course, just a prank made by dropping a large bundle of old glass window panes but for a moment everybody, right up to the Commandant of the College, believed a catastrophe had just taken place.

Nevertheless, the underlying Argentine claim to the Falkland Islands has never been very far from the surface, as a personal experience of mine can illustrate. In 1959, as a 14-year-old newly arrived British citizen of Northern Rhodesia, a land distinctly different in its governance from the then white self-governing semi-apartheid colony of Southern Rhodesia, I had just met my 15-year-old Argentine cousin. The occasion was the first time since 1933 that my father and his brother had met since their separation by the Nazis. She was the epitome of my pre-conception of a Latin girl: she dressed to kill, had dark flashing eyes, a vivacious personality and a huge colonial sense of adventure. She was game to try anything, except kissing – that was definitely taboo; indeed, without a chaperone, she explained, courtship could only be conducted with the approval of both parents. Any close association of any sort was quite out of the question. Men, she intoned, obviously needed 'that sort of thing' and did I not use the local bordello? (Uh, in rural Essex?) She found lots of things very different from Buenos Aires: 'English ice cream was fantastic. Why didn't the English police carry guns? Would they not be murdered after the curfew? And why was all that Argentine steak exported to Britain so expensive when Argentinians paid so little for it?' There was one area thankfully, however, in which we were in total cultural harmony and that was collecting postage stamps. We pored over pages of albums, swapped this for that and enthused about the subject in general. That is, until she came to the page in my album which held a single, solitary stamp of the Falkland Islands. With a gasp she cried: 'The *Malvinas*, you stole them from us!' I was quite taken aback by the venom with which she delivered this declaration and protested that we had done no such thing. To support my case, I invoked the evidence of unbroken British rule in the illustrations of the earliest 1840 Victorian stamps of the Falkland Islands in my 1938 Stanley Gibbons Stamp Catalogue. 'British propaganda!' she hissed. And thus our relationship ended in a state of armed neutrality. She returned to Argentina, injured by the sense of Stanley Gibbons' attempts to subvert the truth of the *Malvinas* sovereignty, I puzzled by the curious passion of her claim.

Indeed, I thought no more of it until, more than twenty-one years later. I had just returned to England from a really relaxing three-week holiday in Tenerife, funded by the sizeable Ministry of Defence Award to Inventors that I had just received for my aircraft recognition project. The holiday had been blissfully free of television, radio and even newspapers. I only had to report in to the Ministry for one Friday of 'work' before enjoying the weekend and that was because I was the function organizer for the office lunching out of one of our colleagues to celebrate his escape from the MoD. There was little chance to peruse any files, only time enough to check the lunch table arrangements, round up the other officers and the Air Marshal and ensure that we got maximum value from the wine-inclusive cost of the chosen menu.

Such posh outings were rare; mostly we staff officers ate sandwiches at our desks in an effort to cope with the deluge of paperwork that attacked us daily. Lunching-out was an infrequent and much anticipated event which burned quite a hole in the wallet; on the positive side, every such outing marked a step closer to one's own escape from the MoD, back to a 'real' uniformed job – hopefully the command of an operational unit somewhere exciting; there was, after all, a war on, albeit a Cold one. We had all joined the armed forces for adventure and the command of men and machines in challenging circumstances, so the end of a three-year-long exercise in dotting 'i's and crossing 't's was always a cause for celebration. This particular Friday, April Fool's Day 1982, was no exception, and as we all tumbled out into Piccadilly, replete and jolly, from the selected Mayfair lunch lasting to 4pm, we had absolutely no inkling that the Argentine invasion of the Falkland Islands was taking place.

Less than 24 hours after returning to the UK, I was to see on my television the shocking humiliation of surrendered Royal Marines lying face down in the streets of Stanley. What I did not know then was that Argentine military preparations for the invasion had gone on for months, if not years and even decades before. Nor did I know that one day I would eventually command some of the heavy artillery that the Argentinians would have to roll out. The military Junta, unfettered by the checks and balances of a democratically elected government, had, under the domestic pressure of its own creation, sought to divert national attention to a popular cause. The unthinkable Gilbert and Sullivan invasion of the Falkland Islands had actually taken place and Britain was in the Nanki Poo. I telephoned my Director at once, to ask what time we should come into work on the Saturday and Sunday, only to be told there was no need; if we were required, we would be called for. After eighteen years of training to be instantly ready for the Russians to roll across Europe, and having participated in numerous colonial independence campaigns to preserve orderly transfers of power upon exit, this was not what I expected to hear. By the time I went into work on the Monday following, a Naval Task Force, fortuitously already at sea, had been withdrawn from a NATO exercise and was already on its way down to the South Atlantic. For the first time in my RAF career, I regretted not accepting my offered place for an officer cadetship at Britannia Royal Naval College, Dartmouth in favour of the place I did accept into the RAF Regiment at the Royal Air Force College, Cranwell, much to the chagrin of my Mum, who was in love with Hornblower and imagined me, M.D.C. Fonfé RN, as his natural successor.

Chapter 4

Operaçion Rosario: Por Las Malvinas son Argentinas

There had, of course, been other invasions of the Falklands. In 1964 a Cessna 172 landed on the island piloted by one splendidly English-named Miguel Fitzgerald, who planted the Argentine flag on the racecourse and claimed the *Malvinas* for the President of Argentina before flying home again.

Then, on 28 September 1966, a much more serious attempt was made. A group calling itself the *El Condor* organization hijacked a DC-4 passenger aircraft of the national airline and landed it on Stanley racecourse, claiming they had come to liberate *Las Islas Malvinas*. After due diplomatic niceties, they were all shipped home, but the aircraft posed a bit of a problem: its undercarriage had sunk into the soft soil so that one wingtip was now almost touching the ground. With much effort, the stricken plane was jacked up out of the quagmire and, with only half a metre of clearance between the racecourse grandstands and the wingtips, it managed to take off safely for home.

Next, in November 1978, an Aero Commander flown by three ardent Argentine nationalists landed outside Port Stanley with the aim of confronting Lord Chalfont, who was visiting the Islands, on the question of sovereignty. The aircraft and its crew were shipped back pronto to Argentina. These actions were all the efforts of cranks. What happened in 1982 was under the jurisdiction of the military Junta, which had usurped power from the civilian government and had taken upon itself the government of Argentina.

Also, for years the Argentinians had kept a tiny, Argentine flag-flying, military-led pseudo-scientific expedition 1,600km from the Falklands in the British South Sandwich Islands, which successive British governments had ignored. In January or early February 1982, the military Junta issued National Strategic Directive 1/82, ordering the establishment of a working committee made up of the commander of V Corps, Major General O.J. Garcia, the head of naval operations, Vice Admiral J.J. Lombardo and a general of the Air Force, Major General S.M. Phessel. The committee was to plan, in the greatest possible secrecy, a joint operation to restore Argentine sovereignty over the Islands. Military Strategic Directive 1/82 laid down the objectives to be achieved.

In the context of Argentine events, I will refer to the islands as the *Malvinas*. This is just to set the events described in context and in no way implies any sympathy or backing for the Argentine cause, which, in my long-held view, has always been a dead duck. When the Islands are safely in British hands, they will be properly described at the Falkland Islands once more.

The Argentine plan called for the *Armada* (Navy) to provide three task forces: one for South Georgia, an amphibious group for the *Malvinas* and finally the High Seas Fleet. Argentine Marines were to capture the San Felipe Lighthouse and the Royal Marines Naval Party 8901 at their barracks at Moody Brook; they were also to secure Port Stanley harbour and town and capture the airfield. The *Ejercito* (Army) was to use two platoons to block the road between Moody Brook and Stanley, while an infantry regiment (equivalent to a British Army battalion) minus one company, was to be landed on Stanley airport to relieve the Naval Amphibious Commando, which was to secure the airfield in the initial landing. The detached company from the infantry regiment was to capture Fox Bay on West Falkland and one platoon of that company was to occupy Goose Green and Darwin. The *Fuerza Aerea* was to support the operation using Stanley airport.

Major General J. Garcia was appointed Commander of the *Malvinas* theatre of operations. Rear Admiral W. Allara was to command the amphibious task force and Brigadier L. Castellanos the aerial task force, while Brigadier A. Dahere was made commander of the land forces and Brigadier M. Menéndez was to become *El Grobenador de las Islas Malvinas, Georgias y Islas Sandwich del Sur*, in place of Sir Rex Hunt. The date of execution was to be 15 May 1982, by which time the 1982 annual intake of national conscripts would have reached a satisfactory state of four months' military training to execute such an operation.

On 24 March Task Force 60, the South Georgia group, consisting of the corvette *Guerrico* and the major polar transport ship *Ara Bahia Paraiso* (the Argentine equivalent of HMS *Endurance*), carrying a Marine detachment under the command of *Capitaine* Alfredo Astiz, had already landed Argentine military forces on South Georgia. HMS *Endurance* had shadowed that operation, but could do little else, although, prompted by Sir Rex Hunt, Lieutenant Mills' fierce resistance with his twenty-three Royal Marines must have taken the Argentinians by surprise, holing the *Guerrico* with an 84mm anti-tank gun and shooting down the first Argentine helicopter of the campaign with small arms fire. Had not so many of the 84mm rounds of ammunition been dud misfires, they may well have sunk the warship too! Later, the British were also to relearn the vulnerability of un-armoured helicopters in the forward edge of the battle area and the thinness of the skins of their warships against cannon fire. Rightly, Lieutenant Mills was awarded a Military Cross for his spirited action.

On 25 March the Order to Prepare was issued by the Junta High Command. The next day the Commanding Officer of 25 Infantry Regiment was informed that D-Day was to be brought forward to six days hence. Officers, NCOs and men, who up to then knew nothing of the intended operation, were given their assigned missions: *Teniente* R. Reyes, with the platoon from C Company, was to capture Sir Rex Hunt, the Governor of the Falkland Islands; Sir Rex was to be captured unhurt and without casualties to the British. *Teniente* Esteban, commanding the balance of C Company, was to capture the settlements of Darwin and Goose Green. The remainder of 25 Regiment was to be flown directly to Stanley airport to relieve 2 Marine Battalion of the defence of the airfield. In addition, 9 Engineer Company was jointly tasked with 25 Regiment to secure Fox Bay, while in Port Stanley itself 181 Military Police Company was to take over the duties of population control from the one and only British policeman on the *Malvinas*. D-Day was now set for 31 March 1982. Aside from a verbal warning order given to the Commander of 8 Infantry Regiment, no other army units were involved with the operation to capture the *Malvinas*.

Task Force 20, the Argentine High Seas Fleet, was led by the flagship aircraft carrier *Vienticinco de Mayo* (formerly HMS *Albion*, which in its previous life had last seen action in Britain's largest-ever Pacific Aircraft Carrier Task Force of six aircraft carriers together, attacking Japanese mainland kamikazi airfields in 1945, thus earning the British the right to sit at the Surrender Table of Japanese formal capitulation). *Vienticinco de Mayo*, with eight Skyhawks, four Grumman S2 Tracker Airborne Early Warning aircraft and some helicopters on board, was already at sea, escorted by four destroyers, *Segui*, *Commodoro Py*, *Piedrabueno* and *Bouchard*, and supported by the oiler *Punta Medanos* and the tug *Sobral*.

Operaçion Rosario finally got under way on the morning of 28 March, when Task Force 40, the amphibious task force, sailed from Puerto Belgrano with the intention of taking the *Malvinas*. The commander of the *Malvinas* theatre of operations, General Garcia, was aboard the destroyer *Santisima Trinidad*. This headquarters ship was escorted by the destroyer *Hercules* and two corvettes with the splendidly British names of *Admiral Drummond* and *Admiral Granville*. On board the Second World War logistic landing ship *Cabo San Antonio* were the naval amphibious forces and the transport platoon of 25 Regiment. Another ship, *Almirante Irizar*, carried the rest of C Company and finally, there was the ex-American submarine, *Santa Fe*.

Due to heavy seas and 40-knot winds on 29 March, General Garcia found it impossible to hold the meeting with his subordinate commanders; instead, he had to content himself with issuing orders and directions by radio. In particular he called for a bloodless operation, for observation of respect for UK emblems and flags, and for the need to exercise care and consideration in dealings with the civil population. A further day of bad weather caused D-Day to be postponed to 2 April. Aboard the *Almirante Irizar*, meanwhile, the Puma helicopter, with which it had been planned to seize Sir Rex's Government House and Moody Brook barracks, was damaged; as a result, tasks had to be exchanged between the Argentine Marines and infantry. By midnight on 1 April, as the ships reached their appointed landing stations, Argentine officers recorded that the troops were gripped by the tension of the historic event that they were about to undertake.

In the event, the tension they experienced on their landings on the *Malvinas* was to prove considerably less gripping than what lay in store for them when the British returned to retake the Falkland Islands a few weeks later.

Meanwhile, on the Argentine mainland, the bulk of 25 Infantry Regiment and the remainder of 9 Engineer Company moved overnight to the airhead at Comodoro Rivadavia, from which they were to be flown to the *Malvinas*. On the Falkland Islands Sir Rex Hunt, informed of the scope and size of the Argentine fleet, announced on local radio at 2015hrs local time: 'There is mounting evidence that the Argentine armed forces are preparing to invade the Falkland Islands'. His forty or so Royal Marines, doubled in number due to a rotational handover of Marines taking place at the time, were dispersed to observation posts overlooking the harbour and to guard the airfield, the road into Stanley and Government House itself.

According to the Argentinians, but unknown to the British, 45 minutes after Sir Rex's broadcast the invasion proper had begun. At 2100hrs on 1 April 1982 the *Santisima Trinidad* landing ship commenced landing the amphibious commando group, which at 2345hrs reported that it had reached the coast without incident. At 0345hrs on 2 April the Argentinians recorded that tactical frogmen had secured the Cap San Felipe lighthouse intact. In fact, Islander Basil Briggs was in the lighthouse at the time and reported ship movements to Sir Rex at 0545hrs before eventually surrendering himself to Argentine soldiers at about 0700hrs. Whatever the time differences, the way was now clear for the invasion proper to begin.

At 0615hrs the first reinforcements of 25 Infantry Regiment took off from Comodoro Rivadavia. Some 15 minutes later the two-pronged amphibious operation was launched. The first five vehicles reached the beach on the north coast of the peninsula without incident in 7 minutes and took up defensive fire positions while the dismounting infantry raced away at full speed to secure the higher ground that dominated the airfield. The Argentinians encountered considerable resistance as the Royal Marines withdrew. The runway itself was blocked by some twenty-five assorted trucks and tractors, but by 0730hrs the officer commanding the infantry was able to report that the airfield was in his hands and ready to accept aircraft. The first Hercules carrying troops of 25 Infantry Regiment landed at 0845hrs. Thereafter the remaining elements of the regiment continued to arrive in an uninterrupted stream of aircraft. As each 'chalk' of personnel arrived, they were immediately deployed to their allocated positions.

The second Marine battalion, for its part, landed at Mullet Creek and raced towards the Moody Brook barracks, arriving at 0635hrs. They raked the deserted barracks with small arms fire and grenades. It was just as well that the Royal Marines were not at home in bed as they would doubtless have experienced very heavy loss of life in an action which is difficult to reconcile with General Garcia's instructions for a bloodless operation. In Stanley town the Argentinians were

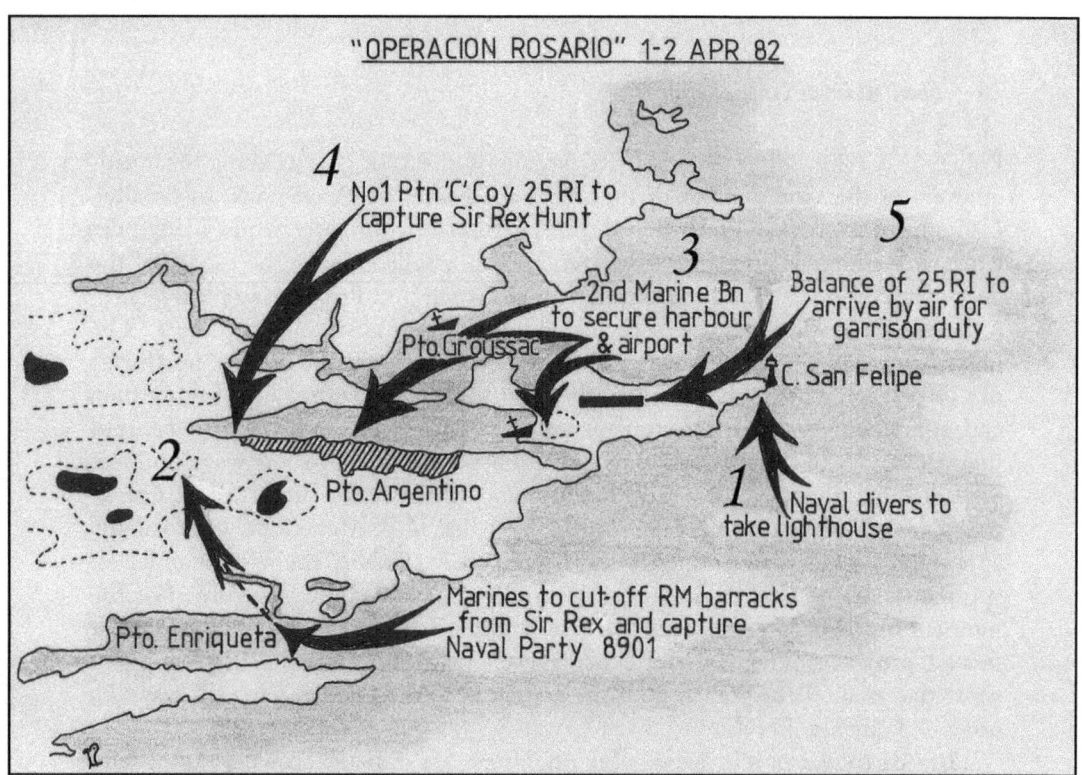

4 No1 Ptn 'C' Coy 25 RI to capture Sir Rex Hunt

5

3 2nd Marine Bn to secure harbour & airport

Balance of 25 RI to arrive by air for garrison duty

Pto. Groussac

C. San Felipe

2

Pto. Argentino

1 Naval divers to take lighthouse

Pto. Enriqueta

Marines to cut-off RM barracks from Sir Rex and capture Naval Party 8901

Map 1. The Argentine invasion of the Falkland Islands, 1–2 April 1982.

engaged in a fierce exchange of fire with Major Norman's Royal Marines guarding Sir Rex and Government House. Several Argentinians were killed in the action that the major was later to describe in a TV interview as 'exhilarating'. At 0800hrs armoured personnel carriers and heavy weapons landed in the face of some fire, but within half an hour the Governor ordered the British forces to surrender. By 0900hrs all resistance had ceased. The Argentinians then captured the radio station and the Cable and Wireless Office, thereby denying London any further reports of activity on the islands. In fact, Sir Rex recalled that it had been almost impossible to make contact with London earlier because of the unfavourable ionosphere for long-range communications anyway. The Argentinians pulled down the British flag and at 1230hrs, in an emotional ceremony, they raised the Argentine flag on the *Malvinas* for the first time. That afternoon 25 Infantry Regiment relieved the Argentine Marines at Stanley airport and there it was to remain, out in the open on the airfield, until it surrendered in June. The amphibious task force re-embarked the Argentine Marines and returned to the mainland. Sir Rex Hunt and his Foreign and Commonwealth staff, plus three wives and the families of the Royal Marines, were repatriated by air to Comodoro Rivadavia, to be joined later by any other Falkland Islanders and others who wished to leave. The next day 181 Military Police Company arrived by Hercules to take on the task of population control, quickly demonstrating to the Islanders the very reason why they had voted not to give up their sovereignty. The Military

Police also relieved 25 Infantry Regiment of the task of guarding the head-quarters of the Commander of the *Malvinas* theatre of Operations. In parallel, C Company embarked on the naval transport *Isla de los Estrados*, while 9 Engineer Company embarked on *Isla Gran Malvina*; both sailed under the escort of the destroyer *Alirante Irizar* for Darwin-Goose Green and Fox Bay respectively.

Goose Green airfield was secured without any opposition on 4 April. The infantry moved out to dig-in and secure the higher ground to the northwest of Goose Green airfield, noting as they did so, the difficulties of bringing men and equipment across the rough terrain. They too were to remain there until their surrender to the British Paras. By 2100hrs on 5 April Fox Bay was occupied. The *Malvinas* theatre of operations command structure for the invasion, *Operaçion Rosario*, was wound up on 7 April. Brigadier M.B. Menéndez was formally appointed Military Governor, with Brigadier A. Daher, the Commander of 9 Infantry Brigade, in command of ground forces under the governor. For the moment the *Malvinas* campaign was over and they settled down to garrison their newest province. The Argentine Army even provided a special handstamp to show that mail correspondence from their new *Islas Malvinas* garrison was '*Sin cargo*, – 'Carriage Free'.

The Argentine public were jubilant. Huge flag-waving crowds, crying and laughing, gathered to greet the news. The song *Las Malvinas son Argentinas* was sung with quadruple the enthusiasm which greeted their football team upon winning the World Cup. Telegrams, letters of congratulation, patriotic poems and offers of volunteers to settle the *Malvinas* poured in from all around the Spanish-speaking world, even from Italy. Commemorative stamps appeared on letters and entire classes of schoolchildren were directed to send their patriotic greetings and paintings through the official mail to the new *Conquistadors*. A sample of children's letters to *El Grobnador* and random soldiers are given in Appendix II.

Fig. 2. Captured Army Post Office 'Carriage free' handstamp.

Chapter 5

Operaçion Reconquista: Plan B

The small *Malvinas* garrison, fewer in number than the islands' civilian population, was an indication that the Junta clearly only expected empty rhetoric from
the United Kingdom, rather than military action. Indeed, beyond placing just one
additional infantry regiment on standby, no serious pre-planning to defend the
Falkland Islands against recovery by the British had taken place. Prime Minister
Margaret Thatcher's response to the occupation came as a surprise. The British
public were stunned and outraged by the humiliating sight of their finest Royal
Marine Commandos held face-down at gun point in the mud in front of the
world's media by a bunch of 'spics'. However, despite the shock and disbelief that
followed, three people had already anticipated the situation, albeit at short notice.
They were the First Sea Lord and Chief of Naval Staff, Sir Henry Leach, the
Prime Minister Margaret Thatcher and the British ambassador to the United
Nations, Sir Anthony Parsons.

On the Wednesday before the invasion, Sir Henry, with the firm evidence of
the amassing Argentine *Armada*, presented himself at a Prime Minister's crisis
meeting in the House of Commons. Significantly, the affair was exclusively a navy
matter, since none of the RAF air transport or bomber fleets had any air-to-air
refuelling capability to cover the distances involved and hence were unable either
to transport any ground reinforcements to the Falkland Islands in time or to
launch attacks on the occupying forces. Only the Royal Navy possessed the
necessary, balanced, equipped, trained and totally integrated long-distance intervention force in the form of the Royal Marines Commando Brigade. Decisively
Sir Henry informed the meeting that not only could the Royal Navy mount a
large task force in response to the impending invasion, but that it *should* do so,
and by the weekend. Thus, even as the Argentine *Armada* was still at sea, orders
went out to assemble a task force, a large part of which just happened to be
together at sea for a NATO exercise. Thereafter, the Prime Minister's part was to
vocalize the indignation of the British public and, most importantly, never to let
herself be deflected by setbacks from the task in hand to recover the Falkland
Islands to full British sovereignty. The Prime Minister's unwavering determination of what was right and just was shared throughout the Task Force, down to
the lowliest soldier, sailor and airman. However, a number of senior officers,
brought up on a British government diet of withdrawals from the Far and Middle
East and Africa, and extensive vacillation in such areas as Suez, Aden and

Rhodesia, were quite ambivalent at the very start. But for the commanding officers of the units involved, this was 'it', exactly what they had trained for a lifetime to do. Having firm resolution coming down the stovepipe from the Prime Minister and First Sea Lord was a new and rewarding experience for the British armed forces, which rose to the occasion.

Meanwhile, across the Atlantic, mindful that it was the isolation of the United States from its allies France and Britain that brought the Suez Crisis of 1956 to its hugely unsatisfactory conclusion, handing the Arab world a 'victory' they never won by force of arms, our third 'man-of-the-moment' Sir Anthony Parsons set about securing his political masterstroke in the form of United Nations Security Council Resolution 502. With the passing of this Resolution, everything which Britain was to do from then on was, diplomatically speaking, with the legal support of the UN: Argentina had invaded a British sovereign territory and it was now legal to boot them out by bullet and bayonet.

Whilst the British may have held the diplomatic cards, the fact of the matter was that the Argentinians were now in physical possession of all of Britain's islands in the South Atlantic, from West Falkland to the most easterly of the South Sandwich Islands. More diplomatic surprises, however, were on the way when the British invoked a treaty giving them access to the huge Second World War-vintage American airfield on the British island of Ascension in mid-Atlantic. Suddenly, about halfway down the full 12,688km distance to the Falkland Islands stood a giant unsinkable aircraft carrier only 5,600km away from the Falklands. Not only that, but Britain had mobilized a sizeable amphibious Task Force and sent it to sea in a breathtakingly short weekend in a blaze of international publicity. In Argentina, however, the people still backed their President exactly as Machiavelli might have predicted. The universal Argentine euphoria generated by the newfound possessions ruled out any chance of the Junta stepping down to any kind of shared sovereignty deal. Instead, the Junta determined to stay.

General Daher, the *Malvinas* land forces commander, went ahead and issued his first Operation Order, 1/82, for the defence of the islands, while on the mainland the Junta issued its own decree, 700/82, to create a new command formation for dealing with the British military response. Vice Admiral J.J. Lombardo was appointed first commander of the newly created South Atlantic theatre of operations and on 5 April the Junta ordered *Operacion Reconquista* to be put into immediate effect. Orders were issued for the *Malvinas* to be reinforced by ten Panhard armoured cars (each mounting a 90mm cannon), eight from 181 Armoured Cavalry Reconnaissance Squadron and two from 9 Infantry Regiment located at Comodoro Rivadavia; additionally, 3 Artillery Group from Paso de los Libres was ordered to move to Bahia Blanca and hence onto Stanley, now renamed 'Puerto Argentino'. It says much for the Argentine organization that within 24 hours of receipt of the orders to move, the first contingents of reinforcements were arriving on the Islands. The sea element of the move was completed

"Bad luck, President Galtieri! We didn't think the British would fight either!"

Fig. 3. Hitler and the Kaiser commiserate with General Galtieri.
(*Cummings/Daily Express/Mirrorpix*)

between 9 and 14 April. Interestingly, the very last reinforcements went not to Stanley but to Fox Bay on West Falkland. Just as the British were forced to hot plan their response to the invasion, so now were the Argentinians forced to hot plan their defences in response to the situation.

The news that the aircraft carriers HMS *Invincible* and HMS *Hermes*, with forty ships in support and five thousand men aboard, were on their way galvanized the Junta into further action. From now on, military assets were to be stripped out of Argentina at an astonishing rate, sometimes overwhelming the ability of the local commanders on the spot to cope. The *Fuerza Aerea* deployed propeller-driven Pucara counter-insurgency ground-attack aircraft, plus the modern Westinghouse TPS 43 long-range air defence radar, and three Oerlikon twin 35mm AA guns with a single 1960s *Superfledermaus* fire control radar to the Islands. The *Armada* deployed a small force of British Gnat-sized Italian Aermacchi ground-attack jet aircraft, an assortment of small support ships and 5 Marine Battalion of Commandos. All naval land forces, plus the additional army forces, were placed under the direct command of Brigadier Daher. On the other hand, 25 Infantry

Regiment, 8 Infantry Regiment, 9 Engineer Company, 181 Military Police Company and the *Fuerza Aerea* at Stanley airport came under the command of the Military Governor, Brigadier Menéndez. This in turn came under the newly created Commander South Atlantic Theatre of Operations, Admiral J.J. Lombardo, back in Buenos Aires. On 9 April Admiral Lombardo visited the *Malvinas* for a briefing by the two brigadiers, Menéndez and Daher, on the measures taken thus far to defend the Islands. He paid particular attention to 'Puerto Argentino', which was considered to be the most important military and political objective for the British. With further public announcements of reinforcements to the British Task Force, and in view of the strategic implications of the British use of Ascension Island, Admiral Lombardo promised to take steps to increase the number of troops on the *Malvinas* even further. The British Task Force was expected to arrive on or after 18 April and therefore reinforcements had to be deployed with extreme urgency. It was not until 15 April that a reliable appraisal on the rate of progress of the British fleet allowed the Argentine battle staff a pause for breath as the forecast earliest date of arrival of the British slipped to 25 April. Back on the Argentine mainland, General Galtieri, the President and Commander-in-Chief of the Argentine Armed Forces, without consulting any of the Army General Staff and without informing the commander of all Argentine forces on the *Malvinas*, assigned 10 Mechanized Infantry Brigade to the Islands. The brigade consisted of 3, 6 and 7 Mechanized Infantry Regiments and included support from Panhard armoured cars of 10 Armoured Cavalry Reconnaissance Squadron and the Brigade Engineer and Communications Companies.

In addition, Galtieri also assigned 3 Artillery Group, equipped with eighteen 105mm pack howitzers, to the *Malvinas* and gave orders for both formations to be moved to the operation zone with the utmost urgency. The consequences that these crossed-wire orders had upon some of the units concerned will be described later. On his return to the mainland, Admiral Lombardo then had the unenviable task of drawing up a new grand plan to consolidate the defence of the *Malvinas* and to prevent the Islands' recovery by the British. His task was to ensure continued Argentine sovereignty of all of the *Malvinas*, South Georgia and the South Sandwich Islands. Although the plan did not reach the Falklands Joint Military Commander or the Governor until 23 April, it is summarized below because it illustrates the intransigence of the Argentine military Junta, even at that early time, to consider any kind of compromise. Critics of the sinking of the Argentine flagship *General Belgrano* should study the Argentine admiral's unequivocal top priority order given in the list below. The individual service missions were as follows:

Armada
1. Use warships to damage, neutralize and **destroy British surface units wherever favourable opportunities arise** [Author's emphasis].

2. Use naval aircraft to attack surface units and aircraft with conventional weapons and missiles.
3. Carry out reconnaissance, antisubmarine and logistic support tasks.

Ejercito
1. Contain, disorganize, repel and annihilate any British attack.
2. Deploy artillery in the coastal defence role against amphibious vehicles and landing craft.
3. Exercise surveillance over the beaches.
4. Maintain a strong air-mobile reserve ready to intervene anywhere on the Islands.

Fuerza Aerea
1. Set up an early warning system to cover beaches, parachute dropping zones and landing areas.
2. Coordinate local air defence.

To meet the requirements for a strategic reserve, the plan called for 4 Airborne Infantry Brigade to be organized into combat groups. The brigade was to be transported to Comodoro Rivadavia and held on permanent standby at the base there. In the event, the tough Para brigade was never deployed, run-of-the-mill 3 Infantry Brigade eventually taking its place. However, between the visits of the Commander South Atlantic Theatre of Operations to the *Malvinas* and the arrival of his plan for their defence on the Islands, considerable upheavals were to take place that would affect the command and control of Argentine forces as they poured in.

First of all, on 12 April the British declared a maritime exclusion zone around the Falkland Islands. At the time it was questionable if there were actually any British forces in the area, but the threat from nuclear submarines was considered to be so real that the *Malvinas* were practically isolated from the mainland and the garrison was placed under siege conditions from that date onwards. Virtually all reinforcements by sea ceased; equipment and personnel henceforth would only arrive by air in 20-ton loads, or 100-man packets, each of which had to be identified, assigned to its tasks and deployed, usually on foot, to each operational location on the Islands. Next the headquarters of 10 Brigade arrived; in a tussle of seniority, Brigadier Menéndez appointed the newly arrived 10 Brigade commander, Brigadier O.L. Joffre, to command the ground forces over Brigadier Daher, whom he sent, along with all his staff and their entire accumulated corporate continuity experiences of the *Malvinas* campaign thus far, back to the mainland. All the main Argentine elements were now in place, as shown on the map below, including the ground-based air defences, whose detailed deployment will be covered in a moment.

Reviewing the developments thus far, the *Malvinas* issue had conveniently provided the classic solution to trouble at home. The small Royal Marines presence

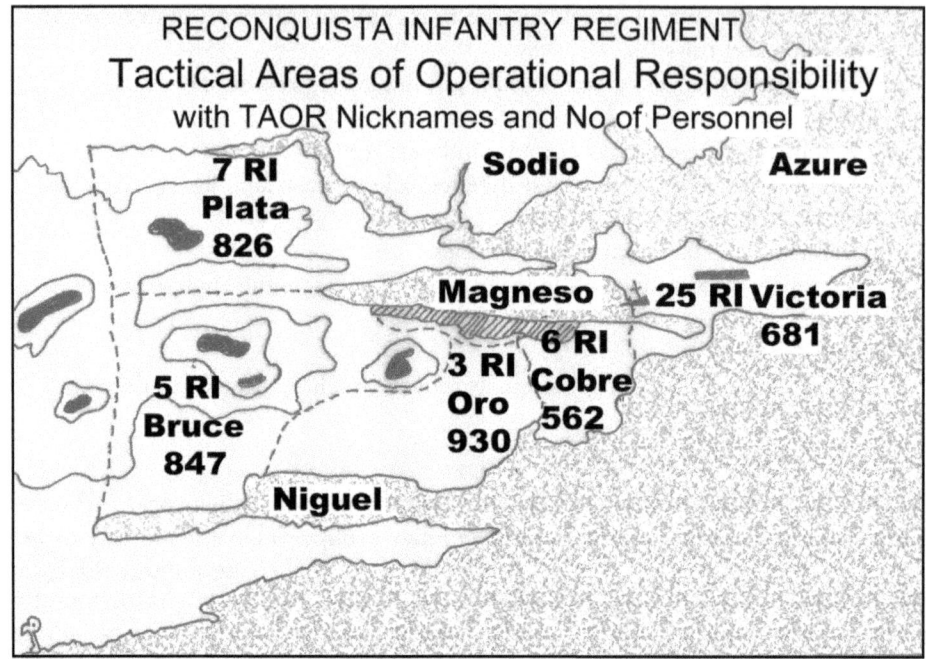

Map 2. *Operacion Reconquista* tactical areas of operational responsibility.

of some forty or so Commandos had been easily overcome without casualties to the British and had been sent back to England, along with Sir Rex Hunt, the British Governor, who departed wearing the full nineteenth-century regalia of plumed pith helmet, gold aiguillettes and sword. The Argentine public relations message was quite clear: the 19th Century sun had finally set on this far corner of the British Empire. The Argentine people were ecstatic. The popularity of the action was confirmed by the joyous, massive crowds calling for General Galtieri to appear at the balcony of the Presidential Palace overlooking the overflowing plazas where, only days before, there had been ugly demonstrations calling for his head for totally different reasons.

It was quite clear from the conduct of the *Malvinas* invasion that the Argentinians never seriously expected to have to defend their position on the Islands militarily. Wrongly, they had assumed that the British reaction, after appropriate protests in the United Nations, would be to let their possession go quietly, just as the Portuguese had let Goa go to India and Zanzibar had been absorbed into Tanzania all those years previously. If the population of the Falkland Islands had been made up of native South American Indians and Hispanic descendants, then such thinking might well have been correct. However, the Falkland Islands Kelpers were all more British than the British. Moreover, they were ingrained with that dour independence and dislike of outside authority, especially military authority, that characterizes islanders all over the world, especially British ones. The original Argentine plan only called for a small, battalion-sized force, provided by 25 Infantry Regiment, supplemented by Military Police from 181 Military Police Company to garrison the Islands. When it was realized that the British were really coming to reclaim the Islands, the Junta hastily poured in men and material. With a large conscript army to call upon from only a few hundred kilometres away, the Argentinians reckoned that saturating the *Malvinas* with troops would be sufficient to persuade the British that a successful counter-invasion mounted from a base more than 11,000km away would be a military improbability. Two significant events would, however, seal the fate of the ten thousand or so Argentinians who were ultimately rushed to the *Malvinas* in response to the sailing of the British Task Force within 48 hours of the Argentine invasion.

The first was that the Argentinians never really appreciated the military implications of that other little British possession in the middle of the Atlantic, Ascension Island. As a mid-point stop, Ascension enabled the British Task Force to reorganize and repack its hastily embarked stores in proper order ready for a major landing. More importantly, its full-length runway in the mid-Atlantic wastes halved the flying distance to the Falkland Islands and this, combined with superb airmanship and an astonishing chain of aerial logistic support from virtu-ally every available air tanker, enabled a British Vulcan bomber, in the twilight of its operational life, to deliver a stick of twenty-one 1,000lb bombs just before dawn on 1 May onto Stanley airport as the opening calling card of an Iron Lady who meant business. Furthermore, by implication, the Vulcan gave notice that the British had the capability to ginger things up a bit for the Junta on its main-land home patch too. And so, a significant number of air defence aircraft, which might otherwise have swayed the battle for air superiority over the *Malvinas*, were held back for the defence of the Argentine Fatherland. This deficiency was somewhat compensated by the deployment of some of the very latest, literally brand new, day-and-night, all-weather ground-based anti-aircraft artillery to the *Malvinas*, the story of which forms the central theme of this book. Equally importantly, Ascension Island also enabled massively long-range maritime aerial reconnaissance sorties to be flown by Victor tanker aircraft and Nimrod maritime patrol aircraft to confirm that the sea approaches to the intended landing zone were clear of all major Argentine naval units for up to 1,600km in any direction. It would also eventually allow Hercules transports to drop vital stores to the Task Force at sea, culminating in the ability to fly single-seat Harrier jet fighter replacements directly from Ascension Island onto the decks of British aircraft carriers at sea, well off the Falkland Islands, using air-to-air refuelling.

The second major factor was the imposition of the 200 nautical mile (NM) total exclusion zone around the Islands, backed up by the threat of nuclear sub-marines, the single most powerful card in the long-range poker game taking place between General Galtieri and Margaret Thatcher. Her ace was finally dealt with the sinking of the *General Belgrano* on 2 May, on only the second day of armed conflict, after which most of the Argentine *Armada* stayed firmly bottled up in port, especially its much-feared aircraft carrier, *Vienticinco de Mayo*. At least in this one far corner of the hostile icy wastes of the Southern Ocean, Britannia once more ruled the waves. Thus, caught in an incredibly long aerial and naval pincer, *Operacion Reconquista* had placed the Argentine garrison, strategically speaking, firmly in an inescapable trap of its own making.

Meanwhile, the Royal Air Force had given no thought to the ground defence of their overcrowded concentration of deployed Victor Tankers, Vulcan bombers, Nimrod maritime patrol aircraft, VC-10 passenger and cargo jets and Hercules C-130 transports, plus numerous helicopters of all three services, jammed cheek-by-jowl on the single runway of the Second World War airfield that constituted Ascension Island, with all the personnel elements pitched in tented enclaves as close to their aircraft as possible, parked by type, on the overcrowded airfield. It was the British Army who initiated the question to the MoD: 'Shouldn't we have some soldiers here just in case the Argentinians land a small force of commandos and have a field day blowing this lot up under our noses?' This eventually percolated down from joint to single service elements of the MoD to the RAF

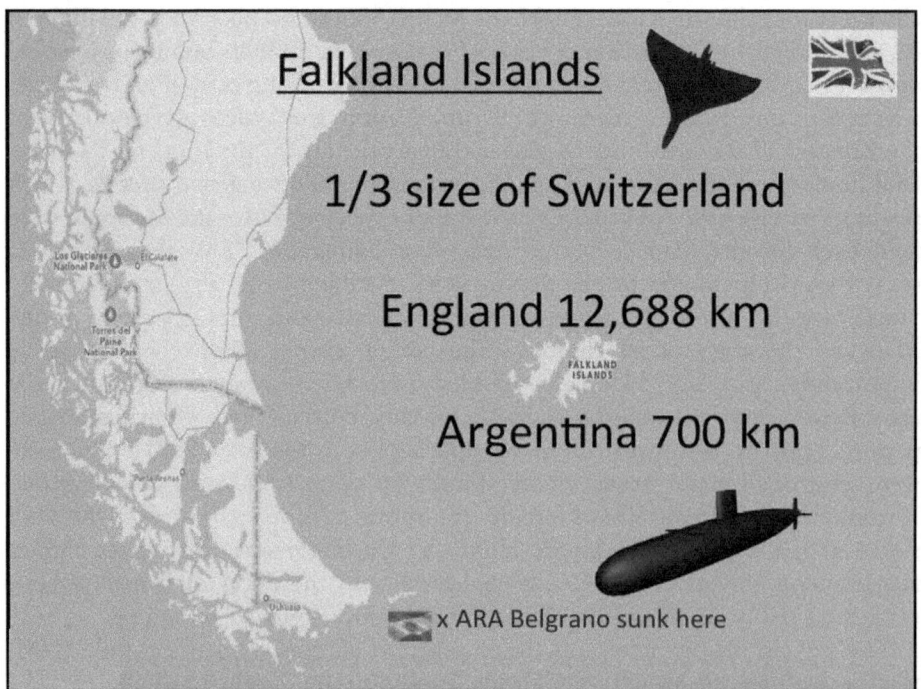

Map 3. The long reach of Britain's aerial and naval pincer arms.

Regiment and on 30 April, a full month after the Argentine invasion, a warning order was at last issued to my old command, 15 Squadron RAF Regiment. Shortly afterwards, a Land Rover-based infantry flight (platoon) of the squadron was dispatched to Ascension with an enhanced command element to organize some kind of force protection for the airbase and provide a quick reaction force under Royal Air Force command. To the chagrin of 15 Squadron, which supplied this little force, no other part of that or any other RAF infantry/armoured unit got further south than Ascension Island.

The next warning order to the RAF Regiment came about through the deployment of six Harrier GR3 ground-attack fighters to HMS *Hermes*. Initially these were sent as replacements for lost Sea Harriers, as they could be armed with Sidewinder missiles and of course had the same 30mm cannon as the Sea Harrier and so could be used as additional air defence fighters for the Fleet. Then the question arose of how to garrison the air defence of the Falklands once the aircraft carriers departed, since Stanley airport was too small for use by the RAF's principal air defence fighter, the F-4 Phantom. The solution would be to deploy the Harrier GR3 armed with Sidewinder ashore, in the air defence role, where they could operate from short (250m) airstrips planted anywhere flat using rapidly assembled aluminum planking. And if the Harriers were ashore, it would be the Air Force's responsibility to protect them, and that would excuse the Army from having to provide any Rapiers for garrison rotation duties once the Islands were repossessed. Because the Harriers were deployed forward, close to the Cold War front line in Germany, 63 Squadron RAF Regiment, a wholly self-sufficient independent unit, equipped with eight Blindfire all-weather Rapier fire units, was tasked with both the defence of the Harrier peacetime airbase at RAF Gutersloh and the alternate protection of the thirty-six Harrier jump-jets when they dispersed forward, off-base, to operate from six spread-out and ever-changing hidden positions in the field to provide close air support for the British Army forward troops. Indeed, when 63 Squadron received its warning order on 7 May to join the thrown-together 5 Brigade, the squadron was actually deployed in the field, exercising air defence of the RAF's helicopter force in Germany. It says much for the high readiness of the squadron under the command of Squadron Leader Loughborough that it was able to recover to base, clean up from the field exercise, bring all its Rapier equipment to full serviceability, equip with Arctic clothing and be ready to roll out of RAF Gutersloh in a 55-vehicle convoy for the UK just 48 hours later, complete with its organic mobile field repair workshops and a full war complement of logistic spares, the latter two to be the cornerstone of both RAF and Army Rapier operational maintenance during the conflict. In addition, they took their tracking simulator and aircraft recognition training kit. The trip through Germany and Belgium was a much-practised breeze of eleven convoy packets, each of five vehicles, all escorted swiftly through Germany and Belgium by police adept at getting NATO military convoys right across their countries painlessly. Not so the British police, who insisted on a single 55-vehicle convoy which, entirely predictably, brought the whole of the morning rush-hour traffic all around London to a complete halt, making its military presence known on every TV and radio traffic report in the land, so the Argentinians would know exactly what was coming their way. On the plus side, stranded motorists waved and cheered the convoy as it went by. Maggie was obviously very visibly 'doing something' about Argentina and doing it pretty impressively at that.

Meanwhile, an advance party flew to the UK, organized the collection of live missiles (the front-line NATO stock in Germany could not be depleted) and prepared the equipment to go on one ship, the *Atlantic Causeway*, accompanied by a small maintenance and security party. The rest of the personnel joined 5 Brigade and embarked with the Welsh and Scots Guards and the Gurkhas on the luxury liner *Queen Elizabeth II*, instantly converted into a troopship just as the *Queen Mary* had been converted in the Second World War. The squadron was further backed up by a small, higher-level operations staff element from the RAF Rapier Force Wing Headquarters. Initially 63 Squadron was part of 5 Brigade but such was the importance of air defence that the Rapiers were transferred to the Commander Land Forces Falkland Islands (CLFFI) as a force asset, with Squadron Leader Chris Feek attached to HMS *Fearless* as the RAF Rapier liaison officer. Once on board the *QEII*, 63 Squadron set up their Rapier tracker trainer, conducted aircraft recognition training and manned 7.62mm and 50-calibre machine guns on the upper decks and trained the Army infantry units to do the same, while 43 Air Defence Battery Royal Artillery manned four Blowpipe shoulder-launched missile points, with a joint air defence command post on the bridge of the *QEII*. During the voyage south the squadron had no idea where at sea its Rapiers might be on the *Atlantic Causeway* or when they might arrive in the Falklands or what their orders were. Indeed, all unit commanders on the *QEII*, including the future CLFFI, Royal Marine General Moore, were virtually incommunicado with anyone, mirroring the Argentine Army force commander's frustrating invasion voyage to the Falkland Islands unable to meet with his commanders scattered across several Argentine warships.

Chapter 6

Argentine Interlude:
Ground-Based Air Defence

The battles to liberate the Falkland Islands are more than well-documented. In fact, it has often been said, cynically, that never before have so many books been written by so few participants and non-participants about such a small campaign. I do not apologize for adding one more; the story that follows is so unique in its subsequent outcome that it needs telling. However, it is not my intention to go into competition with any other books that have been written thus far, the very best of which I consider to be *Razor's Edge: The Unofficial History of the Falklands War* by Hugh Bicheno, a fluent Spanish speaker and British diplomatic intelligence officer of the highest order, who has analysed the second-by-second battle accounts of both sides.

However, Bicheno is not an anti-aircraft man and it is this part of the conflict that I concentrate on, giving only a general view of other events to put the air-ground and ground-air battle into perspective. I was helped enormously by the large volume of operational orders, unit diaries, maps and the like that belonged to the Argentine anti-aircraft gunners and were recovered to the UK, along with the guns, the radars and a huge pile of British-made ammunition that make up the story.

In terms of firepower, the Argentinians deployed to the *Malvinas* the equivalent of the Royal Air Force's entire order of battle of short-range air defence weapons. Anti-aircraft weapons were drawn from all three Argentine armed forces and brought together under the integrated control of the Army's GADA 601. An inventory of Argentine anti-aircraft equipment captured in the Falklands Campaign is given in Appendix III.

The *Armada*'s Marine *Batallón Anti-Aero Nr. 1* deployed three Short Brothers Tigercat surface-to-air missile launchers together with a dozen Swiss/British-made Hispano HS 831 single-barrel, one-man 30mm guns of Second World War design (though upgraded from hand control to powered operation).

The *Fuerza Aerea* also deployed three Tigercat launchers. The system was essentially a dismounted Land Rover trailer version of the Royal Navy's Seacat of the 1960s. The introduction of a pilot flight of three Tigercat launchers into the RAF Regiment in the 1960s gave the missile international terrestrial credibility: if it was good enough for the British, it would be good enough for many

Fig. 4. Tigercat aimer and missile launcher trailers.

overseas customer nations to buy also. Being so tiny and light compared to the then stock-in-trade 3-ton bulk of a four-wheeled 40mm Bofors AA cannon, with its four-wheel 27KVA generator and a ton of ammunition, Tigercat was easily transportable over long distances in all RAF air cargo aircraft and for short distances by nearly all the helicopters then in service. Just three Hercules aircraft loads could provide instant missile air defence at any remote airfield or location. They proved their deterrent value on many overseas show-of-force exercises and, for real, in two far-off international crises in Zambia and Belize.

However, Tigercat is essentially a point defence weapon, which means the system must actually be very close to, or on top of, the target being attacked to be effective, a scenario in which the weapon operator is presented with an aircraft coming right at him. After launching, the subsonic missile is then manually steered by a thumb control via radio link towards the incoming aircraft and the large warhead is exploded by a proximity fuse. Against targets flying at high subsonic speeds and crossing the front of the Tigercat (or Seacat) position, or escaping after weapon delivery, the missile has hardly any effective capability to catch up with a fast-crossing target or a target flying away from the launcher. To be effective in the area defence of, say, a high strategic value airfield facing a dozen or so Harriers, many more than just three Tigercats would have been required, and for this another system, Rapier, was already under advanced development at the time. Tigercat was simply an already in-service Seacat ship system put onto two trailers. Since its missile guidance was visual, the system could only be used in daylight and clear weather.

In its day the Tigercat had served the British well and had had its moments of very effective military deterrence. Disappointingly for its RAF crews, of course, it was never actually fired by them in anger. In the 1960s crisis of Rhodesia's Declaration of Independence, the RAF Regiment Tigercats were rushed to defend Zambia's capital airport in Lusaka for the Commonwealth Heads of Government meeting, which was never attacked. Similarly, in 1977 they were rushed by air across the Atlantic to Belize overnight in order to deter the possibility of an air attack by Guatemalan Air Force Second World War Mustangs attacking Belize's only international airport. Guatemala's claim to Belize was similar to Argentina's over the Falkland Islands and hinged on a supposed status from distant Elizabethan days when it was sufficient simply to plant a flag on a beach somewhere in order to claim an entire continent in the name of a distant sovereign. The Guatemalan response to Tigercat's arrival was a risible protest to the United Nations about the arrival of British intercontinental ballistic missiles, but the immediate presence of the missiles did deter any future thought of invasion.

However, by the mid-1970s Tigercat's days of service were numbered by the introduction of the faster and vastly more accurate all-weather Rapier, while in the Royal Navy Tigercat was being replaced by Rapier's bigger brother, Sea Wolf. By 1979 Rapier had replaced the Tigercat and Bofors 40mm guns in Belize and that deterrence was sufficient for Britain to see the colony safely all the way to independence whilst still managing to sustain reasonably cordial relations with Guatemala.

The story of the RAF Tigercats does not end there, however. They were denied the opportunity to retire gracefully to become the gate guardians for 48 Squadron RAF Regiment, which had operated them for over ten years. Due to Ian Smith's long-running quest for white independence and Rhodesian attacks on Zimbabwean terrorist/liberation army bases inside Zambia, the ex-RAF Regiment Tigercats were hastily refurbished to as-new condition by the manufacturers and sent back to Africa to defend Zambia against Rhodesian cross-border air raids. The Naval Seacats, however, lingered on in a significant number of older Royal Navy warships as their primary anti-aircraft weapon in 1982 where they proved insufficient to prevent any of those ships from being put out of action or sunk.

The Hispano 30mm anti-aircraft gun is an interesting weapon. Originally developed in the Second World War, it has been enhanced only by the replacement of its hand-powered controls with power-operated joystick controls and the replacement of its spider's web gunsight by a predicting reflector gunsight that projects an aiming light-spot that provides aim-off for the gunner based on gyro

Fig. 5. Hispano 30mm trailer-mounted AA gun.

inputs from rates of traverse and elevation. Without accurate range to complete the calculation, this gyro prediction is limited in accuracy, but it is better than gunner guesswork. The Argentine version was mounted on a two-wheel trailer from which it could be pitched-off into action by just one man. A Wankel rotary engine under the driver's seat powered a hydraulic motor to move the gun in azimuth and elevation in response to joystick control. Like the Tigercat, this gun had no radar alerting system to point it in the direction of the target, which therefore had to be acquired visually by the gunner. Except for targets flying straight down the barrel, so to speak, the kill probability is therefore very much a matter of luck, in the order of just 1 or 2 per cent per shell fired. The Hispano would be a good weapon to deploy on something really small like a short bridge, but would need far greater numbers than just twelve to have much value in protecting a larger area like an airfield. Being a small and very portable cannon, it was a much-favoured war trophy for British units to put outside their headquarters as a souvenir of the campaign. One of these guns, along with the personnel and unit records of the Marine *Battalón Anti-Aero* that owned them, was to grace my own squadron headquarters; another went to 1 (Fighter) Squadron's Harriers at RAF Wittering.

The *Fuerza Aerea* created the *Escuadron de Artilleria Anti-Aerea Malvinas* and deployed rather more important ground-based air defence equipment than did the *Armada*. The star of their show was the Westinghouse TPS 43 long-range surveillance radar, which was planted away from the airfield, on top of Canopus Hill, to provide long-range early warning of British attacks out to a range of 300km or more; however, due to severe terrain screening by local mountain ranges, it was blind to low-level flying over most of the *Malvinas* inland. Whilst it provided a measure of early warning, target direction and range could only be passed verbally over wireless or field telephone links to the radar-less Tigercats and Hispano guns. The radar did provide the unexpected bonus of being able to track Royal Navy ships coming in close for nightly shore bombardment, allowing personnel to be warned to take cover and to give ship locations to shore-based artillery to reply; its *pièce de resistance* was to direct the launch of a land-based Exocet dismounted from an Argentine warship to be fired successfully at a British warship, with a little help from French Exocet engineers, or so it is said.

The *Fuerza Aerea* gunners, the Argentine equivalent of the RAF Regiment, were at their base at Mara del Plata when they received orders on 3 April to prepare for combat. They were to deploy nine German Rheinmetall twin 20mm anti-aircraft guns to the *Malvinas*. The guns arrived on the island by Hercules and were placed into their operational positions as underslung loads by Chinook helicopters of *Brigada Aerea VII* between 17 and 19 April. The *Fuerza Aerea* had

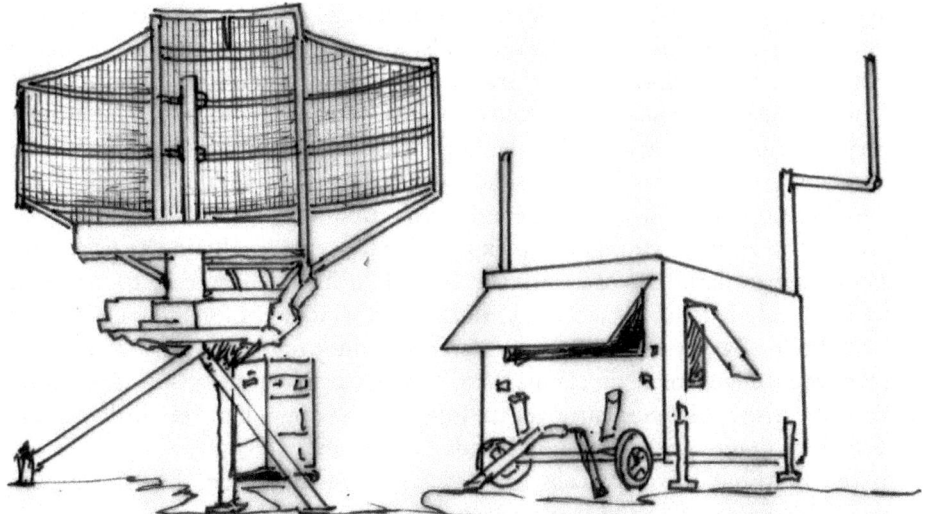

Fig. 6. Westinghouse TPS 43 long-range air defence surveillance radar.

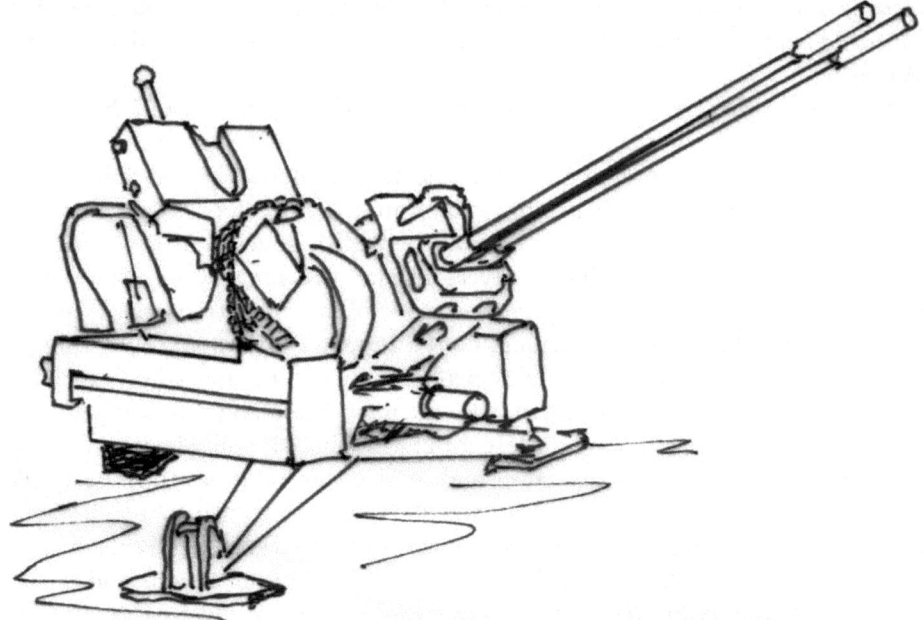

Fig. 7. Rheinmetall twin 20mm trailer-mounted AA gun.

by now quickly discovered that most of the Islands' interior was impassable to heavy wheeled vehicles. These 20mm guns have a maximum effective range of about 2km and are very popular in NATO armies for use as point defence weapons to provide terminal self-protection for small, high-value targets such as bridges, radar stations and temporary concentrations of armour or artillery. On peacetime range practices the Rheinmetalls always look very impressive, firing lots of rounds with a good show of tracer. The guns, however, are optically laid and directed using a joystick; they rely for success on the fact that the target must be very close and coming at it directly; in the Falklands a dustbin-sized and easily moved Israeli Elta or Rasit short-range surveillance radar with a range of 20km was used to provide these guns with verbal direction of where to look for targets. However, the gunners still had to pick up the Harriers visually in the gathering darkness against dark hills or a dark sea. It could not have been easy to maintain constant visual vigilance, especially in those cold, windswept lonely hours of first and last light of every South Atlantic dawn and dusk.

The Argentinians made no claims for kills with the Rheinmetalls. It is possible, in view of conscript service turnover timing, that the crews had very little experience with the guns prior to the Falklands Campaign.

In the first and second weeks of May, after hostilities on the Islands had opened, the *Fuerza Aerea* also procured two batches of Soviet-made shoulder-launched SA7 Strela missiles, roughly equivalent to the American Stinger. These

Fig. 8. Soviet SA7 Strela man-portable shoulder-launched missile.

were deployed to Mount Low; a pair turned up, unfired, at Goose Green and more turned up at Stanley airport, near a twin 35mm Oerlikon cannon that had been overturned by random high-level bombing. However, due to lack of familiarity or training, or perhaps due to the high-speed and low-level Harrier attacks, none of these Russian heat-seeking missiles was successful. Again, it should be stressed that Strela is essentially a point defence, coming-directly-at-you self-defence weapon.

The last *Fuerza Aerea* weapon to be deployed by the Argentinians at Stanley airport was the only one which had the capability to provide any measure of area defence: that battery was a trio of Oerlikon twin 35mm cannon with their 1960s associated Swiss *Superfledermaus* fire-control radar. There was, however, only one

Fig. 9. Oerlikon twin 35mm AA gun common to the Army and Air Force.

Fig. 10. *Fuerza Aerea Superfledermaus* Oerlikon 35mm radar.

such radar. Each gun could be up to 500m from the radar, so the battery footprint on the ground was an entire 1km map square. With an effective range of 4km and a shell self-destruct height of around 18,000ft, it was a fearsome weapon when all three guns under radar control were focused on a single target with great accuracy. However, its target engagement rate was limited to one aircraft at a time in radar mode; in the optical, independent, local control mode, each cannon mount is again only really effective against dead-ahead, approaching targets, as were the other AA guns and Tigercat. For effective operations, at least one, ideally two or even three Oerlikons should be connected to the radar fire-control unit.

The Army, on the other hand, was rather better equipped than the other two services; it was, after all, the senior service in the Junta and that is probably why it had better access to the large sums of money required to buy the most modern electronically controlled anti-aircraft equipment. GADA 601 deployed to the South Atlantic theatre of operations with twelve brand-new Oerlikon twin 35mm AA guns controlled by the then very latest Swiss fire-control radar, the Contraves Skyguard, of which they had six.

The most important advances of the Skyguard over the *Superfledermaus* fire-control system were that it used multi-frequency agile pulse-to-pulse radar against jamming and it had hands-off radar tracking of great accuracy. Accuracy was the system's byword: the guns even had sensors on the ends of the 35mm barrels to measure changing muzzle velocities of individual shells as the barrels loosened-up with heat in combat, resulting in slightly lower muzzle velocities. The radar tracking was paralleled with a TV tracker, either in a fully hands-

Fig. 11. GADA 601 Skyguard-Oerlikon 35mm AA fire-control radar.

off mode or manually controlled by a roller-ball as required, which allowed the tracking radar to be silenced if necessary, giving an attacking aircraft the impression that radar lock had been broken off. The TV display also included a sub-display of the shells going up to the target; this display also worked in reverse to show if the target aircraft fires a missile back at the radar, which would give the crew the chance to engage the incoming missile. The in-house joke was that the radar crews should always chew gum so that they could use it to glue the fire button down, get the hell out of the radar and jump into the safety of their trench outside before the missile hit the radar. More on that little drill later.

Wonderfully, for South Atlantic operations, the Skyguard radar cabin was completely enclosed, cosy, warm and dry, whereas the *Superfledermaus* operators had to stand outside in the blowing Arctic gales. Such was the design foresight of Swiss radar that, as it sank under its 5-ton weight into wet turf in bad weather conditions, a sensor would automatically re-level the radar without the intervention of the crew. And, just in case the radar did miss a late unmasking target, a hapless crewman in a low swivel-chair sat outside, equipped with an electronic pointing device that could put the radar onto a visually acquired target instantly. Each radar could control up to three guns simultaneously, each gun located up to 500m from the radar, giving the same 1km map square footprint as the

Superfledermaus fire unit. Multiple directional targets could be engaged by releasing selected guns to local control. In short, Skyguard was a superbly thought-out state-of-the-art piece of military kit, as reliable as a Swiss watch and it would prove to be the nemesis of Vulcans, Harriers, the Paras and the SAS alike.

In addition, the Army possessed a single Franco-German Roland surface-to-air missile launcher, which they probably fortuitously had for pre-purchase initial operational evaluation purposes. The whole system – surveillance radar, tracking radar, TV tracker, two missile launch tubes, the crew and a power generator – was self-contained and protected from the elements in a container mounted upon a single 5-ton, four-wheeled, heavy truck-towed trailer. In capability and missile performance it pretty well mimicked the British Rapier, except that Rapier was configured on two small two-wheeled trailers for global air transportability, jeep-towed field mobility and easy concealment.

Finally, the Army also deployed three more Tigercats from 602 Mixed Air Defence Artillery Group and a further eight Hispano 30mm guns of the 101 Air Defence Artillery Group. Overall early warning was provided by the *Fuerza Aerea* Westinghouse radar already mentioned, and locally by dustbin-sized, man-portable Elta or Rasit radars used for alerting Blowpipes or Rheinmetall 20mm guns.

These tiny radars, which could change position daily, even hourly, were going to give Harrier pilots a lot of headaches as they were almost invisible to a jet pilot and their locations given by warships offshore, were mostly out of date.

Fig. 12. Roland articulated trailer-mounted missile launcher.

Fig. 13. Rasit dustbin-sized, man-portable AA warning radar.

The final anti-aircraft weapon to be described is the British shoulder-launched Blowpipe, which was operated by the Argentine Army, the Royal Artillery and the Royal Marines. It was at once simple, inexpensive, very fast and left no tell-tale white plume of rocket motor smoke. Like the Tigercat, it had to be steered to the target by means of a thumb-control joystick radio link. However, unlike the Soviet Strela and Stinger, which both trailed white smoke, Blowpipe in flight was virtually invisible to the enemy as its propellant was smokeless, as was British Rapier. Also, not being a heat-seeker, Blowpipe could also be used in daylight, in the ground-role against armour and even as a trench-buster with great effect. Although Blowpipe required a high level of training, both sides very successfully destroyed aircraft with it.

Meanwhile, preparations for the *Malvinas* invasion had been carried out in conditions of the greatest secrecy so that, aside from the Naval Task Force and its Marines, 25 Infantry Regiment and 181 Military Police Company, no other units of the Argentine Army were in any way prepared in anticipation of the

Fig. 14. Blowpipe man-portable shoulder-launched AA missile.

forthcoming operation. Members of the British forces who took part in Operation Corporate may wish to draw some comparisons of their own surprise
notifications and *ad hoc* embarkation experiences in the rush to build up extra
capability for the forthcoming conflict in the Falklands Campaign from this
candid account of GADA 601's deployment to the *Malvinas*.

On 7 April 1982 the Commanding Officer of *Agrupaçion de Artilleria de Defensa
Aerea 601*, GADA 601, *Teniente Coronel* Hector L. Arias, received the order
from the Air Defence Brigade Headquarters to muster and prepare the unit for
an immediate move to the *Malvinas*. He was to have a Roland, Tigercats and
Hispanos attached under his command. All the equipment was to be loaded
aboard the transport vessel *Cordoba* at Mar del Plata, the port just outside Buenos
Aires, during the following night, 8/9 April. *Cordoba* was then to set sail immediately for the *Malvinas*, while the 574 personnel, with their individual small arms
and personal equipment, were to be transported to the *Fuerza Aerea* base at
Comodoro Rivadavia and flown on 11 April directly into the melting pot of the
South Atlantic theatre of operations.

Following receipt of these orders, the GADA 601 commander drew up his
plans to move men and equipment to the *Malvinas*. Firstly, the units were
brought up to their full war establishments of men and ammunition, and then
organized for the move into echelons (or 'chalks' in UK military parlance). From
the outset there were a number of problems; for example, the units did not have
any cold weather clothing for the coming South Atlantic winter. Only after many
demands did the necessary parkas, goggles, gloves and balaclavas finally arrive,
only moments before the unit's departure from the airhead.

A further problem was the almost total lack of information about the characteristics of the *Islas Malvinas* themselves. Un-gridded maps that had been purchased

from the British Directorate of Overseas Survey in the 1960s at the cost of 2 shillings 6 pence each had been reprinted by the Argentine *Instituto Geografico Militar*. For the record, the British ground-attack Harrier pilots embarked on HMS *Hermes* were also to be plagued by the Royal Navy's use of exactly the same un-gridded maps until maps properly gridded by the Royal Engineers Mapping Department were delivered to the ship by air. Unlike the British, who lived on the Islands, the Argentinians had no clue that most of the terrain shown on the maps was totally impassable to almost all wheeled vehicles, especially heavy artillery-towing trucks. It cannot have been easy for the troops to pass exact locations to their higher formation commanders, and grid-less maps must have made calls for artillery fire support and correction very challenging. More Argentine attention was paid to the question of sovereignty than cartography; Argentine naval charts, again copies of British ones published in 1969, went so far as to use the name *Islas Malvinas, Territo Nacional de la Tierra del Fuego, Antarctica e Islas de Atlantico Sur*. In an amusing postscript amid all the Spanish, there was a surviving little footnote in English, which invited users who had a correction or addition to make to annotate the chart and send it to the Director of Overseas Survey at Tolworth in Surrey, who would be most pleased to send the helpful correspondent a free replacement map by return of post.

Back at GADA 601, there was no information on the mission to be assigned to the units, nor any details of the logistic arrangements to support them. All these factors needed to be known in order for commanders at all levels to plan the deployment of a mixed and very large force of highly technical guns and missiles. Luckily the training of officers and Regular non-commissioned officers, NCOs, was excellent. Just two months previously the units had completed all their operational and maintenance courses on the recently delivered Oerlikon twin 35mm guns and their Skyguard radars. Platoon commanders, gun commanders and radar commanders were all highly motivated and had been thoroughly trained by their Swiss instructors. Over the preceding months everyone had been extensively exercised at every level by a series of practice deployments and war games. Before departure, four extra officers and ten extra NCOs were drafted in to man the GADA 601's operation centre. These additional men made it possible to man the operations centre around the clock, without interruption, throughout the six-week battle for the *Malvinas*, to provide early warning of enemy air attack, to control the fire of the various weapons deployed around the islands and, incidentally, to give warning of the approach of warships as they closed in to bombard the Islands with gunfire at night.

The training of the rank and file, on the other hand, was very far from satisfactory. The bulk of the Army was made up of one-year national service conscripts, identified by the year of their birth. Some 50 per cent of the class of 1962 conscripts had already been released from military service in December 1981. Since it was impossible to recall these personnel within the 48hr timescale of the suddenly ordered move to the *Malvinas*, units were brought up to their full war establishments by drafting in class of 1963 conscripts, most of whom had barely completed their initial, most basic, recruit infantry training, let alone any advanced anti-aircraft weapons training.

The actual move of the men was a fairly straightforward affair. They were flown from Mar del Plata to Comodoro Rivadavia by two *Fuerza Aerea* transport aircraft on 12 April and accommodated overnight in the 8 Infantry Regiment barracks. The next day the commanding officer and some of his headquarters staff flew out to the *Malvinas* to carry out reconnaissance and make on-the-spot plans for the air defence of Port Stanley or, as it was now called, 'Puerto Argentino'. The second-in-command (2IC) drew the short straw and stayed behind to supervise the move of the remainder of the unit and its equipment.

The move of the equipment itself to the *Malvinas* was a chapter of order, counter-order and disorder. The equipment, driven down from Mar del Plata, arrived for loading as planned. However, the captain of the *Cordoba*, in the absence of any embarkation and loading priorities, had already taken on board considerable quantities of equipment for a field engineer unit, as well as containers of rations for naval personnel stationed on the Islands. In his opinion, it was impossible to load all the anti-aircraft equipment which he could see lined up on the quayside. Consequently, when the ship set sail on 10 April a number of gun-towing vehicles, two mobile field kitchens and other equipment and stores were left behind. Three days later, on 13 April, *Cordoba* put into *Puerto Deseado*, on the Argentine mainland, about three-quarters of the way to the *Malvinas*. The British had already declared their 200 nautical mile maritime exclusion zone around the Falkland Islands; with the risk of British nuclear submarines lurking around, the Argentine *Armada* decided not to risk the crossing of such a valuable cargo. Over the next two days the rear party of GADA 601, under its 2IC, worked furiously to unload all the equipment. But no sooner was it all unloaded safely onto the quayside than the very next day an order arrived to load it all back onto *Cordoba*; it had been decided to risk running the nuclear submarine blockade after all. As soon as the equipment was safely stowed aboard, yet another order arrived: the guns and radar were all to be unloaded at once, driven by road to Comodoro Rivadavia 300km to the north and then flown to 'Puerto Argentino'. What expletives might have been expressed by the soldiers and the sailors is not recorded but one can easily imagine them. Such is the stuff of the friction of war; the winning trick is to expect it, train for it and rise above it. Of 'can do', there was to be plenty to do on both sides.

Since each Oerlikon cannon weighed over 6 tons and each Skyguard over 5 tons, only one major piece of equipment at a time could be carried in each aircraft; boxes of ammunition and drums of fuel took up the remaining space on each flight. At the mounting airhead, needless to say, GADA 601's carefully calculated loads were competing constantly with the changing theatre priorities as the Argentinians wrestled with the ever-growing problem of sustaining the *Malvinas* garrison by air alone. Nevertheless, due to the initiative and efforts of the rear party and the reconnaissance and planning by their headquarters group already on the Islands, as each load was taken off the aircraft and formed into a workable sub-unit, it was deployed to its operational location with whatever came over the air bridge. Over the next ten days twenty-five Hercules sorties were required to transport some hundred tons of anti-aircraft equipment from Comodoro Rivadavia to 'Puerto Argentino'. Added to the discovery that most of the terrain was impassable to heavy, wheeled trucks and trailers, there was already a heavy demand on the two Chinooks available to position heavy equipment.

The Argentine priorities for deployment were interesting, reflecting the bias of most armies to look after themselves first, already noticeable in these earliest days of the occupation. Notwithstanding that the only remaining link between the Islands and the mainland for the garrison's very survival lay with the airfield, Stanley airport itself was heavily under-defended, with three elderly Tigercats and one elderly *Superfledermaus* controlling two or possibly three Oerlikon twin 35mm guns. The bulk of the most capable air defence assets, the six all-weather Skyguard fire-control radars with their twelve Oerlikon twin 35mm guns and the single Roland missile launcher, plus Tigercats, 30mm Hispanos and Rheinmetall twin 20mm guns, were all used to defend Brigadier Menendez's headquarters in the town and the environment of 'Puerto Argentino' harbour, considered by them to be the most likely targets for air attack. The thought that it might be unlikely that the British would either bomb and shell their kith and kin in Stanley town or storm the beaches of Stanley's harbour in front of the town and thus ravage the Islands' only significantly populated area appears not to have entered the minds of the Argentine High Command. Nor did the thought that since all sea transport, scared of submarines, had evaporated, did the stranded garrison consider that the airfield was now the lynch-pin of their battlefield logistic support.

The only really well-defended airfield was the Pucara forward airstrip at Goose Green. On 17/18 April a complete Army fire unit of one Skyguard and two Oerlikon twin 35mm guns of GADA 601 was flown into position there by Chinook helicopter, to join the six *Fuerza Aerea* twin 20mm Rheinmetall guns already in place.

In an amusing misunderstanding of English translation, the Argentinians re-named the settlement 'Ganso Verde', literally Green Goose. Like so many tiny patches of land with a few houses, it was going to go down in history as yet another far-flung place in the world where relatively few Britons were going to goose another superior enemy into surrender in an amazing feat of arms. As the days of April passed and the British Task Force sailed ever closer, the Argentinians continued to consolidate their positions and dig-in for a winter war, wondering where the first British blow might fall.

Chapter 7

The Softening-up Battle Begins

The softening-up battle for the recovery of the Falkland Islands began with an incredibly long-armed pincer action by two extreme tools of the Cold War reaching across both global hemispheres: a Vulcan nuclear bomber and a nuclear-powered hunter-killer submarine aptly name HMS Conqueror.

The Argentine air defence battle for retention of the *Malvinas* began on 1 May 1982 under the command of GADA 601. With the *Fuerza Aerea*'s TPS 43 long-range radar as its eyes, the *Ejercito* had the strongest air defence: twelve of the best and newest Skyguard-directed Oerlikon twin 35mm guns ranged around 'Puerto Argentino' town and harbour, thickened up with three Marine Tiger-cats, a scattering of 20mm and 30mm guns and one Roland. Also under GADA 601's anti-aircraft control was the entirely Air Force-defended airfield, with its single 20-year-old *Superfledermaus* radar directing just one Oerlikon twin 35mm; the other twin 35mm Oerlikon deployed beyond *Superfledermaus* radar-laying range on an older, earlier generation, airstrip 2km away, in local gunsight-aiming mode; additionally, three Tigercats were deployed, two about a kilometre or so apart at the landward end of the runway and the third 4km away at the tip of the airfield peninsula. This thin, inter-service imbalance of GADA 601 Army and Air Force resources was to continue for another nine days at least.

The British opened their campaign to regain the Falkland Islands in the pre-dawn hours of 1 May 1982, starting with a Vulcan bomber sortie, codenamed Black Buck. Two Vulcan nuclear bombers, in the twilight of their operational lives, XM598 and XM607, hastily reconfigured back to conventional bomb-carrying and with their redundant air-to-air refuelling systems restored, took off from Ascension Island on the night of 30 April, supported by eleven Victor tankers. The lead Vulcan's cabin failed to pressurize after take-off and so XM607, the reserve aircraft for the mission, captained by Flight Lieutenant Martin Withers, took over the task of dropping the opening visiting card of 10 tons of high explosive bombs on Stanley airport as a clear message from the British that the gloves were off.

After refuelling mid-air six times from the string of Victor tankers, with the other five Victors refuelling each other to keep up with the 44 (Rhodesia) Squad-ron Vulcan, it prepared for its bombing run. Considerable mathematical model-ling had determined the optimum height for the attack. A low-level approach would have exposed the aircraft to ground artillery for the shortest time; on the other hand, the aircraft's huge silhouette would have also probably filled the sky, presenting the gunners with the biggest and easiest target aircraft they had ever seen. The bombs also had to be dropped from a reasonable height to ensure good runway penetration and to avoid damage to the aircraft from the explosions. In the end it was decided to carry out the bombing run from just above the published nominal effective fire ceiling for medium calibre anti-aircraft gun engagement zones used by the AA community around the world: 10,000ft. From this height the forward throw of the bombs would carry them the last 3km onto the target, thus allowing the bomber to turn away from the nominal edge of ground-based, short-range, air defence engagement zones.

The Argentinians manning the TPS 43 long-range radar reported that a mysterious blip had appeared briefly and then disappeared again. With the naval blockade in place, there were nightly sometimes unidentified Hercules flights, which were not always pre-announced. The next radar detection was by a 20km range Skyguard radar, which had picked up and tracked a solitary blip approaching from the northeast. The crew of the Vulcan were alerted to the fact that they were being illuminated by a tracking radar by their radar warning receiver fitted in the distinctive bar-shaped aerial on the top of the Vulcan's fin. The Vulcan was also carrying a Westinghouse ALQ-101 jamming pod on the old Skybolt nuclear missile under-wing station and the pod was now activated in response to the threat of AA radars tracking the target. Back on the ground, the Skyguard crews had the option of changing the radar frequencies or even going passive by homing-in and locking onto the source of the jamming, thus giving the bomber the impression that its electronic counter-measures (ECM) had been successful.

The crucial factor, however, had little to do with the nuances of electronic counter-measures, counter-counter-measures, or even counter-counter-counter-measures among competing geeks; the crux of the matter was that nobody had yet identified the target as hostile and so the order to engage was not forthcoming from the AA operations centre. Possibly, at this stage of inexperience in high-threat air defence warfare, nobody had considered the use of ECM to constitute a hostile act, as it did in NATO. One can well imagine the twitch factor as individual duty command post officers wrestled with the decision-making process to fire the very first opening shots of the war as the seconds ticked by. In the end the British made the decision for the Argentine gunners: as soon as the first of the string of twenty-one bombs actually started exploding, they needed no further orders and let fly with everything. Unfortunately for them, thanks to the 3km throw-forward of bombs and the Vulcan being instantly 10 tons lighter, it was already well out of range and in a spectacular climb, pushed up by its mighty engines on full power. Once safely clear of the Falkland Islands, the bomber crew tapped out their secret codeword, Superfuze, in good old-fashioned Morse code on the aircraft's long-range radio and began the long, tiring, haul back to Ascension Island, topped-up all the way back by Victor tankers meeting the Vulcan in stages over the Atlantic wastes. This attack was to enter the record books as the longest ever manned bomber raid in the history of air warfare.

On receipt of the Vulcan's codeword, HMS *Hermes*, now just 100 nautical miles northeast of the Falklands, began the final preparations to launch a series of attacks using twelve Sea Harriers. The attacks against targets at Stanley were planned to divide and distract the air defences as much as possible. Four aircraft, led by Lieutenant Commander Tony Ogilvy, were armed with 1,000-pounders; this formation was to approach Stanley airport from the northeast. At 5km short of the target and just outside effective AA range, the aircraft were to pull up and toss their combined load onto the defences dominating the high ground on Mary Hill and Canopus Hill.

Hopefully, for the 27 seconds or so that it would take the bombs to land on their target, all the AA weapons would be drawn off looking to the northeast at this first wave, while the other aircraft closed in from other directions. The next five aircraft, led by Lieutenant Commander Andy Auld, were split into two groups. As the bombs from the toss-bombers started to explode, the Sea Harriers were to fly straight in, low and fast, from the north and northwest, masked by the land, and drop their BL755 anti-personnel cluster bombs on the runway, airfield buildings and parked aircraft.

Some 4 hours after the Vulcan raid daylight was just breaking and the Argentine gunners were fully keyed up and ready. Despite the distracting manoeuvres of the toss-bombers, a fierce display of tracer rose to greet the second and third waves of Sea Harriers. Without radar lock, most of this fire would have been wasted. Tigercat missiles were also fired, but without effect; the first missile

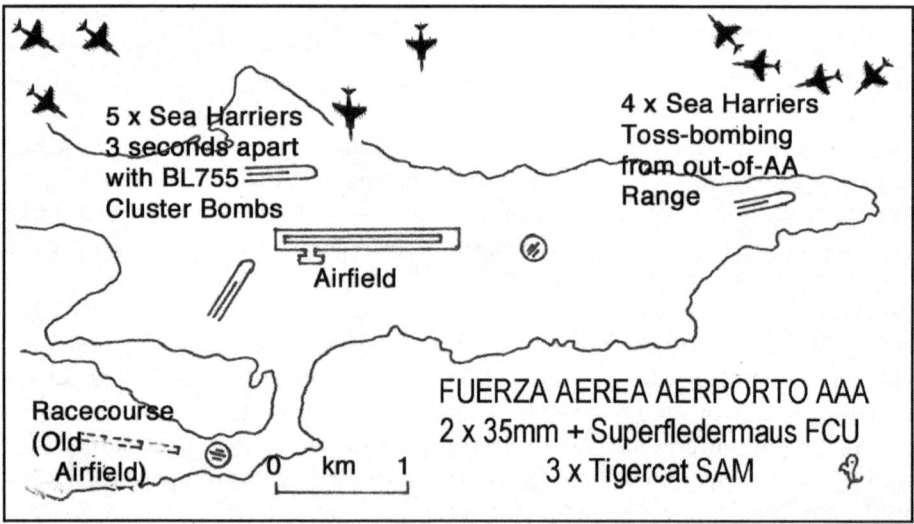

Map 4. Nine Sea Harriers' simultaneous attack on 1 May is all over in 15 seconds.

pulled up sharply into the clouds and after a few seconds of flight blew up, either through malfunction or, more likely, because the missile layer had lost sight of his quarry and terminated the engagement; another missile, launched almost horizontally at the very low-flying Harriers, struck the ground and also exploded harmlessly. Yet another missile, either a Tigercat or a Roland, passed just in front of Flight Lieutenant David Morgan flying at 550 knots over the airfield. Moments later there was a loud bang as a single cannon shell hit the tail of his aircraft, ZA192. His flying controls were still responsive and, as he pulled himself down even lower, his radar warning receiver rasped that he was being tracked by a radar. Morgan opened up the Harrier's airbrakes for a moment to release the radar-deceiving chaff packed inside, then pulled over hard and flew even lower still, finally breaking the lock by dropping behind rising ground, out of line-of-sight, and eventually made his way safely back to his aircraft carrier.

On the ground the crew of the Skyguard-Oerlikon fire unit Bravo 2 saw the flash of the explosion at the rear of the aircraft and what appeared to be bits of aeroplane fall away; they then saw the aircraft roll over onto its back and vanish from view. The crew disengaged the Skyguard and claimed a kill: *Cayo al Mar* – crashed into the sea.

Similarly, the crew of the solitary Roland, which had also been fired, saw a Harrier blip disappear off their radar screen and claimed a possible kill, but with *Sin Information* about the final outcome of the engagement. In the cockpits of their Sea Harriers the pilots doubtless breathed a sigh of relief as they made their way back to land on their carriers, HMS *Illustrious* and HMS *Hermes*, known as 'Herpes' to the RN, and the 'Rat Infested Rust Bucket' to the RAF.

Meanwhile, at Goose Green the defences were at maximum alert, having been tipped off by the earlier Vulcan raid on Stanley airport. Three Sea Harriers, led by Lieutenant Commander Fred Fredriksen, swept in very low and fast down Falkland Sound to hit the grass airfield from the northwest with a total of six BLL755 cluster bombs. Fortunately, just before this first attack of the day, the Argentine air defenders had placed a firing restriction on the Oerlikons to allow a pair of locally based Pucaras to take off. The Sea Harriers were detected late, at a range of about 2km, just a few seconds' flying time, which was not long enough to rescind the restriction order, lay on the guns and fire. The Sea Harriers swept through unscathed, destroying one Pucara. In the words of a report by the *Fuerza Aerea*, one of the bombs hit Lieutenant Jukic's Pucará, which was starting up surrounded by mechanics and gunsmiths. The plane caught fire completely, which caused the gradual explosion of the weapons on board, transforming it into a death trap for those in the area. Lieutenant Daniel Jukic and corporals Mario Duarte, Juan Rodríguez, José Peralta, Miguel Ángel Carrizo, José Maldonado, Agustín Montaño and Andrés Brashich all died in this attack.

The last three Sea Harriers returned safely and that night's intensely watched TV news report by Brian Hanrahan – 'I counted them all out and I counted them

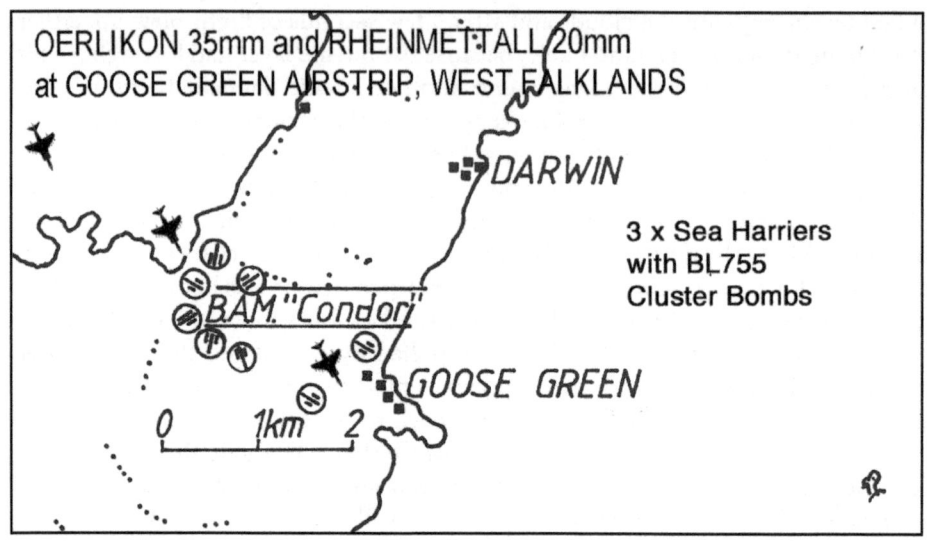

OERLIKON 35mm and RHEINMETTALL 20mm
at GOOSE GREEN AIRSTRIP, WEST FALKLANDS

DARWIN

3 x Sea Harriers
with BL755
Cluster Bombs

B.A.M. "Condor"

GOOSE GREEN

0   1km   2

Map 5. BL755 cluster bomb attack on Goose Green by three Sea Harriers, 1 May.

all back' – had the nation heaving a sigh of pride and relief. Even British helicopters had a share in the excitement of this first day. An armed Royal Navy
Wessex, XS483 of 845 Squadron, temporarily attached to the Exocet-armed
HMS *Glamorgan* for shore bombardment spotting duties off Stanley, reported
that two Tigercats had been fired at it. The Wessex took violent evasive action
and both missiles missed.

During the day the Argentine commanders thought that there might be an
attempted landing at Goose Green and ordered the heavy twin 35mm Oerlikon
guns to be moved to defend the coastline. The weapons were relocated overnight
using a locally requisitioned tractor, siting them either side of the Goose Green
settlement promontory, with the Skyguard radar placed amongst the civilian
buildings. The idea of using anti-aircraft guns in the ground-to-ground role is
not a new one; the Germans in the Second World War famously used their
88mm heavy AA gun as a devastatingly effective anti-tank weapon. The opportunity for *Teniente* Braghini's command to blood his two twin 35mm Oerlikons
and their Skyguard in both the anti-aircraft and ground-to-ground roles at Goose
Green was yet to come. Relative to its size, Goose Green airfield on 21 May was
far better defended against air attack than the thinly spread air defences of Stanley
airport.

In a same-day response to the early morning British aerial assault on the
Malvinas, the Argentinians mounted a fearsomely concentrated attack that afternoon on the Royal Navy Task Force, using Canberra bombers, Skyhawk and
Dagger fighter-bombers, while Mirages provided air defence top cover. Following an air battle between Sea Harriers flown by Lieutenant Steve Thomas and

Flight Lieutenant Paul Barton and two Mirages flown by *Capitain* Cuerva and *Teniente Primero* Perona, the Argentine AA defences were to finally have their first kill.

The two Sea Harriers closed in on the Mirages and in the exchange of missile and cannon fire during a slashing pass, the rear-most Mirage, 1-015, was hit by a Sidewinder. The aircraft exploded in a huge fireball but, as it broke up, the pilot, Perona, miraculously ejected from the wreckage. His parachute deployed properly and, with a further stroke of good fortune, he landed in the shallows of the West Falkland coast. With both ankles injured, he was able to hobble ashore at Pebble Island, another Pucara base. Meanwhile, the leading Mirage, 1-019, dived into the cloud, followed by another Sidewinder. The missile's proximity fuse detonated the missile close enough to rupture the aircraft's fuel tanks. Cuerva turned towards Stanley airport and jettisoned his external fuel tanks as an anticipated crash-landing safety precaution, but the falling tanks were misinterpreted as bombs and his Mirage therefore as an enemy aircraft committing a hostile act. Obviously, Argentine visual aircraft recognition was not sufficiently up to scratch to tell the difference between a Mirage and a Sea Harrier on the Skyguard's TV tracking screen. Understandably, so soon after their morning's experience of the Vulcan and Sea Harriers zipping through unscathed, the gunners were pretty jumpy. Added to this, in an extraordinary procurement omission, the Argentine Skyguard radars were not fitted with Identification Friend or Foe (IFF) equipment and thus, upon seeing what they considered to be a hostile act, the AA defences opened up, destroying the stricken aircraft over Stanley and killing *Capitain* Cuerva in the process. Later, the Scots Guards would, thankfully ineffectually, fire on passing Harriers that had just attacked Argentine enemy positions in their support on the same loose understanding of a hostile act combined with a total lack of aircraft recognition training.

At the end of this day, the opening clash between aircraft and anti-aircraft defences, the Argentinians claimed to have downed two Harriers by two different weapon systems, most likely the same aircraft, whose release of chaff gave the impression of a visually confirmed hit. That aircraft suffered no hindrance to its flying capability and landed safely back on its carrier and the ragged hole in its tail was repaired within hours. The final Argentine score for the day was Enemy Kills: Nil; Own Goals: 1 Mirage. British achievements were an earthquaking Vulcan shake-up, followed by half as much bomb tonnage again delivered by a dozen Sea Harriers, plus a number of enemy kills: two Pucaras on the ground and, in the air, two Mirages, a Skyhawk and a Canberra. It was a good start.

Mindful of the historic nature of this, the glorious first day of the defence of their new *Malvinas* Province, *Grobenador* Menendez directed, in the spirit of all Spanish *Conquistadors* from Cortez to Pizzaro, that his garrison priest, *Capellan Fray* Salvador Santore, set down a record of the historic day's activities and those that followed. The result was a local, A4-sized news-sheet called *La Gaçeta*

Argentina, produced for the benefit of the *Malvinas* troops. In the editorial of the first edition, the *Capellan* spelt out the objectives of the paper: it was to be a source of truth and a reflection of the historical sentiments and social experiences of the *Nuevo Malvinasenses*. He recorded the actions of the first eight days from 1 May onwards with an accuracy which British Intelligence would probably have given its eye teeth for at the time, even down to the detail of individual casualties at various locations and aircraft losses by type and number. The paper also recorded the possibility that the Sea Harrier claimed as a kill might have been downed by either an Oerlikon gun or a missile.

By contrast, the official communiqués issued by the Junta on the mainland for consumption by the world's media were simultaneously claiming that three Sea Harriers and two helicopters had been shot down on Day 1. A complete and slightly rust and water-stained copy of the very first edition of the Good Father's *Gaçeta Argentina*, published on 8 May, is shown in Appendix IV.

No action took place in the air on 2 May, although the Argentinians were to claim, in Official Communique 14, that a further two Sea Harriers had been shot down and six more damaged. With no British losses for a considerable combat effort, there was a huge sigh of relief on the aircraft carriers that everything had got off to a good start with all the efficiency of a peacetime exercise. This changed to a rather more sombre note with the news later in the day that the Argentine cruiser *General Belgrano*, another Second World War survivor, had been sunk by the nuclear submarine HMS *Conqueror* with great loss of life, made significantly greater owing to the watertight doors not being closed-up for action stations – an incomprehensible oversight given that the warship's mission was to sink the British on sight. Closer to the Falklands, two small Argentine patrol craft, *Alfredo Sobral* and *Comodoro Somellara*, were searching under cover of darkness for the crew of the downed Canberra, *Teniente* Eduardo de Ibanez and *Teniente Primero* Mario Gonzalez, whose rescue signal equipment showed them to be north of Stanley. One of the ships was spotted on radar by Lieutenant Commander Chandler in a Royal Navy Sea King. As the helicopter closed to investigate, it was engaged by the ship's 40mm Bofors gun. The shells missed and from a safe distance the helicopter called up HMS *Glasgow* and HMS *Coventry* for two Lynx helicopters. These engaged and sank the first vessel with the Royal Navy's brand-new anti-ship missile, Sea Skua. Whilst the two Lynxes were searching for survivors amid the flotsam, they came under fire from the other patrol vessel, which was duly engaged with a further two Sea Skuas, killing eight Argentine crew, including the captain, and wounding a further six. The *Alfredo Sobral* eventually limped back to Puerto Deseado, on the mainland, two days later. The Canberra bomber crew were never found and the incident, minus any reference to the *Comodoro Somellara*, was reported promptly in *Fray* Santore's *Gaçeta* as well as in Argentine official communiqués.[2] Finally, in mid-afternoon an *Armada*

Aermacchi 339 jet fighter crashed at Stanley, killing the pilot. Clearly the first 16 tons of British bombs had not closed the airfield.

At 0530hrs on 4 May, so *La Gaçeta* reported, another heavy bombardment of the airfield took place by an unidentified bomber. It was, in fact, Black Buck 2, with Vulcan XM607, now preserved at RAF Waddington. The aircraft was captained by Squadron Leader John Reeve of 50 Squadron. None of the Argentine AA forces reported any action against this air raid, which took place from 16,000ft, the twenty-one bombs disrupting flying support activities on the airfield without hitting the runway.

Later in the day, however, a Skyguard-Oerlikon combination was to have its first confirmed kill. Three Sea Harriers, flown by Lieutenant Commander Batt, Lieutenant Taylor and Flight Lieutenant Ball, were to attack parked Pucaras at Goose Green with BL755 cluster bombs and crater the grass airfield with 1,000lb parachute-retarded bombs. This time they came in from the southeast and the Skyguard was up and ready for them. Taylor's aircraft, mortally damaged, disintegrated into a fireball and the remains crashed into the ground at the side of the airfield. Only the tail remained intact. The Argentinians identified the pilot and buried him at Goose Green the same day. To date, according to *La Gaçeta*, the British air raids and naval shore bombardment had killed twelve Argentinians and wounded a further thirty-seven around the Islands. The paper truthfully recorded that the Argentine AA defences had destroyed one Sea Harrier and mentioned that its pilot, *Teniente* Taylor, had been buried at 'Ganso Verde' with *los honores militares*. Meanwhile, back on the mainland, Official Communique 27 was now busily claiming that a total of nine Sea Harriers had been destroyed.

The success of the Swiss radar-directed Oerlikon guns forced an early change in Royal Navy ground-attack tactics. The Task Force commander, Admiral Sandy Woodward, reasoned that in an attrition battle with the Argentinians, he would surely lose; it was therefore necessary to husband the Sea Harriers to cover the eventual British landing, which could not be allowed to fail under any circumstances. Henceforth, low-level attacks over the top of known defended targets were to be avoided wherever possible. In future, high-level bombing or toss-bombing, for which the Sea Harrier had a special bombsight, was to be employed instead. Thus, the Oerlikons, having demonstrated their lethality, forced an inferior tactic on their British enemy by the fourth day of the air-ground war.

For the next eight days bad weather limited air operations against the Islands, though there was much activity at sea, with HMS *Sheffield* sunk. Separately, HMS *Glasgow* was hit by a bomb dropped by a Skyhawk of *Gruppo 5*, flown by *Teniente Primero* Fauste Gavazzi, who was not to enjoy much luck later that day. Firstly, his bomb passed right through the thin-skinned warship, missing all its vital structures, to explode harmlessly in the sea on the other side; next, on his jubilant way home, Gavazzi somehow, inexplicably, flew unannounced through the Skyguard-Oerlikon gun-defended airfield defence zone of 'Ganso Verde' and was promptly shot down and killed. In defence of the gunners, the Skyhawk and both versions of the Harrier can easily, to the untrained eye, be mistaken for one another at many viewing angles. This is the kind of operational accident that aircrew and ground gunners abhor, and the only cure is a rigorous visual aircraft recognition training system to distinguish one squashed fruit fly image from another. Such a high level of visual recognition skill is a constant challenge to full-time aviators and AA gunners alike and was unlikely to have been achieved by one-year national service conscripts within just four months of training; the problem of aircraft recognition, not unique to the Argentinians, will crop up again later in the book.

The next level of friendly aircraft protection against own-goal gunnery, IFF, was not fitted to the Skyguards as a cost-saving exercise, although the cost was outweighed by the expense of just one aircraft lost. The British were not much better: they used a simple IFF unit that was so badly placed in the Harrier cockpits that it was a nightmare to change codes on the ground, let alone in flight. Even when the notoriously unreliable British IFF was working, the signal could be corrupted by mutual interference between two aircraft flying close to each other. Also, the lower they flew for self-protection, the more the protective IFF response signal was screened from the ground below. British helicopters were not fitted with IFF at all either, and this deficiency led directly to a Royal Navy ship-launched own-goal over land later in the campaign. The lack of British helicopter IFF was also to tie British Rapier radars up in knots.

By 12 May a crisis point for the Argentinians was developing. The effectiveness of the total naval blockade, now a month old, had been rammed home by the sinking of *General Belgrano* at sea and by the destruction of smaller Argentine supply vessels whenever they were found. Similarly, in the air the Argentinians felt that the British had already achieved a clear local air superiority which affected the helicopter mobility of their ground forces, even at night. Because of the reduced level of rations available on the Islands, the joint command of the *Malvinas* ordered that troops were to take only one solid meal a day – a development that could not be good for health or morale freezing in the middle of a South Atlantic winter of rain, snow and constant gales.

The deep penetration activities of the Special Air Service and Royal Marines Special Boat Section were also beginning to pay dividends. The Argentinians had become increasingly anxious about the possibility of larger, commando-sized raids in strength or even a major landing. The joint command decided to establish a permanent state of night stand-to and ordered that two-thirds of all personnel were to remain available during the hours of darkness. The threat of enemy night operations also compelled the Argentinians to make frequent changes to the dispositions of their air defence and artillery equipment. Due to the soft terrain, impassable to the great weight of the guns, and the fact that most of the gun-towing vehicles had been left on the mainland, the redeployments had to be carried out by the one and only serviceable Chinook on the Islands, AE521 (the other one, AE520, having been grounded with engine problems near the Governor's Residence at Port Stanley since 2 May). Sir Rex was to tell me later, privately, how he had hoped one day that this and other lightly damaged helicopters might be repaired and put to use for the benefit of the Islanders. Sadly, in their moment of victory, the British forces failed to secure and guard these valuable and vulnerable air assets from their own souvenir-hunting soldiers, who literally picked the great machines to death; only the SAS managed to rescue a flyable UH-1 and a pair of Augusta helicopter gunships for their own use back home.

The *Capellan*'s *Gaçeta Argentina* was also beginning to reflect a more sombre note: the military activities of each of the last five days were covered in just twenty-five lines. Interestingly, the loss of Gavazzi in his Skyhawk at Goose Green was put down to pilot error for entering the free-fire zone of the AA defences. *La Gaçeta* concluded with a warning that personnel were not, under any circumstances, to discuss the military situation on the *Malvinas* with anyone on the mainland when they phoned home.

Bad weather precluded any flying on 13 and 14 May. On 15 May the Argentinians' worst fears about a commando raid were realized when the SAS carried out a textbook attack on Pebble Island, destroying six Pucaras, four Turbo Mentor light attack aircraft and a Skyvan twin-engined transport aircraft on the ground, whilst deciding not to kill the sleeping ground and aircrew tucked up in their sleeping bags as tantamount to cold-blooded murder. At the same time 800 Squadron mounted another inaccurate, high-level bombing raid against Stanley airport and Darwin; thereafter, the technique was discontinued as a serious means of destroying specific targets. Instead, toss-bombing was to be adopted from outside the range of AA ground fire by Sea Harriers, which were at least fitted with a bombsight for the task; this sight proved to give an accuracy of less than 400m. As a further harassing measure, Sea Harriers were to continue to drop single 1,000lb bombs randomly on Stanley airport on their way to their combat air patrol stations. *La Gaçeta* faithfully reported the change in British tactics. The paper then went on to praise the Hercules aircrew of *Grupo Uno de Transporte Aero* for their unceasing efforts, day and night, to bring in tons of supplies from the mainland, and concluded with a summary of the latest football scores on the mainland.

As part of the intelligence build-up to the amphibious landings being finalized for Port San Carlos, a number of Sea Harrier photo-reconnaissance flights took place on 16 May. Flights over Fox Bay, Port King and Goose Green revealed two Argentine supply vessels, the *Rio Caracamia* and the *Bahia Buen Suceso*; both were attacked four hours later by a pair of Sea Harriers commanded by Gordy Batt. These attacks were made at high speed and low level and with great precision. The Argentine gunners responded with vigorous return of anti-aircraft fire. An uncontrollable fire broke out on the *Rio Caracamia* and she was abandoned by her crew, to be sunk a week later by a Lynx with Sea Skua missiles.

Subsequent records showed that another Sea Harrier, ZA191, had suffered a direct hit on its tail that day too, which was then subsequently repaired. Still later in the day, according to *La Gaçeta*, an attack on the airfield at Stanley was repulsed by Argentine AA fire from the ground. The latter 'raids' were in fact combat air patrol (CAP) Sea Harriers dropping off 1,000lb bombs on their way to taking up air patrol positions. However, the initial bombing height of 15,000ft, previously considered safe from gun and missile flight, was now raised to 20,000ft. After the surrender, one of the 6-ton Oerlikon twin 35mm guns at Stanley airport was found to have been turned over by a great force that could only have been a near-miss by a 1,000-pounder; the gun was later shipped to the UK 'as is' and its bent barrels welded together in an 'X' to stand guard outside my 2729 Skyguard-Oerlikon Squadron Commander office at RAF Waddington.

That night the *Fuerza Aerea* TPS 43 air defence radar crew showed their great ingenuity and initiative by passing the range and bearing plot of the British warships as they came in close for their nightly shore bombardment to a battery of Argentine long-range 155mm heavy field guns. Between the efforts of the two, they claimed to be able to get field artillery fire to within 400m of the bombarding ships, forcing yet another reassessment of British tactics.

A further Vulcan attack planned for that night was cancelled. Instead, the aircraft returned to the UK whilst the British contemplated how to deal with the effectiveness of the TPS 43 early warning radar and the Skyguard fire-control radars. The need to mount an anti-radar missile attack against the Argentine radars became paramount. Live firing trials of the daylight-only, TV-guided Anglo-French Martel missile had already taken place with a Vulcan bomber. Further trials were now to take place with a Vulcan carrying up to four American-supplied Shrike self-homing anti-radar missiles on the never-before-used Skybolt missile launch rails on the aircraft.

On 18 May Lieutenant Commander Sharkey Ward and RAF Flight Lieutenant Ian Mortimer were launched in two Sea Harriers to carry out a pre-dawn diversionary attack and drop flares all over the Islands. Ward returned to HMS *Invincible* an hour later to collect six bombs to drop on Stanley airport. Meanwhile, on HMS *Hermes* 800 Squadron was mounting more high-level photo-reconnaissance sorties. None of this activity drew any comment from *La Gaçeta*. Unbeknown to the Argentinians, a most important event was taking place at sea. HMS *Hermes* was being reinforced by four more Sea Harriers and by the first four GR3 ground-attack Harriers of 1 (Fighter) Squadron RAF. Similarly, HMS *Invincible* also received four extra Sea Harriers, all off the *Atlantic Conveyor*.

The newcomers spent 19 May familiarizing themselves with their new surroundings. A pre-dawn attack on a group of Argentine helicopters reported on Mount Kent was postponed due to low cloud and uncertainty about the level of concentration of Argentine anti-aircraft defences in the area. The weather failed to improve and the original plan to drop retarded bombs at very low level was replaced by a high-level, blind bombing mission by four Harriers dropping variable time-fused bombs through the cloud. Later that day the Argentine Joint Chiefs of the General Staff in Buenos Aires issued Official Communiqué 64 to say that two Harriers had bombed an area 100 km from 'Puerto Argentino' but were repelled by anti-aircraft guns. That night the Argentinians also claimed to have used their 155mm field artillery, assisted by the *Fuerza Aerea* TPS 43 air defence radar, to repulse a shore bombardment by the Royal Navy.

The Royal Air Force Harrier GR3s saw their first action in the Falklands Campaign on 20 May. Three Harrier GR3s, flown by the squadron commander, Wing Commander Peter Squire, and his two flight commanders, Squadron Leaders Bob Iveson and Jerry Pook, set out on a ground-attack sortie using BL755 cluster bombs to destroy a fuel dump at Fox Bay. BL755s are particularly suited for dealing with soft targets in high-speed, low-level attacks. As the bomb is released it sows a swathe of bomblets along a 25m-wide strip that is 100m long. The attack was a success but the follow-up missions were going to create a disparate rate of risk-taking between the two Harrier variants, upon the direction of no less than the Task Force commander himself, Admiral Woodward, aboard HMS *Hermes*. Henceforth, all the high-risk, low-level attacks through flak were to be assigned to the Harrier GR3s, and the Sea Harriers were to be conserved and confined to high-altitude CAP, still dropping random 1,000-pounders on Stanley airport on their way to their top cover positions over the aircraft carriers, leaving the eventual beach landings themselves to be covered by the anti-aircraft missiles of the warships escorting the various landing craft until the Royal Artillery Rapier missile launchers were ashore on both arms of the high ground above San Carlos Water.

Some 12,800km away in the UK a curious press release was given out by the British Ministry of Defence. A Sea King helicopter was reported to have got into difficulty on a reconnaissance mission in the vicinity of Tierra del Fuego and was presumed to have got lost and crash-landed whilst attempting an emergency landing in the vicinity of Punta Arenas in Chile. The crew of the helicopter, however, were nowhere to be found. Suspicions about their whereabouts and the true nature of the mission of this helicopter must have posed some problems for the Junta, especially when the Chileans, no great friends of the Argentinians in the oft-disputed border areas in the cone of South America, promptly buried the wreckage with bulldozers in an undisclosed location and released a video of them doing it to the world's TV channels.

The chattering of the paparazzi classes filled the airwaves with conspiratorial theories that would have delighted Ian Fleming, while the Brer Rabbit of British MoD 'He said nuffink', causing the Argentine Junta to put troops on a high defensive alert in the Argentine rear area on the mainland. Perhaps that was all that the British wanted to do: deflect Argentine High Command attention away from what was about to happen next. Scuttlebutt had it that it was a failed SAS raid to destroy the Exocet-carrying Super Etendards at their home base. If that was indeed the plan, the distraction certainly worked. The virtually unopposed initial landings at San Carlos Water made the headlines the next day. The British were back on their own territory and the action now shifted to the beachhead.

Chapter 8

The British Land at San Carlos

In the earliest hours of 21 May, under Commodore Clapp, the naval commander of the amphibious landings, the British slid into the arms of the sheltered, upside-down 'Y' that constituted San Carlos Water and the San Carlos river estuary to land the entire 3 Commando Brigade of Royal Marines, along with 2 Para and 3 Para, using the amphibious assault ships HMS *Intrepid* and HMS *Fearless*, five logistic landing ships (*Sir Geraint, Sir Tristram, Sir Lancelot, Sir Galahad* and *Sir Percivale*), and RFA *Stromness*, plus the civilian ships taken up from trade, namely *Norland, Europic Ferry* and, of course, the famous 'white whale', the P&O cruise ship, *Canberra*.

The beachhead command ship, HMS *Fearless*, landed 40 Commando and 2 Para at Blue Beach, at the head of San Carlos Water, which also housed the San Carlos settlement, with its pier and a , tiny airstrip. The 40 Commando objective was to secure the beachhead and the north–south Verde Mountain ridge to the west, overlooking San Carlos Water, while 2 Para raced south, twice the distance, to secure the east–west ridge of the Sussex Mountains, also overlooking San Carlos Water to the north, and to the south the distant, but not-quite-in-sight Darwin/Goose Green isthmus.

Fearless's sister assault ship HMS *Intrepid* landed 3 Para up the east–west San Carlos river arm of the 'Y' onto Green Beach at Port San Carlos. Meanwhile, RFA *Stromness* landed 45 Commando on Red Beach in Ajax Bay, the location of a disused refrigeration plant, on the landward (inside) arm of Wreck Point Peninsula, which enclosed the other arm of the 'Y'; finally, 42 Commando was ferried off *Canberra* by landing craft to secure Port San Carlos. In the crutch of the 'Y' sat the frigate HMS *Plymouth*, guarding both entrances to the initial landing force sites.

Out in Falkland Sound, the long, wide waterway that divides the major islands of East and West Falkland, were concentrated the anti-aircraft and anti-submarine screen, consisting of the destroyer HMS *Antrim* and the frigates HMS *Argonaut* and HMS *Ardent*, along with the newest, HMS *Broadsword* and HMS *Brilliant*, and finally HMS *Yarmouth* and the RFA *Fort Austin*, the latter being a stores ship, with ammunition and fuel aboard but, in this phase of the operation, employed on anti-submarine duty.

The Commandos immediately secured all the beachheads and the Paras raced out to secure the high ground to north and south, overlooking the beachheads.

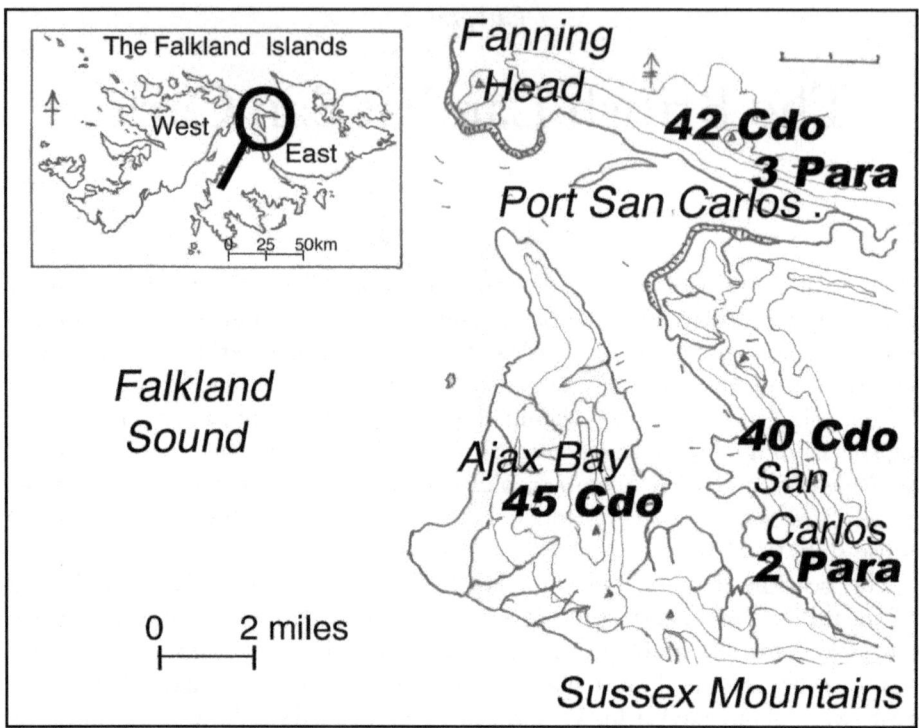

Map 6. Landing destinations for 3 Commando Brigade, 21 May.

A quick look at the map shows how well the landing sites were protected from air and ship view by this high ground on three sides and how the air defence ships and their long-range radars were hemmed-in by the target-masking land masses of East and West Falkland into a 5–10-mile wide neck of water. That the Royal Navy was to achieve this landing and get a brigade of men ashore virtually un-opposed without alerting the Argentine High Command for many hours was a crowning success, overcoming the single most vulnerable moment upon which the whole recovery of the Falkland Islands depended. Argentine intransigence had cast the die that British boots on the ground were the only way to eject the *Ejercito Argentino* and restore the *Islas Malvinas* to their rightful heirs under the name of the Falkland Islands. Now those boots had stepped ashore virtu-ally unopposed and no one had any inkling just how far they were eventually going to have to walk.

The Argentine Army was not wholly unprepared and, like the British, had considered probably around a dozen different landing options. They considered the San Carlos area as one possibility, mainly because of an earlier report on 12 May that the British had already landed there. This may have been one of the many beach inspection patrols by the Royal Marines of the Special Boat Section, who were tasked with checking out numerous possible landing places for suitability. The Argentinians dispatched a reduced company of 601 Commando on a helicopter reconnaissance of the area which, even after a thorough check of the local population, drew a blank. They left behind two parties, one on Fanning Head, critically overlooking the entrance to the 'Y' of San Carlos Water, Ajax Bay and San Carlos, and one on the San Carlos River and Port San Carlos on the other arm of the 'Y'. Each party had a vehicle-mounted radio but only the Fanning Head radio could reach Stanley, the radio in Port San Carlos being completely screened by hills from communicating with anybody. *Teniente* Reyes, from his lookout post on Fanning Head, failed to dig-in or site his heavy machine gun or 81mm mortars properly and was shelled by a pre-landing precautionary bombardment by HMS *Antrim*. The young officer thought this was due to the warship homing in on his radio transmissions, so he closed down his radio. The party was then completely dislodged from Fanning Head by a graveyard-hour, helicopter-landed Royal Marine Special Boat Section clearing patrol led by Spanish-speaking Captain Rod Bell. Two Argentinians were captured and the survivors of the force fled north under Reyes' command, in poor disorder, into the darkness, without radio, machine gun or mortar, eventually losing one man to exposure; another subsequently lost both feet due to gangrene. This extinguished the first opportunity the Argentinians might have had to report the landings and gave the British a clear 6 hours to get everyone ashore.

The rest of the Argentine recce party was under the command of a much more robust young officer, *Teniente* Esteban. He set up his headquarters in Port San Carlos school, occupied positions overlooking the beach and carried out local patrols. At 0230hrs Esteban heard the sound of naval gunfire at Fanning Head but got no contact from the troops there. At first light he could see the ghostly *Canberra* and what he considered to be three warships entering San Carlos entrance, while another warship made its way up towards him in the Port San Carlos Settlement. Still out of contact with the rest of his force and both Goose Green and Stanley, he deployed his men to their positions to await daylight and the arrival of the British. In a spirited action, he was to score the Argentine infantry's first anti-aircraft success of the day, using a light machine gun to fire on an 846 Squadron Sea King ZA296 carrying an under-slung cargo of 81mm ammunition, causing it to shed its load and flee for cover. His next target was the machine gun-armed Gazelle XV411, flown by Sergeants Evans and Cavendish; it too was engaged by small arms. Hit in the tail rotor and gearbox, the Gazelle crashed into the shallows and sank. The crew managed to get ashore in the face of continuing fire but Sergeant Evans died of wounds to his chest and stomach. A few moments later another Gazelle, XX402, carried out a machine-gun and rocket attack on Esteban's position. It too was shot down by machine-gun fire and fell to the ground in flames near Clam Creek, killing Lieutenant Francis and Lance Corporal Griffiths. All the while Esteban's position was under British

81mm mortar fire. A third Gazelle, XX412, flown by Captain Makeig-Jones and Corporal Flemming, now approached the enemy position. According to the Argentinians, it was seriously damaged and withdrew, trailing smoke. In fact, the helicopter managed to get back to *Sir Galahad* and after a few hours a new tail fenestron had been fitted and XX412 was flying again. In the face of a decidedly superior force, having shot down two Gazelles, damaged a third and seen off a Sea King, the enterprising Esteban legged it over the hills to the east, abandoning the wireless vehicle – and the second opportunity to report the start of the landings. Keeping his 44-man command intact and yomping hard, Esteban crossed the Island to reach Douglas Settlement. He was immediately helicoptered back to Stanley to make his report in person and then asked to be returned, with his men, to his regiment at Goose Green as soon as possible.

Now, however, with no Argentinians able to see, assess and report what was happening on the British beachhead and its environs, and crucially without forward air controllers to direct aircraft accurately to attack British targets, the Argentine aircrews were going to have to find their way there unaided, randomly select targets to be attacked and do their best to escape without any idea of the real situation they were flying into. Unknown to them also, ranged above the whole scene, was a bunch of Sidewinder-armed Sea Harriers on combat air patrol, while cluster bomb-armed GR3 RAF Harriers flown by Squadron Leaders Pook and Flying Officer Mark Hare had been busy at dawn destroying one Chinook and two Puma helicopters and nicking the rotor of a fourth helicopter, a UH-1H Iroquois, all dispersed on the ground, hidden in the shadow of Mount Kent and well away from Stanley. Back on HMS *Hermes*, Hare asked Pook if he had noticed any small arms fire, which Pook had not. On their return, Pook's aircraft was found to have only two holes in it, Hare's rather more, but by the next day both Harrier GR3s had been repaired.

While all this was going on, Flight Lieutenant Jeff Glover ended up going on his first-ever operational mission in theatre alone in GR3 Harrier XZ972, his wingman Bob Iveson being called off by aircraft unserviceability just before carrier launch. The luckless Glover was shot down by an Argentine Blowpipe fired by *Caporal Primero* Martinez of 601 Commando of the National Frontier Force[3] whilst attacking Port Howard on West Falkland, in Falkland Sound, about 50km south of the British landings. As one wing folded up and the Harrier started to roll over, Glover ejected sideways immediately. His partially deployed parachute slowed his descent sufficiently that when he hit the water he broke only one arm and collar bone, and injured his shoulder in the process. He was fortuitously rescued by Argentine Commandos in a small rowing boat and treated by them as best they could, before being evacuated to Goose Green overnight. Next morning, he was flown to Stanley and then on to Argentina. He was finally released on 8 July, well after the Argentine surrender. In a completely separate sortie, Steve Thomas, in a Sea Harrier, was also hit by AA fire at Port Howard, which damaged his TACAN navigation system and radio; despite this, he safely returned to his carrier and by the next day the aircraft was fully serviceable. Later in the day Pook was tasked to carry out a GR3 Harrier armed reconnaissance to try to trap enemy transport aircraft believed to be flying out of Dunrose Head airstrip on West Falkland, but nothing was seen.

RAID 1: 0830hrs. No aircraft from the Argentine mainland were to appear over the San Carlos landings or the Royal Navy guard ships just outside in Falkland Sound until 1022hrs. It was up to the *Malvinas* command to inform the Junta of confirmed facts about the scale and location of any landing on the other side of the Sussex Mountains. Not too far away, at Goose Green, Wing Commander Perdoza had ordered an immediate Pucara reconnaissance at 0830hrs against the as-yet unseen and unconfirmed beachhead, which was fortuitously interrupted by naval gunfire from HMS *Ardent*. Flight Lieutenant Benitez had only just got airborne when he had to eject after being hit by a Stinger missile fired by an SAS patrol on the Sussex Mountains, the landmass which shielded San Carlos from view from Goose Green. Two more Pucaras were launched, swept low over the south side of the Sussex Mountains and HMS *Ardent* came into view.

With the rest of the British ships further north in Falkland Sound and San Carlos Water invisible to the Pucaras, they flew in to attack the warship. However, before they were within aircraft cannon range, HMS *Ardent* opened fire with Tigercat, but the pilots managed to out-manoeuvre the outdated missile. Then the Pucaras were attacked by three CAP Sea Harriers. Squadron Leader Tomba was shot down by the 30mm cannon of Lieutenant Commander Sharkey Ward's Sea Harrier. Tomba ejected and walked back to Goose Green, while his wingman, Flying Officer Micheloud, escaped from the Sea Harriers. The outcome was that the Argentinians were still unable to report the extent or dispositions of the British landings.

RAID 2: 0950hrs. Well into the dawning daylight of D-Day at Stanley airport, two naval Aermacchi light attack jet aircraft, equivalent in size and performance to the British Red Arrows Gnat trainer, were ordered to fly an armed reconnaissance mission to San Carlos to find out what was going on. The first aircraft suffered an unserviceability, leaving *Teniente* Grippa to fly out to the area of the landings alone. As he swung into Falkland Sound from its northern entrance, he first came upon a Lynx helicopter, which he was about to engage. Then he spotted HMS *Argonaut* guarding the entrance to San Carlos Water. He attacked the warship immediately with rockets and cannon and then flew up the length of the spine of Wreck Point Peninsula, simultaneously observing warships to his right in Falkland Sound and the amphibious landing ships and transports concealed in San Carlos Water to his left.

Although Grippa was shot at by a Seacat from HMS *Intrepid*, a Blowpipe from a soldier on *Canberra* and small arms from just about every ship with machine

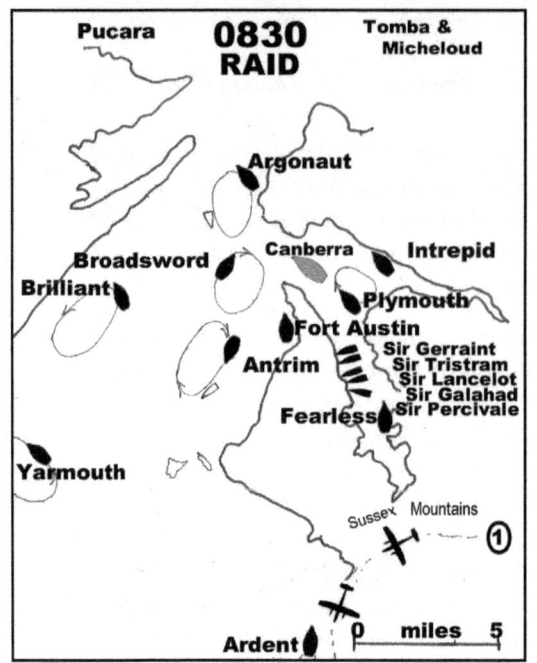

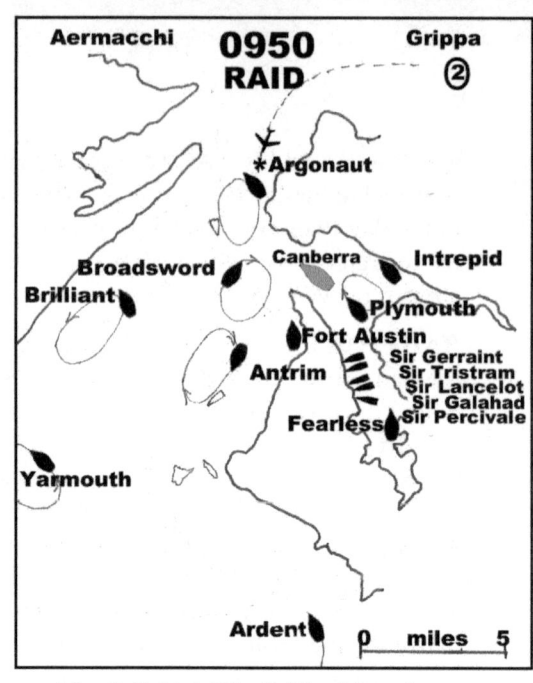

Map 7. Raid 1: The Falkland Sound
air-naval battle, 0830hrs, HMS *Ardent*.

Map 8. Raid 2: The Falkland Sound
air-naval battle, 0950hrs, HMS *Argonaut*.

guns strapped to its railings, he was missed by all. Luckily, there were no British casualties from this uncontrolled fire – what goes up does come down. Coolly, Grippa flew past, counted all the ships and radioed his report to Stanley, galvanizing both the Argentine Air Force and the Air Arm of the Argentine Navy, now also ashore on the mainland, into immediate action, to deal with what was finally and firmly identified as an actual British landing in strength.

RAID 3: 1022hrs. *Fuerza Aerea Grupo 6* Daggers were first off for the 1022–1030hrs raids, eight of the nine aircraft making it to West Falkland, their pilots grateful that they could make the flight to the target area overland. They flew in three groups about 3 minutes apart, screened by Mount Rosalie, to burst into Falkland Sound and their first sight of the warships guarding the entrance to San Carlos Water.

Unmasked late by the mountain, the first three Daggers, led by Flight Lieutenant Moreno, had only split seconds to commit to battle. They headed directly for HMS *Antrim*, whose crew, equally short of time, launched a non-appropriate Sea Slug at them. In return, the ship was hit hard with cannon shells, followed by a single 1,000lb bomb which skipped across the flight deck, smashing its way through the Sea Slug magazine and the guts of the radar, setting off fires but without exploding, but effectively ending *Antrim*'s duty as a long-range air control ship.

RAID 4: 1025hrs. Trailing just 3 minutes behind, at 1025hrs, was the second pair of Daggers led by Dimeglio. They took a slightly greater curve round the

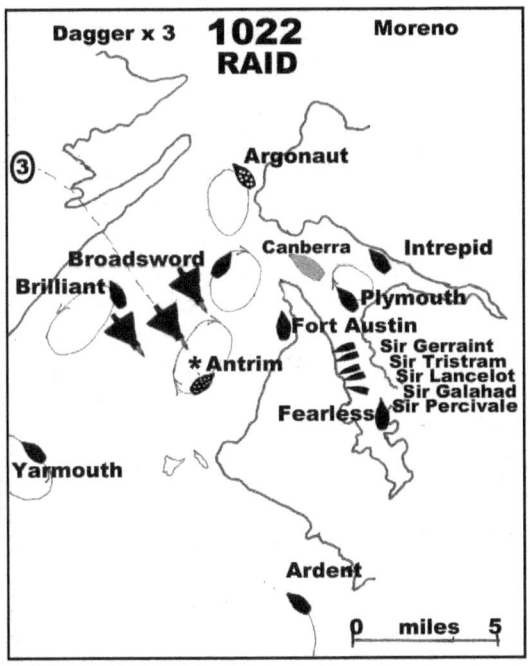

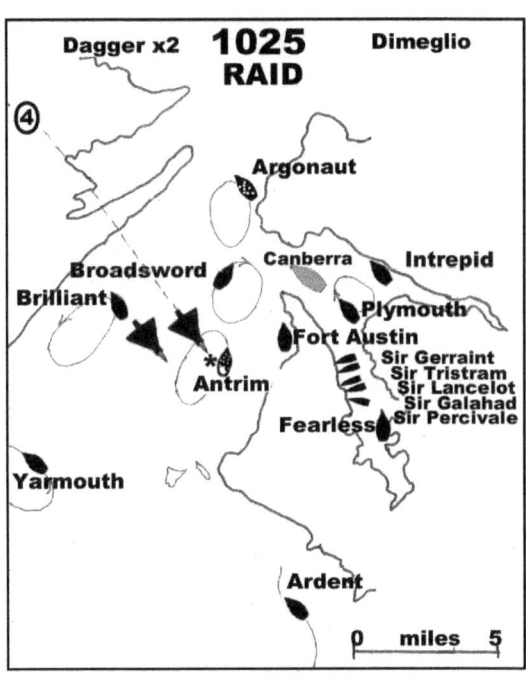

Map 9. Raid 3: The Falkland Sound air-naval battle, 1022hrs, HMS *Antrim*.

Map 10. Raid 4: The Falkland Sound air-naval battle, 1025hrs, HMS *Antrim*.

mountain in time to launch a second attack on *Antrim*. Again there was no time for any kind of target selection or to take a decent few seconds for careful aim. They managed to punch more holes through the warship's thin skin with cannon fire but their bombs missed completely.

RAID 5: 1030hrs. Five minutes later the last three Daggers of *Grupo 6*, led by Flight Lieutenant Rodhe, swept in for the 1030hrs raid; with a few more seconds to spare, they were able to split up. Rodhe engaged HMS *Argonaut* with cannon.

Rodhe then missed with his bomb-load while Pilot Officer Bean aimed his cannon for the ammunition ship RFA *Fort Austin*, tucked in to the opposite shore. Before he had fired many shots, Bean was shot down and killed by a Sea Wolf from HMS *Broadsword*, the Dagger crashing into the sea well short of its target. This led Martinez to attack HMS *Broadsword* a few seconds later with cannon, but his bombs also missed; he was, of course, too late to save the unfortunate Bean.

RAID 6: 1130hrs. With an extra hour of preparation time for their 1130hrs raid, the *Grupo 5* Skyhawks chose to take an even wider loop around Mount Rosalie, skimming over the sea at wave-top level in two formations of three led by Pilot Officers Valesco and Fillipini.

The Skyhawks managed to get two bombs into HMS *Argonaut* below the waterline but neither exploded. However, one entered the engine room, causing an immediate loss of power and steering, while the other destroyed the Sea Cat magazine and set off a major fire. Without steerage, the ship began to drift

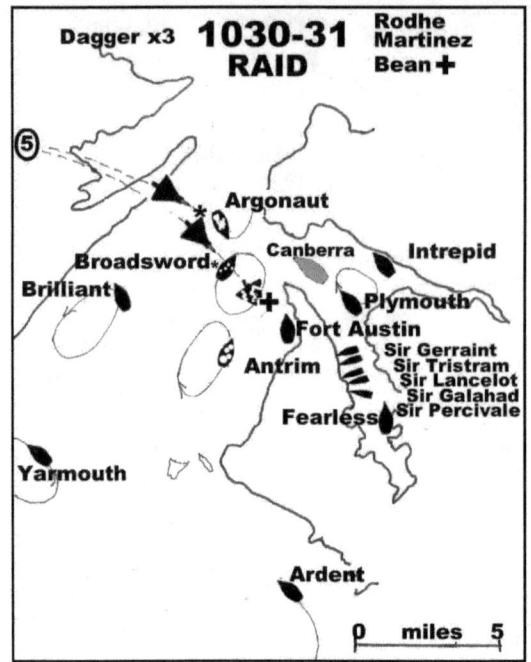

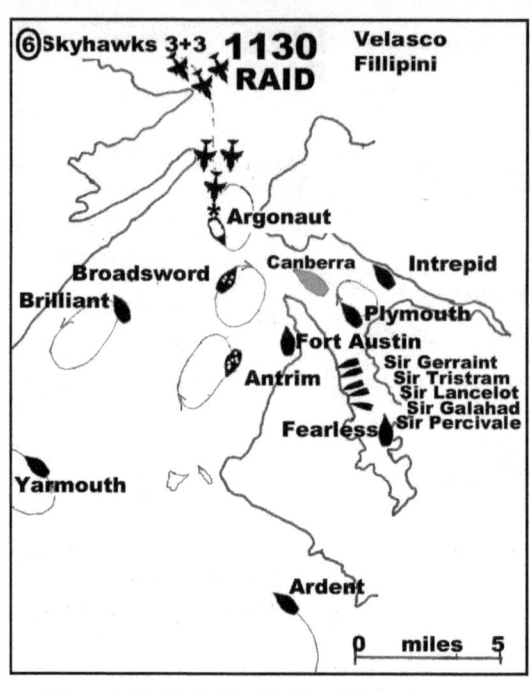

Map 11. Raid 5: The Falkland Sound
air-naval battle, 1030–1031hrs,
HMS *Broadsword* and HMS *Argonaut*.

Map 12. Raid 6: The Falkland Sound
air-naval battle, 1130hrs, HMS *Argonaut*.

towards the rocks of Fanning Head cliffs and was only saved from running aground by the crew's swift action to drop her anchors. That evening she was towed into the shelter of San Carlos, where she remained for the next eight days for the bombs to be defused and removed and for repairs to her propulsion. Effectively, HMS *Argonaut* was out of the war.

RAID 7: 1255hrs. An hour and a half later the 1255hrs raid by four Skyhawks was reduced to two by air-to-air refuelling problems. One expended its bombs uselessly on the abandoned Argentine *Carcaruna* at Port King, mistaking it for a British vessel, leaving Flight Lieutenant Carballo alone to break land cover into Falkland Sound opposite Goose Green, which *Ardent* was continuing to shell. Carballo flew in so low that his fuel tank collided with the ship's radar antenna and all his bombs missed.

RAID 8: 1410hrs. Another hour was to elapse before six *Grupo 6* Daggers could return for their second sortie of the day. Two dropped out with technical problems and a third was shot down by a Sea Harrier on patrol over West Falkland, leaving Flight Lieutenant Mir to lead his three-ship force on yet another attack on HMS *Ardent*, still on Goose Green naval gunfire duties. This time a textbook convergent simultaneous attack paid dividends and they put two bombs into her. One bomb exploded, destroying the helicopter hangar, killing twenty-two of her crew and blowing the Sea Cat launcher over the side, as well as starting a furious fire.

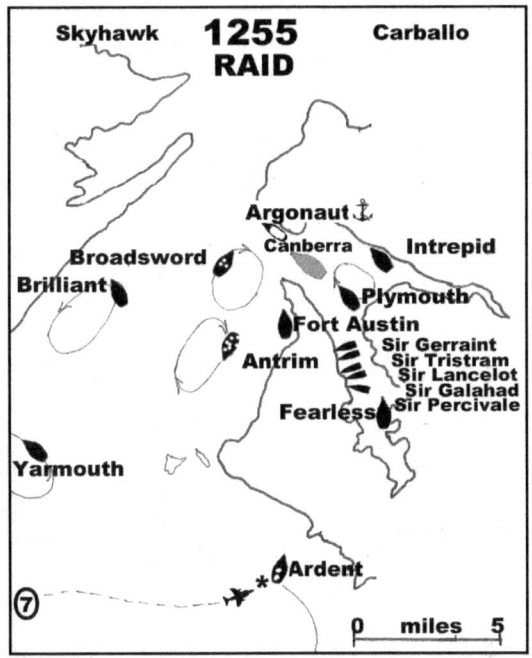

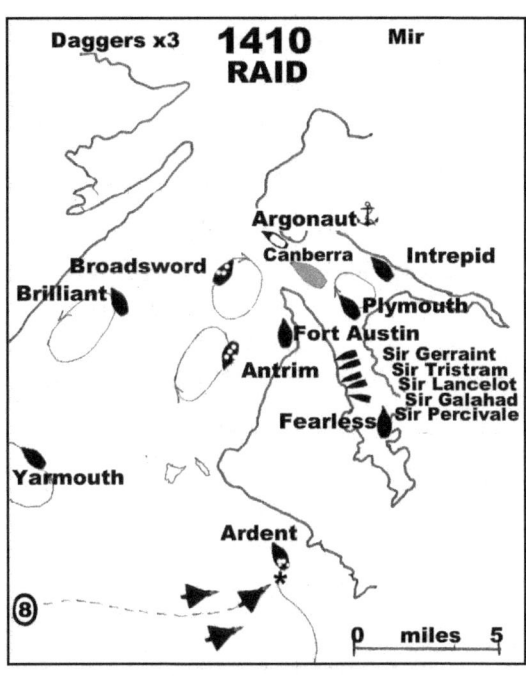

Map 13. Raid 7: The Falkland Sound
air-naval battle, 1255hrs, HMS Ardent.

Map 14. Raid 8: The Falkland Sound
air-naval battle, 1410hrs, HMS *Ardent*.

RAID 9: 1445hrs. Just over half an hour later the next wave of Daggers came tearing up Falkland Sound from the south, passing the elderly HMS *Yarmouth*, aiming for HMS *Brilliant*. Their bombs all missed but their fusillade of cannon fire disabled its fearsome Sea Wolf, punched holes through the Exocet launcher and added another cool-under-fire legend to the Royal Navy's history book. The ship's air defence control centre (ADCC) also took a severe hit. When Commander Sharkey Ward, who had just shot down two Daggers one after the other on combat air patrol, called in to ask if the ADCC had any 'Trade' for him, he was told to wait. Ward challenged the ADCC: 'What do you mean, wait?' 'Well,' replied the wounded Lieutenant Commander Hulme, 'We've just had the ops room strafed with gunfire, with 30mm cannon. The man across the desk from me has lost the top of his head and I've been hit in the arm and I'm just collecting myself.' Within seconds he was back on the radio, directing the Sea Harriers.

RAID 10: 1515hrs. The last air raid of the day at 1515hrs saw the *coup de grâce* of HMS *Ardent* by no fewer than six naval Skyhawks from the flagship *Vienticinco de Mayo*.

These white-painted Skyhawks, put ashore in Rio Grande when the carrier holed up after the loss of the *Belgrano*, were flown by experienced and senior naval carrier pilots who knew their craft. The first trio was led by Commander Phillipi and the second by Commander Rotolo. Most importantly, they were carrying American Mk 82 bombs, fitted with the Mk 15 Snakeye retarder fins specifically designed for low-level delivery. The first trio put several Snakeyes into the already devastated stern of HMS *Ardent*, and more were added by the second trio,

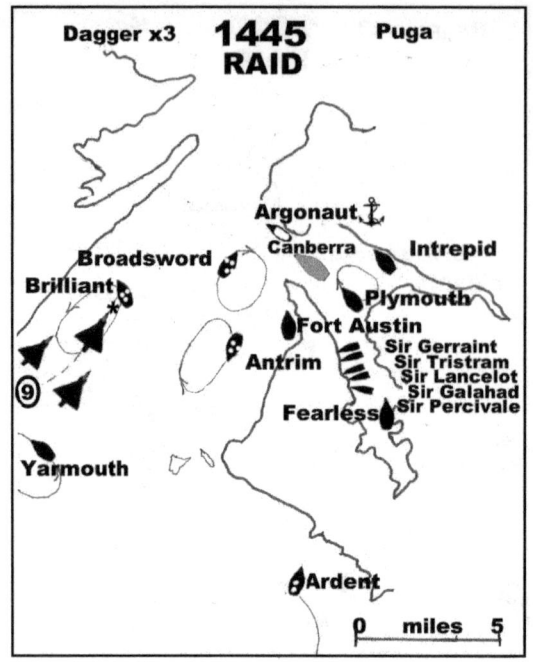

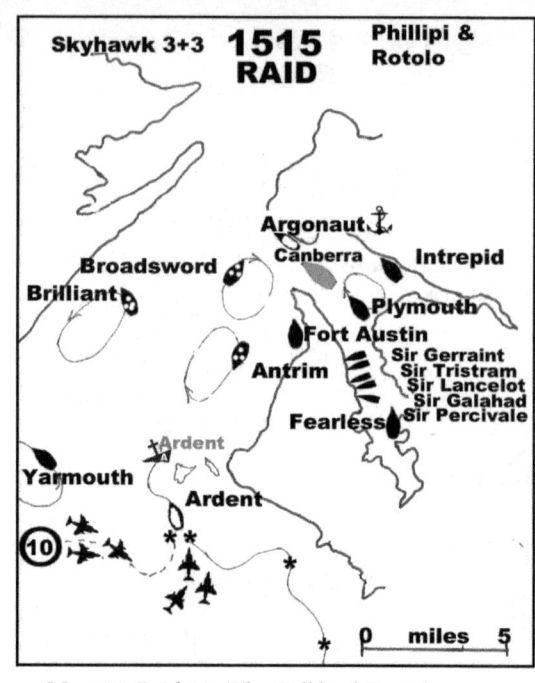

Map 15. Raid 9: The Falkland Sound air-naval battle, 1445hrs, HMS *Brilliant*.

Map 16. Raid 10: The Falkland Sound air-naval battle, 1515hrs, HMS *Ardent*.

which probably also set off the previously unexploded 1,000lb bomb already in her. On the doomed HMS *Ardent*, meanwhile, the crew bravely battled with fire and rising water.

In compensation for the slaughter of HMS *Ardent*, three of the Skyhawks of *Escuadrilla* 3 that had just bombed her were making their escape when they were spotted by a pair of Sea Harriers flown by Lieutenant 'Spag' Morrell, a naval veteran of exchange tours on both Starfighters and RAF GR3 Harriers, and Flight Lieutenant John Leeming, a former Lightning and GR3 Harrier pilot loaned to the Royal Navy. The pair dived into the attack. Morrell fired first and his Sidewinder blew the rear fuselage of one Skyhawk to pieces. *Captain de Corvette* Alberto Phillipi ejected immediately and landed safely in the waters of Port King. Morrell tried to fire his other Sidewinder at the second Skyhawk, but the missile would not launch, so he opened fire with his cannon instead and badly damaged it. The pilot, *Teniente de Norio* Marcelo Arca, realizing that he was losing fuel rapidly, decided to make an emergency landing at Stanley airport. He advertised his non-hostile 'Lame Duck' status to the anti-aircraft gunners by lowering his undercarriage and flying slowly. Eventually, upon making contact with the airfield controller to request clearance for an emergency landing, he was told that his port undercarriage leg was nowhere to be seen. Reluctantly, Arca ejected and, as he hung suspended in space from his parachute, he could see his Skyhawk still flying along sedately. It was left to the AA gunners to bring down the now pilotless and legless aircraft, and it crashed onto the beach at the south side of the airfield. Leeming, meanwhile, dived in cannon firing on the last remaining Skyhawk, which disintegrated into a fireball. The pilot, *Teniente de Frigata* Marcelo Marquez, fell to his death with the shattered, burning debris of his aircraft. HMS *Ardent* lasted bravely through the night and into the next morning before finally sinking beneath the waves in Falkland Sound, much photographed for world news, as she dipped out of sight for ever.

The attack on HMS *Ardent* was the last Argentine air raid of the day. At the beachhead the eight stationary ships, including the 'white whale' *Canberra*, furiously continued to unload men and equipment virtually unhindered. The entire Argentine air action had been against the warships outside, in Falkland Sound. In attacking only the warships, the Argentinians had actually allowed the landing of a full brigade to secure the beachhead to take place, and that failure tracked back to lack of forward observation and total absence of both intelligence-gathering and forward air control.

It is worth now taking a pause for a contemporary review of the effectiveness of the naval surface-to-air defence at the time. Within a battle space of roughly 8 × 15km, filled with multiple fast jets flying at approximately 500 knots, coming in from all directions, and only becoming visible at the last moment, against the eight anti-aircraft missile-armed warships, the action promised to be something akin to the expectation of NATO land airfields in the front line of the Cold War. Stretching in an arc from Norway through central Europe all the way to Turkey, NATO airfield defences were geared up for the Third World War against the Warsaw Pact, with its thousands upon thousands of aircraft. Their airbase battle space was similar in size to this action in Falkland Sound, and they were equipped and practised to handle such similar concentrations of air power in time and space by day and night to those in Falkland Sound. The collective evaluation of their defensive effectiveness was measured in something called the target engagement rate (TER).

For any layout of any number of anti-aircraft weapons, from small cannon to large missiles, it is possible to calculate how many targets might be engaged and destroyed before any aircraft on any radial of attack could release its weapons, be they cannon, rockets or bombs. The distance from the target being attacked is called the line of weapon release. Each of the 360-degree radials of the combined defences would be influenced by the weapon dispositions on the ground, terrain screening of visual and radar detection, the ranges of the radars, the reaction times of the systems and their crews, and the time of flight, range and accuracy of defending cannon shells and missiles. Included in these calculations would be the percentage probability of a single-shot kill: for a visually aimed cannon this could be as low 1–2 per cent; for a radar-directed or infra-red homing missile it could be anything up to 90 per cent.

For combat safety reasons (i.e. to avoid aircraft flying into each other, or flying into the exploding ordnance released by those in front), the peak concentration in attacking such an intensely defended locality commonly worked out at four groups of aircraft coming into the target area from four different directions, one after the other, spaced just seconds apart. Thus for any defensive layout to be effective against a concentrated attack of twelve to sixteen aircraft, a TER of at least four is required on all radials to guarantee the destruction of attacking enemy aircraft before the line of weapon release. This was typically met by between eight and twelve short-range missile firing units, which could be enhanced by mixing in radar-controlled guns and a large number of smaller calibre cannon and man-portable missiles for terminal defence. Number crunching the optimum layouts was typically the task for junior officers, whose job it was to find potential weapon positions and use a theodolite to survey the skyline and calculate radar and visual mask ranges and ultimately the TER; finally the results would be drawn on a map. From this plot, weaknesses in the layout could be identified, so that alternative sites could be found and surveyed and the results recalculated. This kind of analysis was typically performed on a mainframe computer by the Royal Radar Research Establishment (RSRE) at Malvern in Gloucestershire. Back in 1982, however, the RAF Regiment anti-aircraft Rapier squadrons had acquired £20,000 Sun computers, the first 'portable' supercomputer of its day, that could crunch the RSRE-level calculations in the field, using the Rapier squadron's own survey results of all the possible sites, and then recommend the best combinations for a full layout. Better yet, the program could further recommend the next best layouts with progressively fewer and fewer weapons until only the final best site for the last surviving weapon was identified. Feeding the dispositions and radar target unmasking ranges of the Royal Navy warships protecting the landings in Falkland Sound into such a field-deployable, and hence ship-deployable, super-computer would have revealed a TER of mainly ones or even zeros for the ships in Falkland Sound, except around the two Sea Wolf-equipped warships where a TER of two might have been reached wherever the Sea Wolf units of HMS *Brilliant* and HMS *Broadsword* were co-located. As it happened, against the twenty-five or so Argentine aircraft attacking that day, only HMS *Broadsword* was able to make a Sea Wolf kill, destroying a Dagger just as it was attacking RFA *Fort Austin* and killing its pilot, the unfortunate Bean.

With the Argentinians flying similar aircraft to NATO and, with their numbers and availability in the public domain, it was simple matter to surmise that even a South American military dictatorship would likely be capable of flying in attack formations of several aircraft from at least three different directions, just as the British did with their nine Sea Harriers against Stanley on 1 May, three weeks previously. Having freeze-framed the action, this is a capability review of the warships in Falkland Sound and San Carlos Water:

- *Antrim*: 1 × Seacat Launcher, 2 × 20mm Oerlikons, 1 × Sea Slug high-level missile *HIT* by cannon and bombs: *Out of Action*

- *Ardent*: 1 × Seacat Launcher, 2 × 20mm Oerlikons *SUNK*
- *Argonaut*: 3 × Seacat Launchers, 2 × 40mm cannon *HIT* by cannon, rockets and bombs: *Out of Action*
- *Brilliant*: 2 × Sea Wolf Launchers, 2 × 40mm cannon *HIT* by cannon
- *Broadsword*: 2 × Sea Wolf Launchers, 2 × 40mm cannon
- *Fearless*: 2 × Seacat Launchers, 2 × Bofors 40mm
- *Intrepid*: 2 × Seacat Launchers, 2 × Bofors 40mm
- *Yarmouth*: 1 × Seacat Launcher, 2 × 20mm Oerlikons

The few manually aimed 20mm and 40mm guns on the ships, with maximum effective ranges of 2km and 4km respectively, were just as useless as those on the first HMS *Hermes* aircraft carrier, built in 1914 and sunk by Japanese Zeros along with HMS *Prince of Wales* and HMS *Repulse* early in the Second World War. It was these losses of capital warships to air attack that drove British wartime development to install radar-laid anti-aircraft guns on ships, and it was these weapons that morphed into terrestrial radar-directed 40mm Bofors guns for the British Army in the Cold War.

However, guided missiles, smaller and lighter in size, and steered, rather than predicted towards the target, were the way to go. The first generation of British missiles for ship defence was the Seacat: basically a slow, manually steered rocket carrying a massive 50lb warhead. Identical to Tigercat, already covered in detail earlier, it was only effective for a ship's own self-defence if the target was flying directly at it, with little or no crossing component, being far too slow to catch up with modern fast jets passing nearby. The terrestrial version had already been scrapped by the Royal Air Force in 1974 in favour of Rapier, itself derived from Sea Wolf but with a slightly smaller missile and sharing the same type of exceptionally accurate differential tracking radar to guide the missile 'hands-off' to the target. Under this radar control, Sea Wolf and Rapier were outstandingly accurate. I will return to the subject of Rapier radars again, later.

The sum total kill of all this ship-borne anti-aircraft hardware protecting the landings against all the attacking jets in Falkland Sound was a single Dagger shot down by a single Sea Wolf missile fired from HMS *Broadsword*, in return for the sinking of one frigate, HMS *Ardent*, and two further ships, the frigate HMS *Argonaut* and the elderly destroyer HMS *Antrim*, effectively disabled from air defence duties for the remainder of hostilities. While sinking and wrecked warships can be dramatic and emotional affairs, it is worth recording the 1941 riposte of the naval commander of the fateful mass evacuation of British troops defeated in the battle for Crete under intense German air attack. When ordered to withdraw, in order to save the ships, he replied along the lines that 'It has taken the Royal Navy 300 years to win its worldwide reputation; it only takes three years to build a new warship. I'll see this job through.' And so he did, successfully, just as the eight warships in Falkland Sound in 1982 enabled Commodore Clapp in San Carlos Water to get 3 Brigade's amphibious land forces ashore, unharmed and with complete surprise, onto the Falkland Islands, both sides now fully aware of the fact that war is chaotic hell. That none of the enemy jets attacked the actual beachhead on the first day was the Argentinians' second great error of the campaign, their first being to invade the Falkland Islands in the first place.

Before looking at the final aircraft score directly related to the battle space of San Carlos during the landings, there was of course a lot of air-to-air combat by Sea Harriers – a relatively safe exercise compared to ground-attack in the face of fierce flak, thanks to the outstanding reliability of the latest fire-and-forget Sidewinder missile, an exercise that Squadron Leader Jerry Pook would jealously refer to as the 'Sea Harrier Great South Atlantic Turkey Shoot'. To be fair to the Sea Harriers, a goodly number of the Argentine aircraft did fall directly to good old-fashioned Sea Harrier 30mm cannon fired at close quarters, but even that was a one-way shooting exercise, as no single British Harrier was ever to fall directly to any Argentine aircraft in air-to-air combat. However, the Sea Harrier force lost more pilots to operational accidents than combat, making their job just as dangerous.

Contrary to the popular belief that the Argentine *Malvinas* garrison did not know about the British landings, a full report of the day's activities appeared the very next day in the *Malvinas Capallan*'s new news-sheet, *La Gaçeta Argentina Ediçion Espeçial, Anno 1, Nro 5*. A five-line editorial gloried in the valour of the Argentine soldiers, sailors and airmen defending their territory and their home-land against the enemy. *La Gaçeta* then went on to list all of the major actions of the day and factually spelt out the bad news as well as the good, including:

- admitting that an amphibious landing had taken place;
- describing a British diversionary attack on Darwin;
- acknowledging the destruction of Argentine Chinook, Puma and Iroquois helicopters at Mount Kent and the Pucaras at Goose Green;
- reporting a counter-attack by the Argentine Navy Aermacchi against the British landing force;
- confirming the destruction of one Harrier by Blowpipe and the capture of its pilot; and
- giving details of further counter-attacks by the *Fuerza Aerea*, with reference to the loss of several aircraft.

Back on the mainland, the Argentine media, especially the tabloid press, were making such wild and unsubstantiated claims of success that the Junta took the unusual step, in its own Official Communiqué 82, of warning publishers that they would be held responsible for the veracity of any statements they printed. As soon as Esteban arrived back in 'Puerto Argentino', his patrol report was published in full, without editorial comment, in a special edition of *La Gaçeta, Anno 1, Nro 7*. For the action Esteban and one of his soldiers, *Cabo* Hugo Codoy, were each awarded the Argentine Medal for Valour in Combat. The report listed with great accuracy the ships taking part in the San Carlos landings. The Argentine anti-aircraft gunners, however, were only able to claim one GR3 Harrier kill 50km from the beachhead, and that, ironically, was to a British-made Blowpipe, plus, of course, shooting down a crippled Skyhawk whose pilot had already safely ejected, following fatal cannon fire damage from a Sea Harrier on combat air patrol. The final D-Day score is summarized below:

D-Day British losses
2 × armed Gazelles to small-arms ground fire
1 × armed Gazelle damaged by small-arms ground fire but repaired the same day
1 × Sea King undamaged but shed its load of 81mm mortar ammunition
1 × warship sunk
2 × warships rendered non-effective
Fatal casualties on many warships and Gazelle helicopters
Elsewhere:
   1 × GR3 Harrier lost to Argentine Blowpipe, pilot Glover captured

D-Day Argentine losses
1 × Dagger to Sea Wolf by HMS *Broadsword*, pilot Bean killed
1 × Pucara to SAS Stinger, pilot Benitez ejects, to walk back to Goose Green
1 × Pucara to Sea Harrier CAP, pilot Tomba ejects successfully and survives
5 × Skyhawks to Sea Harrier CAP
4 × Daggers to Sea Harrier CAP
Elsewhere:
   1 × Chinook to GR3 Harrier ground attack
   1 × Puma to GR3 Harrier ground attack
   1 × UH1-1H Iroquois main rotor damaged by GR3 Harrier ground attack
   1 × Puma to Sea Harrier CAP

One must conclude that the majority of Seacat-equipped ships were woefully under-armed against aircraft attacks that leaked through overhead combat air patrols. In hindsight, all the warships damaged or sunk could have been saved by an Admiral Fisher-like throwing of all the radar-less guns and Seacats overboard and replacing the lot with a like number of inexpensive (and already then in-service), triple-mount Blowpipe launchers or, better still, the more expensive, latest version of Stingers. (It is not too late to do this for all today's warships; the Blowpipe replacement of today, Starstreak, is a fearsomely effective, superbly flexible, long-range, day-and-night, terminal defence anti-aircraft weapon, equally effective as an anti-suicide, high-speed, attack-boat swarm killer with triple the range and accuracy of the current family of radarless 'Modern' 20mm cannon still in vogue today.)

Against all this, the British Commando Brigade, with its Royal Marines and Paras, was ashore, the high ground all around secured and the immediate beach-head area now free of enemy. With Sea Harriers patrolling overhead, both Argentine Pucaras and helicopters would in future be very wary of flying in daylight; similarly, British Gazelles would refrain from playing at helicopter gunships. That night the transport ships *Canberra* and *Norland* slunk out of San Carlos for safety, without unloading stores for the forces ashore, including vital radio batteries and ammunition not carried by the men, plus at least two weeks' rations for the entire brigade. The Royal Navy's next task was to get the thousands of tons of logistic equipment, fuel, food and ammunition ashore. This would then enable the fleet of heavy-lift RAF Chinook helicopters, then still at sea on *Atlantic Conveyor*, to come in and support an overland advance of 65km across East Falkland, to break the Argentine siege of Port Stanley and its environs.

As D-Day closed, the next phase of the ground-vs-air battle was to begin with the landing of the twelve Rapier fire units of T Battery Royal Artillery. Due to the terrain being completely impassable to wheeled transport, each Rapier would have to be helicoptered into position, without its support vehicles, onto the higher ground surrounding the 'Y' arms of the waters of Ajax Bay, San Carlos and Port San Carlos. The plan was for the Army Rapiers to free the Royal Navy from being hemmed in, acting as duty targets in the confined space of Falkland Sound and San Carlos Water, as soon as possible.

Chapter 9

British Beachhead Consolidation

The days after the successful landings were enormously busy, with Commodore Clapp working all-out to get the tens of thousands of tons of British war materiel ashore, handicapped by the loss of some of his night-vision equipped helicopters to Special Forces insertions and recovery. His other concern was his vulnerability to the threat of Argentine air attacks. Most urgent, therefore, was the deployment of the twelve Rapier fire units of T Battery, 12 Regiment, Royal Artillery. In the planning process for the landings, the optimum layout for the deployment to cover the beachhead inside San Carlos Water had been carried out for the Army by the RSRE in Malvern. While the Rapiers were being set up, the Royal Navy and RAF Harriers were out on a big push, keeping Argentine heads down and hopefully paralysing their opportunities to develop any kind of a counter-attack against the beachhead.

First off on 22 May was a simultaneous battle-four formation attack on Goose Green by GR3 Harriers from HMS *Hermes*, planned and led by Squadron Leader Pook. Instead of one pair trailing the other, and thereby only the first pair possibly surprising the enemy anti-aircraft gunners, leaving the second pair to bear the brunt of their wrath, the plan was for all four aircraft to come in together, more or less abreast, drop their weapons on their allocated targets and then fan out to exit as far apart and as low and fast as possible, hopefully before any of the defenders could pick them up. So low were the experienced GR3 Harrier pilots flying that navigation was by memorizing distinct features along a straight line drawn on a map; these features had to be guaranteed to be seen, in the right order, in the tunnel vision of high-speed flight at very low level, sandwiched between the ground and a low flat layer of stratus cloud. Conveniently, just where the cloud thinned out, the formation burst out into the open, flashing across Darwin Beach, with Goose Green dead ahead. Neither radar signals nor flak greeted them. In Pook's own words:

> I snapped up to a hundred feet above the terrain, feeling horribly exposed to every gun on the Isthmus. Ignoring the Pucaras on the north side of the airfield, I recognized some camouflaged vehicles by a hedge. This was my target. I pickled and dropped my right wing to look back towards Bob and see the fall of my cluster bombs.

The Skyguard radar was clearly caught off-guard, along with the pair of Oerlikon twin 35s, fearsome only under full radar direction. Also wrong-footed were the

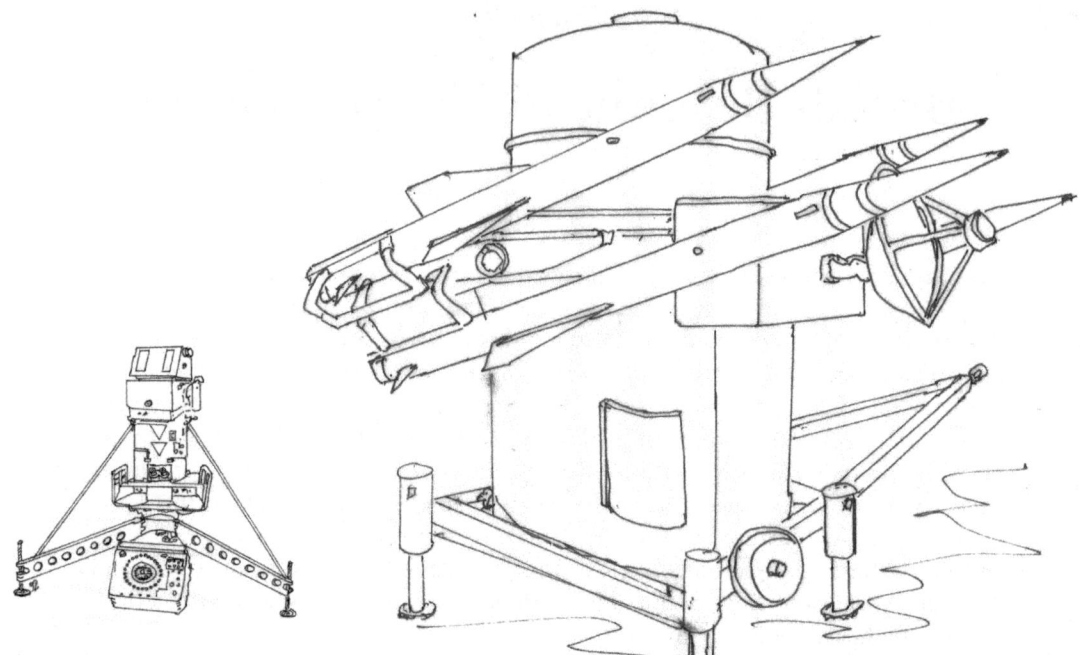

Fig. 15. T Bty 12 Regt RA Rapier B1 lightweight trailer with optical tracker.

six one-man Rheinmetall twin 20mm cannon crews, each sitting in their ground-level seats strung out in the open on the north side of the airfield. As soon as the jets roared past and the cluster bombs started going off, the gunners let rip in a visually spectacularly but ineffective fusillade of lost initiative. Pook continues:

> As my head turned, somebody switched all the lights on. The sky around me lit up with multiple flashes, a dozen huge flashbulbs going off simultaneously. The accompanying crackle told me that this was heavy calibre flak, and they had got my range. 'Jesus Christ – these guys take offence easily!'

Iveson later told Pook that he was sure to have been hit with shell bursts all around the aircraft. Streaking-out low over the tussock grass at 550 knots (over 600mph, 1,100kph) for a full minute, Pook put himself 16km beyond the target before calling the others for a join-up and mutual external inspection for damage. There was none. The speed and ferocity of the raid had totally overcome the much-feared Argentine Goose Green defences. It is worth mentioning here that 20mm and 35mm shells do not explode unless they actually physically make contact with a part of the aircraft; if they miss, they will fly out to maximum trajectory, which is four to five times beyond maximum effective range, and then self-destruct to reduce the possibility of shells falling amongst friendly forces. What the pilots would have seen was the white-hot burning magnesium tracer flare in each shell or their self-destructing explosions; the crackle would have been the supersonic crack made by the multiple 35mm cannon shells which leave the guns with muzzle velocities of Mach 3, each passing shell loudly and clearly audible in the cockpit. Twelve 20mm barrels also make a lot of noise, four 35mm ones more so. Clearly the firing was too wild and too late; in this battle, the Argentine gunners lost big time. However, despite the British success of getting to the target and back, unscathed in the face of fierce flak, the bomb release mechanism of one Harrier had failed to operate, not for the first time, so only 75 per cent of the bombs were delivered – not that the Argentinians on the ground would have noticed any difference in the terrifying experience as a hugely long and wide carpet of continuously merged BL755 cluster-bomb sub-munitions explosions rippled across Goose Green airfield.

Meanwhile, deep in San Carlos Water, the Rapiers were being landed by Mexi-floats, great slab-pontoons that formed a key part of the kit carried inside the amphibious warfare ships, HMS *Fearless* and HMS *Intrepid*. Mexi-floats, powered by powerful outboard motors, transferred equipment from ship to shore, one load being, for example, a Rapier fire unit comprising a launcher trailer and a missile trailer of reloads, plus their powerful V8-engined 1-ton Land Rover towing trucks. Since most of the Rapier sites were totally inaccessible to wheeled vehicles of any kind, due to the exceptionally difficult trackless terrain of soft peat bog and heather (think of the wildest and wettest parts of Dartmoor or the North Yorkshire moors in an exceptionally miserable mid-winter), positioning the launchers had to be by helicopter under-slung load, plus their six-man crews and all the now loose Rapier accessories, along with personal weapons, ammunition and kit.

The 1970s build of Rapier Field Standard B was about as reliable as the electronics in the Harrier: they were of the same vintage, needing constant attention and spares every day. Unlike the Harriers on an aircraft carrier, with spares and technicians to immediate hand, each of the twelve Rapiers would sit isolated in its combat location, far away from each other, and away from their few spare and stretched diagnostic technicians. If a Rapier did not work right away upon start-up, with no wheeled transport access and a shortage of helicopter availability there would inevitably be a significant delay before the forward repair team could visit the remote site. Without their vehicle-borne diagnostic tester and a truck-and-trailer load of spares, they would have to diagnose the fault as best they could manually, which would be followed a further delay as they went back to locate and return with the appropriate spares. Competing demands had led the senior Royal Navy Load-Master on Ascension Island to take a not unnatural but totally ignorant logistic decision that three Rapier truck-mounted workshops and additional spares vehicles, however mobile, were not part of the front-line equipment to be crammed into the beach landing order of equipment for the amphibious rush to war. This meant that T Battery went to war with a logistic, maintenance and repair nightmare handicap from the start. Finally, there was Rapier's insatiable demand for fuel to power the launcher generator all day (it would have been double, if they had taken Blindfire radars like the RAF) and run the radio truck's V8 engine with its built-in radio battery charger. In NATO a well-practised, daily flow of Land Rover-transported jerry cans would be run to the nearest military dump or even civilian petrol pump to keep Rapiers running in the field. In the Falklands, Rapier's fuel needs placed a relentless demand on helicopter lift, a demand that was to dog all of the widely dispersed Rapiers, irrespective of Service.

With warships still covering the movement of transport ships outside the pro-tected waters of San Carlos, it was the Royal Navy that would continue to bear the brunt of the attacking Argentine aircraft while Rapier deployed. It should be made clear here that it was never intended for Rapier to provide any measure of air defence to cover the ocean side of Falkland Sound, where the warships escorted the transport ships in and out of the hidden beachhead inland, now mainly under the cover of darkness. Rapier's layout was optimized to cover the inside of San Carlos Water, where the beachhead was and where the forward Harrier strip would be shortly. As soon as the first Rapiers came on-line, their next problem surfaced.

Their short-range, kilowatt-powered surveillance radars shared the same frequency band as the megawatt-powered warship radars and were thus totally swamped by interference. The consequence of this was not that they could not fire; it was that the system was unable to calculate if the target being engaged was inside the performance envelope of the missile, so the operators, instead of being given a clear 'Wait' for a target coming in range, or an 'In Cover' to prompt a missile launch or an 'Out of Cover' indication to select a different target, the system instead reported a laconic, flashing, 'Wait' and 'Don't Know', leaving the decision to fire to the operator's commander. Without the fallback of a ring of manned and trained observation posts from the long-gone, radar-less gun days, Royal Artillery Rapier operators were backed into a guess-and-shoot mode. There was no loss of missile-in-flight accuracy; it was simply down to guesswork if it would reach the target or not.

And, of course, no radar also meant no electronic IFF, placing the final, fast-moving 'Fire! or don't fire!' decision, based on visual recognition, on the shoulders of young soldiers. Visually, Skyhawks and Harriers at 10km distance look as small as fruit flies and appear very similar at many viewing angles. A further complication was that neither side's helicopters had IFF and so, when the Rapier surveillance radars did work, they would distractingly lock up on every friendly helicopter flying in the vicinity. Whilst both sides did employ identical Chinooks, their other helicopters were thankfully quite distinctly different. My only personal contribution to Galtieri's downfall, for which I previously claimed a small but important part, was to ensure that no British Rapiers or Blowpipes mirrored the earlier fatal Goose Green Skyguard-Oerlikon Harrier-Skyhawk misidentification. Unfortunately, such anti-aircraft visual aircraft recognition discipline did not extend to the Scots Guards, who fired willy-nilly at every passing jet.[4]

Later in the afternoon two Sea Harriers flying combat air patrol over the Choiseul Sound opposite Goose Green spotted the wake of a small warship zipping along on the waters below. They dived down and found it to be a West German-built, 90-ton coastal patrol craft armed with a 20mm cannon, the *Prefecture Naval Argentina's*[5] *Rio Iguazu*. The vessel was on its way to Goose Green with Pucara aircraft spares and 105mm pack howitzers on board. It is just as well they were not 155mm artillery pieces, whose ammunition had already been pre-positioned at Goose Green. The 155s would have brought the beachhead within artillery range and upped the ante considerably. Royal Navy pilot Rod Frederik-son and his wingman strafed *Rio Iguazu* with 30mm Sea Harrier cannon, forcing the captain hurriedly to beach his craft at Button Bay, the crew running ashore for their own safety. However, the ship's part in the campaign was by no means over. The next day British intelligence reported that Argentinians had been seen reoccupying the vessel, some apparently carrying shoulder-launched missiles, so HMS *Hermes'* pilots were to give it a wide berth. Some two weeks later, when the British were in control of the general area, a party of sappers were on board the vessel assessing it for salvage, when the beached ship was pounced upon by Sea Harriers from HMS *Invincible* and shot-up again, ground intelligence exchange between the two aircraft carriers apparently being non-existent.[6] Luckily, the sappers survived.

At last light there was another incident involving another beached ship. Three Argentine Pumas, flying under the cover of the gathering pre-evening gloom, were on an ammunition resupply run from Stanley to Port Howard, carrying an urgently requested load of British-made Blowpipe missiles for 5 Infantry Regiment. Mistaking the wreck of an unknown vessel in the dark for a British warship, they fled back to Goose Green, where they were told it was the abandoned 8,000-ton cargo vessel, *Rio Carcamia*. They were not the only ones to misidentify the vessel; over the course of the next few weeks the *Rio Carcamia* was to be attacked by the *Fuerza Aerea* and by British naval gunfire, and was finally sunk by Sea Skuas launched by a Lynx from HMS *Antelope*, putting paid to Commodore Clapp's hope of using it as a naval prize for British coastal resupply later. The Puma diversion to Goose Green would cost the Argentinians the loss of two of the three helicopters the very next day.

Meanwhile, the final attack on 22 May was to be a night raid by four Sea Harriers on a toss-bombing mission to deliver a fan of 1,000lb bombs to deter the Argentinians from landing fighter-bombers overnight on Stanley airport. The method of delivery would ensure that the Sea Harriers kept out of range of the night-capable Oerlikons. Second off the carrier, HMS *Hermes*, was Lieutenant

Commander Gordy Batt, in Sea Harrier ZA192, which had been previously damaged by Argentine anti-aircraft fire on 1 May. As he lifted over the ramp the fully fuelled-up and bombed-up Harrier exploded, the wreckage plunging into the sea in front of ship and its remains ploughed under by the propellers of the on-rushing *Hermes*. The two Sea Harriers that remained aboard the carrier, their pilots somewhat subdued by the suddenness and violence of what they had just witnessed, launched one after the other and then joined up with the first one and disappeared into the night on their mission to keep the Argentinians awake on helpless stand-to. The large bombs rained down randomly all over the air-field. The Argentine ground-attack aircraft never materialized overnight and the three Sea Harrier pilots, minus their popular comrade, all recovered back to HMS *Hermes*, job done. The day, however, ended with one bit of good news: an Argentine report was intercepted that a British Harrier pilot had been captured; this could only be Jeff Glover, whose fate up to this date was not known.

The next day, 23 May, promised to be a 'Counter-Air Day', attacking Stanley airport again, plus minor airstrips that could be used by Pucara reinforcements to harass the beachhead and finally by jumping on any Argentine helicopters that might be moving reinforcements and weapons around the Islands. The first British success involved the delayed mission of the three Argentine Pumas holed up on Goose Green, which were attempting to deliver their Blowpipes to Port Howard. As the Pumas set off again, they were bounced by Sea Harriers on combat air patrol. High above Shag Cove, Flight Lieutenants Leeming and Morgan, both RAF pilots on exchange tours with the Royal Navy, had spotted the first helicopter flying low over the water. As Morgan dived in head-on to confirm his identification, the pilot of the first helicopter took such wild evasive action that he crashed into the ground, the Puma exploding into a ball of fire. The next Puma tried to take cover in a ravine near Shag Cove, pursued by Sea Harrier cannon fire. After being hit, the helicopter burst into flames and finally disintegrated in a huge explosion. Only Puma AE508 escaped and survived to deliver its load of British-made Blowpipes to Port Howard.

In parallel, aboard HMS *Hermes* four GR3 Harriers were being prepared for the first-ever low-level attack on Stanley airport since 1 May; the aim was to drop penetrating 1,000lb retarded bombs onto the runway. This would mean two pairs of Harriers flying down the length of the runway, high enough to ensure the bombs would penetrate the concrete, and with the pairs far enough apart so that the second pair would not fly into the explosions and debris of the first pair's bombs. Since the only photos of the airfield were microscopic ones taken by Sea Harriers from 20,000ft during their 'cookie-dropping' runs on their way to CAP positions, there was a great need to both properly assess the target, and update the positions of enemy anti-aircraft artillery, plus anything else worth destroying. Squadron Leader Pook volunteered to do a high-speed photo-recce run through the target area at first photographic light, about two hours before dawn. This would enable the attack pilots to study their targets accurately beforehand, plan and memorize exactly what they were to hit and where, in the tunnel vision of a single, high-speed pass. After much discussion with the Sea Harrier pilots, who normally came in from the sea and used their radars to identify the exact point of their landfall, a capability the GR3s did not have, Pook carefully plotted an over-land route through the valley of the Murrell River that avoided the anti-aircraft guns and missiles of Stanley town and harbour; moreover, the route would be easy to navigate with the maximum protection of being out of sight until almost on top of the target. Even so, in order for the fan of cameras in the GR3 recce pod to take good photographs, he would have to slow down to 420 knots and climb to 250ft over the target. It was a risk worth taking, given the improvement in accurate target selection it would bring to the attacking jets. Indeed, in the Cold War theatre, virtually all planned GR3 attacks were guided to pinpoint accuracy with photos taken and developed and made available to the pilots in less than 20 minutes. So skilled were both the RAF photo-interpreters and the RAF pilots that they usually worked directly off the negatives, enlarged prints being usually only reserved for Army commanders in the field. However, in the dismissive Royal Navy battle management style of HMS *Hermes* towards the RAF GR3 pilots, the recce mission was cancelled and the attack hour brought forward with-out explanation. After much fruitless arguing to the contrary with OC 1 Squadron, Wing Commander Peter Squire, the best Harrier squadron commander in the entire RAF Harrier Force, who would eventually rise to become Chief of the Royal Air Force Air Staff, HMS *Hermes'* captain agreed to add two Sea Harriers to the mission for the purposes of 'flak suppression' by approaching from the opposite, northern, end of the airfield, out of range of the feared Skyguard-Oerlikons, of course, and tossing in air-burst bombs which could land anywhere within half a kilometre of where they were aimed at, a form of 'Russian roulette' that the Argentine anti-aircraft gunners had endured for the last three weeks. So Pook stayed back, grounded, while Squadron Leader Iveson led the first GR3 pair, followed by Mark Hare leading the second pair. On the way in the first pair were greeted by intense flak alerted by the Navy 'suppression'. Unintentionally, the Harrier pairs had also closed up inside the considered safe distance, so that Hare actually flew through Iveson's bomb explosion, making for a magnificently spectacular head-up display film record. However, Hare came through the explosions unscathed. Between them, the Harriers managed to crater the runway twice, but only enough to deny the Argentinians the use of the airfield for a couple of hours. Far more disruptive and fear-instilling were the cluster bombs that followed, since these covered a great area, thus discouraging all but essential personnel from movement. All six Harriers returned unscathed but still no wiser about the enemy dispositions. One Sea Harrier also brought back a centre-line bomb which would not release; the pilot, Neal Thomas, made a risky but skilled vertical landing with the bomb still attached, there being just a few inches' clearance between the deck and the bomb.

Meanwhile, outside San Carlos the Seacat-armed HMS *Antelope* and the Sea Wolf-armed HMS *Broadsword* came under sudden air attack by four Skyhawks of *Grupo 5* led by *Teniente* Carballo, springing out from the cover of land to the east. Two 1,000lb bombs went into HMS *Antelope* and two more skipped over HMS *Broadsword* and exploded harmlessly in the sea beyond. The damaged HMS *Antelope* took refuge deep in San Carlos Water, in Ajax Bay, just offshore from 45 Commando. That night the bomb inside her hull exploded, killing Staff Sergeant Prescott of the Royal Engineers, who was attempting to defuse it. The night explosion broke the warship's back. However, the reared-up stern and bow refused to sink quickly, providing further iconic images of the agonizing death of a Royal Navy warship at war in full view of the troops it had been protecting. Just as the sudden appearance of GR3 Harriers at Goose Green earlier, springing out at very high speed from behind rising ground cover and concentrating aircraft in time and space, won the British their anti-aircraft battle against the Argentinians, this time the identical tactics worked in favour of the Argentinians against the combined British efforts of small arms, ship cannon fire, Seacat, Sea Wolf and Rapier, all of which only brought down two attackers between them.

Rapier's day was supposed to be 24 May, when seven Daggers of *Grupo 6* at last entered the confines of San Carlos Water at midday to concentrate on the Logistic Landing Ships (LSLs) tied up in a neat row in Ajax Bay. The attack provided some of the best and most spectacular video footage of screaming jets flying past, low and fast, well below bridge height, as they missed RFA *Fort Austin* (the ammunition ship), *Stromness* (the repair ship) and the returned commercial ferry, *Norland*, with their bombs. Three of the Daggers were shot down outside the area by Sea Harrier Sidewinders. An hour later five Skyhawks from *Grupo 5* attacked, again without success, one of them being downed by several conflicting weapon systems all claiming to have killed Pilot Officer Bono in his Skyhawk. This attack was followed by three further Skyhawks of *Grupo 4*, led by Vazquez, who had previously skipped a bomb over HMS *Glasgow*; this time, they put two 1,000lb bombs straight into the LSL *Sir Lancelot* and another one into the LSL *Sir Galahad*. Again, British Lady Luck was to overcome Argentine pluck when none of the bombs exploded, sparing the lives from incineration of some 300 embarked men, the combined manpower of the Royal Marines Commando Logistics Regiment and the Royal Corps of Transport's Port Detachment hard at work on board, unloading the ships; this was due to Argentine oversight in bomb fuse-timing as the bombs came to rest deep inside both ships. Thanks to the BBC blurting out the good news about Argentine bombs failing to explode, the Welsh Guards were to have no such luck when the hapless LSL *Sir Galahad* took yet more hits from further Skyhawk attacks later on in the campaign. Tragically for the Welsh Guards, those bombs did explode.

Just about every ship and shore-based weapon that saw the attackers opened up in a frenzy of feel-good fire, mostly with zero probability of ever hitting any target and worse, with absolutely no fire discipline where the fall of shot might land, amongst friendly forces ashore or on ships. That no British troops or sailors were killed or valuable helicopters downed was luck in spades. The action, of course, was a visual and audio treat, made more exciting by a soundtrack of crackling small arms fire from ground troops on the opposite sides of San Carlos Water, punctuated by the deeper and slower snarling chatter of 20mm, 30mm and 40mm cannon, the whoosh of passing short, fat, slow missiles and the flash of dazzlingly fast slim ones. In the aftermath of the day, multiple competing claims for kills were made by the Royal Navy and the Royal Artillery. For all that, only two Argentine aircraft were lost to anti-aircraft fire: one crashed into San Carlos Water and the other flew, unseen and uncounted, into a distant mountainside in low cloud, well beyond the scene of action, its wreckage and pilot not discovered until years later. However, the much-anticipated slaughter promised by Rapier's forty-four ready-to-fire missiles and a further 156 reloads failed to materialize. Back at the Paris Air Show, an un-attributable flyer was circulated among the spectators stating that it had taken Rapier more than seventy missiles to down just one enemy aircraft. Later in the campaign, LSL *Sir Galahad* and LSL *Sir Lancelot*'s own pathetic Seacats and single, visually aimed, Second World War-era Bofors 40mm self-defence guns, supported by four Rapier fire units, were to disappoint again, this time with fatal consequences, almost unhinging the entire campaign. It was also the last massed Argentine mainland raid against the Islands.

At this point it is worth pausing the action to examine a few more of the historical factors that were to come together to work against the optimum performance of the Rapier and reduce its effectiveness to way below the great expectations bestowed upon it. I cover these not in any sense of inter-Service rivalry or holier-than-thou crowing. It is, nevertheless, a fact of life that, in the extraordinary circumstances of this particular deployment, the frictions of war, Murphy's Laws,[7] came sharply into focus, to the detriment of the optimum use of Rapier as a weapon. Such is the penalty of a come-as-you-are unplanned party, without a pre-prepared contingency plan. The later arrival of 63 Squadron RAF Regiment, also equipped with Rapiers and deployed with 5 Brigade to Sid's Harrier Strip being constructed ashore for land-based Harrier operations, was to suffer a totally different set of stupid institutional failures, but since they were still at sea at this stage of the events, the review will be confined to the first wave of Rapiers of T Battery, 12 Regiment RA already ashore at San Carlos.The first factor was that, unlike the RAF, which had the ultra-accurate, ECM-resistant Blindfire tracking radar on a one-to-one basis for each Rapier launcher, the Army scale of Blindfire radars was just 25 per cent, i.e., one for every fourth launcher. This day-and-night radar was designed to simultaneously track both the target and the missile in-flight and bring them together for the kill, 'hands off'. Indeed,

Blindfire was so accurate it would even kill the small, expensive, radio-controlled practice drone targets with a single shot. Consequently, RAF units only assigned two missiles a year for Blindfire live firings. The bulk of training missiles, actually stock turnover to maintain up-to-date fresh missiles for the Cold War, were fired on a scale of one per operator per year in the alternative, reversionary, daylight-only optical mode. In this mode Rapier operators have to track the targets in an optical sight, using a joystick with great skill; in addition, the operators have to ignore the distracting gyrations of the missile, whose rearward facing magnesium flares are also seen in their optical field of view. The missile itself, however, is controlled by a co-axial TV camera parallel to the optics, via a radio command link. Few operators actually hit the small practice drones or aircraft towed-targets. The miss-distance is measured by a Geiger counter inside the target that senses the passing radioactivity of a nose plug of depleted uranium on the tip of the missile. Anything closer than 30ft is considered a probable hit on a full-size aircraft and units compete intensely to achieve the overall smallest miss-distances at missile practice firing camps.

The Blindfire radar, however, could also do without the Rapier surveillance radar data as it had the option to be manually slaved to a selected target using the optical tracker head under the Rapier commander's control and thus provide all the missing range, speed and direction details to the computer for a successful 'hands-off' and lethally unemotional engagement. This is because Blindfire operated in a totally different radar frequency band from the surveillance radars

Fig. 16. 63 Sqn RAF Regiment Blindfire Rapier in all-weather configuration.

and those of the Task Force warships. Furthermore, with such a high-powered, focused pencil beam, Blindfire radar signals were almost totally impervious to electronic jamming and would only alert the enemy radar warning receiver of the actual aircraft being engaged, not those of its companions. To sum up, the RAF operated a 100 per cent Blindfire Rapier force, whereas the Army depended on human skills in the optical manual tracking mode for their primary operations.

Much smoke and mirrors energy was also devoted to the 'sensitivity' of Rapier to the damp atmosphere of its transport ships in transit to the Falklands. This was patent nonsense; the equipment had been rigorously tested by Joint Service Trials in Arctic cold, desert heat and jungle damp conditions for months in the field prior to entering service. Instead, the in-service lifestyles of the two Rapier units that went to war should be examined. All the RAF Rapiers were committed to the highest value airbases in Germany and the UK, either those with nuclear weapons or air defence fighters. As such, they were held at the highest daily-reported readiness states of equipment serviceability, manning and training, and its men were never taken away from their primary mission for use as supplementary infantry, such as Northern Ireland; the RAF Regiment had mechanized infantry squadrons that were dismounted into Land Rovers to undertake that role. Whilst the Army Rapiers on the NATO front line in Germany were also held at high readiness and free of Irish distractions, the UK-based Army Rapier Regiment, whilst nominally available for worldwide deployments, was also the first reserve for maintaining the NATO front line; in addition, four of its Rapier fire units were on permanent rotational loan to the Royal School of Artillery for officer and NCO training; these, therefore, were not lavished with the same care as the fire units permanently assigned to (some would say 'lovingly owned' by) the permanent crews of the front-line units. Moreover, being in training use, the School Rapiers had priority of spares and mobile workshop throughput over the donating UK Regiment. The Germany Regiment and RAF Germany always took the highest priority for everything Rapier, leaving the UK Regiment in a perpetual state of catch-up. With a centralized thirty-six Rapier servicing system already under huge logistic strain, it was prone to suffer what the Air Force would call the Hangar Queen Syndrome, where at least one piece of equipment would be so cannibalized for 'borrowed' spares to keep the others running that it would almost take a factory rebuild to ever get it back into firing condition.

Other differences between the Services came into play. The RAF units were permanently garrisoned at the airfields they were to defend; like the Army, they rolled out into the field for deployment, but always within in logistic support range of a well-hardened base, whereas the thirty-six Army Rapiers would be spread out in greater numbers over a much larger and fluid battlefield area. RAF personnel were also individually posted in and out in a steady trickle throughout the year, whereas the UK and Germany Rapier regiments would periodically swap geographical locations. Gunners new to RAF Rapier first went to an RAF

Rapier training unit with its very own organic establishment of Rapiers, and so they arrived at the front line fully trained ready for war, whereas in the Army a select number of officers and NCOs went to the Royal School of Artillery to be trained as instructors-in-gunnery (IGs), qualified to instruct on every anti-aircraft weapon system then in service. In the Army IGs in Rapier regiments carried out *ab initio* Rapier training at unit level so that within any unit there was always an element of untrained personnel in the establishment. A further burden was that long-term, unfit personnel, and those nearing the end of their military service, would also be sent back from the Germany front line, to be carried by the UK units, which also bore the brunt of Army-wide recruiting shortages; in short, a tough call for all the UK Rapier battery commanders.

A logistic difference was also to mar the Army Falklands deployment. Because of geographical separation and isolation of RAF airbases, every 8-fire unit Rapier squadron had its own fully organic mobile field repair workshops and spare parts stock, whereas the three 12-fire unit UK batteries shared a centralized mobile workshop and spares facility on a regimental, 36-fire unit basis which, to be fair, is how they were structured to operate, full-on, in the Third World War. This meant that the deploying T Battery went to war with a thrown-together Rapier second-line field mobile workshop and spare parts stock under its full command that was separated from T Battery and held back, out of their control, and left behind on Ascension Island. Returning to Rapier's supposed delicacy and vulnerability to damp, the RAF Rapiers were subjected to exactly the same humidity conditions on the voyage south and suffered not; however, the eight Rapiers of 63 Squadron RAF Regiment landed at San Carlos on 1 June complete with all their mobile workshops and second-line field repairable spares. Within 24 hours of landing, 63 Squadron was up and running and within 48 hours had cleared all of T Battery's backlog of accumulated unserviceable sub-units in a mini-marathon of mutual cooperation but, by then, the 'Great South Atlantic Turkey Shoot' was largely over. The whole of the San Carlos Rapier engagement zone now consisted of twenty Rapier fire units with eighty ready-to-fire missiles on the beams, all just gagging for enemy aircraft to appear. But never again would the campaign see such intense concentrations of Argentine air power directed at the Falkland Islands; had they done so and entered the now-in place joint Army-RAF missile engagement zone, the telling of Rapier's story might have been all the more glorious. However, while the British continued to pound the trapped *Malvinas* garrison, the Argentine effort now switched to going all out to sink the aircraft carriers of the Task Force with their last remaining card: the Exocet anti-ship missile.

The *Fuerza Aerea* gunners were also demonstrating their initiative: in Choiseul Sound, the sea approach to Goose Green, an Argentine salvage party set out to rescue the two 105mm pack howitzers aboard the beached Coastguard vessel under the cover of Soviet-made SA-7 Strela shoulder-launched missiles manned by NCOs of the *Fuerza Aerea*. The party was recovered by two Bell 212 helicopters at dusk, when the risk of interception by Harriers was considered minimal.

At Stanley airport, meanwhile, Wing Commander Squire, Squadron Leader Iveson and Flight Lieutenants Harper and Hare were tasked to attack the runway with 1,000lb retarded bombs. They flew in low immediately after air-burst, variable-time fused bombs tossed in by a pair of 800 Squadron Sea Harriers some 20 seconds earlier had exploded amongst the defending Argentinians. Despite three hits, the runway survived intact, and so did all the aircraft in what must be regarded as a classic airfield attack: lots of aircraft arriving from all directions all at once. The elderly Tigercats, radar-less 20mm and single barrel one-man 30mm guns, the one elderly *Fuerza Aerea Superfledermaus* fire-control radar with just two or three Oerlikon twin 35mm guns, and possibly one Skyguard with two more Oerlikon twin 35s were simply not quick enough to cope with the sudden concentration of air power. Later, Wing Commander Squire was to comment that the Argentine anti-aircraft fire was not as fierce as he had expected it to be. But then the bulk of the best anti-aircraft weapons were still uselessly protecting Stanley town and harbour. Also, Squire may not have realized that the Argentinians were only using one tracer round in every clip of seven shells. Much of the fire, therefore, would have been invisible.

The question of visibility of 35mm tracer ammunition would come up again once the Oerlikons were in British hands. At the first post-war refurbishment test-firing of the equipment, I commented to Wing Commander Spike Jones of the British Manufacture and Research Company (BMARC) in Grantham, which manufactured Oerlikon ammunition for worldwide use, that the tracer was rather hard to see; he told me that the Argentinians had especially requested that the tracer element in their ammunition order be reduced so that it would not give away the location of the firing guns. Later, the Argentinians were to mix solid-shot bright tracer training shells with every two or three high explosive rounds so that they could at least see the path of their gunfire, allowing a lucky hit of solid shot to pass straight through the odd Harrier without exploding – possibly what did for Squadron Leader Pook later.

The next day, 25 May, in addition to being the name of their *Armada*'s flagship aircraft carrier, *Vienticinco de Mayo*, now timidly holed up in port to escape the spectre of British nuclear submarines, was also Argentina's National Day and to mark it *Armada Argentino* Skyhawks and Super Etendards mounted all-out concentrated attacks on the Royal Navy far out at sea. Salvatore Santore's *La Gaçeta Argentina* opened with an editorial on the heroic revolution of 1810 and the final liberation of Argentina from colonial Spain by General San Martin in 1817, naturally without mentioning the hugely significant British contribution to their independence by the Royal Navy. The *Malvinas* garrison chaplain drew a parallel in the present conflict, describing it as 'the final recovery of the vestiges of one of its colonized territories, a confrontation with one of the modern monsters that had taken away certain lands by force'.

In the same vein *La Gaçeta* recorded the speech of *El Senor Grobernador Militar de los Islas Malvinas, Georgias del Sur y Sandwich del Sur* (rather rich, seeing that the British were already back in possession of the last two groups of islands):

> Sailors, Airmen and Soldiers, on this twenty-fifth Day of May 1982, we find ourselves, as we did on that day exactly one hundred and seventy-two years ago, fighting to build a proud, sovereign Nation. Like our ancestors, we have left our families, our houses, our towns and cities, to run and fight to defend our beloved fatherland. To my men on this glorious twenty-fifth of May, when Argentina finds itself at war for a right and just cause, I beg you to sacrifice yourselves to attain honourable victory and I ask God for his protection for you all on this day. Long Live Argentina.

After the war, the *Malvinas* chaplain, Salvador Santore, would complain bitterly that at Mass, a large number of conscripts were coming to him asking for an excuse to avoid battle, rather than for absolution of their sins in case they were killed. If nothing else, his experience validates the saying that one volunteer is worth ten pressed men, many of the Argentine soldiers having been compulsorily conscripted only four months previously.

Meanwhile, HMS *Coventry* was on picket duty off Pebble Island, positioned to draw Argentine air attacks away from the beachhead; she got off to a good start by downing a Skyhawk of *Grupo 4* with a Sea Dart, killing Flight Lieutenant Palaver. However, the professional *Armada* and *Fuerza Aerea* aircrew officer corps were made of stern stuff and would give it their all in the spirit of their founding forefathers in their next aerial assaults. By the end of the day HMS *Coventry* would manage to fire another Sea Dart and down one more Skyhawk from *Grupo 5*, the pilot, Flight Lieutenant Garcia, ejecting safely, only to die in the cold South Atlantic waters, while the remaining two weaving Skyhawks of the formation confused the accompanying HMS *Broadsword*'s automated Sea Wolf system, which shut itself down at this most critical moment of the anti-aircraft battle. By the time the missile system had rebooted, *Coventry* was between the Skyhawks and *Broadsword*, blocking her Sea Wolf engagement and allowing *Teniente Primero* Valesco in his Skyhawk to deliver three 1,000lb bombs which exploded deep inside *Coventry*'s hull, explosions from which she never recovered, first burning and then capsizing, before sinking from the mortal damage. Meanwhile, over in San Carlos Water, Rapier was to have a good day, bringing down a Skyhawk from which Pilot Officer Lucero ejected.

Much further out at sea the MV *Atlantic Conveyor* was hit and set on fire by *Capitain de Corbeta* Robert Curilovic and *Teniente de Navio* Julio Barraza, who had been air-to-air refuelled by Hercules tanker and launched two Exocets from their Super Etendard jets from a range of about 50km at what they thought was either

HMS *Hermes* or HMS *Invincible*. In a way, *Atlantic Conveyor* was a sort of aircraft carrier, albeit carrying well wrapped-up aircraft. Luckily, she had already launched off all her attrition replacement Harriers but she was still carrying four Chinook heavy lift helicopters, six Wessex helicopters and one Lynx, along with a large supply of BL755 cluster bombs for the GR3 Harriers and enough tents and field living equipment to shelter 4,500 personnel ashore. At a stroke, the British plan to retake the Islands had to be rewritten. In the stricken ship that lay burning from stem to stern were the helicopters with which it was intended to leapfrog across the Falklands. Luckily, one Chinook just happened to be airborne on a flight test at the time; with not enough fuel to go anywhere, it made an emergency landing on HMS *Hermes*, where the Royal Navy gave serious consideration to pushing it overboard from the crowded deck, until common sense prevailed.[8] However, as a result of the attack, which was meant for the two aircraft carriers, the Task Force commander decided to put a further 100 nautical miles between himself and the Argentine mainland, considerably reducing Harrier time in the skies over the Islands.

Concurrent with the loss of the MV *Atlantic Conveyor*, the Harriers mounted three more successive raids on Stanley airport to keep the anti-aircraft guns and missile crews there busy, without taking any hits to their aircraft. First off was a six-aircraft attack in two waves of three aircraft abreast, the outer two GR3s taking their cue from a Sea Harrier (which was fitted with a toss-bombing bomb-sight) and together tossing nine 1,000lb bombs in two neat flying formations of bombs towards the airfield. As the bombs started going off, at least three Tiger-cats in different positions and even the one distant Roland launched missiles, together with an assortment of tracers of various calibres all fired in fruitless pursuit of the departing Harriers. Next in were two further Harrier GR3s, this time tossing their bombs in without the benefit of Sea Harrier guidance. The pair then quickly returned to HMS *Hermes* to refuel and rearm. However, one Harrier went unserviceable, leaving the other to repeat the harassment, keep everyone's heads down and stir up the Argentine anti-aircraft defences once again. In a postscript to this attack, the commanding officer of GADA 601 records in his Order of the Day 9/82 the death of one of the gun crew on an Oerlikon of Bravo Battery's Skyguard at the airport; it was rather a lot of effort just to kill one man. The same Order of the Day then directed the crews not to toast the soles of their boots in front of a fire to dry them, as this caused severe deterioration; instead, when putting on damp boots, they were to wrap their socks in dry newspaper first, as this would absorb the moisture.

Later on, we would find the damaged Oerlikon, displaced by a large explosion and barrels bent, whilst nearby, in boxes, were a pair of brand-new Soviet Strela shoulder-launched missiles, clearly a replacement for the loss of the only Oerlikon cannon ever found to have been damaged in action.

Despite the grievous losses of the two British ships on Argentina's National Day, the Harriers kept up the pressure on the next day, 26 May. Two Harrier GR3s were scrambled to undertake an armed reconnaissance sortie, which had to be aborted because the IFF on both Harriers failed their pre take-off check, making the aircraft vulnerable to being shot down by their own Task Force ships. Next off, with Squadron Leader Pook's earlier, good quality target photography of the troop concentrations at Port Howard to go on, Squadron Leader Iveson and his wingman found their targets easily, describing the attack on personnel as 'a bit like murder'. Upon their return, Squadron Leaders Pook and Iveson then flew an armed reconnaissance sortie over the high ground overlooking Ajax Bay in the hope of locating enemy artillery on the reverse slopes of the high ground, but found none. After another turn around on HMS *Hermes*, Pook and Hare carried out a 50km line search from Estancia House to the outskirts of Stanley. Mindful of the flak concentration around Stanley town, the pair swept a little wide and in so doing, Pook spotted an Argentine Puma helicopter on the south side of Mount Kent. As he dived in to bracket the grounded Puma with two BL755 cluster bombs, a missile smoke trail passed above him and fell away to the rear. After weapon delivery, Pook tipped his Harrier's wing down to look back to see his handiwork of flashing explosions of cluster bomblets creep up to and then envelop the hapless helicopter, causing it to explode in a large fireball.

Back in Buenos Aires, the Joint Chiefs of Staffs released Communique 84, claiming that three Harriers had been shot down by the Argentine anti-aircraft guns in the 'Puerto Argentino' zone, bringing the total claimed by them as destroyed to twenty-three. For the other side, the British reckoned Argentine losses stood at fifty-seven aircraft to date. Never again were the Argentinians to mount frontal air assaults *en masse* on such a scale again; later, both sides would recognize Argentina's National Day as a turning point in the air war. However, the anti-aircraft gunners had only lost one Oerlikon; moreover, they had huge piles of ready-use ammunition to hand and were far from being minded to ease off; indeed, they were to remain alert and undefeated, adding aggressive and effective ground-to-ground firing at the advancing British troops to their combat actions right up to the very last hours of the campaign.

The planned British breakout from the beachhead by Chinook helicopters was now well and truly scuppered by the loss of the MV *Atlantic Conveyor*. Also, there remained on the flank of the beachhead a sizeable threat from the Pucara base at Goose Green, well protected as it was by six twin 20mm Rheinmetall guns with their own organic little Israeli Elta alerting radar plus, of course, the fearsome and now battle-proven pair of Oerlikon twin 35mm anti-aircraft guns with their lethality-enhancing Skyguard radar, with a score of two aircraft already shot down. Brigadier Julian Thompson and his staff of 3 Commando Brigade could see no alternative to the Commandos and Paras having to march the 66km to Stanley. The Argentine *Malvinas* military commanders also were contemplating their own helicopter losses and were now avoiding the risk of flying the remaining machines in daylight due to the fatal bounces by Harriers prowling around. The Argentine High Command also considered the option of foot-slogging to attack the British beachhead from Goose Green but rejected the idea of a fight at the end of an exhausting march as suicidal. The Argentinians, however, rated a British attack on Goose Green as highly likely, so much so that the *Malvinas* commander specifically requested a reinforcing air-drop of Argentina's crack parachute battalion of 500 men onto Lafonia. That request was refused and so Argentina's best-trained and toughest infantry battalion remained at home for the duration of the *Malvinas* war. For his part, Brigadier Thompson assessed that the threat of a counter-attack was too great to ignore and he decided to await the arrival of 5 Infantry Brigade before dealing with Goose Green. Just then, Thompson was summoned to the satellite communications terminal at Ajax Bay to receive clear and unequivocal orders from Northwood to attack the Argentine forces at Darwin and Goose Green. The intelligence assessment of enemy strength was estimated at three infantry companies, with half a dozen anti-aircraft guns, about 400 men in all. An earlier assessment by D Squadron SAS, who had carried out a reconnaissance there on 21 May, reported that the area was defended by one company, about 160 men. This may well have been the case at the time but, at every opportunity, the Argentinians had been busily beefing up the Goose Green garrison, adding three 105mm pack howitzer artillery pieces to the defences, plus the instructional staff of their equivalent of the RAF Regiment airfield protection force already deployed there with two 81mm mortars and an additional enhanced company-sized number of Special Forces troops. On the British side Lieutenant Colonel 'H' Jones was itching to get on and do what he 'had been waiting for twenty years to do', when the Argentinians were notified by the treacherous BBC World News that Goose Green and Darwin were about to be attacked. It would be an understatement to say that the British victory was snatched from the jaws of defeat, in the most studied and written about, complicated and under-supported envelopment of a superior enemy force ever conducted by the Parachute Regiment, which stretched both sides to their absolute limits. The British Paras won through, however, because they were made of sterner stuff, their soldiers and junior commanders especially, honed by forty years of continuous campaigning overseas to high levels of experience, initiative and determination at every level of rank, against tough enemies, whereas the Argentine Army had only had its own 'dirty war' hapless civilian population to practice upon. Winning is much about the will-power to determine who gives up and, in this case it was the Argentinians who blinked first. For the record, the two Goose Green infantry commanders were subsequently dishonourably cashiered. I will not attempt yet another in-depth rewrite on this battle. Instead, my focus will be on the air-to-ground and ground-to-air elements as each side at Goose Green was attacked by the aircraft of the other side; in this, also, the British came out on top.

Chapter 10

The Battle for Goose Green Airfield

The battle for Goose Green is an interesting airfield defence battle worthy of great study as it contains plenty of valuable lessons for future so-called Expeditionary Air Warfare, where flying and fighting takes place in difficult, distant, ground situations in which neither side has total control of either or both the ground and the airspace above. It is also interesting because both sides were more or less equally matched in terms of mortars, artillery, air defence and offensive air attacks in support. Discounting the one hundred or so air operations personnel but including a further hundred *Fuerza Aerea* infantry and Military Police, the Argentinians had over 1,000 trained soldiers deployed against a total British force of 576, of whom 513 were Paras, a defensive advantage of two to one. Only in 7.62mm infantry machine guns did the British out-gun the Argentinians by thirty-five machine guns to seventeen, and then only because the CO of 2 Para, Lieutenant Colonel 'H' Jones, in a smart trick well worth remembering, ordered all-new machine guns for his entire battalion just before departure and cleverly did not return the old ones in the rush of embarking.

In the air, the British fielded only two Scout helicopters (one of which was shot down by a Pucara), one Gazelle and one Sea King in the battle against the Argentinians, who threw six Vietnam-era Huey UH-1s, a Puma and two Hirondo Augusta gunships into the fray. In terms of close air support at Goose Green, the Argentinians launched seventeen aircraft in six ground-attack air raids, while the British launched ten Harriers in five raids, the Argentinians delivering cannon-fire and napalm and the British delivering cannon fire, rockets and cluster bombs, all pretty terrifying anti-personnel weapons launched close-in, very much like the ground-attack aircraft of the Second World War. Weather played a huge part, with luck heavily favouring the British, who only lost two sorties to weather, whereas a planned attack by six Skyhawks that, if they had been successful, might have put the Paras into full 'shock and awe' on Day 1, was blanked off by heavy low cloud, forcing them back to base, leaving just three Harriers in the last twilight minutes before dark of Day 2 to deliver their 'shock and awe' at a finely balanced moment to the Argentinians instead.

Rather than speculate on alternative possibilities, I will instead draw out 'lessons learned', although the MoD at the time declared there was nothing new to be learned! I am a great fan of the astronaut Neil Armstrong's dismissal of a TV armchair host's 'chatterbate' question about what might have happened on the moon if he had used up the last few remaining seconds of landing thruster fuel before actually touching down, to which he replied dryly: 'Well, it didn't happen, so there's no point in talking about it.' The fact is that in the first serious contest for ownership of this bit of ground, known to the Argentine invading force as *Fuerza Aerea BAM Condor* at 'Ganso Verde', their occupation was doomed and it returned to British possession to become Goose Green once again in just two days of short, sharp fighting; a stunning victory was won by 2 Para, taking prisoner over a thousand men, a full 10 per cent of the entire *Malvinas* garrison. The success of the action fully justifies every aspect of the heavy investment in the rigorous selection and elite training of the Parachute Regiment, placing them right up there with the Spartans at Troy, with their popular, posthumous VC-winning commander, Lieutenant Colonel 'H' Jones, as Achilles and the level-headed Major Chris Keeble identifiable as the wily Odysseus.

After two days of fierce fighting both sides ended up firing just about everything they had. The final casualties were fifty-five Argentinians killed in action (including two pilots) and ninety wounded, compared to the British with eighteen killed[9] and thirty-nine wounded. The key to victory was that the willpower of a smaller, but intensively trained and hugely physically fit, homogenous, competitively selected, all-volunteer force of a single British battalion, with global combat experience, broke the will of a largely conscripted and inexperienced defensive force that was twice the size but made up of fragmented parts of units from four different battalions thrown together in an under-unified command of Argentinians, many fractions of which individually fought as well and as bravely as any Para. And therein lies a warning for future expeditionary air deployments deep inland, in territory not wholly controlled by the host nation, however friendly. At fighting man level, junior British military leadership is at the cutting edge of a fierce meritocracy, in which authority is earned, whereas in virtually every conscript army in the world, the officers tend to be privileged and detached, while most NCOs are corpulent, bureaucratic and corrupt. Be the air power a projection by a single nation, a multinational, multi-lingual alliance such as NATO or, more complicated still, a coalition of willing but disparate forces of many nations volunteering units to the United Nations on rotational duties, their superior numbers will be hugely less effective if they have never worked together and trained together and integrated well. Indeed, they are likely to lose to hard men of volunteer armies, Special Forces or suicidally intentioned, heavily armed, asymmetrically structured, unconventional assaults by rag-tag irregulars of great ingenuity, determination and suicidal courage.

For the most incisive analysis of a blow-by-blow account, carefully linking every element of the British advance with a detailed person-by-person report of the actions of Argentine and British soldiers, I would hugely recommend to the reader Hugh Bicheno's book, *Razor's Edge*.[10] In my book, however, the main theme is what happened to all that Argentine booty afterwards. I will therefore just take readers on a quick gallop over the Goose Green airfield to set the anti-aircraft and ground-attack elements of it into proper context. Lining up the hardware first:

Artillery Support

The Argentinians had three 105mm light guns salvaged from the beached *Rio Iguaza* and a goodly supply of pre-positioned 105mm ammunition. They had also pre-positioned 155mm artillery ammunition at Goose Green but by then they no longer had the helicopter capacity to bring forward just one such heavy gun, which could have threatened the beachhead itself. The 105s were commanded by the very competent *Teniente* Chanampa of *Grupo Artilleria 4*, who moved his guns about the busy battlefield with great panache and initiative, using tractors and Land Rovers confiscated from Falkland Islanders.

The British had a like number of 105mm light guns, which were pre-positioned behind the Sussex Mountains by helicopter but were dependent on air supply and resupply for ammunition. Ammunition was in incredibly short supply following the destruction of the initial stockpile landed at Ajax Bay by a Skyhawk flown by Flying Officer Velasco on 27 May. As an aside, two other bombs dropped by Velasco had fallen, without exploding, into the abandoned Ajax Bay refrigeration plant being used as a field hospital. One lodged in the roof and was famously made safe by an RAF bomb disposal officer who spent the night alongside the bomb, reassuring the medics below that it was safe to continue their work, before defusing the bomb safely in daylight. The ammunition shortage at Sussex Mountains was not really made good until the battle was nearly over and all the Para support weapons – GPMG(SF)s, Milan anti-tank missiles and 81mm mortars – had been helicoptered forward for the final stages of the battle.

Anti-Aircraft Weapons

The Argentine Army initially deployed a pair of twin 35mm Oerlikons by Chinook onto the airfield, where they were separated by some 500m from their Skyguard fire-control radar commanded by another extremely professional and competent young officer, *Teniente* Braghini. This lethally accurate combination had already destroyed one Sea Harrier on 4 May and an Argentine Skyhawk on 12 May. After the San Carlos landings, the threat of a British beach landing at Goose Green, mounted from Falkland Sound, was considered a very real one and the twin 35s were redeployed 100m apart on either side of the promontory in front of the Goose Green Settlement buildings, to face a seaborne assault that never came, such an approach being rejected by the British due to the dense inshore kelp fields. This positioning considerably reduced the guns' all-round coverage due to screening of large parts of their firing arc by the settlement buildings. The Skyguard was also placed near the buildings but as both the radar and the TV tracking systems could see over the top of most of the low-roofed buildings, the Skyguard was able to focus the two guns on Squadron Leader Iveson's GR3 Harrier during the forthcoming battle and shoot him down. This was one of only two Argentine anti-aircraft successes in the battle for Goose Green, the other British loss being a rare, air-to-air engagement, in which a Pucara shot down a Scout helicopter, killing the pilot, Lieutenant Nunn.

In addition, the *Fuerza Aerea* deployed six one-man, hydraulically powered but visually aimed twin 20mm Rheinmetall AA guns in a kilometre-long arc on the northwest (open) side of the airfield, along with a portable alerting Elta or Rasit radar. Finally, just before the battle, a *Fuerza Aerea* anti-aircraft section, which had provided AA cover for the unloading of the 105mm light guns from the beached *Rio Iguazu*, added its Soviet-made Strela shoulder-launched missiles to the Goose Green air defence inventory.

On the British side, the Paras were supported by the Royal Marine Air Defence Troop equipped with Blowpipes, who gave hair-raising near-misses to two Pucaras at Camilla Creek and were to bring down an Aermacchi naval jet at Goose Green. Finally, the Paras themselves were to bring down a Pucara at point-blank range with small arms fire. From all this, it can be seen that the defending Argentinians and the assaulting Paras were each attacked at Goose Green by the other's aircraft and both sides had successes in shooting them down. With so much already written about the battle of Goose Green, I will only cover the battle in brief chronological order so that the anti-aircraft actions of both sides can be put into context.

Overnight, on 26/27 May 2 Para had advanced on foot from San Carlos to within 8km of Goose Green, every man overburdened with as much extra mortar and machine-gun ammunition as they could possibly carry, and lay concealed in the lee of the Sussex Mountains. At first light on this day the equally overloaded 45 Commando headed out of the beachhead in the opposite direction, to 'yomp' on foot across East Falkland to Douglas Settlement, while 3 Para, similarly overloaded, began their famous 'tab' across the island towards Teal Inlet, to bring the Argentinians ringing the high ground above Stanley to battle, both units demonstrating the value and flexibility of elite forces over line infantry when push comes to shove. The Argentinians had considered a similar option, in reverse, to counter-attack the British beachhead but lost the initiative after deciding that a cross-island foot-march with a fire-fight at the end would be just too difficult. Based on their previous Falkland Islands platoon-sized rotations, the Royal Marines were well aware, in advance, of the difficult Falklands terrain and had brought along their arctic warfare BV-206 all-terrain tracked personnel carriers, now totally loaded-up with ammunition and field rations. In addition, the Islanders themselves were also to throw in their rather unsung and under-reported logistic support in the form of tractors with trailers and farm Land Rovers, along with their intimate knowledge of which tracks were passable or not, to support the foot-slogging advance. In parallel, an air-bridge, a fraction of the capacity of the Chinook and Wessex helicopters lost on the *Atlantic Conveyor*, would fly artillery and ammunition forward as well. The simultaneous, three-pronged British breakout was to seize the initiative from the Argentinians so that, from now on, they could only react to but not create new operational circumstances.

At Camilla Creek 2 Para's 50-year-old RAF forward air controller had been evacuated to the rear as an early casualty and was thus unable to direct the first Harrier attacks supporting the 2 Para advance on Goose Green. First off to Goose Green were a pair of GR3 Harriers, led by the boss of 1 Squadron, Peter Squire, who 'stooged around' at 5,000ft waiting for the replacement FAC to be able to see through the mountain-top clouds, but lack of visibility at low level prevented either the Harriers or the FAC from seeing anything to attack, so the two jets dejectedly returned to HMS *Hermes*.

At around noon, HMS *Hermes* received an air tasking order indicating that the Paras at Goose Green 'were in need of urgent support'. This was the kind of language used in NATO to indicate that friendly forces are in dire need and that desperate measures might be required. Unknown to the Harrier pilots, this was not actually the case. On the ground the 2 Para observation posts were still moving into position on high ground, ahead of the main attack, which had not yet even started. The link-up with the FAC had failed, so that, without prior photo-reconnaissance, which was consistently refused by the Naval Task Force commander, finding targets was going to be a hard task. Indeed, the wily *Teniente* Chanampa had hidden his guns way up the isthmus, level with Burnside House, and on his first pass Iveson reported that he could not see anything; on the next pass he dropped his cluster bombs on enemy troops he could see and, on the third pass, still looking for targets to strafe with cannon, he had by now thoroughly stirred up the wildly shooting 20mm Rheinmetalls. Meanwhile, the deadly accurate Skyguard, under the command of *Teniente* Braghini, locked the twin 35mm Oerlikons onto Iveson's Harrier and Braghini let rip. Harrier XZ988 was hit and mortally damaged, fortunately for Iveson, in the rear. All sorts of cockpit warning lamps came on but, as the aircraft was still stable, Iveson let it fly as far from Goose Green as it would go. When the controls froze, Iveson ejected seconds before the Harrier disintegrated in a great fireball upon impact with the ground. The FAC reported the aircraft hit and the pilot's ejection, but did not make any mention of a parachute. The squadron leader, partially blinded by the ejection, mistook sheep for Argentinians and ran away from them, eventually hiding up in a vacated but fully furnished farm called Paragon House, about 10km from Goose Green. He made a brief transmission on his personal locator beacon, which was picked up by a Sea Harrier on combat air patrol high above and was enough to galvanize 1 Squadron RAF into believing he was still alive. A helicopter search-and-rescue mission was rejected by the Royal Navy as too risky but at last light Squadron Leader Pook was allowed to fly a reconnaissance mission to Goose Green, with the unwritten part of his plan to scout around to try to make contact with Iveson. He arrived in the area just as an Argentine air raid was taking place at Ajax Bay in San Carlos Water. With Pook beginning his photo run at 15,000ft, *Teniente* Braghini easily had the Harrier in his TV tracker sights and opened fire, the tracers flashing close by the cockpit just as Pook's radar warning receiver burst into life. Breaking away at maximum speed, Pook fled from the flak; he made some optimistic calls to Iveson on the rescue frequency but heard no reply. Making his way back to HMS *Hermes* to land in the dark, he made a mental note to add another 5,000ft when overflying Goose Green. Iveson, meanwhile, survived on a diet of tinned beans that he found in the deserted farmhouse – famously part of the fare that the Harrier force enjoyed on exercises in the field; he was rescued days later by an Army Gazelle.

To best appreciate this famous battle, I rely heavily on map illustrations. Unfortunately, such detailed information was not available to Colonel Jones or his 3 Brigade Commander, Brigadier Julian Thompson. For this, I blame the Royal Navy for the fundamental failure of not permitting the Harriers to get low-level, timely, tactical target imagery to either the RAF ground-attack pilots or the soldiers fighting on the ground when both aircraft carriers and both kinds of Harriers were fully equipped to do.

The most important feature of Darwin-Goose Green is that it is a 2-mile wide, 4-mile long isthmus that joins East Falkland to the north with Lafonia to the south (Map 17 covers the battleground). Lafonia is named after Samuel Lafone, an asset stripper who landed a party of Argentine *gauchos* to round up and sell the wild cattle that roamed the southern half of East Falkland Island. To mark his boundary, he planted a straight line of gorse bushes from Brenton Loch across Middle Hill and Darwin Hill to the beach of Darwin Harbour, providing one of the many thin threads to the claim that Argentina 'owned' the Islands. Brenton Loch gives access, through much kelp, out into Falkland Sound, while from Darwin Harbour there is water access all the way to Stanley and other points, such as Fitzroy and Bluff Cove, all of which feature later in the campaign.

Since the battle of Goose Green proceeded from north to south, the locations that feature in the battle begin with the Sussex Mountains, off the top of the map to the north, behind which lie the waters of San Carlos and the British beachhead. The easiest access to the isthmus from the north is through Low Pass, a neck of land between Camilla Creek and another equally narrow route around the pond just north of Burnside House. Further south, more than two-thirds of the way across the isthmus is a small ridge named No Name Ridge.

Going further south there is substantial rising ground across the isthmus, with the two higher points named Middle Hill and Darwin Hill. This high ground completely overlooks the race course, fenced meadow land, Goose Green airfield (also fenced) and the Goose Green settlement, itself on a small peninsula and with rather more houses than Darwin. Halfway between Goose Green and Darwin

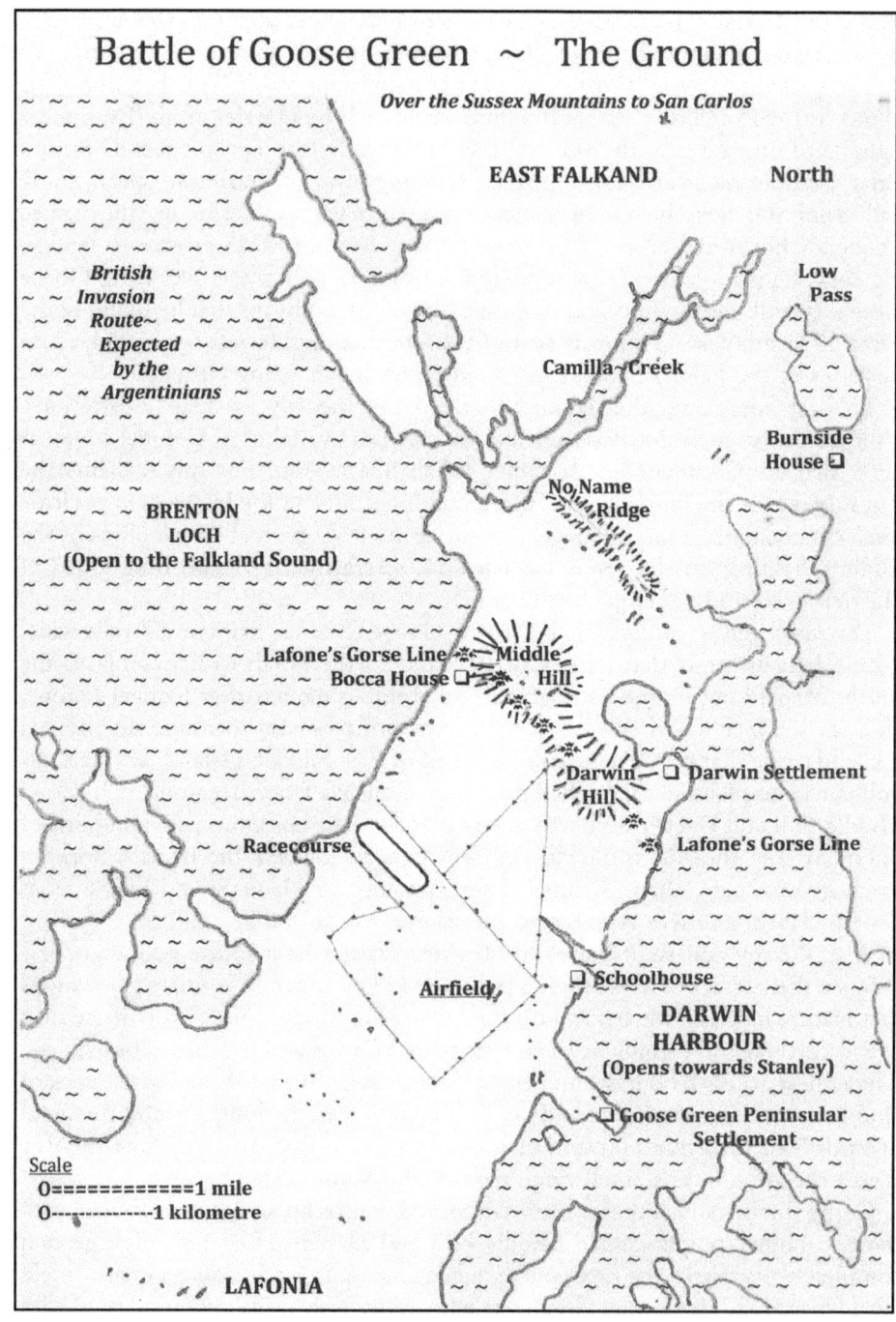

Map 17. The main physical features of the geography of Goose Green.

there was a schoolhouse overlooking a small creek; it was in this building that the residents of both settlements were incarcerated once the campaign began. To the south there was Lafonia, an extensive area of rather flat ground and many lakes.

Goose Green airfield was simply a well-flattened grass area with no formally prepared runways. A windsock informed pilots of the wind direction and a small shed housed fire extinguishers and fuel drums for visiting light aircraft.

The first weakness of the defence of the *Fuerza Aerea* Pucara forward operating base, *BAM Condor*, was its fragmented structure under *Vice-Commodoro* Pedroza and *Teniente Coronel* Piaggi, 12 Infantry Regiment Commander, both hamstrung by incomplete communications and fractions of units of mixed experience which had not worked together before. In addition to Piaggi's own full A Company of the 12 Infantry Regiment, with their 81mm mortars, there were the air operations and aircraft maintenance staff, six *Fuerza Aerea* twin 20mm AA guns, *Fuerza Aerea* infantry with two more 81mm mortars, Air Police and the *Ejercito*'s GADA 601 Skyguard-Oerlikon fire unit consisting of its control radar and two twin 35mm Oerlikons. As the British beachhead developed, it became clear that *BAM Condor* was going to be attacked, so bit-part reinforcements were rushed in from the 8, 12 and 25 Infantry Regiments (8 RI, 12 RI, 25 RI), including the 105mm howitzers and some *Fuerza Aerea* shoulder-launched Strela missiles.

The initial Argentine expectation was a sea landing. Brenton Loch beach was mined and strung with 125kg remote detonation aircraft bombs covered by the twin 35mm Skyguard-Oerlikons in dual AA-cum-ground role. Minefields to the immediate north and south of the airfield protected its flanks and these, in turn, were covered by an arc of six twin 20mm Rheinmetall AA guns, and another minefield combination closed the box on the settlement promontory to the east. A Company 12 RI, its HQ and reinforcements from 25 RI occupied the largest east–west ridge formed by Middle and Darwin Hill, with further infantry and two 81mm mortars deployed on the next, northerly, No Name Ridge. More mines and aircraft bombs were strung out on both ridges and to the far south. Further north still, reconnaissance patrols were deployed to cover the narrowest land approaches to the isthmus, the 500m-wide Low Pass and Burnside House. Another important reinforcement was the arrival of the 105mm howitzers deployed forward of No Name Ridge. Once battle with the Paras was joined, two further enhanced, platoon-sized combat teams were flown by helicopter into Lafonia under great risk of interception by Harriers, one team arriving in the morning and the other in the afternoon, respectively dropped off between 5 and 8km south of the bottom edge of the map. The first reinforcement arrived just in time to take part in the battle and the other more or less in time for the surrender.

For the bare bones of Jones's six-phase plan, see Map 19. He was to advance down the isthmus, two companies up and one company back, through the narrow neck of Low Pass, with the fourth company skirting down the highly indented

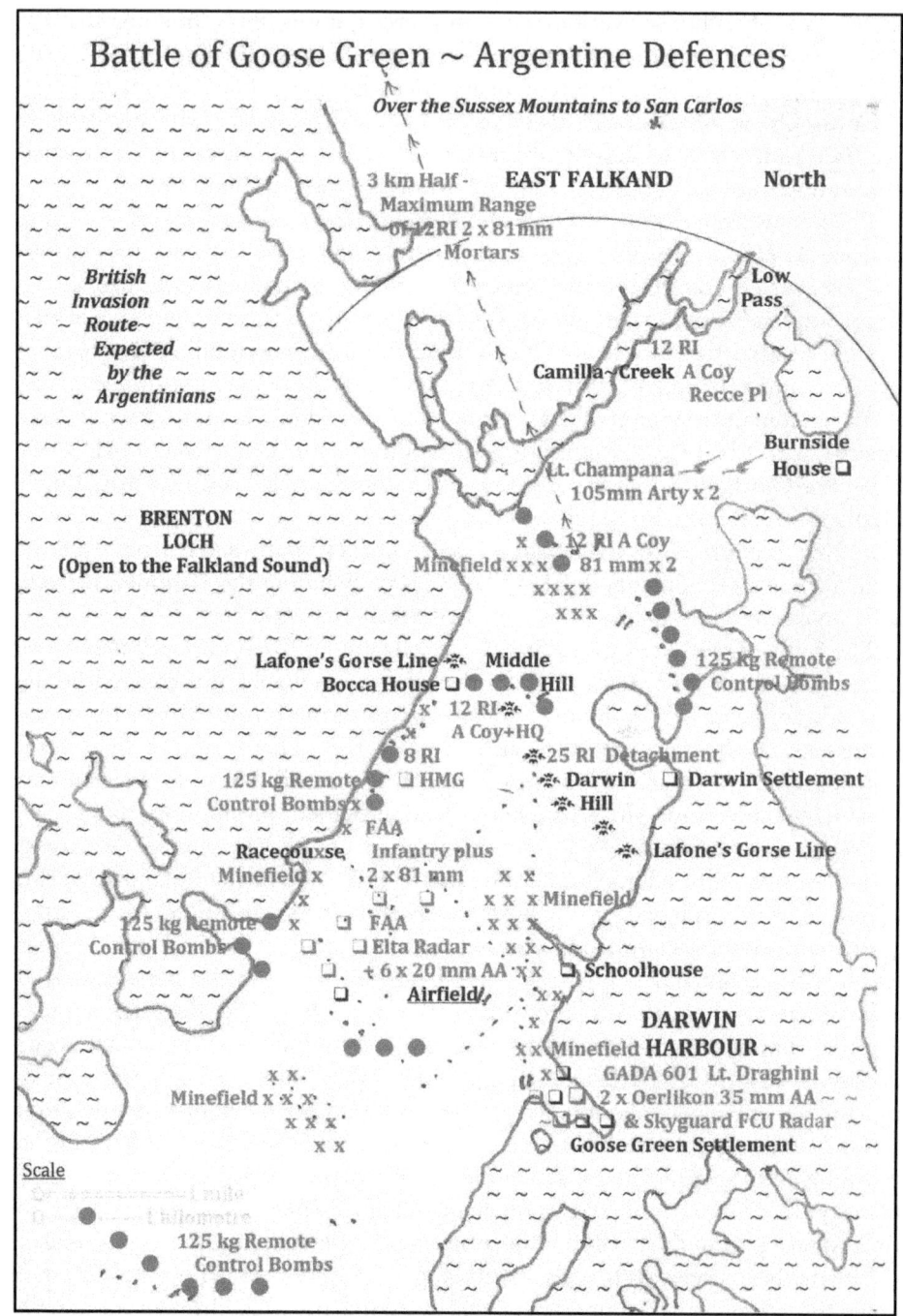

Map 18. Argentine major dispositions before the battle of Goose Green.

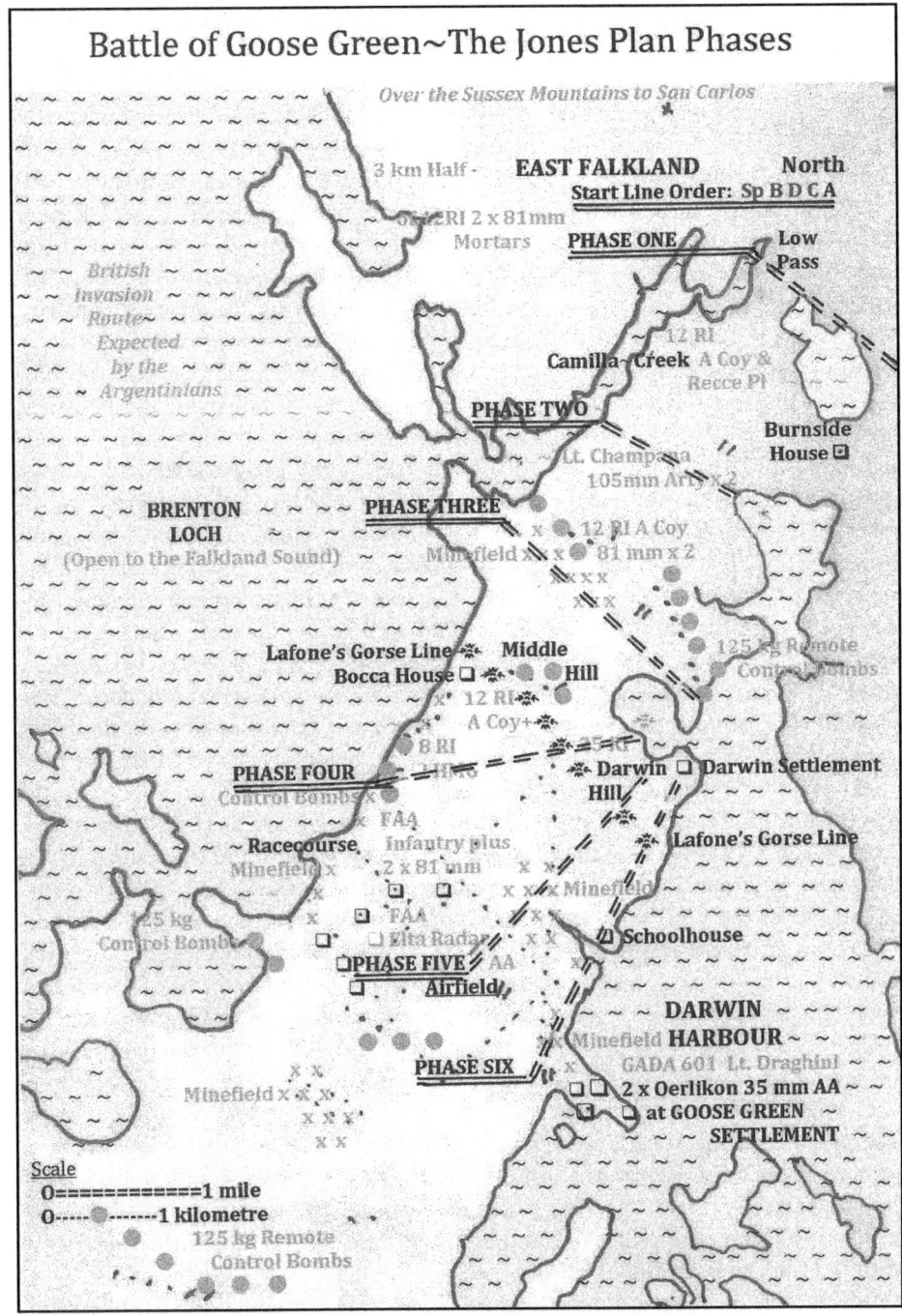

Battle of Goose Green~The Jones Plan Phases

Over the Sussex Mountains to San Carlos

3 km Half - **EAST FALKLAND** **North**
Start Line Order: Sp B D C A

12 RI 2 x 81mm
Mortars **PHASE ONE** **Low Pass**

British
invasion
Route
Expected
by the
Argentinians

12 RI

Camilla Creek A Coy & Recce Pl

PHASE TWO

Burnside House ▣

Lt. Champana
105mm Arty x 2

BRENTON LOCH **PHASE THREE**
(Open to the Falkland Sound)

x 12 RI A Coy
Minefield x x 81 mm x 2
x x x
x x

Lafone's Gorse Line **Middle**
Bocca House ▢ **Hill**
x 12 RI
A Coy+
8 RI

125 kg Remote
Control Bombs

PHASE FOUR
Control Bombs x

Darwin ▢ **Darwin Settlement**
Darwin Hill

FAA
Racecourse Infantry plus
Minefield x 2 x 81 mm x x
x x x x Minefield **Lafone's Gorse Line**

25 kg
Control Bombs FAA
Elta Radar x x **Schoolhouse**

PHASE FIVE AA
Airfield

DARWIN
Minefield **HARBOUR**

PHASE SIX GADA 601 Lt. Draghini
▢ ▢ 2 x Oerlikon 35 mm AA
▢ ▢ at **GOOSE GREEN**
SETTLEMENT

Minefield x x x
x x x
x x

Scale
0=============1 mile
0-----●-------1 kilometre
● 125 kg Remote
Control Bombs

Map 19. The six phase objectives of Jones's battle plan.

Darwin Harbour coastline, clearing his other flank as it went, starting at Burnside House.

He would leave his two 81mm mortars, one-third of his normal firepower, at the start line and set up his four machine guns alongside them in the sustained-fire (GPMG SF) mode to provide flanking fire support from the west side of Camilla Creek. At the phase two line he would bring the fourth company up the middle of the first two, assaulting any enemy troops found on No Name Ridge.

Even before the battle began Jones lost his experienced RAF forward air controller; this turned out to be a blessing in disguise because his Army FAC replacement, unable to bring in the Harriers to soften-up the Argentinians the day before the battle due to weather, bumped into an Argentine reconnaissance patrol equipped with one of the only two jeep-mounted Argentine radios on its way back to Goose Green. After a brief fire-fight, the patrol surrendered to the FAC, so that another chance was lost to the Argentinians of getting early warning of Jones's initial actions. Indeed, although the enemy commander had moved most of his forces forward of the highest Middle Hill/Darwin Hill ground to the lesser No Name Ridge, that force did not stand-to when Burnside House, or rather the trenches around it, were shot-up and grenaded by A Company opening Jones's battle an hour late at 0300hrs. Luckily, the British residents were un-harmed. Even after the GPMG SFs opened up 15 minutes later, the Argentine front line had not stood-to properly and their first line of defence collapsed as Phase 2 began. Sadly, parts of the advancing companies crossed paths and engaged each other – not a good start for the Phase Three assault. Middle Hill/Darwin Hill was what the Germans call the *Schwerpunkt*[11] of the battle. Earlier, a fleet of nine Argentine helicopters had dropped off a half company-sized battle group from 25 RI, which reinforced the defenders of Darwin Hill. Already late starting, the 2 Para battle stalled for a moment and while it did, the enterprising *Teniente* Chanampa got his 105mm howitzers, intact, back through the confusion and set up in the rear of the battlefield, once more facing the Paras; he was to repeat this rearward leapfrog twice more. With two of his advancing companies stalled, and his other company halted on a previously ordered phase line, Jones personally leapt forward to get phase three unscrambled and lost his life when he charged a rat's nest of enemy machine guns suddenly revealed in the darkness. In the taking of Middle Hill/Darwin Hill the Argentinians lost nearly a hundred men: twenty killed, thirty-seven wounded and forty prisoners. However, when the Paras went southwards, onto the forward slope of the hill, they were met by a barrage of AA gunfire from the airfield and took more casualties there than any-where else in the battle. Clearly a phase four frontal crossing of the open ground of the airfield was not going to happen as the Paras unscrambled themselves on Middle Hill/Darwin Hill.

Only when the Paras brought forward their support weapons to Middle Hill/Darwin Hill did the situation change, as their long-range Milan anti-tank missiles

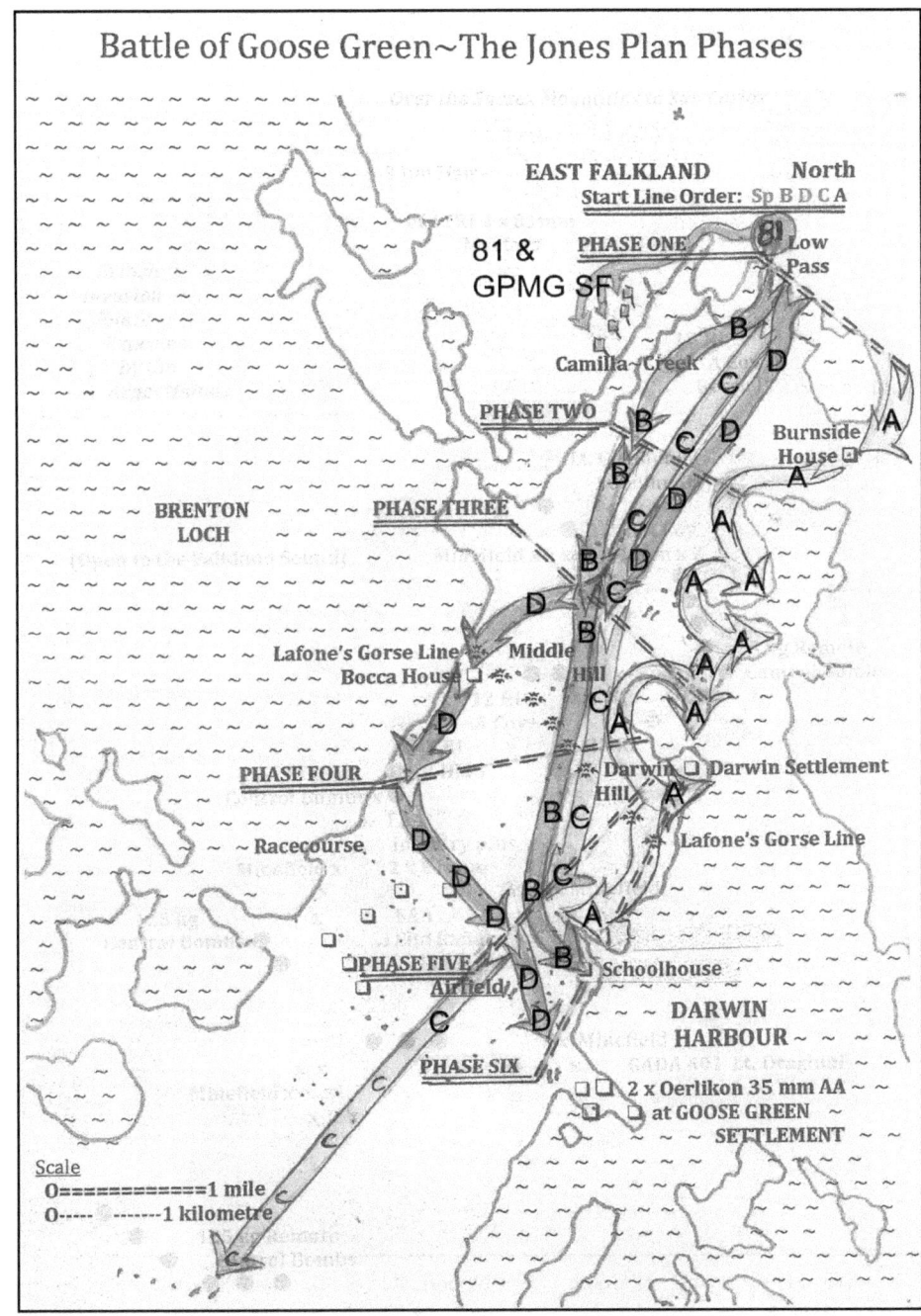

Map 20. Jones's planned four-company moves over six phases.

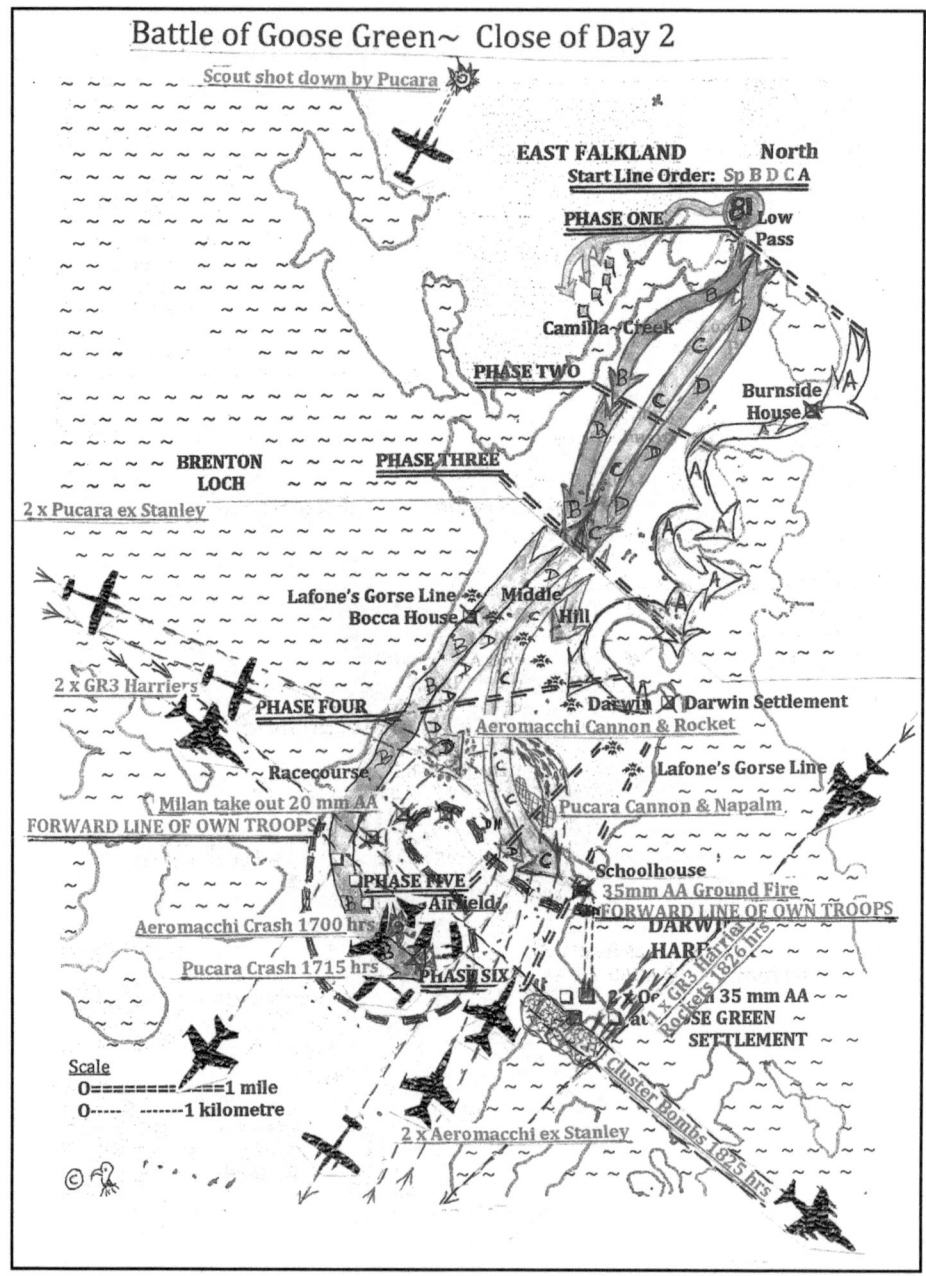

Map 21. Air attacks on Goose Green by both sides within hours of each other.

took out the nearest three twin 20mm cannon on the airfield. GPMG sustained fire from Middle Hill/Darwin Hill then made the open airfield extremely inhospitable, forcing the AA gunners to abandon their remaining three twin 20mm cannon and for the *Fuerza Aerea* infantry to abandon their two 81mm mortars and retreat towards Goose Green settlement, now home to three 105mm howitzers as well as the fearsome twin 35mm Oerlikons. This in turn opened up a flanking opportunity for B Company to slip along the northwest side of the airfield and switch to Jones's planned advance line of D Company. On the airfield in the late afternoon B Company under the cool Major Crossland suddenly found itself showered by an exploding Aermacchi shot down by a Blowpipe, followed 15 minutes later by a Pucara cartwheeling over their heads, to break-up and cover them with fuel, which luckily did not ignite. From the Paras' point of view things were not going well: they were getting shot-up by the Argentine Navy and Air Force and were facing a great concentration of 105mm and 35mm firepower from the Goose Green settlement corner. In addition, they were low on ammunition, low on radio batteries and vulnerable to overnight counter-attack. The Argentine commander saw things differently. He had just witnessed two aircraft from his side wrecked as they crashed into the centre of his patch; he was dominated by heavy fire from high ground that was essential to his defence but that was now held by the enemy, and he was hemmed in on all sides, with his back to a small promontory, from which there was no escape route out. Moreover, the majority of his own surviving 12 RI troops were first-year conscripts with less than six months' service and he felt they were not up to mounting a counter-attack in daylight, let alone at night. To sharpen the negative assessment of his situation, a pair of Harriers shrieked in only an hour after the two Argentine air crashes, laying a carpet of cluster bomb explosions in the shallows, right alongside the length of his last stand on the promontory, followed seconds later by a fusillade of seventy-two rockets from a third Harrier chopping up the end of the pro-montory, all three Harriers disappearing into the deepening darkness with nary a pop from any of his hitherto mighty air defences. Into this gloomy picture stepped the acting commanding officer of 2 Para, Major Chris Keeble, making his staff college-trained review of how the battle might be seen from the enemy commander's perspective and proposing an Argentine surrender against the possibility that the next morning's Harriers would not bother with a firepower demonstration on the beach but would come in, bang on target, for real. The surrender offer was accepted. At dawn, well over a thousand men marched away into captivity, leaving the iconic image of their paraded impedimenta on the airfield to wow the world with the Paras' magnificent feat of arms. Lieutenant Colonel 'H' Jones and Sergeant Ian McKay were each awarded the Victoria Cross posthumously. Piaggi and his second-in-command were cashiered and 'Ganso Verde' became Goose Green once again. It was a hard-fought, finely balanced, airfield defence battle by any standards. Total unconditional surrender of the remainder of the Argentine garrison was now just a fortnight away, but there was a lot more flak to come and some very tough nuts ahead yet to be cracked.

The lessons of the battle are clear. Prior intelligence of enemy dispositions based on low-level photo-reconnaissance is absolutely essential, marked on maps and made available down to section level. Vehicle patrols close to the front line are an invitation to ambush and capture; active foot patrols and covert observation posts should have warned of the Para advance. Ground vital to the defence should be held at all costs: in this case the high ground of Middle Hill/Darwin Hill and the two narrow bottlenecks of land at Low Pass and Burnside; once these fell, the initiative passed to the British. However, back on *BAM Condor* airbase there were still more than enough trained soldiers between the Air Force infantry, 20mm gunners and the rump of 12 RI to have executed an immediate counterattack and maintained an aggressive Argentine stance: speed and aggression save lives in the longer run. In multi-service and multi-national deployments liaison officers should glue each other's units together. At Goose Green the late injection by a formation of nine helicopters, not once but twice, of fully worked up, near company-sized combat teams from 25 RI, only the first of which made their way with all speed to the front line, caused the Paras on Darwin Hill to recoil, but not to break as 12 RI had already abandoned Middle Hill next to it, thanks to earlier British aggression. Finally, one wonders why there was not a taxi rank of at least one Sea Harrier and one GR3 Harrier on combat air patrol 20,000ft above, solely dedicated to the battlefield, to keep Pucaras and Aermacchis and the eighteen close-in helicopter sorties away from the Goose Green airspace, instead of frittering the carrier's scarce air resources chasing will o' the wisp targets elsewhere, all over the Islands, particularly when naval gunfire support to the Goose Green battle had to be withdrawn in daylight.

Back in the UK jubilation followed the publication of the picture showing a sea of Argentine helmets and rifles surrendered to 2 Para on Goose Green airfield, and more than vindicated the humility of the earlier images of just a dozen or so Royal Marines lying face down in the dirt outside Stanley.

Meanwhile, on Ascension Island further trouble was brewing for the Argentinians as the first Shrike anti-missile armed Vulcan, Black Buck 4, captained by Squadron Leader C.N. McDougall, launched into the air with its armada of Victor tankers. Unfortunately, this whole carefully choreographed aerial assembly unravelled early when the hose-drum unit of the first refuelling Victor failed to operate and forced the entire extremely complicated sortie to be cancelled.

In Stanley *La Gaçeta Argentina* faithfully recorded the cessation of Argentine military activity at Darwin-Goose Green, but on the mainland Official Communiqué 107 admitted only to 'losing radio contact after the Argentine forces resisted attack by two thousand men transported by helicopter and supported by anti-aircraft guns' (of which the British had absolutely none). No further

A bare Oerlikon gun and crew, dropped off by Chinook at Goose Green, in what they stood up in. Note the complete absence of camouflage and the one-man bivouac. This photograph was on an undeveloped film roll found in captured Skyguard radar.

The supposedly silenced Goose Green Oerlikon gun was fired again at Sid's Strip forward operating base by Flying Officer Peter Kaye following its relocation by Chinook in late 1982. At the time it was the best condition cannon on the Island. *(Flying Officer Peter Kaye RAF Regt)*

The Goose Green gun, the best on the Island, was the sorriest-looking gun of all to arrive at RAF Waddington. It turned out that the crew shipping the gun out of the Falklands, ignorant of how to unload the ammunition, decided to cut off the whole section with an acetylene torch. An exploding shell blew off the welder's hand.

Although looking terrible, with its barrels badly bent and rear tyres blasted by the explosion which turned the gun over, probably from a random 1,000lb bomb tossed into Stanley, killing a number of its crew, this battle-damaged gun was easily repaired.

The first four Oerlikon twin 35s out of the Faldingworth factory, refurbished to squeaky-clean, brand-new, fully warrantied, zero hours, zero rounds fired condition, with the Swiss BMARCO Ltd technical team that did the job and the author, Martin Frey and Spike Jones.

The new Director of the RAF Regiment, Air Commodore Dempster Anderson, seen here in deep consultation with Martin Frey and the author in Switzerland, brought refreshing energy and charm to speed up the Byzantine into-service process.

2729 Sqn Regular Cadre Qualification Firing at HMS *Cambridge*. An exceptional Regular RAF Band of Brothers from seven different trade groups become one as live-firing qualified crew and instructors on the Skyguard-Oerlikon weapon system. Back row, left to right: Fg Off Johnston; the author; Cpl Holmwood; Cpl Hamilton; F Sgt Bolding; F Sgt Wilson; Cpl Duffy; Sgt Matthews. Front row, left to right: F Sgt Kavanagh; F Sgt Collins; Sgt Hughes; Cpl Knott; Cpl Clements; F Sgt Coupe.

The 2729 Squadron Regular Cadre live-firing to qualify. The twin cannons vomit empty shell cases from a half-second burst tearing away at Mach 3 to the target in an unforgettable experience of roaring metal and cordite scent ...

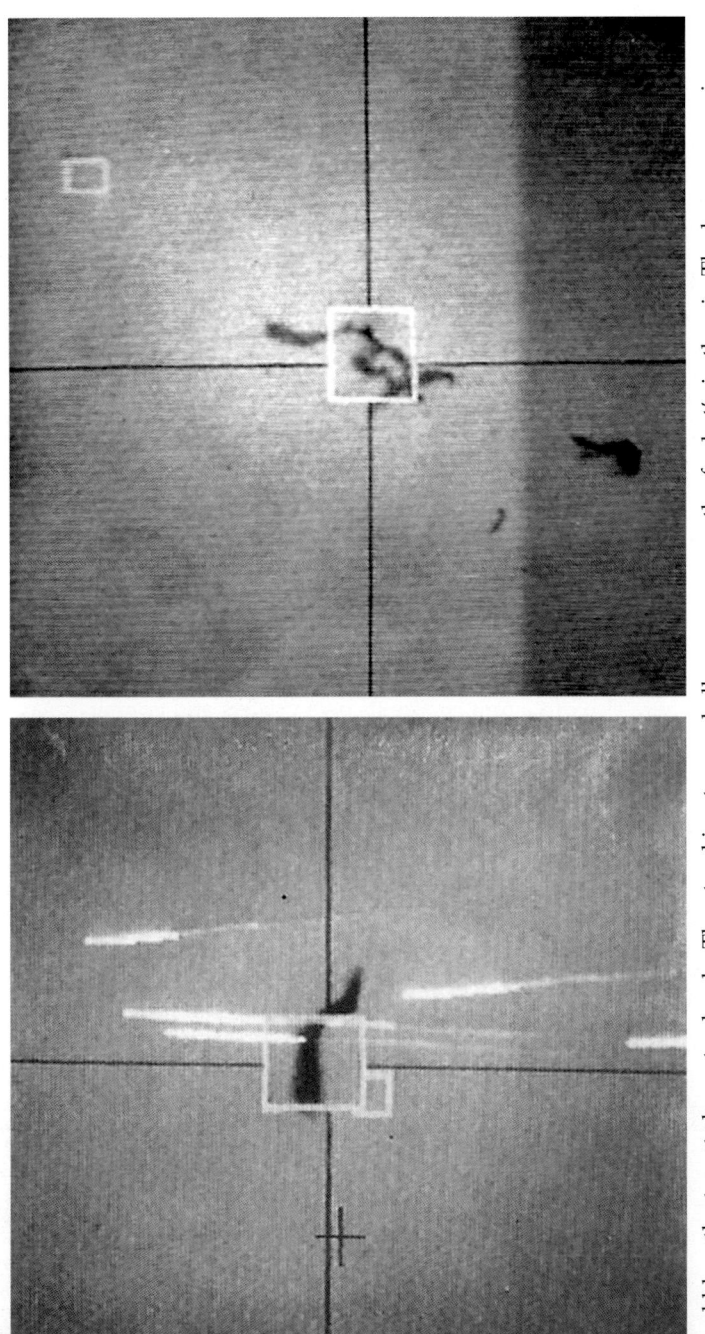

... and blow the target sleeve to shreds. The streaking tracer shells are one seventh of what's in the air. The large square is what the hands-off TV tracker is following; the small square shows what the radar is locked onto; both can be corrected by manual intervention. An air sentry crewman outside can also inject a late, close-in target at any time.

The author pictured giving a tv interview. Media interest in the captured equipment entering service was a huge boon to good relations with our host RAF base and the Royal Navy and Royal Artillery ranges, and assisted our recruiting of civilian Reserve Forces volunteers enormously.

Recruit selection team problem-solving challenges. We based our gender neutral, social status neutral and previous military rank neutral recruiting on the best meld of officer and airmen selection procedures rolled into a live-in weekend of taster gun drills, briefings, initiative tests and interviews. Nowhere else can a unit choose its own officers and gunners!

Our first ten recruits. They trained together, starting on Lesson 1 on the deployment and operation of the 6-ton Oerlikon twin 35mm gun before any other aspect of training, and were ready to fire it after nine weeks of part-time training. After that they could learn to march!

All recruit training starts with the 6-ton Oerlikon. It's hands-on, out-of-the box training, with all the right things to hand in the right places so that it becomes instinctive; with fearsome power-operated heavy metal flying around, the pass mark is a civvy culture-shocking 100 per cent.

As soon as gunners are Oerlikon qualified, the most motivated and talented can move up to the Skyguard radar, the source of the killer accuracy of the entire fire unit. Ease of into-action and operation lead to 'Star Wars' shooting games with a for-real fire button that can unleash a hundred shells into a metre cube in two seconds.

After just nine weeks we had an operational crew ready to fire. The intense training on real kit motivates the 'no bull-and-bullshit' transition from civilian to Oerlikon gunner like no other military training, the dressing smartly, knowing who is what rank and saluting being learnt by observation and osmosis. It helped having brand-new everything, from guns to trucks to radars to clothing.

Visits by more VIPs than I have experienced anywhere in thirty-six years of service motivated and sharpened up the volunteers' deployments to a very high standard.

The chance discovery of a Second World War bomber aircraft dispersal underground crew shelter blessed this on-base Skyguard deployment site in the middle of a minefield, offering crew accommodation out of the occasional Arctic blast.

It's always a surprise to find a silver-service bunker lunch – a bit like enjoying roast lamb in a nuclear submarine directly under the hull of an Argentine cruiser. Here Station Commander Gp Capt Bonner hosts Royal Canadian Artillery officers with RAF Regt Wg Cdr Wallis and the next officer to command 2729, Sqn Ldr Kemp.

With the Oerlikon twin 35s, everything comes in pairs. On the left, front to back, Cpl Stafford with his son-in-law J/T Easton; on the right, front to back, mum Cpl Steele with son LAC Steele. The middle pair in the back row are the Gallaghers, sister and brother; the middle pair in the front row are the brothers Saxby. And, of course, their cannon is called Two Sisters.

As a unit that chose its own officers, and with the ability to accelerate the highly motivated and able in our civilian ranks, we preferred home-grown ingrained Skyguard-Oerlikon talent to parachuted-in pre-conceiving ex-Regulars, so we commissioned sparingly. Here I am pinning our first rank, Pilot Officer Steve Howard.

My absolute best recruit was Sir Rex Hunt. In a wonderful twist of irony, he became the Honorary Air Commodore of a squadron constituted from the ex-Argentine spoils of war that had defiled his governorship of the Falkland Islands. As a Second World War Typhoon ground attack pilot as well, there was no one better fitted to the role.

The winning team. Hand on heart, I can say that none of this extraordinary adventure of technical delight, exponential introduction to real staff work in a first tour in the MoD and an amazing command of a NATO-assigned unit would have been possible without the equally iconoclastic support from my now lifelong friend Martin Frey of Oerlikon.

Argentine official communiqué would mention the battle of Goose Green again.[12] For the record, Braghini's Skyguard radar was so perforated by Para small arms fire that it never returned to British service. The Oerlikon guns, however, were returned to operational service in the RAF. One gun was named Goose Green and carried the badge of 2 Para in honour of this battle. Cannon, after all, are the battle colours of every artillery unit, and captured ones even more so. For the victors this cannon truly deserved its battlefield name in honour of its captors.

Chapter 11

The Last Three Days of May

After 29 May, following the liberation of Goose Green, the British counter-airfield attacks intensified. It was decided to subject the Argentinians to continual harassment throughout the day, taking good care to avoid the anti-aircraft defences. At noon, Rapier also had its day, shooting down a *Grupo 6* Dagger, killing the *Fuerza Aerea* pilot, Bernhard. Then, in mid-afternoon the Royal Navy lost a Sea Harrier when it slid sideways off the aircraft carrier's deck as the ship rolled in heavy seas. The pilot, Lieutenant Commander Braithwaite, ejected into the water, from which he was immediately rescued. Meanwhile, inland, Squadron Leader Iveson was plucked out of hiding following his post-Goose Green ejection escapade by a Gazelle and taken to HMS *Fearless*.

It is worth quickly switching now to review the parallel British breakout from the San Carlos beachhead by the Royal Marines and Paras and to identify some of the key geographic features that were to figure in the next battles with the Argentinians on the hills blocking their way and their view of Stanley. By now, also, it was clear to the Argentinians that Stanley airport, with its vital nightly runs of C130 Hercules transport aircraft bringing in ammunition, weapons and Special Forces and taking casualties back to the mainland, was more important than Stanley town and harbour. Thus the anti-aircraft defences at the airport were much thickened up and, where roads allowed, weapons and radars were moved about without recourse to their rapidly diminishing force of helicopters. They did this at night, making it all the more imperative for the British to locate and target the long-range, early warning Westinghouse TPS 43 surveillance radar, as well as the accurate Oerlikon gun-directing Skyguard radars and the one Roland missile launcher. The map below shows the planned overland foot-slogging routes of the advancing British forces and the names of key features in the forthcoming battles. Parallel to the marches, sea-transport helped to build forward depots of ammunition, food and fuel, while helicopters transported artillery using the two British surviving Chinooks; in addition, of course, there was the famous flying logistic column of Falkland Islanders driving an assortment of farm Land Rovers, tractors and trailers loaded with military supplies.

Towards the end of the day on 29 May two GR3 Harriers flown by Harris and Rochfort were tasked to seek out and destroy an enemy radar in the hills to the north of Stanley airport. This was one of many radar missions, the target locations being provided by accurate six-figure grid references based on ship-borne

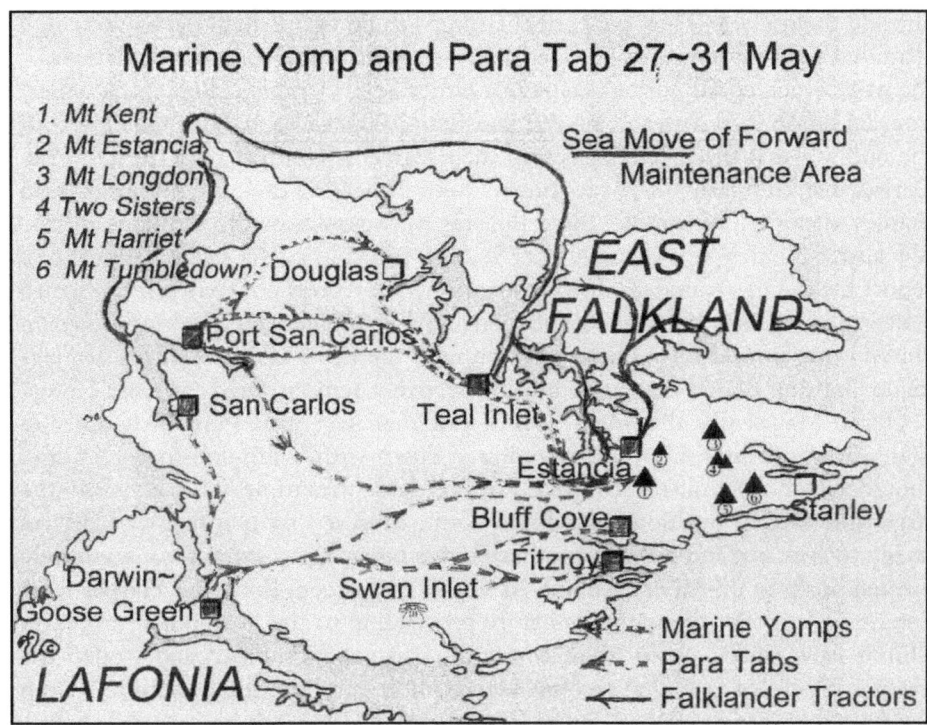

Map 22. 'No Picnic': the Para tab and Royal Marine yomp routes.

radar signal intercepts. In all probability the targets were the tiny, man-portable *Elta* or *Rasit* alerting radars used by the 20mm and 30mm guns of the *Fuerza Aerea* and *Batallón Anti-Aero* of the Argentine Marines. Being so small and movable, there was little chance of finding them to attack in a high-speed, low-level pass without prior and timely photo reconnaissance. In the event, Rochfort's aircraft went unserviceable with a fuel leak before take-off and after much fruitless searching in what was known to be a militarily quiet area, Harris returned to the aircraft carrier with his weapon load intact. The final mission of the day was for two GR3 Harriers flown by OC 1 Squadron and Hare to attack dug-in Argentine troops on Mount Kent with rockets and cannon. Mount Kent was the first and most heavily fortified peak on the route to Stanley and was thus a key Argentine position to be softened-up ready for 45 Commando, Royal Marines. The day ended with the news of Squadron Leader Iveson's rescue by Gazelle reaching 1 Squadron.

The Argentinians, meanwhile, having suffered severe aircraft losses penetrating hostile and concentrated air defence zones around the beachhead, and suffering the tiring effect of continuous, random air and naval bombardment throughout each 24-hour period, decided to retaliate and carry out some bombing from high altitude themselves. They attacked that night using two British-made, very high altitude Canberra bombers, vestiges of less strained Anglo-Argentine relations of the past, which could not be reached by either Sea Harriers or Rapiers. A typical internal bomb load for each aircraft was four 1,000lb iron bombs. One effect of the raid was that the British dispersed their scarce helicopters away from the San Carlos area. Similarly, the Argentinians were dispersing their aircraft away from Stanley airport: for example, three Pucaras were now noted to be flying off the old airfield which was actually the Stanley racecourse. *La Gaçeta Argentina*'s report for the day rounded off with a warning for troops not to touch or disturb a new type of Israeli-supplied anti-personnel bomblet, described as brown in colour with conical fins. These were, in fact, the sub-munitions of the British-made Hunting BL755 cluster bomb, so effectively demonstrated at Goose Green.

On 30 May it was the SAS's turn to catch an Argentine Puma helicopter in their early morning flak trap, bringing it down with a fire-and-forget Stinger shoulder-launched missile. Two GR3 Harriers, meantime, also attacked the Argentine dug-in positions on Mount Kent, followed by two further Harriers trying to seek out and destroy another elusive radar, again given as an accurately located position on Mount Round. As nothing was seen, Pook and Harper were determined to take photographs before proceeding to the next 'radar' target on Mount Low where, again, they saw nothing, so they bombed and strafed the given grid reference, taking reconnaissance photographs at the same time. When the pictures were developed, no radar was revealed but one picture did show a very well camouflaged Rheinmetall twin 20mm cannon at the rear of Mount Round. However, none of the Harriers thus far had drawn any flak from this or any other anti-aircraft weapon on this day.

The next sortie was to be a trial of the newly delivered laser-guided bomb. Because there was a problem getting the right sort of batteries to the forward air controllers equipped with laser target designators as they yomped and tabbed across East Falkland towards Stanley, it was recalled that a qualified weapons instructor in the UK had briefed that the laser range-finder built into the nose of the GR3 Harrier could be used to illuminate the target for the bomb laser-seeker to home onto. So off went the pair, one to illuminate and the other to deliver the bomb onto Stanley, all from a great height, out of the range of anti-aircraft fire. As it turned out, the brief was a bum steer; the laser was in fact not compatible[13] with the bomb and a valuable, futuristic, pin-point bomb was wasted.

The final GR3 Harrier sortie of the day fell to Pook and Rochfort in the gloom of descending darkness: a rocket and cannon attack on enemy helicopters reported to be bringing in reinforcements onto Mount Harriet. Due to inadequacies of intelligence about enemy dispositions and a dearth of photo-reconnaissance missions, compounded by lack of communications with forward air controllers, the pair closed in on the given target area, additionally dogged by intermittent radio failure and bad light, without seeing any helicopters. Just past his planned navigational pick-up point, Pook felt a 'thump' in the rear of his aircraft and assumed it was small arms fire as his wingman called out 'Jerry, you are losing fuel.'

However, on this day the Skyguard-Oerlikon 35mm fire unit *Bravo Uno* of *GADA* 601 claimed a hit.[14] It is quite possible that Pook would have been unaware of the fire because, as discussed above, much of the Argentine ammunition was either high explosive without tracer or high explosive with tracer reduced visibility, and so they added high visibility, solid-shot training tracer shells to their clips. Such a round would hit without exploding but would be enough to bore a large hole through any fuel system. The Skyguard radar, on the other hand, could 'see' shells in flight, both on radar and on the TV tracking display, and would also 'see' the fuel leak. Notwithstanding this confirmation of a hit, Pook pressed on regardless and, together with Rochfort, tore into a head-to-head attack on the Argentine artillery from opposite sides of the mountain with rockets, each breaking left at the last second. Pook's next action was the drill for losing fuel: that is, to go as fast and as high as he could in the direction of home. He briefly considered making a run to land at San Carlos but, mindful of the two own goals of the Argentine gunners, he did not wish to share a similar fate at the hands of equally trigger-happy British sailors and soldiers, and so he headed for home on the aircraft carrier HMS *Hermes*, over 100 nautical miles away, out in the cold, dark wastes of the Southern Ocean. Dogged again by dodgy radio, he sped onwards and upwards alone, while Rochfort had a devil of a time catching up on Pook's high-speed, full-throttle dash for safety. With Pook unable to communicate by radio, Rochfort had already called up HMS *Hermes* for help and several helicopters, one of which was carrying Squadron Leader Iveson back to his ship, were on their way. As his fuel ran out, Pook glided down to a more pilot-friendly altitude and ejected, to be rescued almost immediately by the nearest anti-submarine Sea King helicopter, arriving back on HMS *Hermes* soggy and wet just in time to meet Iveson, who had just landed on the carrier. Pook reported[15] that they shook hands warmly and exchanged words along the lines: 'Jerry, you're all wet – been for a swim?' to elicit the response: 'Something like that. I understand you've been taking a few days off in the country – you lazy sod!'

However, there was no time to follow this cheery reunion with a celebratory beer because at that moment the carrier group came under an impressively coordinated bomb and Exocet attack. Fortuitously, the guard ship HMS *Exeter* brought down two Skyhawks with Sea Dart and the last known air-launched Exocet, fired from maximum range, failed to reach any targets. That made the day for both pilots, which ended with a message from the UK Headquarters at Northwood to say that the Harrier laser range-finder was, after all, not compatible with laser-guided bombs.

Meanwhile, close to midnight on Ascension Island Black Buck 5, the first Vulcan to be armed with two Shrike anti-radiation missiles, together with its armada of air-to-air Victor tankers, was being launched for a radar suppression mission against the *Fuerza Aerea* Westinghouse TPS 43 long-range surveillance radar. Around roughly the same time the said radar was busy tracking Royal Navy warships making a nuisance of themselves with a shore bombardment. The radar crew passed the ship coordinates to the Argentine 155mm artillery battery to carry out retaliatory return fire into the early hours until the ships withdrew as darkness ended.

Indeed, the dark hours of 31 May were to be busy as at Darwin and Goose Green the Argentine Canberras were doing their utmost to play the British at their own game of high-level harassing bombing from above the ceiling of the ground-based anti-aircraft defences. Meanwhile, 200 nautical miles from the Falklands, the Vulcan dropped down to 300ft to slip under the radar cover of the TPS 43. At 23 nautical miles the Vulcan pulled up to 16,000ft for its final attack phase, to coincide with a coordinated raid by Sea Harriers.

The 801 Squadron aircraft carried out two toss-bombing sorties. Each pair of aircraft was armed with either two variable-timed bombs or two conventional iron bombs. The aim was to keep the Argentinians transmitting long enough for the Shrikes to home in and destroy the radar set. As the Vulcan climbed up to its missile launch altitude, hopefully out of range of the one Roland and the Skyguard-directed Oerlikons, its radar warning receiver detected the TPS 43 but the transmissions promptly ceased. Both sides, now more confident and experienced, played out their respective electronic warfare counter-measures. The Argentinians turned down the power of their radar, hoping they could lure the bomber down into range of the Oerlikons. For the next 40 minutes the cat and mouse game continued before the Vulcan picked up the TPS 43 again. Both Shrikes were launched. One missile fell short, just too far away to damage to the radar; the other struck the base of a wall of sand-filled oil drums and sandbags protecting the lower body of the radar and a shower of shrapnel sliced through pressurized waveguide tubing to the aerial and cut the main signal data cable to the control cabin. Radar transmissions ceased immediately and the Vulcan crew could only assume success. For their part, the radar crew received a replacement waveguide section on the next nightly Hercules run into Stanley and repaired the cut cable in such a way that they could, in future, cut radar transmissions remotely from their control cabin, obviating the need for a man to run between the two halves of the radar. Both parties commemorated the raid in rather splendid paintings of the event as seen from their respective perspectives, which can be seen online.

The last day of May ended with a bit of a flap, as RAF pilots are wont to say, and it was all down to a lack of Royal Navy intelligence communication and coordination between the two aircraft carriers. After the Vulcan attack, one of the Sea Harriers on combat air patrol photographed what the pilot thought were a pair of Super Etendards on Stanley airfield. Two more Sea Harriers were diverted to have a look and visually confirmed the sightings. These reports from

HMS *Invincible*, which only carried Sea Harriers, were forwarded to the flagship, HMS *Hermes*, at once. Super Etendards[16] at the end of the Stanley runway brought both carriers within unrefuelled range of these powerful aircraft. Unsurprisingly, the Task Force commander, Admiral Woodward, ordered an immediate, all-out attack on Stanley. The commanding officer of 1 Squadron, Peter Squire, took this rushed priority mission upon himself, with Hare as his wingman. The Royal Navy contribution to the attack was to be two toss-bombing Sea Harriers throwing in bombs from outside the range of the 35mm Oerlikons; in fact, all that the Russian roulette randomness of this kind of bombing did was to place the entire Stanley air defences at the peak of alertness and readiness for action. Squire had previously commented that there did not seem to be much flak at Stanley, but on this day he and Hare flew into everything the Argentinians could throw into the sky. Both Harriers delivered their rockets, firing as they turned away to avoid flying over the entirety of the now bolstered-up and very hostile airfield anti-aircraft guns and missiles. Both GR3 Harriers were hit, the Boss's so severely damaged that it would take five days to patch up all the damage and replace the engine entirely, while Hare took a cannon shell hit directly in the centre of his armoured windshield, which was ultimately repaired with copious quantities of Araldite. *La Gaçeta Argentina* faithfully recorded the day's fighting and claimed that the two Harriers, seen to be taking hits, had been shot down. The claim, however, was truthfully withdrawn in a later edition of *La Gaçeta*. This raid left 1 Squadron with just one serviceable GR3 Harrier and that was flown off next by pilot Peter Harris to carry out a hazardous solo rocket attack on Argentine positions on the hills to the west of Stanley. Thankfully he returned safely to HMS *Hermes*.

After just ten days of ground attack, 1 Squadron ended the month with three of its six aircraft shot down, two seriously damaged and just one left flyable. Fortuitously, no pilots lost their lives. Only one pilot, the unlucky Glover, solo on his first ever operational combat sortie, ended up as a POW for the duration. The Argentine anti-aircraft force had certainly done its job and the king of the ground-air-ground battlefield was the Skyguard radar-directed twin 35mm Oerlikon cannon.

However, more GR3 Harriers were on their long way south, sipping fuel from a string of tankers, all the way down from Ascension Island to the British aircraft carriers off the Falkland Islands. A Royal Marine Special Forces cartoon about the Vulcan raid appeared as an imagined conversation between two Argentine conscripts cowering in a slit trench: 'If that is the size of their aircraft, my God, what is the size of their aircraft carrier?' Well, Ascension Island, like Malta in the Second World War, was that giant, unsinkable aircraft carrier and it was doing a truly great job converting the Vulcan heavy bomber XM597, with a new crew, into an even more powerful, flak-suppressing, rocket-firing, over-sized, ground-attack fighter, now armed with four Shrike missiles.

Chapter 12

The Last Days of Argentine Rule

The first day of June began with a delayed start to air activity due to bad weather, which was just as well because in the previous 48 hours the entire hardware of the RAF's Rapier surface-to-air system had been unloaded from MV *Atlantic Causeway* and sat uselessly on the verges of the dirt track leading out of Green Beach waiting for its crews to arrive. Luckily, Squadron Leader Chris Feek, now the Falkland Islands' Force Commander's Rapier Liaison Officer on HMS *Fearless*, became personally involved in the disembarkation of the entire squadron's equipment of launchers, radars, trucks, spares, mobile workshops and missiles, using a landing craft and a pair of Mexi-floats from HMS *Fearless* onto Green Beach, along with the five RAF personnel who had travelled with the kit. It had taken 24 hours to unload everything and park it all on either side of the only track leading out of the landing area. Next to arrive was MV *Norland*. On Feek's initiative, he got A Flight of 63 Squadron married up with its equipment, while the commanding officer, Squadron Leader Ian Loughborough, was still afloat incommunicado somewhere at sea. However, this unloading only took place after the entire Gurkha battalion had gone ashore first, the infantry being given a higher unloading priority into a rear area secure from any Argentine ground attack but still demonstrably vulnerable to air attack. Thus there was no possibility of any of the ships present or the unloading soldiers being provided with an instant, dense, air defence boost within about 20 minutes of the first Rapier crews coming ashore to cover the vulnerable landing of the infantry battalion. Luckily the Argentinians missed their chance.

In mid-morning a task came in for two Harriers to attack another elusive radar location, given as a six-figure grid reference to a portacabin some 24km behind the forward line of advancing British troops. Two Harriers, one RAF GR3 flown by OC 1 Squadron, Wing Commander Peter Squire, and one RN Sea Harrier, flown by RAF pilot Hall on loan service to the Navy, set off in search of the chimera; finding nothing, they released their rockets at the precisely given grid reference. Out at sea, OC 801 Squadron, Lieutenant Commander 'Sharkey' Ward, off HMS *Invincible*, was low on fuel and nearing the end of his high-level combat air patrol when he was vectored onto a 'slow-moving target' presumed to be an even more elusive C-130 Hercules. He had more success than the radar hunters and connected by radar with an Argentine Hercules C-130. His first Sidewinder fell short into the sea. As a test pilot for Sea Harrier into-service trials, Ward was both skilled and ruthless and he pressed on, even shorter of fuel, to close the range for his second Sidewinder, which hit the Hercules in one engine but did not bring it down. Finally Ward came to such close quarters that he could hose the Hercules fuselage with cannon fire at point-blank range and duly sent Wing Commander Meisner and his hapless crew of seven cartwheeling in the burning Hercules down to their deaths in the sea.

Then, early in the afternoon it was the turn of the Argentine flak for success. Another HMS *Invincible* Sea Harrier pilot, RAF Flight Lieutenant Mortimer, also on loan service to the Navy, watched a missile from GADA 601's one and only Roland launcher wend its way upwards, past its supposed 12,000ft ceiling, to smack into his aircraft despite his best efforts to out-climb and out-manoeuvre it. He ejected over the sea and was seen to fall by parachute into the water. The Argentinians immediately sent a Pucara and a helicopter to search for him but both of them were seen off by Sea Harriers without being shot down. After a very long and cold 8 hours in his dinghy, Mortimer was finally rescued under cover of darkness by a British helicopter. At more or less last light two of the Harrier GR3 reinforcements, just flown-in as battle replacements from Ascension Island by pilots Mike Beech and Murdo McCleod of 3 Squadron RAF, were cruising at about 14,000ft over Sapper Hill, the Roland's favourite spot to gain a bit of extra height. Sure enough, the Roland greeted them with an upwardly-spiralling missile which, luckily, they were able to outrun, the reinforcement pilots learning their first lesson to add their own safety margins to missile performance limits published in defence journals. (The experience rather mirrored a Rapier success a decade earlier in the hands of Iranian operators in the days when Iran was pro-Western. For weeks the Iranian border was being overflown by an Iraqi jet. At the suggestion of the RAF Regiment training officer in Iran, the Rapier was heli-coptered to a bordering mountain top and took out the Iraqi IL 28 Beagle bomber at 20,000ft, making it Rapier's first-ever operational aircraft kill.)

Luckily, appalling weather on the following day, 2 June, allowed the *Canberra* to come into San Carlos Water. Again the same priority problem arose as the infantry went ashore first, before the four Rapier crews of B Flight and the 63 Squadron command element were allowed to go. And so, for a second day running, again there was no possibility of any of the ships being provided with an instant, dense, on-the-spot air defence cover within about 20 minutes of the Rapier crews coming ashore to cover the vulnerable landing of the second and third infantry battalions. Had there been an Argentine air raid, the Army Rapiers on the mountain tops then covered by low cloud above San Carlos Water would have been useless without the Blindfire that the RAF were equipped with. The frustration of the RAF Rapier squadron commander at the ignorance of 5 Brigade landing without protection against air attack was palpable. Indeed, it was an early sign of a problem that was to manifest itself in the next beach landing by one of these self-same infantry battalions within the coming week and would almost negate the entire liberation effort. As OC 63 Squadron hugely and kindly understated in his War Diary:

> As we came closer to the time to go ashore, I had expected to receive some orders, but this was not to be. Circumstances beyond my control dictated the order that the Sqn went ashore and it was totally in the wrong order. By the time I arrived A Flt was deploying. So much for orders, reconnaissance and the standard operational deployment sequence. It was, I suppose, inevitable as events moved so quickly and Amphibious Operations can change the whole sequence of events for a small unit.[17]

Meanwhile, despite the weather Pook was to take the newly arrived and somewhat chastened Harrier GR3 pilot, McCleod, on a familiarization flight as his wingman, to hunt for another phantom radar to the far north of the Islands, well away from any known flak. From a safe height of 20,000ft they descended together through very thick cloud, itself a hazardous task, with always a risk of collision. At just 500ft there was still no sign of the ground, so they tentatively crept lower still, down to 300ft, when the ocean below appeared for a fleeting moment. Finally, at a very scary 100ft, still only glimpsing flashes of ocean below, Pook called it a day and they both returned, with great relief, to the safety of HMS *Hermes*, ending British flying for the day.

The RAF Rapiers, however, continued to deploy and by the end of the day six Rapier fire units were up and running in position. No reconnaissance had been possible prior to deployment. Six of the eight Rapier sites had required helicopter support as they were largely inaccessible from the ground. Up to four Sea King helicopters were working for the squadron at any one time, since each fire unit comprised five underslung loads. Although the squadron had no previous experience in helicopter-transported operations, they learned quickly under the pressure of operational necessity and it went exceptionally well, with no equipment damaged. By the evening of 2 June, Squadron Leader Loughborough was able to hold his first squadron Orders Group in the field with his officers and Rapier commanders at the Harrier forward airstrip, nicknamed Sid's Strip after its naval commander. With 75 per cent of the Harrier forward operating base's day-and-night, all-weather, close air defence in place, the British air superiority noose tightened further around the Argentinians' neck as the Harrier and helicopter strip was now ready and open for business to accept jets the very next day. The 800ft aluminum plank strip provided a landing pad, parking space for four Harriers, refuelling for Harriers and helicopters, and a firm platform for the GR3's INAS inertial navigation system to be set up accurately. The following day the last two Rapiers came on-line with the arrival of the last of the squadron's men.

There was never any shortage of spares on 63 Squadron as their second line workshop included an optical repair vehicle and two electronic repair vehicles, which also provided vital engineering support to the twelve optical-only Rapiers of the Royal Artillery's T Battery. Given the inaccessibility of the Rapier sites to wheeled vehicles, the operating techniques of the forward repair teams had to be changed to suit helicopter operations. Initially, a Sea King helicopter would lift the two engineers with their specialist repair trailer to the location of the unserviceable fire unit. Later, only the smaller Wessex helicopters were available and the repair trailer could not be taken. This delayed rectification since the team did not have the full range of spares or test equipment with them and this necessitated replacement spares being ferried to them by further helicopter flights following diagnosis.

Overall, the squadron was able to maintain six or seven Rapier fire units at full Blindfire capability, with all the lethal enhancement of accuracy that the tracking radar brought, with the remaining one or two Rapiers in the reversionary, and less lethal, manual-tracking optical mode for the remainder of the campaign. This was not altogether surprising, as the independent unit was manned, equipped, trained and well-practiced to operate in exactly the kind of isolated and remote geographic position it now found itself in. More's the pity it was not deployed with 3 Commando Brigade from the start. After the Argentine surrender, 63 Squadron was then required to stay on in the Falklands as the first garrison air defence unit at Stanley airport and was to return many times in a cycle of RAF Rapier squadron rotations that were to last for over twenty years.

Still on the same day the Argentine Canberra bombers, on the other hand, with their two-man crews, were less constrained by weather and three of them paid the British on Mount Kent a pre-dawn visit; in the darkness and flying at low level at 400 knots, they drew some AA fire but escaped intact, leaving the startled staff of the forward British Headquarters there to give some thought to key asset dispersal.

Notwithstanding the dreadful weather, following the restoration of the Argentine TPS 43 from its last Shrike attack, another Vulcan, Black Buck 6, was already wending its way down south, this time armed with four Shrike missiles. In the early hours of 3 June the TPS 43 was switched off as soon as the Vulcan closed in on the target area. The Vulcan loitered off the island for nearly an hour, trying to tempt any radar to switch on. At last, at around 06:30 local time, the Vulcan crew were alerted by the buzz of a Skyguard/Oerlikon fire-control radar of GADA 601's Alpha Battery on the aircraft's radar warning receiver. The Skyguard radar was locked onto the Vulcan, though it remained out of Oerlikon cannon range, and two Shrikes were launched. Although the Skyguard has a TV camera co-axially mounted with the tracking radar, it was still dark, so the crew could not see the Vulcan, only knowing the radar was locked on. However, the radar also has a special sub-circuit to detect missiles launched towards it, together with an audio alarm and a display of the actual radar returns of any inbound missile on the side of the TV screen. The drill is to switch target radar lock from the aircraft onto the incoming missile, ensure both Oerlikon gun mounts are slaved for a radar-controlled firing, press the fire button and hold it down for continuous fire until the missile is destroyed.

With only seconds to play with, the anti-radiation missile drill has a lot of elements to react to and coordinate quickly; completing them in time is a matter of considerable practice and the luck of the devil. What is certain is that the Argentine crew switched the radar off, followed within seconds by the closest Shrike striking the ground just 2m from the radar. The resultant explosion, debris and shrapnel killed the fire unit commander, *Teniente* Alejandro Dachary, the radar operator, *Sergeanti Primero* Reno Blanco, and two conscripts, *Soldados del [19]62* Oscar Diarte and Jorg Llames, as well as shredding the electronics on that side of the radar. Despite other AA guns firing, the Vulcan made a successful escape. Since no other radars dared to illuminate themselves for the remaining two Shrikes on board, the aircrew set course for home, towards their much-needed next air-to-air refuelling rendezvous. The Skyguard crew were buried the same day.

For this action the Vulcan commander, Squadron Leader N. McDougal, was awarded the Distinguished Flying Cross. Interestingly, only after I corresponded with the Vulcan crew of 44 (Rhodesia) Squadron through their Aircrew Association some thirty years later did they learn the full outcome of the success of their raid; previously, they were only told that Skyguard had simply gone off the air. Both wrecked Skyguards, this one and the Goose Green one shot-up by the Paras, were eventually recovered to RAF Waddington and stripped for valuable spare parts. Later still, their intact lower trailer bodies were purchased back by Oerlikon and fully rebuilt as operational radars.

Excitement for the Vulcan crew, however, continued. On the return leg, it broke the refuelling probe during a tanking link-up with a supporting Victor, presenting the crew with the choice of either ditching in mid-Atlantic with no prospect of rescue, or making a run for the nearest dry land, which happened to be Brazil. To reduce embarrassment, they fired off the two remaining Shrike missiles, but one mis-fired and refused to leave the rails. Requesting an emergency landing as anonymously as possible, they touched down on Rio de Janeiro airport with just enough fuel to clear the aircraft off the end of the main runway. The event made international headline news; the Brazilian authorities impounded the aircraft for the duration of the conflict and when it was all over allowed the crew and their repaired aircraft to return home. Thus, Vulcan XM597 is better remembered for its Brazilian adventure than for its Skyguard kill. However, the teeth of the GADA 601's AA defences were far from being pulled; a Royal Navy Lynx, piloted by Lieutenant Commander Moody and Lieutenant O'Collard, narrowly missed a land-based Argentine missile as the helicopter passed within 3km of Cape Pembroke, the extreme tip of the Stanley airport peninsula. It could have been a Tigercat, a Roland or a Soviet-made SA-7

EJERCITO ARGENTINO
GADA 601

107

M E M O R A N D U M

PUERTO ARGENTINO, *03* de Junio de 1982.-

PRODUCIDO POR: J GADA 601

PARA CONOCIMIENTO DE: Todo el personal de la Unidad

1. El suscripto pone en conocimiento de todo el personal de la Unidad
   que, en el día de la fecha, siendo las 0630 hs se produjo un ataque aéreo enemigo sobre la posición de fuego de la 1/A/GADA 601.
   (A mitad de camino entre PUERTO ARGENTINO y el AEROPUERTO)

2. Como consecuencia del mismo se produjo la baja instantánea del J
   Sec, Tte D ALEJANDRO DACHARY, El Subof Operador del DT, Sarg 1ro
   RENE PASCUAL BLANCO y de los soldados c/62 DIARTE Oscar y LLAMAS
   Jorge.

3. Los mencionados Cuadros y Tropa murieron heroicamente en su
   puesto de combate y combatiendo ya que en ese momento la Sección
   tenía adquirido el blanco lista para abrir el fuego.

4. Se aprecia que el ataque consistió en el lanzamiento de un cohete
   o de un misil, lanzado por un avión que sobrevoló la posición
   aproximadamente a una altura de 500 a 1.000 m.
   El cohete o misil hizo impacto a escasos 2 m de altura sobre el
   DT y sus esquirlas y onda expansiva produjeron la destrucción
   parcial del DT.

5. La Sección, demostrando un alto espíritu de lucha, continúa en su
   puesto para cumplir la misión que tiene asignada.

6. Los señores JJ Ba(s) y JJ Sec(s) al promediar la tarde del día de
   la fecha recibirán órdenes a fin de aplicar las medidas adecuadas
   contra este tipo de acciones del enemigo.

V I V A   L A   P A T R I A

HECTOR LUBIN ARIAS
TENIENTE CORONEL
JEFE GADA 601

Fig. 17. GADA 601 action report on 3 June Vulcan attack on Skyguard radar.

Strela similar to a Stinger but that matters not much because, whatever it was, it missed anyway.

The weather continued to worsen into the developing day, earning 3 June the Royal Navy met man's ultimate accolade of being a 'Zebra's Arsehole' of a South Atlantic weather depression; in other words, no flying would take place all day. However, 1 Squadron was briefed that the Argentinians, having run out of air-launched Exocets, had now removed a missile from a warship and were planning to launch it from a trailer as a shore defence against Royal Navy ships providing naval gunfire support from the sea. Pook was finally going to be tasked to conduct one of those all-important solo, pre-attack, photo-recce flights that he'd been pressing for throughout the campaign. It would take him right through the centre of the rat's nest of concentrated, radar-directed flak that was now Stanley airport. Because of the importance of photographs to back up a visual Exocet launcher sighting, the mission would have to be flown at 250ft with his speed reduced to ensure no picture blurring. However, Pook's recce flight through Stanley airport's main AA defences could not be flown on the morning of 4 June because of appalling fog and clinging low cloud all the way down to ground level.

Meanwhile, the two elements of the British Armed Forces which vied with each other for success in every possible climatic and terrain training environment, the Royal Marines and the Paras, were proving the value of their ethos and training as they yomped and tabbed over the bleak Falklands terrain, into the teeth of icy, driving winds spattered with sleet, doing what the Argentinians had backed down from doing earlier: crossing the inhospitable Falkland Islands on foot and taking the fight to the enemy. Not so the proud Regiments of Foot, pulled suddenly from London Ceremonial duty and equipped with embarrassingly low levels of infantry 'light scales' of weapons and fitness, more suited to a quick air inser tion on to some laid-back Caribbean island ex-colony, and failing even to match the Paras' short march over the Sussex Hills from San Carlos to Goose Green. Thus the ill-prepared and thrown-together 5 Brigade, its infantry selected for prestigious regimental status rather than recent high rotational operational preparedness, was in no state to follow the Marines and Paras on foot, and so a Plan B emerged.

On the intelligence of a local Islander, a random opportunity to make a phone call from an isolated but working red telephone box in the middle of nowhere (preceded by a mad whip around amongst the troops in the field to find the necessary UK 10p coins to operate the remote pay phone) enabled a call to be made to an equally remote Islander settlement close to the current Argentine front line; this established that there were no Argentine forces actually deployed at either Fitzroy or Bluff Cove, where the Argentinians had previously expected a British landing to take place. Thus, Plan B evolved: 2 Para, having crushed a superior force at Goose Green, would 'tab' on foot across the Island towards Fitzroy and

Bluff Cove, whilst the two Guards battalions, Welsh and Scots, would be transported there by sea, under cover of darkness, in two logistic landing ships. As a precaution, a troop of Army Rapiers would be deployed forward nearly 80km from their tenuous support at San Carlos, with a troop of Blowpipe shoulder-launched missiles split between the two ships to back up the ship's next-to-useless single, slow-firing 40mm Bofors AA guns.

In the midst of all this ground action on the mountains and lesser hills surrounding Stanley, a tiny marginal break in the weather on 5 June enabled Harrier GR3 reinforcements to pre-position two aircraft at immediate readiness at Sid's Strip. In transit, the head-up display of one failed in mid-cloud flight, demanding a very high level of blind flying skills on basic look-in, look-down instruments. As they crossed East Falkland the weather worsened, and they only just managed to get down onto Sid's Strip, coming very close to losing both aircraft before the weather closed down completely, trapping them there overnight. Back on HMS *Hermes*, a Hunt-the-New-Exocet photo-reconnaissance mission to locate a land-based launcher on Hooker Point was declared 'On'. The plan was that pilot Hare would be the rabbit to have the Argentinians looking up, while Pook, the crafty fox, would flash in at high speed from the opposite direction. Hare's instructions were to come in from the southeast, from the sea, high enough to be seen on every Argentine radar screen and then, at the last moment, at the very edge of the flak zone, shed chaff and turn away, diving low and out of sight. Meanwhile, Pook, who would normally have flown at 250ft to enable the recce cameras to get good camera coverage, would fly as low as he dared – which, for a specialist aircrew member like him, would be very, very low indeed. With one wing banked up to raise the camera viewing angle on the other side to compensate for the absence of height, it was tricky to fly thus, delicately balanced, at high speed, hiding behind any tiny rise in ground or outcrop of rock at the same time as visually searching the ground ahead. In just 120 seconds his fly-by, timed to the second, was flown and he was in and out of the flak zone before any gunner could open fire. Of the Exocet there was no sign. And so low and fast was the fly-by that Pook's recce camera caught the astonished faces of Argentine troops looking the Harrier camera lens straight in the eye over the tops of their slit trenches at Air Raid Red stand-to. Upon his return, as no Exocet launcher had been detected, Pook was ordered by the admiral to fly a repeat mission to look again immediately but his bacon was saved by the winter weather clamping right down for the rest of the day.

In the small hours of 6 June the only British 'Blue-on-Blue' anti-aircraft action of the campaign took place in total darkness. At around 0400hrs HMS *Cardiff* detected a low, slow-flying aircraft just south of Mount Pleasant, unaware that it was one of many helicopters on a Special Forces insertion support mission. The British Army Gazelle was, in fact, carrying radio equipment to set up a relay station to enable the 5 Brigade landings at Fitzroy and Bluff Cove to communicate with the Land Forces Commander back at Port San Carlos. The helicopter's crew of three were killed and it was to take several years for the Royal Navy to formally admit the error caused by almost non-existent intelligence sharing and lack of IFF electronic identification equipment aboard helicopters.

On this day also Squire, OC 1 Squadron, and one of the new reinforcement pilots were launched in improved weather conditions around midday to re-run Pook's Exocet search, again out-running the surprised flak gunners before they could fire a single shot. The only scare for Squire was that as he cleared the airfield he nearly flew into a pair of radio masts not shown on any map. The great achievement of the day, however, was that on the strength of Pook's critical photography showing dug-in troops, Squire was able to deliver a swathe of cluster bombs right on top of the Argentinians' heads with pinpoint accuracy, exactly as the Harrier force was trained to do in war, despite the resistance of the Royal Navy to such essential pre-attack reconnaissance.

The next day, 7 June, began with a Sea Dart missile fired by HMS *Exeter* bringing down an Argentine Learjet Command Post aircraft flying at 40,000ft over Pebble Island. It was exactly the right weapon for the task. Back on HMS *Hermes*, two pairs of GR3 Harriers were due to be launched: one pair to be pre-positioned at Sid's Strip, to be on immediate on-call for close air support to ground troops, capable of arriving within just minutes of such a call – again the bread and butter of the Harrier Force; the other pair were sent to seek out and destroy a 155mm artillery gun with rockets. The gun was reported to be on the rear slope of Sapper Hill, without, of course, any previous photo-recce evidence to crank up the attack-planning accuracy. In the event, the launch of both GR3 pairs was mixed-in with the launch of Sea Harriers going on combat air patrol. As luck would have it, one GR3 in each pair experienced a major unserviceability just before launch, and so the two aircraft which made it into the air were briefed for two totally different missions and were already 100km apart; they now had to bring themselves together to rebrief in-flight and execute the 155mm artillery task first. Their attack was successful in that the rockets were delivered to the given grid reference, although no artillery was seen. The reason was simple: it wasn't there. The guns hid in Stanley town during the day to avoid exactly such attacks. However, the sparkle of exploding rockets was seen by a Sea Harrier on patrol far above, causing the pilot to report that he was being engaged by flak from a new location. The same Sea Harrier then reported seeing a missile, possibly a Roland, being fired at the departing GR3s but falling away behind. An inspection of the GR3s on HMS *Hermes* revealed one bullet hole in one aircraft, so they had definitely been shot at.

At 0322hrs on the following day, 8 June, whilst HMS *Yarmouth* was shelling the Argentinians, the air defenders of GADA 601 radar got her range and bearing and gave it to the long-range Army guns, which were able to bracket the ship with six rounds of 155mm shells and rattle her topsides with airburst shrapnel. The RAF were not too happy either, beginning the day with a write-off crash-landing by Peter Squire when the aluminum planking he was landing on at Sid's Strip billowed up into the air towards the Harrier, which smashed into the ground, dropping its nose wheel right into an RAF Regiment Rapier crew trench. Shaken, the pilot climbed out of the Harrier cockpit, and in a very British, carry-on-regardless way, was handed a steaming mug of hot sweet tea by the Rapier crew. With the Harrier strip out of action, there was to be no more flying from it that day and nor would that particular Harrier ever fly again.

Meanwhile, over at Bluff Cove and Fitzroy, there was developing what the American Marines would call a clusterfuck, a coming-together of multiple military frictions that had been brewing up for days and had the potential to unhinge the entire operation to recover the Falkland Islands. It had begun with the delayed loading and departure of one of the landing ships due to the lateness of the 5 Brigade field ambulance unit, so the landing ship was still just offshore, in plain sight of the Argentinians at Bluff Cove, as daylight broke. Next, a number of infantry landing craft, critically pre-positioned to pick up and land other forces, had been hijacked for a private variation of the overall landing plan, which seriously delayed the landing craft from doing their planned job of unloading the ship. Worse still, the major infantry unit on board one landing ship refused to disembark and hike some 16km to link up with the Paras because a short-cut bridge was down. Instead, they demanded to be taken further round the coast to be landed nearer their objective. On top of that, Rapier followed Murphy's First Law, demonstrating that if it could go wrong, it would, closely followed by Murphy's Second Law, which was if it was going to go wrong, it would do so at such a time as to maximize the inconveniences, in this case, in the middle of an air raid.

The cumulative result of all this friction of war was that when the mid-winter daylight finally broke, there were two British landing ships sitting offshore, right where the Argentine Junta had most expected them to be for the main thrust of the British landings. The *Fuerza Aerea* reacted instantly and rushed in a quartet of heavily armed Skyhawks from the mainland 600 km away towards the hapless ships. Three made the final distance to the target. Thanks to the BBC's 'impartial' publicity about Argentine bombs failing to go off inside British ships, these bombs were properly armed and exploded in the heart of LSL *Sir Galahad*, killing a large number of soldiers who should not have been on board and exploding the petrol tanks of vehicles which should have been ashore. LSL *Sir Tristram* at Fitzroy, however, had largely disembarked its load and, while she took serious blows, she was empty of the kind of cargoes which, once set afire, had turned her sister ship into a towering inferno. The attack served to remind the British how lucky they were that the Argentinians had attacked warships and not transports during the critical landings at San Carlos Bay. The burning vessels could be clearly seen from Argentine positions on high ground and *La Gaçeta* reported '*el enemigo ha sufrida approximadamento 600 bajas*', a mis-evaluation the British were very keen that the Argentinians should continue to labour under for as long as possible. This was why no announcement about the total number of casualties was made in London and why next-of-kin were notified individually and privately. The bitter-sweet upside of the day was that all three Skyhawks were downed after their attack, by Sea Harriers on combat air patrol using Sidewinder missiles and the Skyhawk pilots killed.

The débâcle caused a serious pause in the stupendous forward momentum of 3 Brigade operations in rolling-up the Argentine front line on the direct approaches to Stanley, as all the scarce helicopters were diverted to recover casualties and reconstitute shattered sub-units back into fighting formations, all conducted in appalling weather conditions in winter, without sleeping bags or bivouac shelter for anyone in either brigade, over the next two days. Notwithstanding this huge setback, the soldiers themselves from both brigades, once they got going again and were in contact with the well dug-in enemy surrounded by anti-personnel minefields and equipped with the latest night-vision goggles and a raft-full of machine guns of every kind, never wavered in their tenacity, pluck and bravery. They won a complicated, major pincer action, fought mainly in the dark, at bayonet-close quarters, in exceedingly difficult, uphill, rocky broken ground, against all odds and won.

Next day, with Sid's Strip miraculously repaired by the ubiquitous Royal Engineers, Sea Harriers could now triple their effective time on overhead combat air patrol, whilst the RAF GR3s were used to mount several close-support sorties against the Argentinians dug-in on Sapper Hill and Mount Longdon. Two attacking GR3 Harriers met with intense ground fire, and the hydraulics of one were so badly damaged that the pilot had to crank the undercarriage down manually. At Port Harriet House a Scout helicopter was engaged by an Argentine Blowpipe which missed the aircraft by just metres.

With the British inexorably closing in for the final assault on the Argentine positions overlooking Stanley, the artillery from each side spent the day trying to eliminate the other in counter-battery tasks. At 11:25 the Argentinians reported that an air attack on their positions had been made by two Harriers, at least one of which they claimed to have shot down in flames with anti-aircraft fire. Neither side made mention of any specific anti-aircraft weapon system; the British did, however, acknowledge that a Harrier, XV919, had indeed been hit by small arms fire, damaging a hot air duct which, in turn, caused a hydraulic oil fire to start during its vertical landing on HMS *Hermes*. The fire was extinguished and the aircraft quickly repaired. RAF Rapier's excitement for the day was that an Argentine medical officer walked up to the fire unit at Windy Gap and surrendered. As a result of the information he supplied, the Royal Marines were able to capture several more Argentine soldiers hiding in a house some 8km inland. During this period it had been assessed that the Harrier strip at Port San Carlos was a likely target for a ground troops or Special Forces' attack, but no such attack ever materialized.

On 10 June, as the land battle for the Islands intensified, detailed Argentine records of events began to dry up as their situation became more desperate. *La Gaçeta* and mainland official Argentine communiqués made just one-line references to British attacks on their positions and claimed that they had been repulsed, without mentioning either personnel casualties or materiel losses. They also mentioned Pucara attacks on British positions on Mount Kent, which actually did take place.

The next aerial assault on Stanley airport came on 11 June. Black Buck 7, Vulcan XM607 under command of Flight Lieutenant Martin Withers, who returned to deliver a rolling thunder stick of twenty-one 1,000lb bombs that ran up the Stanley airport beach. As before, four Sea Harriers, each armed with three 1,000lb, radar-fused, air-burst bombs, also attacked the airfield, the twelve bombs adding further mayhem below. As Auld, Blissett, Morrell and Thomas approached to toss in their bombs from just outside anti-aircraft range, they were greeted by streams of gun tracer, Blowpipes, Tigercats and SA-7 Strelas. One Pucara of *Grupo 3* was destroyed, but these raids did not prevent the Pucara squadron from mounting another attack on the British at last light the same evening. *La Gaçeta*'s only other news was that a hospital ship, *Ara Bahia Paraiso*, formerly used as a landing ship in the Argentine South Georgia operation, and suspected by the British of transporting Exocets removed from Argentine warships for use on land, would soon be at anchor in Stanley harbour.

British helicopters were receiving their fair share of attention from GADA 601's anti-aircraft artillery. Wessex XT484 was tasked to carry out an AS-12 precision missile attack on Stanley police station, thought to be in use by Argentine military staff. The helicopter met fierce anti-aircraft fire from Cortley Hill to the north of Stanley harbour, and launched its attack from a range of 5km. The first missile missed and the second fell into the sea. *La Gaçeta* reported this as an attack against the hospital ship in the harbour by a Gazelle using American Hot anti-tank missiles, highlighting the poor quality of their visual aircraft recognition. The Wessex withdrew, undamaged, to return to its hide at Teal Inlet. A pair of Lynx helicopters from HMS *Minerva* and HMS *Exeter* were also busy. They flew chaff deception missions to mislead the Argentinians into thinking that perhaps a major helicopter assault was taking place near Port Stanley. The mission was considered a success because a significant number of radars, the Roland and Skyguards were locked up tracking the helicopters outside AA gunfire range, without any forthcoming flak. Harrier GR3s were also busy, with Squire and Hare bombing gun emplacements on Mount Longdon. They reported three Blowpipe missiles had been fired at them, the nearest exploding within 30m of one of the aircraft, luckily without damaging it.

Overnight, a brilliant night attack by the Royal Marines and Paras secured Mount Kent and Mount Longdon. The Argentine anti-aircraft gunners, however, were far from neutralized. Given that the Skyguard radars were at the heart of the Oerlikon twin 35mm guns' accuracy and lethality, at long, long last, just two days before the Argentine surrender, a Harrier was modified to carry two Shrike anti-radar missiles. In the event the missiles were never used. With Argentine troops beginning to abandon their positions in daylight and fall back into Stanley town, it was the actions of the *Marine Batallón Anti-Aero* that qualified for the day's eulogy in *La Gaçeta* that evening. It was, however, to be the *Capellan*'s last word; he was captured and interrogated by the RAF Regiment's Spanish-speaking intelligence officer, Flight Lieutenant Guy Bransby, and sent packing, back to Argentina, along with his crated *Virgin Mary of the Malvinas*, which the Friar had hoped to leave behind, permanently installed, in Stanley Cathedral. That evening the TPS 43 radar went off the air for the last time, victim not to mighty Vulcan Shrikes, but to pin-point conventional field artillery fire, killing just one more hapless Argentine conscript crew member. Enough was enough: the survivors turned off the radar. Finally, there was a ferocious overnight ground action by the 35mm Oerlikons deployed on the peninsula across the water from Stanley harbour.

As 3 Brigade's Paras and Commandos and 5 Brigade's Scots Guards and the surviving Welsh Guards massed around the Argentine occupied heights overlooking Stanley, D Squadron SAS and a commando troop of the SBS found themselves on the flanking ridge opposite an Argentine deployment of 35mm anti-aircraft guns across the waters of Stanley harbour. The SAS knew that the night would be taken up with an all-out night attack against the Argentine heights overlooking Stanley and that their friends in 3 Para were to assault a front more or less the other side of Mount Longdon, while 2 Para were to do the same on Wireless Ridge. The operational scene-setting, therefore, was that anything the SAS and SBS could do to divert Argentine attention and resources, especially counter-attacking infantry reserves and heavy artillery fire, away from the Paras, Marines and Guards would be of great help to them.

In the event the SAS and SBS men stirred up a veritable hornet's nest of night-long, heavy Argentine anti-aircraft fire from a pair of fearsome Oerlikon 35mm twin cannon firing directly at them, over open sights, the impact of which they were lucky to survive. Even the Argentine hospital ship in the harbour joined in this caper to use its solitary searchlight to try to illuminate the British Special Forces, thus breaching the Geneva Convention by effectively taking part in the battle. The whole lopsided firefight – 7.62mm rifles versus 35mm and 155mm cannon – was very intense and marked the penultimate grand finale of Argentine combat by the Oerlikons in the battle for the *Malvinas*. The diversionary attack played a critical success in the Argentine High Command's decision not to commit its reserves to bolster-up and counter-attack the British now attacking the heights overlooking Stanley.

Finally, the last action of the Oerlikon twin 35s was, as it had been at Goose Green, a ground action against 2 Para. The Oerlikons of Bravo Battery, at the suggestion of their own *Teniente* commander, took over an artillery fire mission from 4 Artillery Group, whose 105mm and 155mm guns had all been neutralized by British counter-battery efforts. The fire mission was against groups of British troops who could be seen occupying the high ground abandoned by the retreating 7 Infantry Regiment; the target happened to be 2 Para, once again.

Despite this accurate Oerlikon intervention in their support, the Argentine infantry line broke across a wide front, becoming a tsunami wave of retreating, defeated soldiery headed downhill in plain sight of all, into Stanley town. In the air the last British Harrier sortie of the campaign was flown by three Harrier GR3s piloted by Wing Commander Squire, OC 1 Squadron, Squadron Leader Harris and Flight Lieutenant Gilcrest. Their mission: the long-awaited laser-guided smart-bomb attack on an individual 155mm artillery piece. As they neared their target, the forward air controller on the ground, armed at last with a working laser target marker and a fully charged battery, saw white Argentine surrender flags appearing around Stanley and cancelled the mission. All the Argentine impedimenta of war of over ten thousand men, ranging from personal equipment to heavy artillery pieces, to helicopters, radars and ammunition, were abandoned on the battlefields where they were last used.

The formal surrender, completed in a few words and without pomp, was followed by a massive effort to repatriate the invaders as quickly as possible, lending irony to a North Sea ferry company's motto to 'Set You Free'. The *Malvinas* were once again, properly, the Falkland Islands and Sir Rex Hunt returned to take up his interrupted Governorship of British kith and kin. The Union Jack that now flew at Government House was the same one that had been hoisted after the recovery of South Georgia. The Falklands Campaign, an extraordinary feat of arms, was over.

It is, perhaps, now a good time to review the achievements of the bomber 'heavies'. On one side the British-made Canberras of the *Fuerza Aerea* flew a total of fifty-four sorties, half of them at night; they delivered 100,000lb of bombs and lost two aircraft to missiles. The Vulcans of the Royal Air Force made five sorties over the Falkland Islands and delivered 63,000lb of bombs, along with two Shrike missions, one of which disabled the TPS 43 radar for a day while the other destroyed a Skyguard anti-aircraft fire-control radar and killed its four-man crew.

In their Official Communiqués the Argentine Junta claimed twenty-nine Harriers and nine helicopters shot down; in the Argentine post-Junta Lessons Learned Report, these figures were reduced by their Army Anti-Aircraft Artillery Group, GADA 601, which had command of all ground-based anti-aircraft systems, down to eight Harriers and three Argentine own goals (see Appendix V).

The British acknowledged losses to AA fire were five Harriers destroyed, two Harriers seriously damaged and one Gazelle own goal, plus two Gazelles shot down by Argentine small arms fire during the initial landings, and one Scout shot down by a Pucara. It does not include Harrier losses due to mid-air collisions, sliding off the carrier deck or crashing onto lifting airstrip matting.

In this campaign the Argentine anti-aircraft gunners had been in action, at battle stations, without break from 04:40 on 1 May until noon on 14 June. On average they had been brought to Air Raid Red ten times each day. GADA 601, with its 462 men and a further 112 under command, had lost in combat one officer, two NCOs and six soldiers killed, with a further officer, six NCOs and twenty-six soldiers wounded, a rate of 7.3 per cent casualties out of a total of 574 personnel employed directly on anti-aircraft duties. The Rapier and Blowpipe crews suffered no casualties. If there was a lesson to be learned, it was the wrong assumption by the nominally Joint Service Command of the Argentine forces that the bulk of the air defence artillery was there for the protection of the Army, when in fact the *schwerpunkt* of the ground-to-air battle was the airhead at Stanley airport. The initial assumption was that as the Air Force had its own air defence equipment, it would be responsible for itself. It is worth studying the relative anti-aircraft dispositions at the start and finish of the campaign in the four maps that follow.

Overall, the Argentine anti-aircraft gunners achieved their mission. They caused casualties to attacking Harriers, denied the Vulcans, Sea Harriers and Harrier GR3s their freedom to attack at will and forced wildly inaccurate, inferior, toss-bombing and other weapon delivery means upon them. The anti-aircraft radars, large and small, with the exception of two Skyguards, survived much of

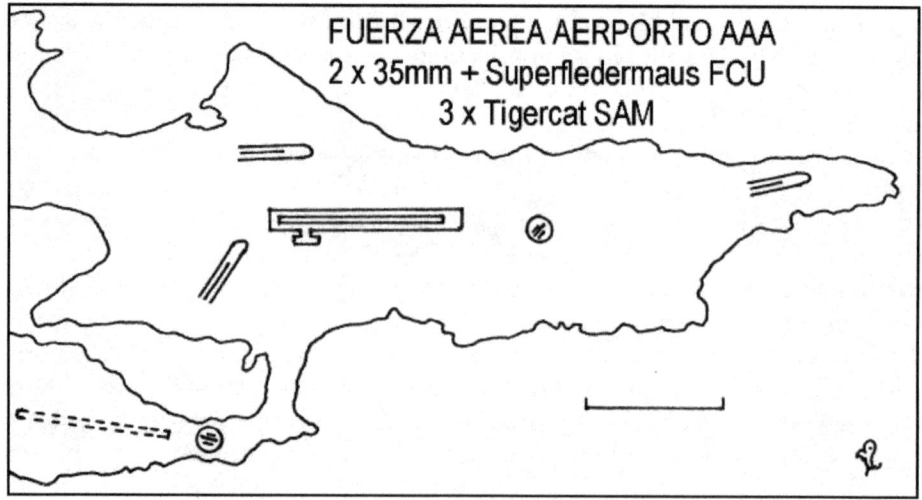

Map 23. Stanley airport initial air defences: the first air raid on 1 May 1982.

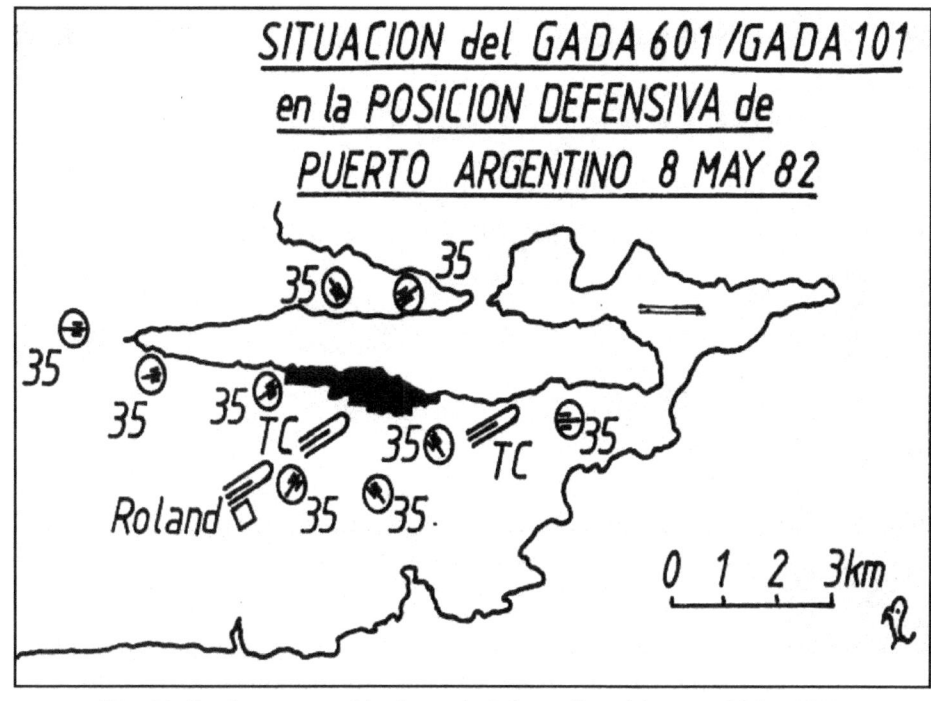

Map 24. Stanley town and harbour air defence dispositions on 8 May 1982.

Map 25. Argentine plot of Vulcan, Harrier and naval gunfire hits on Stanley airport.

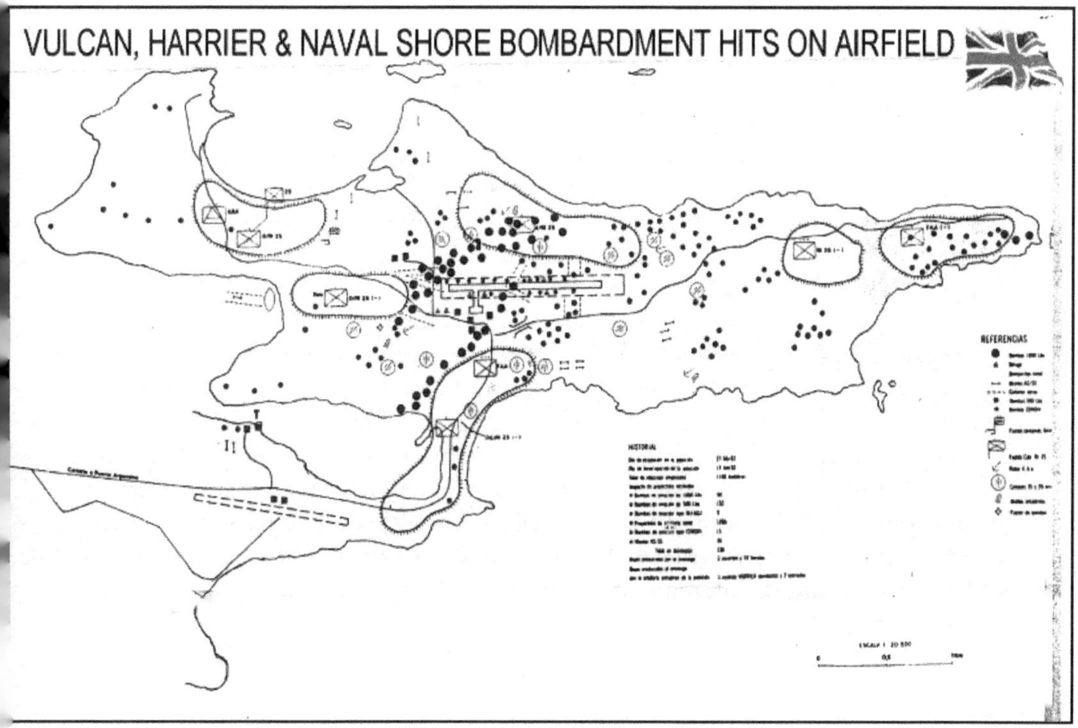

Map 26. Argentine final air defence of Stanley airport, 14 June 1982.

the flak suppression directed at them, only becoming non-effective when the infantry and other front-line forces around them collapsed or surrendered. They also kept Stanley airport open to the very end. In the words of their ill-fated commanding general and former governor of the *Malvinas*, the Argentine anti-aircraft gunners were the only Argentine forces in the campaign not to be beaten directly by the British and they can take pride in being the first and last to fire on the enemy.

As it turned out, ultimately, these same Oerlikon twin 35mm anti-aircraft cannon were only silenced temporarily; shortly they would begin nearly a decade of further British service in the defence of two important NATO bases, as well as introducing women into combat roles in the Royal Auxiliary Air Force Regiment Reserves decades ahead of the Regular Royal Air Force. The Skyguard radars, however, given the global spread of the Oerlikon twin 35mm cannon and its Skyguard fire-control radar in potentially hostile hands, would go on for even longer, past the fortieth anniversary of the Falklands Campaign, and continues to this day to train NATO aircrews in electronic counter-measures.

Meanwhile, following the Argentine surrender and return of its personnel to Argentina with little more than the clothes they stood up in, the RAF Harriers and RAF Rapiers were redeployed to Stanley airport, which became RAF Stanley. By the end of June, San Carlos was almost deserted and everything was taking place at Stanley. Reconnaissance for the Rapier redeployment to Stanley started in mid-June, with key officers commuting to Stanley by Chinook helicopter. Everything Rapier was done by 63 Squadron RAF Regiment in the correct operational sequence, quite differently from the initial deployment on 1 June, when no deployments orders were forthcoming, no reconnaissance had taken place and no proper site selection had been possible. Nor had the most capable Blindfire Rapier been deployed forward to protect the advancing ground forces head-quarters or the beachhead to cover the ill-fated landings of 5 Brigade.

RAF Rapier remained in action at San Carlos until 09:00 on 30 June. A small advance party deployed to the airfield at Stanley by Chinook helicopter. The remainder of the squadron and all of the equipment were loaded on to RFA *Sir Lancelot*. The ship then sailed round to Stanley harbour, where it anchored at 11:00 on 2 July. After unloading, the fire units deployed to sites around the airfield. On this occasion three of the sites required helicopter support to deploy. The first units were operational on that day and the remainder the following day. The RAF Blindfire Rapier squadrons remained fully deployed on rotation well into the next three decades in the Falkland Islands.

Following the Argentine surrender on 14 June there remained an air threat, although no further attacks took place. There was also a threat from land mines. Records of where the Argentinians had placed mines were sparse. The movement of several fire units was severely restricted because of potential mines in those areas. Also, many of the vacated Argentine defences had been booby-trapped. By early July a severe winter had set in. Snow, ice and very strong winds posed prob-lems, causing damage to accommodation tents. The thaw, wind and rain which then followed posed different problems, with tracks becoming deep, slushy, mud trails. Gradually the supply chain improved and meals went from composite field rations to fresh food. A system of rest and recuperation was introduced which enabled personnel to have a two-day break on a ship in the harbour, primarily the accommodation ship *Rangatira*, which spent 14 months at Port Stanley while the new airfield was being built.

By mid-July all the 5 Brigade units that had originally deployed with the squad-ron were returning home, but no decision had been made about 63 Squadron's return. Numerous rumours started to circulate at RAF Gütersloh and on the squadron, including one that the squadron was to remain deployed for six months. Naturally this affected morale. Eventually a decision was made, but the closure of the runway for upgrading from 14 to 29 August to allow all-weather Phantom F-4 air defence fighters to operate from Stanley on six-week rotations further delayed the squadron's return. Finally, 37 Squadron RAF Regiment took over responsibility for the Rapier defence of RAF Stanley in early September. The handover took place in two halves, which enabled half the squadron to leave RAF Stanley on 4 September and the second half on 12 September. Both elements spent 48 hours on Ascension Island in order to unwind (known today as 'decompression') and the last elements of 63 Squadron arrived back at RAF Gütersloh on 15 September to a well-deserved tumultuous welcome. Thus ended a unique RAF Regiment deployment that had lasted 4 months, as elaborated in Squadron Leader Loughborough's book.

For me, the real heroes of this campaign were the Harrier GR3 pilots of 1 Squadron and the supplementary 3 Squadron who undertook the difficult and dangerous job of bombing, strafing and rocketing Argentine ground forces at low-level, in the face of furious flak, in extremely difficult terrain and often positively dangerous weather conditions, over and over again, with no break. For 1 Squadron to be reduced to just one Harrier without a single pilot fatality speaks of luck and skill in spades. With replacement aircraft and additional pilots, they continued to fly the most challengingly dangerous missions of the Falklands Campaign, day in and day out, for the duration of the conflict, constantly made more difficult by an ill-concealed senior naval contempt for the RAF. As an anti-aircraft professional in command of the very self-same Oerlikons, I understand exactly what they had to fly through and, as an infantry squadron commander charged with Harrier protection in the field, I have long marvelled at the speed and professionalism with which Harrier pilots set out to find and photograph the enemy and, within minutes of studying the negatives, to launch fully briefed ground-attack fighters into the air to wipe out those self-same enemy with pin-point accuracy, over and over, each pilot flying five or six times a day, from a hide in the woods. I just hope that the naval frictions evident in the Falklands Campaign are not carried forward into future RAF carrier flying in the mixed RN/RAF force of new F35 jump-jets, costing £100 million each, on our two new super-carriers.

Chapter 13

After the Surrender

Within fourteen days of the Argentine surrender, the first of the British soldiers, sailors and airmen who had taken part in the liberation of the Falkland Islands were being replaced by garrison forces. One of these junior officer replacements was Flying Officer Peter Kaye, formerly an infantry flight commander of mine on 15 Squadron RAF Regiment, a squadron I had previously commanded. Now he was the field operations officer to 3 (Fighter) Squadron RAF, also equipped with GR3 Harriers, which had come to replace 1 Squadron. Kaye was responsible for organizing the ground defence of the Harrier squadron site at Sid's Strip, Port San Carlos. He takes up the story himself:

During my ten weeks in the Falklands, with the Argentinians safely back on the mainland, there was not much to do, so I looked around for other diversions. The Islands were strewn with a fascinating range of weapons to stimulate the inquisitive military mind. The anti-aircraft guns interested me most, as there were several different types; the most powerful and impressive of these were the twin barrelled 35mm Oerlikons. After an initial inspection, it seemed to me that, despite the rust which bound the working parts solid on most guns, they could be made to work.

Fortuitously, at this stage, I was sent to Sid's Strip to look at the possibility of this diversionary airfield becoming a fully fledged Harrier field site, complete with some sort of defence. The nearest two anti-aircraft cannon were at Goose Green; they stood in the village square in a compound of collected Argentine impedimenta which, incidentally, also contained every conceivable munition and equipment. The whole junkyard was fenced off by using the most available material handy locally, namely hundreds of Argentine 7.62mm FAL self-loading rifles, stabbed, at one-foot intervals, barrel-first, into the peat turf and joined together by mine tape wrapped around the rifle butts to form a fence. Knowing how much care we took of our rifles in the RAF Regiment, it was quite a painful sight to behold. I set to work on these two Oerlikons at once and arranged for them to be lifted out, with their associated generators, by a Chinook of 18 Squadron.

At the first attempt to raise one of the Oerlikons, the lifting strops were found to be too short; it looked as if the gun would tilt and poke its barrels up through the floor of the helicopter into the cockpit. The loadmaster threw me down a set of longer strops and I climbed back up on the gun to connect them to the helicopter hook. In the air all helicopters generate so much static electricity that they have to be earthed with a special chain before anything on the ground can be attached to them for lifting. Somehow, I must have touched the Chinook a split second before the chain properly earthed; I received the most enormous, heart-stopping shock, through my arm and across my chest and was flung bodily off the gun to the ground. At the next and more careful attempt, I managed to connect up the strops correctly and the first gun was flown to the Harrier strip, followed shortly by the second gun and the two generators. I sited the Oerlikons realistically, one on each side of the strip. Initially they would serve as decoys until I could get them going again. Overall, this first pair were probably the best guns on the Island; they certainly had not been silenced by either Harrier attacks or small arms fire from 2 Para.[18]

My Island hosts, with whom I was billeted at Goose Green, told me that on one of the first Harrier passes over the Argentine positions, a cluster bomb (a special effects bomb which dispenses hundreds of anti-personnel bomblets over an area the size of a football pitch) landed on an Argentine bivouac area and killed and injured almost forty troops. The Islanders reported a marked and sombre change in the attitude of the soldiers. A captured diary spoke of the horror of arms and legs everywhere and an official Argentine communiqué even went so far as to claim the weapons were against the Geneva Convention (which, incidentally, they were not). One consequence of the raid was that all the inhabitants of Darwin and Goose Green were rounded up and incarcerated in the Village Hall where they remained until they were literally liberated by 2 Para.

Peter continued:

Initially, my problems were many: there were no cleaning kits and no pamphlets to explain how to set up and use the equipment. During the next few weeks, I travelled back and forth to Stanley where most of the anti-aircraft guns were to be found. I procured the use of a Scout helicopter and used it to scour the Island for more guns; in all, from the air, I located fourteen guns plus nine generators. Before I could inspect the weapons on the ground, however, I had to have each site cleared by a bomb disposal team for mines and booby-traps, of which there were many, placed quite deviously, on various items of Argentine equipment. Paradoxically, the Islanders found all sorts of uses for captured war material. At Goose Green, I vividly recall the incongruity of a little old lady planting out the season's cress seeds. To make a nice neat hole in the peaty soil, she carefully prodded the seed in with the sharp end of a live round of Argentine rifle ammunition. On my way to Stanley Town, I found a nearly intact gun and generator abandoned in the travelling position at the roadside. It too was lifted by Chinook to Sid's Strip.

Slowly but surely, I built up a stock of spare parts for the guns. I took a new top cover from one gun, and found various new spares, including breach blocks, springs and tools, still wrapped in greaseproof paper. But, without a pamphlet, I had no way of telling what was missing from any given gun, other than by comparing it with another. The task was made harder because the *Fuerza Aerea* guns were an earlier 001 model, whereas the Army guns were built to the 002 standard[19] and were less than a year old. The break came when the RAF Regiment officer I was ultimately to replace, Flight Lieutenant Chris Miller of 1 Squadron, gave me a set of three gun manuals in Spanish as his parting gift. There were quite a few illustrations in the manual and from the gist of the text, I became even more impressed with the gun. At Headquarters Land Forces Falkland Islands, HQ LFFI, Captain Jeffrey Gordozo of the 4/7 Royal Dragoon Guards agreed to translate parts of the manual for me.

One bright and sunny morning, the Land Forces Commander, Major General David Thorn, late Royal Anglian Regiment, came to visit the diversionary airstrip at Port San Carlos. I showed him around and steered him towards the three Oerlikons now positioned at the end of the airstrip. I explained to the General the problems I was having in getting them going and he said that he would help. He did. On my return to Stanley, I was met by a Major John Charteris of the Royal Scots, now Training Major at HQ LFFI and a Chief Petty Officer, CPO Harcus RN, from the Logistic Landing Ship, *Sir Bedivere*. He had come to talk to me about 'the Guns'. I told them all I knew about the Oerlikons, their ammunition and operation, and explained I was positive they could be made serviceable. He told me that HQ LFFI was about to send eight thousand rounds of 35mm ammunition back to the UK for sale but, as a result of what I told him, he would ensure the ammunition would now be held back for use by my three guns. CPO Harcus put me in touch with a Lieutenant Dan of the *Stena Inspector*, an RN requisitioned oil-rig workboat. Two weeks later, Dan sent me two gunnery artificers, CPO Horrocks and Whittall. During this period, the Queens Own Highlanders also found a complete set of 35mm gun manuals in English, and it says much for inter-service cooperation that these were now sent to me. On close examination of the manuals, it soon became apparent that the 35mm Oerlikon gun was quite a piece of equipment. I gave the manuals to the two CPOs, introduced them to the guns and let them get on with their work.

During my hunt for more guns, I came across another pair of Oerlikons in the sand dunes at Stanley airport, near the lighthouse. Both appeared to have been badly damaged by a series of large explosions, probably from aerial

bombs or naval shore bombardments. Behind the dunes lay the gun generators and, beyond them, about a quarter of an acre of ammunition. Nearby,
I noticed an uncharacteristically straight line running along the base of the
sand dune. When I dusted it down, a long green metal box revealed itself.
Inside were two brand-new Soviet-made SA7 Strela missiles. Everybody
got very excited about these and they were taken back to HQ LFFI for
evaluation. I can only presume they had been deployed to bolster up the
Argentine air defences after the two Oerlikon guns had been silenced.[20]

Within two weeks of starting work, the CPOs had the most complete gun
ready for firing. By robbing other guns around the islands, a serviceable
XABA gunsight was reconstructed, complete with ground-to-ground firing
reticle. The electrical traverse and elevation servos and ammunition feed
mechanisms were now all in working order. There had been a slight problem
with the generator; it was found to have petrol in the sump instead of oil, but
this was soon rectified. The firing was arranged so that the gun pointed out
to sea on a fixed bearing. The template used to mark out the danger zone
for the 35mm ammunition was 13km long and 27,000ft high; super-velocity
ammunition certainly goes a long way. A new batch of ammunition was
declared safe by an ammunition technical officer and loaded onto the gun.
The electrical firing button was found to be unserviceable so the foot-firing
pedal was used instead. We successfully fired 180 rounds, on both single-
shot and automatic. We had to end the practice at this stage as the barrels
became too hot for safety.[21]

The results of the firings were signalled off to London. A decision was
made to send one of the guns to the Royal School of Artillery for further
refurbishment with a possible view to returning them to the Falkland Islands
with Royal Artillery crews to defend Port San Carlos. [Author's note: I took
the gun off the RSA, so that never happened.] The generators and guns were
rounded up and stored at Moody Brook Camp, pending shipment on the
Contender Bazant, a requisitioned container ship converted to provide a
Harrier and helicopter landing deck to become RFA *Argus*. Unfortunately,
I was not able to clear all the shells out of the automatic ammunition feed
after the firings although, obviously, the cannon themselves had been unloaded and made safe. The captain of the ship refused to have the gun aboard
with ammunition in place. A technician, tasked to make the gun safe, could
not work out how to remove the shells from the power-operated automatic
loader. He decided that the best course of action was to cut that whole
section of the gun ammunition feed away with an oxyacetylene torch. Some-
time during the operation, the flame touched one of the live shells and it
exploded, blowing off his hand. Shortly afterwards, I left the island and was
not to see these guns again for five years, when I visited Mike Fonfé at
RAF Waddington.

The RAF Regiment's pre-association with the Oerlikons, however, did not cease there. Flight Sergeant Bolding, commanding a Rapier detachment on a remote site at RAF Stanley, had located an Oerlikon gun generator and, being very resourceful, he fired it up to power the detachment's kettle, video recorder and TV! He would later be posted to the new Skyguard Squadron as one of its radar and gunnery instructors and was thus reunited with 'his' generator.

It is also interesting to note that nobody had tried to connect the Oerlikon guns to a Skyguard fire-control radar to turn them back into the lethal Skyhawk and Harrier killers they had proved to be. Peter at that time was an infantry officer and not an air defence instructor-in-gunnery versed in the mysterious world of wriggly amps that made up the Rapier side of the RAF Regiment. Had I known back in 1982 of his Oerlikon initiatives, I would have pushed hard to have him posted to the new Skyguard Squadron as its training officer and possible future commanding officer. There is an irony in that the Goose Green Oerlikons, considered by Kaye to be the best undamaged ones available, survived the campaign relatively unscathed only to be seriously damaged by an ignorant Brit who ordered the use of an oxyacetylene torch because, at the moment of shipping to the UK, no one immediately around knew how to unload the automatic feed. The feed had a 10hp clockwork motor to power it when there was no electrical power available. Unloading has to be done absolutely by the book as any shortcut would relentlessly draw a hand or forearm into the works, almost certainly leading to injuries worthy of amputation. And so, the most pristine gun from the Goose Green battlefield turned up at RAF Waddington more seriously damaged than the other heavily damaged one that had been turned over by a close call with a 1,000lb bomb dropped from 20,000ft, only suffering two bent barrels and 10m of generator cable ripped off.

Chapter 14

Opportunity Knocks

After my photographic foray into Soho, the RAF Regiment began regular rotations of Rapier squadrons to the South Atlantic. With each squadron rotation, I requested each unit in turn to send me a 'Bluey', that MoD free aerogram for deployed members of the armed forces, with a set of the latest Falkland Island postage stamps on it and franked with that unit's date stamp. Over the years the Blueys piled up, making a unique historical and attractive addition to my philatelic collection. I also changed jobs within the Directorate, taking on responsibility for future equipment; this was very interesting work for which my Royal School of Artillery multi-weapon training was most appropriate. It brought me into contact with officers who were planning operational requirements five, ten and even twenty years ahead, for which a sound understanding of the technical and developmental issues was needed. The work was very demanding as each new idea had to be exposed to the full scrutiny of the supporting branches who would be responsible for procurement, evaluation, employment, maintenance, logistics, training, operational use and, most importantly, funding.

One of the consequences of all this consultative work is that MoD files tend to be rather fat. Typically, we would limit a file to a hundred enclosures. If a new letter referred to a document in an earlier file, the two files would be delivered, fully cross-referenced by an army of clerks, to one's desk, along with multiple bundles of files on other subjects requiring attention. The total mail for the day could be two or three in-trays, each more than a foot high, making the poor incumbent invisible behind his columns of bumpf. One morning, about eight months after the Falklands Campaign and about nine inches down into my second pile of bumpf for the day, out popped a 100+-paged inventory of every item of equipment captured from the Argentinians. With it was a letter from the MoD Central Staffs, inviting all to peruse the list with a view to formalizing the disposal of the captured equipment. What had happened is that in the immediate aftermath of the campaign the major participating units and after them the rotating garrison units had, over the course of months, 'claimed' a considerable number of bits of Argentine kit as war trophies. Artillery pieces, armoured cars, rifles, machine guns and even entire aircraft were shipped home with great initiative and ingenuity to adorn the headquarters and museums of the three Services.

Many items abandoned under the unconditional surrender were among the best of foreign equipment and here was an opportunity to study hardware manufactured by rivals to British industry without the niceties of commercial restrictions. There were also large numbers of items that were common to our own British inventories and it was thought that some of these could be used to top up our own operational stocks. The MoD Central Staffs, senior in policy-making power to the individual Single Service staffs, therefore resolved to create some ground rules for the allocation of booty and to take a grip on the free-booting, grab-what-you-can of what, in legal terms, was actually now British government property. Every unit was required to declare its trophies, and these, along with all that still remained on the Islands, now constituted the inventory on my desk. All MoD organizations, formations and units were invited to bid for the Argentine equipment under one of five allocation priorities. Top of the league was operational use, followed by research, evaluation, and then unit war trophies with, lastly, military museums.

Idly I scanned the pages, more as a relief and change of routine than anything else. It was hugely interesting: American amphibious trucks, the DUKWs of the Second World War D-Day landing vintage, mixed in with tons of corned beef (Fray Bentos, presumably), Mercedes Jeeps, Browning .50 calibre machine guns, 105mm howitzers, Tigercat missiles, manpack radios, rifles and radars. Might there just be something, I mused, that the RAF Regiment could make use of? There were plenty of Tigercats and a goodly supply of missiles; but we had retired ours years ago, for the reasons stated earlier. However, I did bid for one for our regimental museum and another for 63 Squadron. There were also plenty of Rheinmetall twin 20mm cannon but as they were without radar direction and had no all-weather capability, they had hit nothing; I knew the Royal Air Force interest in them therefore would be nil. For the same reason I ignored the many Hispano 30mm cannon, though I did remark to myself that the quantities were quite astonishing. Then I came to the part that showed five Skyguard all-weather fire-control radars and about seven Oerlikon twin 35mm anti-aircraft field guns. These latter weapons, I knew, had just about the highest rate of fire of any large calibre anti-aircraft weapon. At this time the Argentine Army's report on the campaign had not yet been made public, so information on the Skyguard system was limited to general information in the military press. However, my professional interest was piqued when I noticed that many of the radars and some of the guns were already in the UK. A few preliminary phone calls to the various 'owners' revealed that most of the twin 35mm cannon were in good condition. The best report came from the Royal School of Artillery; their Corps of Royal Electrical and Mechanical Engineers workshops had already completely refurbished a pair of guns in the follow-up to Flying Officer Peter Kaye's live-firing in the Falklands. The School intended to carry out further evaluation firings. However, they did admit that without a Skyguard, their evaluation would be less than complete. Speaking to them as an instructor-in-gunnery and alumni of the School myself, they agreed that if the RAF could find a Skyguard radar, they would be willing to release 'their' guns for any trial I might be able to arrange. The Royal Artillery gunners also gave me a lead on the whereabouts of the 35mm ammunition in the custody of the Royal Army Ordnance Corps; the latter revealed that to prevent unauthorized use of untested explosives, their brief was to dump any ammunition not required by the British Forces in the deep ocean. A swift MoD signal from my lowly RAF staff appointment to the Army Logistic Executive froze all 35mm ammunition disposal, pending possible use by the RAF. This was my first serious appreciation of the power of a junior staff officer's pen on a signal signed off as 'From: MoDUK(Air)'.

One tip-off led to another; a further gun was located at the Royal Radar Research and Development Establishment (RARDE) at Fort Halstead. My enquiry revealed that RARDE intended to use the gun for research; there could be no question of its release. When pressed further, however, a spokesman explained that actually only one 35mm barrel was required; this was for a series of clinical firings to complete a computer data base they held of the trajectory details of every calibre of artillery shells worldwide. When I explained that the RAF might want a complete gun mounting for a dynamic, operational evaluation firing trial, which at that time only existed in my head, RARDE agreed to keep the gun in an operational condition and even offered to service it.

Next call was to the Harrier squadron at RAF Wittering. 1 Squadron was very proud of its Oerlikon twin 35mm trophy and, yes, it was in excellent condition; they had carefully chosen the best one for themselves whilst in the Falkland Islands, given how many times the Oerlikons had fired at them. Finally, the Royal Ordnance Depot at Donnington, which was acting as a clearing house for captured equipment, confirmed that they had at least six artillery pieces with twin barrels. They also mentioned that some cannon did not have barrels and that they were unsure of the actual calibres of many of the various guns they had custody of. I therefore talked-up my School of Artillery qualification and volunteered myself to be invited to the ordnance depot to verify that what was shown on the Central Staff inventory was indeed accurate and up to date.

As I commuted daily to the MoD from my home in Marlow, 2 hours each way, the rudiments of a plan began to come together. I have always regretted not jotting these initial thoughts down on the back of a cigarette packet, on a serviette, or even on a table cloth or some other interesting surface which I could later have framed as a good conversation piece. However, I don't smoke and posh silver service lunches were rare events in the life of a junior staff officer. In fact, on the train between Paddington and Maidenhead I penned out the bones of a proposal to utilize the captured equipment on just four sheets of Ministry of Defence paper. I was to find out later that at Air Force Board level, where such ideas go for ultimate approval, four sheets of paper were all that would be allowed. In between the two lots of four-page papers over the next two years, a couple of foot-high files on the subject of Skyguard-Oerlikons would eventually fill my MoD office filing cabinet.

It was quite out of the question to consider raising a new unit with Regular manpower because a manpower ceiling had been imposed on all three Services as a means of controlling rising costs. The only realistic option would be to use part-time reserve forces. Unlike the Army, which maintained a reserve of over 50,000 Territorial Volunteers, and the Navy, which had its Royal Naval Volunteer Reserve, the Air Force's Reserve, the Royal Auxiliary Air Force, was just over 1,000 personnel strong, having been savagely decimated in the Defence Review of 1957. More than twenty years later, in 1979, half a dozen RAuxAF Regiment infantry squadrons, so-called field squadrons, each of around 160 men, were raised for airbase protection in the UK against Russian Special Forces. It seemed to me that a seventh squadron might be acceptable, with part-timers put in charge of the modern, multi-million pound, battle-proven and very effective equipment. By the time I reached Marlow, my first draft plan had emerged as a squadron of three Skyguards and six Oerlikon all-weather AA guns to defend an airbase in the UK. The squadron would have fourteen Regulars, the same as the auxiliary field squadrons. The unit would be comparable in size to the six-gun Bofors 40mm AA gun squadrons we used to deploy to Belize before the arrival of Tigercat and Rapier. The key difference, however, between the Bofors and the Oerlikons was, of course, the proven lethality of Skyguard radar direction, which had outperformed even Rapier in that campaign.

Up to this moment in time, around February 1983, nobody higher in rank than me was aware of my idea. Before I went further, I needed to see if the Air Force policy staff would support the possibility. I already knew we were reporting to NATO that while we, the UK, agreed we should have ground-based air defences on at least another four airfields, we simply did not have the resources just yet, so I went to see Wing Commander Air Plans, John May, whose role was to ensure that RAF short-term finances would meet the next few years' projects; he confirmed both the operational requirement and the lack of funds, and then took me round to see a senior civil servant in the Defence Secretariat who was responsible for briefing the Armed Forces Minister on air matters. He thought that the idea to utilize the Argentine equipment to provide a low-cost means of meeting a commitment to NATO to strengthen the air defences of the UK, a move which both Labour and Conservative governments had been making since 1976, would be viewed with favour. With Plans and Policy support in hand, there remained the operational requirements and engineering staffs to consult. There was, of course, no Air Staff Requirement, that trigger for industry to develop a product, for a gun-based, ground-based air defence system.

As early as the 1960s there had been a considerable debate about guns-versus-missiles to replace the British Army and RAF Regiment's ageing 40mm Bofors guns and the Army's Thunderbird medium surface-to-air long-range missile. The solution was to replace Bofors guns with the shoulder-launched Blowpipe missiles and replace Thunderbird with the smaller but much more numerous Rapier, which was small enough to be towed by a Land Rover. The savings in manpower were dramatic and the leap forward in lethality, the target engagement rate, was enormous. In cash terms Blowpipe cost peanuts but in radar, missile and launcher development Rapier was to be the MoD's first ever billion-pound, long-term project, with three incremental development stages for Rapier planned over twenty years, each stage involving totally new ground equipment but using the same missile. In the event Rapier was to serve for fifty years. Of course, the gun fraternity wishes persisted but it was clear that adding radar and computing power to guns was as expensive as a missile system, but with shorter range, greater transportability weight and a much larger manpower bill compared to a more capable missile system. In contrast, other nations, with cheap conscript armies and no empire overseas to defend, tended to keep their older, radar-less or primitive radar-directed gun systems going for longer, topping up their defences with smaller numbers of missile systems. Given that Warsaw Pact, Russian-led Communist air forces hugely outnumbered the aircraft numbers of NATO, maximum kill capability at minimum cost ruled the day. The only Western nation able to afford an up-to-date, truly modern mix of missiles and radar-controlled guns was Switzerland; as neutrals, they exported their best gun products to NATO nations and other countries friendly to the West and bought Rapier with the proceeds.

Thus, when push came to shove, the operational requirements staff agreed that the requirement was for an all-weather, day-and-night, ground-based air defence, rather than guns or missiles *per se*, the actual means being a matter of affordability. And since I was bringing about £15 million worth of hardware to the table for free, they would support the concept. That now just left the engineering staffs to convince.

Radars in the West tend to be very international, with manufacturers cherry-picking the best components from multiple manufacturers in many countries. For example, they might buy the core of the radar, the microwave power tube, from one country, a ready-made signal processor from another country and so on, and then assemble the whole as a turnkey equipment under their own brand name for sale. Indeed, some of the defence supply chains are so long that in one famous example British tanks actually ran on Russian ball-bearings. After that discovery, the MoD required suppliers to declare the total supply chain source of all components. The Royal Signals and Radar Establishment at Malvern already had a Skyguard radar and so it was easy for me to ask an engineer there, Squadron Leader John Symonds, whom I had known from my officer cadet days at the RAF College Cranwell, for a formal appraisal of the captured radar. His off-the-cuff response was that it was the best-designed mobile radar he had ever seen and that two of them had been running at Malvern for eight months already, without any requirement for spare parts. In terms of capability, the radar was hugely more advanced than the Rapier radar and its reliability spoke for itself. He then confessed that they actually had four radars, but two of them were severely damaged. Better than that, he informed me that there was a fifth Skyguard at RAF Scampton, near Lincoln, and suggested we should meet there to look at it.

Thus armed with verbal support from the four quarters necessary to fly the project, I tidied up my notes into a proper Service Paper, with introduction, aim, arguments in favour and against, conclusion and recommendation, now proposing four radars and eight guns, and sought an audience with my director. Formal access to the director for a junior staffer was, of course, through my immediate wing commander boss, who happened to be a high flier and very open to innovations and new ideas. The deputy director, Group Captain Phillip Gibson, on the other hand, was a Sandhurst officer and leading equestrian of the old school, who had served in such places as Egypt and the Sudan. Indeed, he had been the aide de camp to the British Governor of the Sudan and had even kept a horse outside his room in the officers' mess there. Regimental scuttlebutt was that he'd actually ridden it at the battle of Omdurman with Churchill, which was clearly untrue! At Cranwell he had been the most senior RAF Regiment officer at the college, known to all cadets there as 'King Rock', whilst I was the most junior RAF Regiment cadet present. He would, I knew, be less than enthusiastic about any new-fangled, electronically controlled gadgetry. And in his company I always felt slightly unskittled, standing to attention in front of him, even now. This, I think, derived from our very first encounter, which happened to be on my very first parade at the RAF College when, with us new arrivals still in civilian clothes, he bellowed out to the 6ft 4in college warrant officer, 'Who is that scruffy-looking cadet at the end of that rank, there?' 'That, Sir, is your newest RAF Regiment cadet, Fonfé!' the warrant officer bellowed back. Since then, I had served under Gibson as a pilot officer on active service in the last and bloody days of our withdrawal from Aden in 1967. And now, fifteen years later, with both of us three ranks higher, I was sure he still regarded me as a miscreant cadet. It was with some relief on that day, therefore, to find the group captain out of the office.

I was thus able to put my ideas directly to the director, Air Commodore Roy Strickland, who was what I would call a 'man's man', the epitome of Trenchard's founding philosophy for the Royal Air Force that any airmen, irrespective of social background and education, should, with appropriate training provided by the RAF, be able to rise to the highest rank. Strickland had joined as a 14-year-old boy engineering apprentice, a 'brat' in Air Force parlance, during the Second World War and had worked his way up through a commission at Sandhurst, where RAF Regiment officers were trained in the 1950s, then through the RAF Staff College, all the way up to his present appointment, just one rank below our two-star Commandant General. Roy had three characteristics I admired: first, he always heard his junior officers right out to the end, without interruption; secondly, by deft questioning, he pared the most intractable technical modern equipment problem down to its barest bones, as often as not, through an analogy with the mechanics of a motor car; and finally, once he had decided on a course of action and given his orders, he would back his officers to the hilt in their execution.

True to form, I outlined my proposal to utilize the Argentine equipment without interruption. At the end he agreed that there could be some merit in exploring the possibility further and he would direct Gibson, when he returned, to undertake a feasibility study, subject only to the condition that other on-going staff work in the Directorate was not to suffer; if any extra work was required, he reiterated, it had to be done by me on a voluntary basis.

The die was cast. My project was launched and I would do all in my power to make it feasible.

Chapter 15

The Feasibility Study

Before Group Captain Gibson could start the Feasibility Study, it seemed prudent to assemble all the captured Argentine equipment in one place. RAF Waddington near Lincoln was the base from which the Vulcan attacks against Stanley had been mounted. By coincidence, Waddington was also considered to be the next most important RAF base to be given its own low-level air defence since it was already nominated to be the main operating base for the RAF's then most expensive aircraft ever, the £60 million airborne early warning (AEW) Nimrod. The base had just run down its four Vulcan nuclear bomber squadrons but many of the support personnel were still in post, tidying up the loose ends of the redundant bomber force. I was keenly aware that misinformed and disparaging opinions about the use of 'old' anti-aircraft guns might be put about by the older generation of RAF Regiment officers, whose experience was limited to their radar-less, Second World War design, vintage Bofors guns. Then there were the 'Rapiercrats' who might add their own opinions to that scuttlebutt and between them thus possibly torpedo the project before it got off the ground. I therefore avoided gathering the equipment at our regimental depot. Instead, on the authority of Air Plans, I gave out instructions to move all the as yet uncommitted Oerlikon guns and their power supply generators to RAF Waddington. I issued one further instruction, on the grounds of not alerting the Argentinians, that the movement, storage location and possible intended use of the equipment was to be kept secret.

Within days the first five guns and generators had arrived and were spirited away into Waddington's now vacated nuclear bomb storage shelters; there was nowhere in the RAF more secure than that and the station's personnel were well used to keeping secrets secret. Further luck was with me. The guns were placed in the care of Warrant Officer Terry Lattimer, the nuclear weapons chief armourer. Without any bombs to look after, the Oerlikons were manna from heaven to keep his now idle armourers awaiting posting, busy with a worthwhile job and he set them to work at once. For the first time since they were abandoned on the Falklands battlefields, the Oerlikons received their first proper maintenance as his so-called 'black hand gangers' set-to with a will. Their labours were to do as much to preserve the weapons from deterioration as to make them very presentable as well-greased and clean operating machinery to any doubters seeing the booty for the first time. Much later it was to be my pleasure to recruit Lattimer's daughter Paige into the Royal Auxiliary Air Force Regiment as one of our first ten female Oerlikon gunners under my command.

In the meantime, another colleague pointed me in the direction of the British Manufacture and Research Company (BMARCO), just 27km away at Grantham, and informed me that it was the UK subsidiary of parent company Oerlikon-Buhrle Gmbh, of Zurich, Switzerland. BMARCO manufactured, amongst other sizes of ammunition, the 35mm shells for the Argentine guns. I was also informed that Oerlikon maintained a training centre for gun and maintenance crews for overseas customers at another former nuclear bomb base nearby, ex-RAF Faldingworth. Being a training man myself, I thought I'd open up my contact with the company at a working level and called the Faldingworth Training Centre. By chance, it was also the day that the Radar Research Establishment RAF engineer Squadron Leader John Symonds was with me for an intended visit to RAF Scampton to view the captured Skyguard radar there. As luck would have it, I was put through to one Herr Martin Frey, who happened to be the head of Oerlikon's overseas training department and I invited him to join us to inspect the Skyguard radar at RAF Scampton.

Herr Frey was everybody's preconception of what a Swiss banker might look like: a penetratingly alert, tubby chap with a salt-and-pepper goatee beard and a sharp Armani light grey suit. He was also a man after my own heart, an enthusiast for solving intractable problems by cutting through protocol with the sharpness of a Swiss Army knife. We took an instant liking to each other as he explained what, from a company point of view, he saw as the essential steps to be taken if the Royal Air Force were serious about putting the captured equipment back into operational use. First, he explained, it was the company's understanding from their Argentine customer contacts that the guns and radars had all been disabled and, to make doubly sure they could not be reused, the equipment was booby-trapped as well. Their feedback was that primed hand grenades had been placed in the internal compartments of the guns and radars in such a way that when the access hatches were opened, the live grenades would fall out and explode. Before anything could be done, therefore, the company would require an assurance that they had been made safe from booby-traps. In the event the armourers found nothing; we could only assume that some hapless Argentine conscripts, when tasked to do the job by their officers, had taken the easier option of running down the hill away from the advancing British infantry, safe in the knowledge that they would never see the guns or radars again.

Martin Frey then went on to explain that, obviously, the company's UK subsidiary, BMARCO, as a major UK heavy weapons manufacturer, would carry out any necessary refurbishment of the guns, but the radars would probably have to go to Switzerland. He explained the principles of operation of the gun-radar combination and stressed the important part that the Skyguard played in the overall lethality of the system. It was vital, he stated firmly, that he needed to see a captured Skyguard because that was the single most expensive item in the whole weapon system. Martin then launched into a technical briefing about the weapon system, followed by an explanation of how the company trained its customers up as instructors who, in turn, would then train their own personnel. Technical training for engineers followed the same principles. Finally, he outlined the Swiss Army concept of maintenance support for the equipment based on four levels:

- Echelon One – maintenance in action in the field;
- Echelon Two – repair from a vehicle-mounted field workshop;
- Echelon Three – arsenal maintenance in a fixed base workshop such as an airbase; and
- Echelon Four – factory support.

It was a very slick presentation which answered most of the unasked questions that I and engineer John Symonds had framed up beforehand. Clearly, even with the short notice and a cold call from me, Martin knew his stuff and was very keen to explore and support the advance of my project. (Later, when I recounted the events of the day to my mother, she very succinctly observed: 'Of course they were happy to help you; they will have sold the support for the same equipment twice!') At the end of the briefing John and I were each presented with that thing on every Cub Scout's Xmas wish list: the tiniest of Swiss Army knives. Despite its small size, it housed a razor-sharp blade, a nail file and a miniature pair of scissors. Later I was to joke with Martin that the size of the Swiss Army knife being presented seemed to signal the commercial progress of the project, as each time we met the knife presented was bigger than the previous one. (In a word of advice to the British armaments industry: if you want to hand out a freebie that is really appreciated, forget the coffee mugs, desk accessories and fancy pennants – the one thing that will never get binned is a Swiss Army knife.)

To round off the day, Martin, John and I went off to RAF Waddington to inspect the guns. They gleamed with new paint and freshly applied grease on polished steel. A cursory glance revealed that the greatest deficiency appeared to be the removal of easily detachable parts, in particular the £10,000 Ferranti gyro-predicting gunsight, probably removed by battlefield trophy hunters. However, the company insisted that if a proper feasibility study were to be carried out, they would have to be closely inspected by Oerlikon engineers.

We then went to RAF Scampton to view the Skyguard. Martin, in his Armani suit, stepped up to the radar, lifted up a small panel and pressed a button. The generator coughed into life and settled into the steady air-cooled beat of a VW Porsche engine. Then, singlehandedly, Martin unlocked and swung out a pair of outriggers, one on each side of the radar and pressed another button. Hey presto: three hydraulic jacks powered themselves down until the radar trailer wheels were clear of the ground, jiggled around for a few moments and then stopped when the radar was perfectly level. Martin then undid a latch above the radar cabin door on each side, stood back and eased the cabin roof open, pressed another button and the entire surveillance radar aerial, the tracking radar aerial and the tracking TV mount rose quietly under hydraulic pressure into their operating positions. Climbing up into the now revealed radar crew cabin previously occupied by the aerial assembly, he leaned up and freed the aerial azimuth and elevation travelling locks, closed the cabin roof, sat down on the operator's bench and pressed the radar start button. Everything came to life; he pressed another button marked 'Self-test' and various lights flashed on and off, which meant something to Martin. After a couple of minutes he grinned at us and said the magic words: 'Mike, this radar is fully operational.' He then rummaged around in a door pocket compartment and pulled out a sheaf of paper, with neatly written up figures in rows of different coloured ink, and four ball point pens, one each in red, blue, green and black. 'Good boys,' he sighed, and then turned to us and said something like 'Shall we now enter the upper windspeed and direction data for 14 June 1982 into the computer? The Argentinians seemed to have been interrupted.' Secretly, Martin was delighted, as it was he who had trained the Argentinians, just as he would later train us, to use a different colour pen for each altitude line entry on the meteorological balloon tracking data form so that the figures would not be mixed up while keying them in to the digital computer, which in turn fed azimuth and elevation prediction data to the guns to get them on target. We were very impressed with the Skyguard's self-levelling mechanism, mentally recalling the messing around we had on Rapier trying to level the four corner jacks of the launcher and snatch-lifting the 250kg generator off its mount, to then drag it 15m away, before starting the Hillman Imp 'little screamer' petrol engine.

Martin then went on to say with a dead-straight poker-face that there were three things seriously wrong. 'What?' we anxiously enquired. 'Well,' he said, 'firstly, the generator engine is pinking. You must be using shit 80 octane British Army fuel. This radar has a Porsche engine and that demands the best quality 98 octane five-star petrol if you want the engine to last.' Next, he said he was cross that the Argentinians had failed to enter the met data for the last day of the war, so how could they expect to hit anything, and finally he grinned and said: 'All we need now is the gun and some ammunition and we are ready to shoot down a few Red Arrows.' I was, to use one of my gunner's more ghastly expressions, completely gobsmacked at the ease of the Skyguard's setting-up for operations.

In a quieter moment Martin explained the reason for the Swiss pursuit of easy operation. In the Swiss Army every male had to do military national service from the age of 18 to age 40. In the first year, in just four months of full-time military service, they would cover all the infantry skills, nuclear, biological and chemical personal survival drills and be appointed to a specific crewman task in the Skyguard-Oerlikon combination, which they had to master completely, before being sent home with all their personal kit, including a rifle and 200 rounds of ammunition. A year later they would be recalled for one week of refresher training, a full week of rigorous field deployments with little sleep and lots of challenging setbacks to overcome, finishing off the last week with short rest, debrief and clean-up, to put the kit to bed for another year. With forty-nine weeks between field deployments, the Swiss military equipment had to be both user-friendly to long absences and exceptionally reliable. If soldiers had no ambitions of command, they could simply repeat this process on an annual basis and remain as privates in the same crew position for the next twenty-two years, by which time they were able to do the job blindfolded. On the other hand, if they had ambition, they could come back for another four-month block of training to take them up a rank. The other feature of the system is that all the employees of a factory, for example, would all join the same unit. Indeed, the Oerlikon factory staff virtually ran the Swiss Army anti-aircraft artillery, which, of course, made for a very short chain of staffing any improvements and eliminating things like a four-jack trailer. (The final build of Rapier trailer took twenty years to get to three jacks.) The Swiss equipment, therefore, was built to exceptionally high standards of quality control to guarantee switch-on working after forty-nine weeks of storage and trouble-free working during a week of refresher training and a further week of intense field use. And with nuclear shelters mandatorily built into every home and block of flats, the huge, active-and-trained, citizen army and air force guaranteed the Swiss their neutrality by force of arms through two world wars and the Cold War. For me, there would be some good reading as to how I might structure the manning and training of our own Oerlikon crews. Overall, I was now very confident the Royal Air Force would, if only it could be so persuaded, have a virtually new all-weather, powerful and battle-proven close air defence system for the UK airfield hosting its newest, most important and most expensive Nimrod AEW aircraft at next to no cost. The next action, therefore, was to make the as yet unaware Group Captain Gibson aware of his new, formal, Feasibility Study – but this, I found out upon my return, the Director had already done.

Group Captain Gibson was not impressed but he called the interested parties together to report their findings. Wing Commander John May (Air Plans) led the way by stating the operational need and our commitment to NATO to provide more air defence for close protection of strategic airfields. Squadron Leader Symonds reported that from a Royal Signals and Radar Research Establishment engineering point of view, we had inherited a very fine, very advanced fire-control radar of great reliability and user simplicity, which had been specifically designed to be operated by part-time personnel with long intervals between training. Moreover, he went on, the Swiss maintenance philosophy could economically and efficiently be adopted by the RAF without difficulty. I reported that we had inspected both radars and guns and had visited Oerlikon's international training centre only a few kilometres from RAF Waddington, which could be the conduit for both training and factory level maintenance support if needed. Finally, with

Oerlikon in the UK being represented by the British heavy arms and large calibre ammunition manufacturer BMARCO, also nearby at Grantham, there was the possibility of emulating the Swiss and recruiting factory personnel into the unit. Gibson seemed relieved at the positive outcome of the meeting and two actions came out of it. The first was that the Feasibility Study was now formally constituted and, second, that the RAF should now make a bid to the Central Staffs to take possession of all Oerlikon and Skyguard materiel captured in the Falklands Campaign on the basis of a formal operational requirement. He instructed me to prepare the minutes of the meeting and issue the appropriate signal messages to all those concerned, with the Director's rider that this work was to be done after all my normal duties had been completed, i.e. in my own time. As I had 4 hours of daily travel time cooped up in a railway carriage, this was not too onerous. Later, I was able to turn this 'own time' directive to my advantage and qualify for yet another MoD Bright Ideas cash prize.

The first task was to take formal possession of all the Skyguard radars and the Oerlikon guns. I went to see the controller of logistics in the MoD Central Staffs, Wing Commander Harcourt-Smith, who remembered me as an officer cadet at Cranwell. He scanned the minutes of the Feasibility Study meeting, freshly written by me on the train home and noted that the words Feasibility Study now began with capital letters. He agreed that the minutes constituted sufficient authority for him to issue a formal equipment allocation to the Air Force Department and thus under my direct control in the MoD, on the condition that if they did not enter service, the items were to be returned to the original trophy 'owners'. At my suggestion he agreed to sign off the reallocation signal from the Central Staffs to overrule any single-Service problems. I also suggested a follow-up order to the current holders to deliver the equipment directly to RAF Waddington under a secrecy caveat, removing me as an individual from the firing line of any ire that might follow and minimizing the risk of alerting any possible detractors until the Feasibility Study had established all the facts and reported its recommendations.

Over the next few days the phone buzzed with protests from now lower-priority trophy-holders who had helped themselves to stuff off the battlefield in the free-for-all that followed the campaign. Patiently and, I hope kindly, I explained that the operational imperative was just too great to allow a £3 million radar and a £750,000 double cannon to sit outside a unit headquarters or in a regimental museum as an ornament. More protests arose from Headquarters Strike Command that RAF Waddington was on the run-down of personnel and could not possibly cope with looking after all this additional equipment without a formal increase in manpower establishment. Clearly not everybody was as enthusiastic as Warrant Officer Lattimer. It took some weeks to get round all the objectors and allay their fears about the amount of work that might be involved. While all this was going on, Lattimer's team had gone ahead and given the first

6-ton cannon mount a 300-manhour new coat of paint as part of its long-term preservation. While I understood the formal whinge, I knew that at the coalface, the men at Waddington were not going anywhere for several more months; indeed, they just quietly got on with the clean-up and ultimately were to repaint all but three of the cannon. In fact I intervened to stop the repainting of the last three because they were Argentine Air Force guns and each was already beautifully adorned with the proud words 'Fuerza Aerea' on each side and I wanted to keep this as a public relations reminder of who lost the war. The work the Waddington men did made an enormous saving in the overall cost of refurbishing the guns. It was also a great boost to my morale to find such enthusiasm for getting on with the job so far from the MoD paper battlefield and I am pleased to report that Terry Lattimer was eventually to take himself to Buckingham Palace to receive a just reward for his efforts. That weekend, on the M4 motorway, I passed an articulated Army lorry carrying one of 'my' Oerlikon guns on its way to join my growing arsenal of heavy anti-aircraft artillery at RAF Waddington; the sight made my day.

Of all of the previous owners, the Royal Signal and Radar Research Establishment, essentially a civilian scientist-run organization at Malvern, argued most loudly to retain their share of the booty. The radar was essential for research; then it was essential for technical intelligence, closely followed by commercial intelligence and then, well, for everything. Thank goodness the allocating directive had come from the over-arching Central Staffs and the staff at Malvern were simply ordered to release the Skyguard radars, period. It says much for their good grace that, having lost the case to retain a superbly engineered and easy-to-use research tool, they generously threw in a whole pile of new spare parts they had already purchased out of their own budget for long-term maintenance. I was especially keen to maintain good relations and the friendships I had built up over the years with them through my involvement in the Rapier Arctic trials and particularly their development of computer-aided deployment site analysis for our RAF Rapier squadrons. It gave me great pleasure to invite these boffins to witness the real purpose of the equipment by coming to a live firing camp to see us shooting down every target.

On the subject of spares, on Martin Frey's next visit he let fall that approximately £250,000 of field maintenance spares were missing off the battlefield. Unlike Rapier, Oerlikon spares were held forward on the generator trailer, packaged in rugged, waterproof, suitcase-like pull-out drawers on each generator, along with all the tools that were needed to fit them. All a technician had to do was turn-up at the gun, if necessary walking all the way, and carry out the repair, the spares and tools already being to hand at each fire unit. Now that I knew that the Land Forces Command Ordnance Depot at Donnington in the Midlands was the collection point for all the Falklands booty, it was time to make another visit and look through their piles of miscellaneous loose items. While that day out only located three out of a total of 144 missing aluminum spares cases, I could see why such a handy container full of mechanics tools should disappear into personal shipments home. The good news was that I discovered that two of the cannon listed as 30mm guns were in fact, upon inspection, a further two Oerlikon twin 35s. Better still, I was able to identify five further generator trailers, which meant that all the guns could now be powered up, even if they were minus those attractive spares and tool boxes. Continuing my rummage of literally piles of unsorted military stores on the shed floor, I saw a goodly number of the very latest American night-vision goggles mixed in with largely junk, so I fished them out and added them to my operational necessity list. In my previous service in Northern Ireland I had run experimental trials with these devices and found that by wearing them one could actually see the flight path of bullets leaving one's own gun and see the heat strike of where the bullets hit the ground, and thus one could actually shoot lethally accurately from the hip at night more easily than taking careful aim in daylight. No wonder the Scots Guards had such a tough time on Mount Tumbledown. And so, in the final dish-out of booty, I got a dozen sets of the very latest night-vision goggles so we could drive our Oerlikon trucks about and deploy radars and guns in total blackout. Altogether it had been a very worthwhile day. Finally, mindful of the importance of a trophy or two, I also made a bid for a single barrel 30mm Hispano anti-aircraft gun, the direct descendent of its unpowered cousin manned by the RAF Regiment in North Africa and Burma in the dark days of the 1940s.

At around this time I was to win over Group Captain Gibson, who now became an active supporter of the project, still disguised as a Feasibility Study. Earlier in my MoD tour he had been tasked to review a trial whereby part-time personnel were being trained to operate the Rapier missile system. Being the kind of leader he was, of course, he was determined to have a go at everything the part-timers had learned to do. So naturally, he had a go at hauling out a cable with a 55-pin connector at each end and tried humping the 250kg Rapier generator back onto its latches at the rear of the launcher, plus the fun and games of trying to level four jacks with four people, all of which I think he found quite daunting. Of course, the boys forgave him for his poor aircraft recognition because gone were the Dakota DC3s and Vampires of his youth and now aircraft even changed shape as they flew along. However, the one skill Gibson absolutely could not master was the Rapier optical target tracker, basically a times-ten magnification periscope controlled by a joystick that, unlike every other radio-control model and computer game controller on the planet, did not actually move. It was a pressure joystick and it controlled rates of elevation and azimuth; applying pressure set the optics moving and they would continue to move at the set speed, even hands off. To correct the tracking, all one had to do was apply a little pressure in the desired new direction and relax as the electronics took up the new rates of movement. Despite considerable ribald soldierly advice from the trained reservists, this skill was simply beyond Gibson's comprehension, which only put the part-timers higher up in his assessment scale of what auxiliary personnel were capable of mastering; in short, he came away most impressed.

Fast forward now to Group Captain Gibson's first viewing of a Skyguard. He was presented with basically a box on wheels and, on being guided around to open a hatch here and swing an outrigger there, unlatching one half of the box-body and then simply pressing buttons in appropriate places, he transformed the box into a fully functional radar. He was impressed. Best of all, however, was the radar tracker; with this, by means of a roller-ball, he could designate a target that looked like a caterpillar-trail on the radar screen and transform it, at the touch of a button, to a Red Arrows jet doing aerobatics in the deadly crosswires of the co-axial television tracker. And when the aircraft came within range of a gun, not fitted on this day, a light illuminated and all he had to do was press Fire and the jet was doomed. We then explained that the Skyguard also had some other tricks up its sleeve: if it were jammed, this button would change frequency. If the target launched a missile at the radar, that button would jump from tracking the aircraft to tracking the incoming missile so we could shoot the incoming missile down. And, while this explanation was going on, the Red Arrow remained in the deadly TV crosswires, even after we turned the radar off, because the TV electronics kept tracking the target hands-off, while the Red Arrow turned and twisted its way round the next season's aerobatic display routine. No words were necessary; I knew Gibson was hooked on the kit and he was on-side.

Chapter 16

More Grubbing About on the Battlefield

The business of the missing field maintenance spares and tool boxes was a worry to me, given their cost of replacement. My guess was that when the guns were recovered from the battlefield, only the major assembly of the four-wheeled cannon was collected up. The ancillary boxes were probably dug-in for protection or, at the very least, dispersed and concealed around the gun positions. Without knowing what a complete and illustrated gun box looked like, it would be difficult for troops on the opposite side of the planet to even know what to look for. Moreover, there were the very real hazards of unmarked minefields and confirmed reports of booby-traps that could hardly be ignored. Using the authority of the MoD once again to direct lesser formations, endorsed now a little more enthusiastically by the group captain, I requested RAF Regiment squadrons manning Rapier on rotation in the Falkland Islands to undertake a detailed search for the missing accessories. Martin Frey provided photographs of the gun boxes with illustrated inventories of their contents, whilst the intelligence staffs provided maps of where they thought the equipment had been deployed during the campaign, since at that time I was unaware of Peter Kaye's efforts.

The RAF Regiment gunners set to with a will, tramping the Falklands for 'Fonfé's Flak'. However, only one further gun box was located and that was being used as a duckboard at Squadron Leader Martin Hooker's 63 Squadron Rapier tactical headquarters in the Stanley mud. Apparently, he was standing on it at the time he was telling his Rapier fire unit commanders what to search for. Martin did, however, recover a number of gun generators quietly burbling away in various locations, running kettles, video tape players and even tent heaters. At £120,000 each they were definitely worth recovering. One further twin 35mm cannon, but with only one barrel (and therefore assumed to be a single barrel Hispano), was located outside Black Eagle Camp, where it had stood as a war trophy since the end of the campaign. Huge credit is due to Martin Hooker and the others, who not only located the equipment but arranged for its extraction, usually by Chinook, the only means available.

A follow-on Rapier squadron commander and friend of mine, Squadron Leader Dick Moore, later to be Commandant General of the RAF Regiment, had an amusing search for the Goose Green guns, both he and I being unaware that

Peter Kaye had already moved them to Sid's Strip at San Carlos. At my request, 1 Squadron, its Harriers now back at RAF Wittering, had gone through their campaign photo-reconnaissance library and extracted two photographs of Goose Green; these were printed out for me at almost 1m square in size. One was a very detailed close-up, showing in great detail a few settlement houses, a grass airfield, a hut for fuel and fire extinguishers and a beach; the other was a very high-level picture, taken from 20,000ft. While the latter clearly covered the area, one would have needed a microscope to even make out a house, let alone a cannon. In answer to my question about why one was so detailed and the other from so high, it was explained that after losing two Harriers to Oerlikons by flying low over Goose Green, everyone since either gave the place a wide berth or flew so high over the top as to be out of reach of the guns. Not having been down to the South Atlantic myself, I accepted the pictures in good faith and sent them down to Dick. If nothing else, they proved that the presence of the Oerlikons had forced a change to inferior tactics upon us, the enemy.

Back in the South Atlantic, Dick Moore tasked a helicopter for the search mission and was hovering around Goose Green, trying to orientate the air photo with the ground. The pilot turned the helicopter round this way and that and Dick turned the photo round and round, but the image simply did not fit the ground. At one time they thought perhaps the photo had been printed back to front and did some mental, spatial transformations but still nothing matched. Frustrated, they decided to land and consult a local. In the way of islanders everywhere, the local took his time studying the picture for a long while; finally, whilst probably regarding the two military personnel standing by the helicopter as complete idiots, he slowly declared it to be Pebble Island, about 50km away. I was assured by 1 Squadron that the regrettable misnaming of the Pebble Island airfield as Goose Green had absolutely nothing to do with their losing their prize Oerlikon war trophy to a bunch of 'rock apes' from the RAF Regiment. One good thing, however, did come out of Dick's embarrassing flight to Goose Green; elsewhere on the Island they located the fourteenth Oerlikon gun, making it just two short of the number needed for two independent squadrons. In the grand mix of Argentine Air Force and Army Oerlikons there were minor differences: the newer Army guns were powered by Porsche air-cooled engines, the older Air Force ones by less powerful VW camper van flat four engines running on lower-grade petrol, not that a layman could tell the difference. I also discovered that although the advertised configuration for the Skyguard was to control two Oerlikons, it was actually hard-wired in its computer configuration to control up to three, so I altered the refurbishment to cater for four Skyguards and twelve guns and adjusted the Auxiliary manning accordingly in my next iteration of the project plan.

There remained one more Oerlikon gun to recover to make the total fifteen: the one in the Fleet Air Arm Museum at RNAS Yeovilton. I took an afternoon off to visit it and it was in the best condition of any I had seen, complete with its generator and all twelve gun spares and maintenance boxes complete on board, a treasure indeed. I mentioned the MoD Central Staffs' policy regarding the allocation of Argentine booty against scaled priorities to the museum staff and heard my words fall upon stone-deaf ears. I could also feel myself getting into deeper and hotter water with this senior Royal Navy officer, who obviously held RAF crabs in contempt. I felt myself being drawn away from Peter Squire's professional cool to Jerry Pook's unconcealed frustration but held myself in check by enquiring who might be the right person to address this conundrum. 'See the First Sea Lord; he is President of the Fleet Air Arm Museum' was the reply. I decided there and then that was no need to follow this up any further and meekly asked if I might instead go over and photograph the Pucara on display in order to update the accuracy of my aircraft recognition slides. This I did and consoled myself that fourteen out of fifteen cannon was still a pretty good haul.

Back in London, the Swiss, through BMARCO's aviation sales manager, retired Wing Commander 'Spike' Jones, had come to present a formal proposal to survey the captured equipment. The task would take two weeks; at Swiss rates of pay, travel, accommodation and subsistence, the cost would be a neat £100,000. I was stumped, because the one thing my Feasibility Study did not have was cash up front nor, incidentally, did I have an MoD procurement executive department to write up any contract, let alone pay for it. Also, having worked in so many budget-cutting exercises in my short time in the MoD, I realized the near-impossibility of pulling any money out of thin air. Spike must have read my face as he only left me with a marginally larger Swiss Army knife than the one Martin Frey had given me. I dared not run this seemingly intractable problem past the group captain in case the Director picked up on it. I could even hear in my head his likely response: 'That's it, Mick. No money. Now get back to your job.' Instead, I tidied up my office, cleared out all the accumulated unwashed coffee cups, washed and dried them and took a later and slower train home to mull over the problem. I woke up at Slough, three stops from home, with a start. In my sideways-thinking sub-consciousness, I recalled that Spike had said the BMARCO-made Oerlikon ammunition cost £50 a shot. We had recovered over 40,000, worth some £2 million, about twice as much as we expected to use in training over ten years, even allowing for a large war reserve. How about, I mused to myself, horse-trading some of the pristine, surplus, ex-Argentine, BMARCO-manufactured 35mm ammunition back to them in exchange for two weeks' work? After all, was not the MoD already flogging off other usable ammunition calibres on the world market. With that idea dancing like a sugar plum in my head, I slept like a baby, remembering to wake up in Marlow.

Next day I contacted RAF Waddington's armourers and they confirmed both the quantities and the new condition of the ammunition stock which I had by then stockpiled under RAF care, in order to have it taken on charge and stored to our normal high standards under my direct control. I then called the RAF Supply Branch and explained I wanted to draw out 2,000 rounds of ammunition to transfer to BMARCO as payment in lieu of cash for the factory inspection of the equipment. Impossible, I was told; the only way they could remove the ammunition off charge was for us to go to war, fire it in training, or have it dumped at sea as no longer required; in short, it was a complete dead end. Next I tried the Air Force's civilian finance branch, the dreaded F11(Air), famous even in Trenchard's formative time in the 1920s for parsimony and inflexibility. Could they sign off 2,000 rounds of 35mm ammunition worth a hundred-grand to BMARCO? 'Absolutely not!' came the reply. 'We only deal in money.' Another definitely dead end. Under pressure to deliver a mainstream task by noon, I therefore completed that work on time as I still had a real job to do. The Director, I was sure, would be watching me closely for any fall-off in performance. In a rather uncharacteristic fit of pique, therefore, I dashed off a grumpy review of my seemingly intractable hundred-grand problem on a hand-written memo pad, Mod Form 4a, signed it off, sent it to the Head of Air Force Finance with a priority label on it and went for a run around St James's Park to cool my heels. Upon my return, my office mate, Sandy Davie, conveniently responsible for Auxiliaries in the RAF Regiment, greeted me with 'Aaah, I've just had a phone call from the PA to the Head of Air Force Finance. Would this Squadron Leader Fonfé fellow please report to the Head of Air Force Finance at 3pm.' My heart sank, knees went weak and I gulped. I had clearly overstepped the mark and could already imagine the stand-to-attention dressing-down I would deservedly get from my Director, if not an immediate posting out of the MoD. 'Never mind,' said Sandy. 'It's not a court martial offence, so you'll still get paid at the end of the month, even if you are posted to Timbuktu' – or words to that effect. With a lead ball bouncing away in my gut, I dragged myself reluctantly to the MoD Main Building, with its two bare-breasted statues flanking the main entrance. Even the in-house joke about bigger boobs being made inside failed to lift my dread. I arrived in good time and was waved to a seat; it felt like waiting outside the headmaster's study for six of the best. Spot on time, I was ushered into the largest office I had seen so far in my time in the MoD. At the end of a huge and beautiful mahogany table, possibly a captain's table recovered from some great ocean liner, sat a large decanter of sherry and two giant sherry glasses. At the opposite end sat a mature, grey-haired lady, who could have been Golda Meir's younger sister. 'Come in, my boy,' she boomed. 'Have yourself a sherry, then come and sit here and tell me what this is all about.' It took me quite aback. I was grateful for a gulp of sherry while the lady's cool grey eyes appraised me without any sign of disapproval. Taking a deep breath, I launched into a rapid review of the project to return the captured artillery to operational use, the great windfall of £30 million worth of equipment now assembled at RAF Waddington and the intractability of both logisticians and financiers to write off £100,000 of captured ammunition in exchange for a thorough technical inspection of nearly new equipment. Like our Director, she heard me out completely without interruption and then said, with a twinkle in her eye, that it was the most interesting story she had heard in a long time and, yes, I had come to exactly the right person in the MoD, since she was responsible for signing-off gifts of military hardware to museums, worthy causes and even deserving foreign nations, on behalf of the government. There was just one small problem: the limit of her gifting powers was £50,000; above that, she had to go to the Treasury for approval and that could be tricky. Impetuously I blurted out, 'Ma'am, the ammunition is second hand. Could we value it at half price?' And with no further ado, she replied that that was a brilliant idea and suggested she should phrase the reason for the transfer of 2,000 rounds of captured ammunition to BMARCO as an 'MoD gift in return for services rendered following the Falklands Campaign'; she then called her PA in, had it typed up, signed and stamped and placed in my hands, with CC copies to the finance and logistics branches. Finally, I suddenly saw a way to recover the Royal Naval Air Service Museum Oerlikon gun. Meekly I enquired if Treasury approval had been given for the £¾ million Oerlikon gun in the Yeovilton Museum. 'Absolutely not' was her reply. 'If that had been handed over underhandedly, such a large value item would definitely warrant a Treasury inquiry as to how it came about.' Saying no more, I thanked her for her fantastic support and left a very happy man.

In jubilation, I skipped all the way back to our offices in the Metropole Building, briefed Sandy on the extraordinary turn of events and cracked open a 50ml miniature bottle of brandy and poured it into our office coffee in celebration. Just then, Group Captain Gibson wandered in, demanding to know what the outbreak of morale was all about, so we sat him down and placed a brandied coffee in his hand, while I rummaged around for the one King Edward cigar we kept hidden for really big emergencies and told him that I had found a very unusual way to finance the detailed Oerlikon factory assessment of the captured equipment, leaving out any mention of my memo, the sherry and the Yeovilton cannon.

Later in the day, in my politest-ever phone call to Yeovilton, I whispered that a Treasury inquiry would likely follow if the Oerlikon cannon in their possession was not delivered to the RAF as per the MoD Central Staffs' allocation signal. The Saturday afternoon of the following weekend I saw passing me on the opposite side of the M4 motorway another Oerlikon twin 35mm AA gun complete with generator on a Royal Navy low-loader, presumably heading towards RAF Waddington. Score: fifteen out of fifteen. However, there was one final sequel to this last gun. On the way up Lincoln Hill the low-loader skidded on the smooth wet tarmac and demolished a lamppost. The *Lincolnshire Echo* reported the accident with the gleeful headline 'Argie Gun Attacks Lincolnshire Lamp Post'. I just loved it.

My next call was to Spike of BMARCO, to tell him he could have a hundred-grand's worth of his pristine new 35mm ammunition back in exchange for the Oerlikon factory inspection. He wasn't quite as enthusiastic as I expected him to be and promised to come back to me in a couple of hours. Just 15 minutes later he was back on the line and said Oerlikon had agreed to the deal but would only accept the ammunition back in lieu of payment if the Royal Air Force did not go ahead and put the guns and radars back into operational service. Henceforth, Spike informed me, the company codename for the British Skyguard-Oerlikon introduction into RAF service was 'Project Angel' and he asked me how soon I could deliver all the gun and generator equipment in my hands to Faldingworth so they could begin the factory inspection right away. I checked with Warrant Officer Lattimer and he could deliver the first cannon the next morning, so I asked him to liaise with Faldingworth directly and arranged to meet Spike there the following week, asking also if I could I bring my group captain with me.

Chapter 17

Project Angel is Born

I imagined the Project Angel Oerlikon factory inspection would be something between a car MOT certificate test and an Automobile Association condition report for a prospective car buyer. When I got there, both Spike from Grantham and Martin from Switzerland were already present and they took Group Captain Gibson and I on a tour of the Faldingworth workshops. I was astonished to see three 6-ton gun mounts already stripped down to the bearing ring on the trailer chassis, with all the major components – the cannon, power ammunition feeds, control boxes, electric motors and so on – all neatly laid out on the floor, while at the workbench behind each gun three or four engineers in immaculately clean pale blue overalls were busy stripping down each major assembly into its individual component parts. I was quite taken aback and I think so was Group Captain Gibson, who anxiously enquired if the ammunition deal had really paid for all this very technical work to be done. I was saved from the need to gulp and flannel my way through this one by Martin Frey and Spike inviting us to a briefing, followed up by lunch.

Martin led the briefing. Starting with praise for the cleaning, de-rusting, greasing and painting already done by the RAF, Martin went on to explain that, given that the equipment had come off a pretty fierce battlefield, in order for Oerlikon to be satisfied that everything about the equipment was in order and safe, and that it would perform for us with the reliability the Swiss expected, it was necessary to strip down and inspect everything, right down to individual component level. Any part, no matter how small, that was less than functionally perfect would be recorded by individual part number, and from this, they would have an exact inventory and therefore cost of what was required to refurbish each gun. The same would apply to missing items which had been removed by squirrelling soldiers as trophies, such as gunsights and spares-cum-toolboxes, or parts that had been damaged in battle or by accident or neglect. Once the costed inventory was complete, the equipment would be reassembled back to the same level as the RAF had delivered it to them for the inspection. All this work, Martin explained, would enable the company to give us an exact cost, guaranteed to be without cost or time over-runs, and to deliver refurbished equipment back to us 'as new' with zero hours of run time and a full one-year warranty, as if we were the original buyers. And, of course, this would include all 144 battlefield spare parts and tool boxes to be carried on the generators of the twelve guns. The end result would be a formal costed proposal supplied by the company to enable an exact contract for parts, labour and warranty to be drawn up by the UK Ministry of Defence. The same process would be applied to the Skyguard radars and they would recommend the same scale of first, second and third level echelons of spares and tools as for the Argentinians, who had proved that the quantities were sufficient to fight a serious war with. Indeed, the scales recommended were common to both the Swiss Army and the other forty or so customer countries that had already bought the equipment.

At this point Martin enquired if we would like to send our fourteen Regular RAF personnel to Switzerland or have Swiss instructors come to the UK. Much as I would have loved two months in a hotel in Zurich, with all meals, travel and accommodation paid for, to do the training, it was obvious that the most economical option was to have the Swiss come to the UK because the instructors could be accommodated at the company facility at Faldingworth and they could easily travel to Waddington daily. That settled, I suggested to Gibson that we should go for a UK training and manuals package to be included in the overall refurbishment proposal so that we would have a single, so-called 'turn-key' contract cost to cover everything, which he agreed to. It was also a turning point in our relationship, for I sensed he no longer viewed me as a miscreant Cranwell cadet. Finally, Martin Frey made his day and presented Group Captain Gibson with a Swiss Army knife, tactfully visibly much larger than the one he gave me.

Back at the MoD, my service paper on the proposed formation of a new RAuxAF Regiment squadron to man the captured equipment at RAF Waddington had completed its circulation at wing commander level. It was now necessary to flesh it out in more detail, including a progress report on the conduct of the Feasibility Study. The paper at group captain level would include the expectation that the RAF would now get a £30 million squadron fully sustainable for ten years and equipped with refurbished and warrantied 'as new' battle-proven ex-Argentine radars and guns. Regular RAF personnel would be trained at minimal expense in the UK. Currently, the only unknown was the exact cost of the total project but it would be less than 10 per cent, i.e. no more than £3 million. The paper provided for Regular RAF personnel to train RAuxAF Regiment gunners and also to train RAuxAF tradesmen armourers, vehicle mechanics, generator mechanics, radar technicians, logisticians, clerks, a cook and even a medic. And, as a final cost-saver, the hundred or so personal weapons provided for them would be ex-Argentine rifles and machine guns taken out of the 10,000 or more left behind in the Falklands. Group Captain Gibson signed off the paper and it went on its rounds to all the appropriate group captains in the MoD Central Staffs, MoDUK(Air), Headquarters Strike Command for operational matters and Support Command for logistic and training matters.

In the month allowed for all the group captains to respond, it was time to address how this unit was to be funded, as clearly no directive from on high had anticipated the possibility of a new unit in the Annual Defence Estimates. The only possibility was the chimera of the so-called 'MoD Underspend'. If any MoD project was not running exactly to cost for any one of a hundred thousand different reasons, there would be small and large amounts of cash left unspent in the current year's allocation. Unlike a commercial business, which would simply leave the money in the bank, the Treasury claws it all back, thus reducing its borrowing needs for the following year. As a result, all government departments keep a close eye on the underspend pot and within their respective organizations develop priority lists of where such monies can be moved across projects and spent quickly against the year-end deadline. The absolutely critical factor to understand is that underspend cash has to be billed, processed and paid in the current financial year; there is absolutely no carry-forward. In parallel, the MoD bids for the next year's Defence Estimates have also to be agreed. Even at the height of the Cold War expenditure had to be constantly reviewed and either pruned back or increases authorized, usually more of the former than the latter. At the highest level, overrunning costs or a really big expenditure by one Service (like replacing the failed Nimrod AEW aircraft project with an off-the-shelf buy of the American Boeing 707 AWACS) could result in future cost cuts for the other two Services. Similarly, within each Service there would be competing demands that constantly have to be updated, fine-tuned and resolved. The plans and finance departments work these issues through committees and working groups attended by all the parties affected. As a staff officer, I attended a number of these scrutiny meetings as the aide to the Director or Deputy Director as appropriate. An up-and-coming underspend scrutiny meeting had been called to cull several millions off the wish-list bids which, naturally, exceeded the size of the pot available. Within days of the two-week Oerlikon factory inspection being completed, the final 'turn-key' price was in: £1.25 million, a third of what we had expected. And so, Group Captain Gibson and I prepared ourselves for this meeting, which was held at air commodore (One Star) rank level, with the group captain representing Director RAF Regiment and me as his aide.

On the day of the scrutiny meeting, the aim was to pare some £300 million worth of bids down to the £50 million or so of real money that was actually available. It was a fascinating exercise in the application of power and the ability of money to make things happen or not. In just a few minutes some MoD project might bear fruit immediately, while another might be postponed for another year, or years, or even for ever. I watched as millions of pounds on the hopeful list were pared down: £300 million, £294 million, £198 million, £75 million …

With the books just about balanced, the chairman then drew attention to the fact that whilst everybody present was there to cut the bids down, the contrary RAF Regiment, as usual, had brought their man along to slip in a new bid. The inter-branch bantering remark drew a little laugh and he allocated 2 minutes for everyone to hear out our case, pointedly sitting back to examine his watch. I had rehearsed for this moment over and over and quickly reminded the meeting that the government had committed itself to NATO to provide four more Rapier squadrons for the UK at a cost of £200 million[22] and, as was already clear from the bid cuts just agreed, that was just not going to happen. However, thanks to the Argentine defeat in the Falklands, they had not only abandoned £30 million worth of the latest Swiss, nearly brand new, all-weather Skyguard radar-directed Oerlikon twin 35mm anti-aircraft artillery that had done better than Rapier, but it had now all been recovered and cleaned-up at RAF Waddington. The equipment had just had a 100 per cent factory-level inspection at a cost of £100,000, which we got for free by horse trading some 2,000 rounds of brand new ammunition out of our £2 million stockpile of captured ammunition and we now had an accurate cost to refurbish everything to factory-new standard with a one year warranty that included all the spares, tools, technician and gunner training to launch an RAuxAF Regiment squadron with fourteen Regular RAF personnel and some 100 or so part-time Reservists, following-on from the success of our six other Reserve squadrons, all for a cost of just £1.25 million. So please, could we have £1.25 million in real money right now? Finally, Gibson drew the committee's attention to consider the following quid-pro-quo. Each airbase that fully met all of its NATO criteria, which included all-weather defence, qualified for a £100 million[23] infrastructure refund from the NATO budget. If the Argentine kit was declared as operationally available to the NATO order of battle for the defence of RAF Waddington, there would be a £100 million NATO refund to the UK Defence Budget. The group captain then went on to explain that he had personally witnessed the thoroughness of the survey and reminded the committee that the Argentinians had just paid for the work without knowing it, which drew a modest laugh. Everyone nodded their approval of £1.25 million for Project Angel and without further comment or ceremony proceeded to the next bid. It was indeed an exhilarating moment. A very pleased Group Captain Gibson reported back to the Director with the news that 'Fonfé's Mad Project' was now fully funded.

I rang Spike to tell him that I now had the cash to proceed with Project Angel, subject to the condition that all the work had to be completed, with bills presented to the Ministry of Defence and fully paid to Oerlikon, by 31 March. A meeting with Oerlikon as soon as possible was agreed but Spike said that I should first go to the factory at BMARCO immediately as they had something important to show me. He would not elaborate any further over the phone so I travelled to Lincolnshire once more.

At the BMARCO Faldingworth facility there is a 75m proof-firing range for quality assurance testing of ammunition lots of every calibre. The range is completely enclosed in a large concrete tunnel that I suspect once stored ready-to-drop hydrogen bombs. Now the far end was closed off by a solid block of steel that had once been the bow armour of the German pocket battleship *Tirpitz*. One of the Argentine cannons had been removed from its mobile twin mount and was now bolted down on a fixed stand, with sensor wires attached to various places along its length. I was invited to inspect the bore through a 10ft endoscope. The bore gleamed brightly, as good as any Bofors 40mm barrel I had inspected in my time as a junior officer in Belize, and I said as much. Not so, Spike explained. The Swiss were very unhappy. Could I look again at the tiny pockmarks of corrosion, which I did, and yes, I could see them; they were typical of a cannon in service. The Swiss disagreed and went on to say that throughout its life the barrel should be free of any pockmarking. They had tried every stiffness of wire brush and even chemicals to remove the pocks with corrosive chemicals. What to do? Being a soldier and not an engineer, I asked if they had considered firing a shell through the barrel; surely that would sweep the inside as clean as a whistle. Their reply was to express concern that resistance to the passage of the shell through the barrel might cause it to burst. The penny finally dropped: they wanted the MoD, aka me, to take responsibility for the possibility of a burst barrel. Also going through my mind was the sudden possibility that I might need to bring forward the twenty-four replacement barrels that I had factored in to budget for in about ten years hence. The concrete tunnel made the test safe from the worst possible mishap, so I made a squadron leader-like decision and ordered the Swiss to fire the cannon. We watched from behind a foot of armoured glass and naturally, to heighten the tension, there had to be a count-down: Three-Two-One-Fire!

After a flash and bang, the cannon was still there, barrel intact. The endoscope was produced and the inside of the bore gleamed even more brightly. I was content but the Swiss were not. The muzzle velocity of the shell was down by a third from normal; the shell had shed its copper driving band and had actually hit the armoured bow plate sideways. Again, they looked to me for instructions to fire more shells and suggested an operational burst, to which I agreed. The burst was duly fired and again the Swiss engineers pored over the results: muzzle velocity was now back up to par but the tiny pockmarks stubbornly remained. From my Bofors days I recalled that we retained a spare barrel which we would hold back for operational use only and would use older barrels for exercises and training. Not necessary, said the Swiss; their barrels were manufactured to last the entire operational life of the cannon, hence their unhappiness with pock-marks, however tiny. In the end, I said that provided the cannon hit their targets, I personally would accept the status quo and review the need for replacement barrels early, after say ten years of operational use, when we could fund new barrels if required. The Swiss nodded in somewhat unhappy agreement and we went our separate ways.

A week or so later, ahead of the next meeting between the Directorate and the company, Spike tipped me off that Oerlikon's head of quality assurance, who was also a senior commanding general in Swiss Army air defence, wished to meet the Director of the RAF Regiment, his opposite number, personally. Given the importance of the meeting, I decided I needed to upgrade the coffee break and brought in my silver service and best coffee cups from home and invested a couple of pounds in decent biscuits. What transpired between the two one-stars was that Oerlikon wished to make an immediate gift of twenty-four brand-new barrels to the RAF Regiment on the condition that if the cannon did not enter service, we should return them to the company. In a light-hearted parry, the Swiss said the gift was because the Argentinians had failed to follow their excellent Swiss training by not cleaning the guns after their last use. So, in the end we got new barrels for every cannon and I now had twenty-four barrels-worth of spare cash in my forward budget and the Swiss were happy because they were delivering truly zero hours brand new equipment to us.

On the MoD side I made a considerable effort to explain to the Swiss the workings of the British parliamentary system of fund voting and the significance of the end of the financial year. This was new territory to the Swiss, who by national nature were not given to debit budgeting and whose oil-rich customers always paid money up-front. If a customer country was short of cash, they would be directed to a Swiss bank for a loan and Oerlikon would still be paid up-front, in hard cash. Nevertheless, with the head of Oerlikon quality assurance present, the importance of completing the task in the financial year was taken on board. The task could certainly be done; all that was required was a written go-ahead from whoever would sign the contract. Clearly they were used to dealing with foreign military dictatorships, so some further explanation of the workings of the British MoD was required. Our RAF Director controlled no budgets; the financial procedures between air operations staffs, planning staffs, financial staffs and the Mod procurement executive were explained. The Swiss took careful notes and confirmed that for their part they could start work at once. Indeed, in view of the short time scale allowed, they felt that they really ought to have started work already; the plan was that the guns would be refurbished by BMARCO and the radars by another Oerlikon subsidiary, Contraves Gmbh in Bavaria, just across the border from their Swiss factory at Oerlikon, a suburb of Zurich. Before they departed, there was one other matter that had to be settled and that was the end user certificate. In view of Switzerland's neutrality, strict control was kept over sales of armaments. To ensure that Swiss equipment was not sold downstream to unauthorized customers, the Swiss retained a say over whom their equipment might later be sold to. None of the gun parts could cross Switzerland's borders without this certificate. They produced an example and asked if they might take a signed copy back. In the end, as I was the only one currently running this project and that as I personally had already done a cashless hundred-grand deal, I took another squadron leader-like decision and signed it, shook hands and hoped it would not come back to haunt me. It never did.

Back in the office, there was another two days' mainstream work to clear before I could address Skyguard again. There were now two immediate Project Angel problems. The first was to find a department in MoD(PE) to raise the contracts to actually spend the £1.25 million I had secured on paper. The other was that if we were to meet the underspend time scale, the radars would have to be pre-positioned in Germany. I decided to do the easiest task first. Movement of RAF equipment was the responsibility of the RAF Supply Branch, which kept track of the Air Force's entire inventory and moved it about; in service slang, the branch was split into bean counters and movers. The movers took pride in getting any-thing to anywhere,[24] so I consulted a mover of my rank in the MoD and he pointed me at a sergeant in the RAF section of NATO Rheindahlen Head-quarters in Germany, who only required a signal order from me to say where and when the equipment was to be collected from, its size and weight, and where it was going to, and ditto for the return journey. He would see to all the customs paperwork for crossing multiple international borders, cargo security in transit, the physical vehicle transport, convoy arrangements, driver accommodation and so on. In accordance with his instructions, I sent off a quarter-page MoD signal and it all happened. The next time I was to see the radars, they were all safely inside a Swiss factory in Germany. The difference between shifting kit as a unit commander and shifting kit as a staff officer was chalk and cheese; I definitely appreciated being a cheese for a change.

Finding an MoD(PE) department to take on the contractual responsibility for the captured equipment was by far the most difficult problem I had had to deal with to date. Because a normal MoD(PE) project spans such wide aspects as quality assurance, design approval, design control, acceptance-into-service, geo-graphic reliability trials in hot, wet, temperate and arctic conditions, spares, repairs and support-in-service, in contractual terms all these aspects are covered in a logical, set sequence that has been perfected over the years. Maximum rational-ization ensures that where more than one of the armed forces uses the same equipment, there is only one MoD(PE) department that buys it. So, in MOD(PE) the Army buys all vehicles, the Air Force all furniture and the Navy all food. Each Service contributes servicemen of appropriate specializations to each of the MoD(PE) departments, which are essentially run by civil servants. Notwithstand-ing the risks inherent in all three Services working on really big projects in the forefront of high technology areas, often where no man has been before, overall the system works well, avoids duplication and ensures both the armed forces and the taxpayer get best value for money.

My difficulty was that no radar-controlled anti-aircraft gun had been in terres-trial service since the 40mm Bofors gun was retired ten years previously. We had procurement executives for radars and for artillery pieces but there was no PE for a radar-controlled artillery piece. The start point for a suitable PE project manager was the fabled MoD Green Book, a confidential telephone directory including a potted summary of the terms of reference of every staff officer in the MoD. The Air Force's department of land-based radars looked most promising.

They dealt with everything from over-the-horizon missile attack warning radars, to long-range radars for directing fighter aircraft, to mobile, wheeled air traffic control radars not unlike the Skyguard. Preliminary enquiries looked favourable and I was passed up the chain of command to the one-star air commodore who was deputy head of the department. I suspect he was sympathetic to the requirement because I wore a light blue uniform like him. Not so his civil servant superior, who was absolutely adamant that because the radar was part of a gun weapon system, it was properly the responsibility of the artillery weapons department. In short, the Skyguard radar could not possibly be his area of responsibility. Period.

Off I went at the next opportunity to steal a spare moment in my day-to-day primary responsibilities to visit the PE heavy weapons department; at least they were sympathetic. Clearly such matters as cannon and their ammunition proofing were right up their street and while they were quite busy with several new items entering service, they were honour-bound to see to the gun aspects of the Skyguard-Oerlikon 35mm AA system. However, the radar was all 'wriggly amps' and thus outside their field of expertise. I would have to go elsewhere. Back I went to the Air Force radar department to propose that now they only had to look after the radar, not the guns. Absolutely not; his department could not countenance having anything to do with a radar which was, in his eyes, a subsidiary part of a complete weapon system. I then tried the Air Force's airborne radar department which, I reasoned, day-to-day dealt with radars connected to aircraft cannon and missiles. Request declined: my guns did not fly!

I was beginning to become an angry young man again, which might not do my career any good. Here I was, with over a million pounds in my budget and £30 million of hardware in my hands, facing a jobs-worth battle with civil servants outranking me by many pay grades. I decided to have one more go at the weapons end of the MoD(PE) spectrum, this time armed with a letter signed off by the Director RAF Regiment himself, to his opposite number in the heavy weapons PE. The post was at that time actually filled by a serving Army officer and I duly made an appointment with his PA. As I sat outside his office, that headmaster's study feeling flitted through my mind, only to be interrupted by a 'Hi Mike, what's our RAF Rapiercrat doing in the Army's Heavy Artillery Department?' It was Peter Woodger, our civil servant head of the Joint Army-RAF Rapier Guided Weapons Project, whose meetings I often attended in my main job. Briefly, I outlined my experiences and frustrations of the last four days. His reaction was magnanimous, to say the least. The problem was not a gun or a radar, he declared. As far as he was concerned, the Skyguard-Oerlikon combination was a guided weapon: the radar guided the gun at the target and the gun shot it down. He offered to take over the MoD(PE) responsibility for the entire system then and there and just asked for a couple of days to square it away with his junior minister. I never did get to see the heavy guns man and within a day Peter announced he was now my MoD(PE) project manager. I went in to brief my Director and told him we now had an MoD(PE) department to do our procurement. And the really good news was that it was the same department I already dealt with for Rapier.

In the meantime, all the other group captains had responded to our Deputy Director's iteration of my paper about the formation of a new squadron to man the Argentine guns. Nobody was against the idea and many had useful points to make, which had to be resolved to obtain full agreement. Then, my next task was to shorten and concentrate the facts and arguments in a paper not longer than eight pages for circulation to all the air commodores. This was to be the Director RAF Regiment's very last task before retirement and I arranged for it to be the very last document that he would sign as a serving officer, on his last day, in his last hour in the Royal Air Force, before Air Commodore Roy Strickland walked out of the Ministry of Defence Metropole Building into retirement, at the end of a distinguished career for a man who joined the RAF as a 14-year-old boy entrant in the Second World War.

About this time I was to acquire another ally in Project Angel: no less a figure than the Minister of Defence Procurement, Lord Trefgarne himself. Each year, in the inter-governmental exchanges of information, the British Government would inform the NATO Council of Ministers about their achievements (or otherwise) in meeting NATO force goals agreed within the Alliance. Because some assets, such as Rapier, had been taken out of the NATO order of battle in order to prosecute the Falklands Campaign, there was obviously a need to show NATO that the situation was being restored to normal as soon as possible after the event. If the Skyguard-Oerlikon system could be declared, then clearly the government would have demonstrated its resolve to meet its commitment to NATO. Most of this was all pretty high-flying stuff dealt with by civil servants who managed the higher strategic and political aspects of the MoD machine. To cut a long story short, the air commodore circulation was approved in a trice, and on that basis, Lord Trefgarne made an announcement in the House of Lords to the effect that 'plans were now in hand for the Royal Auxiliary Air Force to use captured Argentine anti-aircraft equipment'. It's not every day a lowly squadron leader's handiwork gets a mention in Hansard, let alone the House of Lords. My Mum was most impressed and thought perhaps I was right not to have joined the Royal Navy after all.

The end of the financial year, however, was marching ever closer. Having secured a slice of the underspend pie, I still needed the Air Force's own finance department to sign off that there was an operationally justified need for the money to be spent. This was probably the most critical governmental check-and-balance in the military system. Air marshals may decide they need this or that but built into the system is a core of hard-headed accountants who audit every intent for spending against laid-down objectives and priorities decided by each Service, the Ministry of Defence and Parliament as a whole. These financiers are experts in operational policy and priorities; they know little about the actual equipment and are solely concerned with the correctness of the spending in line with stated defence objectives. The nub of the problem was that, whilst a statement about the intended use of the Argentine equipment had been made in Parliament, was this a duly stated fact of Air Force policy? I could see a bit of 'Yes, Minister' entering my experience orbit. It was a chicken-and-egg situation because the Air Force Board, as the top uniformed part of the Air Staff for formally endorsing the creation of a new unit in its order of battle had not yet actually been consulted. With captured equipment, these two stages were out of step; nevertheless, in order to spend real money, all the ticks had to be in all the financiers' boxes before funds could be released; quite the opposite from the way the Oerlikons were purchased on the whim of a junta general who could sign a Swiss bank loan to buy 'his' fancy and then hand the problem of paying the interest and the bank loan back to his country's exchequer.

Happily, our new RAF Regiment Director, Air Commodore Dempster Anderson, waded into the problem with enthusiasm and irresistible charm. He took a whole day out from his new office to discuss the proper financing actions for the formation of a new squadron with the financiers. Here, he explained to the financial wizard, with charm turned up to 110 per cent boost, was a totally unique opportunity for the Royal Air Force to take a complete, ready-made weapon system straight into service without the MoD ever having had to spend a penny on the expensive preambles to a new procurement. What was needed was vision, flexibility of outlook and the breadth of mind to seize the advantage of this once-only chance of some much-needed and virtually free all-weather air defence. If a policy statement was needed, he would provide it; if a guarantee was required that the small number of Regulars needed to form the squadron would be found from within the RAF's current manpower ceiling, he would provide it; if confirmation was needed that the Swiss could undertake the work in the remaining weeks of the current financial year, he would provide it; whatever obstacle was offered by the financiers, the air commodore charmed it away. The clincher was that the equipment had been bought with the blood of more than 250 British servicemen who did not return from the Falklands; surely we could not dishonour them over a bureaucratic jobs-worth point of procedure. The very next morning the financier's formal release letter to spend the refurbishment funds were delivered to the air commodore's desk by courier.

At last, with the written financial approval to proceed with the refurbishment in hand, I rang the civil servant recently appointed by the MoD(PE) Guided Weapons Director as the Skyguard project manager. Tom was one of those mature civil servants not much impressed by exuberant young 'RAF crabs' stirring up work in the Army department and he popped my balloon with a laconic 'Oka-ay. Have you got the requisition?' I didn't quite twig at first and reiterated that I now had the Air Finance Department's approval to go ahead with the spend. He repeated the demand for a requisition, followed by a slowly delivered explanation that he could not write a contract to buy anything until the RAF handed him a requisition stating exactly what he had to buy in a contract. I protested that we already had a hundred-plus page itemized list of everything we needed, from the smallest screw to the last training manual, all provided by Oerlikon. No, that was a shopping list from the contractor, not an instruction from the Royal Air Force to buy it all, not an RAF requisition form 1234 (or whatever number it is). Not unexpectedly, my two follow-up questions were to ask which Air Force department might raise such a requisition and how long this all might take: 'Several months, maybe as many as six' was his reply. Now I understood the reason for his total lack of urgency. In MoD(PE) experience, *Mañana* was clearly an emergency and there was absolutely no chance of me getting the required paperwork done in the current financial year, let alone have a contractor complete the actual work. Trying not to show my frustration, I asked him to explain the entire paper trail between the requisition, the contract and the actual bill-settling payment to the contractor. 'Well, that would take some time,' he replied. My blood up, I told him I'd be there in half an hour, put on my running shorts, grabbed a pocket notebook and pen and ran the 6km to his office.

Mollified by a mug of MoD(PE) tea, I sat out his explanation, taking copious notes and making sure I had the correct MoD Green Book job title and phone number of every person in the emerging bureaucratic chain of events between the requisition and the contract. Byzantine would be an understatement: the RAF supply branch that dealt with radars would have to requisition the radar parts; the branch that dealt with mechanical armaments, i.e. everything from handguns to aircraft cannon, would have to requisition the gun parts. The requisitions then had to go to the finance branch to sign off that funds were authorized and agreed in principle to make the purchase; the MoD(PE) would then sign them to agree that they would now undertake the contractual arrangements and send the paperwork back to the finance branch who would in turn confirm that the earmarked funds were still available (and had not been hijacked by another Air Force department on a higher priority) and authorized the MoD(PE) to now go ahead and raise the contract to buy the goods and services on the requisition. Finally the draft contract would go back to the finance branch for final approval, whereupon the contract would then be issued to the manufacturer to deliver the goods. He ended by reminding me that if the work was not completed by the end of the financial year, there would be no money to pay Oerlikon and enquired, somewhat smugly, if I would like coffee instead of tea. Small wonder he was so relaxed, which only made me more determined to pull this off.

I ran back to my office, skipped the shower and stayed in my running kit, to much nose-wrinkling by my office mate, and called the first Green Book number in my notebook: the RAF supply branch in Harrogate, North Yorkshire. Over the phone they agreed to the urgency of my request and could raise the requisition right there and then but first needed to see the financial release letter that my Director had received. No, it was not good enough simply to give them a file reference, date, and name and appointment of signatory; it absolutely had to be the letter itself. I mulled this one over quickly: a day in the out registry, another day in the hands of the Post Office, another day in Harrogate being signed and stamped, yet another day in the post back to me ... lucky to be done in four working days. Maybe this was not going to work. I consulted the suppliers once more, who said that while they had to see the actual financial document, a facsimile copy would be acceptable as they had such a machine in their building. (Remember this was the early 1980s. A facsimile machine was a seriously expensive, large and slow rotary scanning drum device used by those in the news industry like Reuters to transmit photographs around the world, not the domestic cheap and cheerful machines we would all own at home a decade later.) They also mentioned that I could use such a machine belonging to their opposite number in MoD Main Building, and even offered to alert the operator to my priority need. With said document in hand, I literally ran over to Main Building in my running kit and sent my first-ever fax. However, because the return document, the RAF requisition form, was a formal, auditable financial document, that form had to be the original as it would carry the office stamps and signatures of each department that authorized each step in the process.

The original signed requisition document was in Yorkshire, and I was too junior a staff officer to order an MoD courier; it would also take me too long on a Friday afternoon to explain the need to the top of my command chain to get the necessary approval. A quicker solution was needed. Our regimental depot was at RAF Catterick, an hour's drive from Harrogate. What I needed was an RAF Regiment gunner-driver and a Land Rover pretty damned quick. It was time to call in a favour owed. I called a fellow squadron leader in command of a 164-man field squadron on a 'no names, no pack drill' basis: 'Could I borrow a gunner for a round trip between Harrogate and London, like right now, today?' The groan at the other end of the line was palpable. I recalled from my own experience in command the inconvenience and trouble caused by such requests to divert a man and a vehicle on an operational unit onto some no-notice staff officer's job on a whim; such demands usually came from a higher-ranking officer who had neglected to think ahead and hence had missed the schedule of a proper courier, so his poor time management would become our priority task. Yes, I knew it was Friday afternoon and yes, it was really important for the RAF, not for me personally, and don't forget the favour owed. I was asked for an hour's grace and five minutes later he rang back.

With laughter coming down the phone, I got my A-OK. One of his gunners had had a vasectomy on the RAF and now wanted it reversed. But the RAF only did one-way snips; reverse vasectomies were not counted as duty medical care.

Gunner X had a private appointment in Harley Street for his operation and would be delighted to get a duty 500-mile round trip for free, given that he was already shelling-out mega-bucks for the private operation. If I could send a priority tasking signal from MoDUK(Air) that would cover the squadron commander's vehicle authorization, copied to Command and Group Headquarters and the station commander, he could be on his way within 10 minutes. Said signal sent, I rang Harrogate; they had a man on the gate with the signed requisition to meet Gunner X and I had the document in my hand that evening.

On Monday morning I took the 05.30 train from home, presented the signed RAF requisition to the surprised finance officer, who signed and stamped it with the First Approval, ran over to MoD(PE) to have it signed and stamped by my equally surprised project manager, ran back to the even more surprised finance officer who signed and stamped the Second Approval, ran back to the now totally bemused project manager, who simply attached the full Oerlikon fully costed proposal as the draft contract, duly signed and stamped, then back I ran to the finance branch for their final stamped Third Approval, finally returning to the MoD(PE) for them to issue the contract. I then limped back to my office at the end of the day's half-marathon with my file copy of the BMARCO-Oerlikon contract, the other copies having already been faxed to Spike Jones in Grantham and Martin Frey in Switzerland. Once more showered and smelling like a rose, and back in my civil servant blue suit (we sadly don't wear uniform in the MoD, probably because it would show up how few of us there were amongst so many civil servants), I went in to see my Director to give him the good news that the refurbishment and training contract had been successfully let. The following morning the Swiss refurbishment team arrived at Faldingworth, along with the first four twin 6-ton guns and their generators trucked over from RAF Waddington. The job was on and with typical Swiss thoroughness, they set to work at once.

Chapter 18

Proof Test Firing at Manorbier

With just eleven weeks to go to the end of the financial year, BMARCO had their work cut out, as the contract also included a live firing demonstration of a refurbished radar connected to three refurbished cannon. We held frequent meetings to review the progress of work. BMARCO invited the three key MoD desk level players (me, Squadron Leader John Symonds and MoD(PE) project manager Tom McGann) to Zurich to inspect the progress of the Skyguard refurbishment across the border in Germany. Like the guns, the radars were stripped down mechanically, while all the electronic boards were taken out for factory quality assurance testing and bullet holes sealed and painted over once it was established that nothing was damaged between the entry and exit points. Any bullets lodged anywhere were also removed, lest they broke free later and caused foreign object damage to the radar. We also had a tour of the Oerlikon machine tools works, which was the heavy metal engineering department of the company that made top quality, large, machine tools much-prized in engineering workshops around the world. Being the manufacturer of machine tools, it was logical for the company to make armaments, particularly cannon, for which it became famous in the Second World War as the definitive Oerlikon gun manufacturer. The company takes its name from the Zurich suburb of Oerlikon, which is to Switzerland what Sheffield is to England and Sollingen is to Germany.

The factory was most impressive; everywhere in the works was immaculate and clean. The workers on the metal cutting, boring, grinding and turning machines all wore fresh, clean, white overalls over a shirt and tie. We watched a 35mm gun chassis being fabricated out of sheet steel on a huge engineer's plane table; the welder would do a welding run of about a metre, tap the slag off with a small hammer and then sweep it into a bin with a dustpan and brush, before welding the next stretch. When the workers broke off for lunch, they would go for a shower first, then have the same lunch in the same canteen as all the foremen and senior managers (hence the dress code of shirt and tie), and then go back to work in their clean overalls, fresh every day. Quality exuded everywhere; it was clearly a very wealthy, top-notch company which also owned Bally Shoes and Pilatus Aircraft, all renowned for product quality. It was all very impressive but as we were fielding a weapons system, it was clear that we wanted to see our refurbished equipment at work on our own territory and this required a UK ground-to-air range. Britain's wartime anti-aircraft range was located on a remote Welsh coastal cliffside near the village of Manorbier. In its heyday its throughput was a simultaneous live firing of up to thirty-six anti-aircraft guns in three tiers of twelve on the cliffside shooting at windsock targets towed several kilomtres behind the fastest aircraft in service. Now the site was in post-war decline, with only a few derelict, brick-built office buildings and unheated and unlit corrugated iron workshop hangars still standing. Its use now was limited to small numbers of shoulder-launched Blowpipe firings at radio-controlled model aircraft; however, the Royal Artillery confirmed that it still retained its full Second World War legal status as a declared danger area with powers to exclude shipping and aircraft from a space large enough to fire anti-aircraft guns up to 40mm in calibre. This could be made available for our 35mm live firing. I had in fact used the range myself during my earlier days of Bofors gun training and was very pleased to see that the range warden was none other than an old acquaintance from my Royal School of Artillery days, Master Gunner Roe. He in turn was quite excited to see real guns on his patch again, instead of the tiny spliff-like Blowpipe missiles fired off the shoulder of a single soldier. The RAF still retained a high-speed sleeve-towing capability with Canberra jet bombers and these could be made available for the proof firings, which were to be conducted as a company demonstration; the company would run the range, provide the safety equipment to ensure the guns could never be pointed outside the published danger area, and man the guns. My contribution would be to get the equipment to the range on the appointed day. The Argentinians generously provided the ammunition. As the day approached, Warrant Officer Lattimer at RAF Waddington arranged for the three guns and generators to be transported on low-loaders (as they had not yet been militarily taken on as legally registered for road use by the Army), while my part was to make a phone call and send a tasking signal to my RAF Movements man in Germany; that fixed the delivery of the radars directly to Manorbier and then their onward move back to RAF Waddington. The firings were to be witnessed by the AOC 11 Group, Air Vice Marshal Ken Hayr, under whose command all the air defence resources of the UK fell, plus the Commandant General of the RAF Regiment, Air Vice Marshal John Howe, also a distinguished pilot, plus all the key staff officers in the MoD that I had had to deal with to get this far. All of this organization fell upon Wing Commander Spike Jones, the air salesman of BMARCO, himself a well-known Hunter fighter jet pilot and former commander of the same 1 Squadron that had latterly flown Harriers in the Falklands. The official host for the firing was Major General Donald Isles, managing director of BMARCO; the head of quality assurance of the Oerlikon Group and part-time general in Swiss air defence, Herr Burghi, was also going to be there. It was going to be quite a high profile event and all I had to do was turn up with my clip-board to tick-off my instructor-in-gunnery check list that the equipment was going to do what it was supposed to do, i.e. shoot down target sleeves instead of planes.

In the event the whole show was very slickly executed, not surprising since all the employees at Oerlikon in Switzerland were lifelong Oerlikon gunners, commanders and officers in Swiss air defence regiments. Travelling down to Wales in civilian clothing, on the almost empty branch line train to Manorbier, I fell into conversation with another passenger who, from his dress, was clearly Swiss. He introduced himself as Herr Ziegentahler and turned out to be the commander of a Skyguard-Oerlikon unit in the Swiss Army, so we had a lot of common ground to chat about, as Switzerland was also in the process of buying Rapier. Later, talking to the Swiss refurbishment team who were to crew the guns for the live-firing, it turned out that Herr Ziegentahler was apparently the most pernickety fine-tuner of gun-radar alignment, bearing in mind the two were up to 500m apart, so much so that the tiniest tweak of adjustment was nicknamed a 'Ziegentahler' by the Swiss gun and radar crews. Soon I was to discover what this meant in execution-of-mission terms.

On the appointed demonstration day in March 1984, the Welsh weather did its usual thing and clamped down low over the hills, obscuring the mountains. Then the Canberra jet declared it too was grounded and that said goodbye to the target sleeves we were due to shoot at. Next the RAF executive jet that the military VIPs were due to arrive in could only get as near as Plymouth, so their journey had to be completed by a low-flying RAF air-sea rescue Sea King helicopter whistled-up at the last moment. As the weather was so awful, Spike suggested we started off with a ground-to-ground firing demonstration. Some 2,000m away they had set up a wooden, 1m cube, with ten mixed sheets of steel and aluminium spaced out vertically in the box to represent the various layers of internal construction of an aircraft. The first firing of the demonstration was a single shot from a single barrel of one of the three guns linked up to the Skyguard radar. There was a sharp crack from the gun and less than a second later a bright flash at the box target, followed by a 2-second delay for the boom of the explosion to reach us. The box was then brought to the assembled spectators and each person was given a totally shredded sheet of metal still smelling of explosive to inspect. For the next ground firing display the company whipped a tarpaulin cover off a detached Fiat G-91 fighter cockpit positioned even further away than the box target. This was to be a demonstration of the fire-power of a one-second burst by both barrels of a single gun mount, about thirty-six shells in all. This time, in place of a discernable bang, there was a roar from the 6-ton mounting vomiting empty shell cases forward of the cannon at a phenomenal rate, a straight line of white tracer to the target and a glitter of soundless explosions as the entire cockpit vanished from view. Ken Hayr's jaw dropped down in shocked surprise as the cockpit disintegrated. Again, the shattered remains of the cockpit were brought up close for inspection and I could see from the various pilots' faces an immediate appreciation that the twin 35mm Oerlikon was definitely not a Bofors pop-gun of their older generation of flying experience against flak.

Meanwhile, the Swiss, mindful of the vagaries of Welsh weather following a tip-off from Welshman Spike Jones, had arranged their own sleeve target towing aircraft, a company product, the Pilatus Porter. This was a super-short take-off and landing, rugged mountain and outback bush aircraft which I guess had probably brought the Swiss VIPs over by air. This aircraft was now invisible, somewhere overhead in the murk above, circling the range under the radar direction of the Skyguard, in ever lower passes. We were informed that as soon as the VIPs could see the sleeve target trailing several kilometres behind the Pilatus drop into sight out of the bottom of the cloud, it would be engaged by a radar-directed firing of all three twin 35mm Oerlikons. Sure enough, as soon as the bright orange sleeve appeared, there was a tremendous rolling thunder of gunfire and a pyramid of tracer rose from three corners of a kilometre square to come together in a pinpoint of glittering flashes on the sleeve target, followed by further, pale distant flashes a long way beyond the target as the remaining, un-exploded shells self-destructed to remove the danger of them falling amongst friendly troops below. The Pilatus then flew the shredded sleeve low over the VIPs, to drop it in front of the spectator line, while an operator popped out of the Skyguard clutching Polaroid snaps of the target kill photographed on the Skyguard TV tracking screen. The Pilatus disappeared into the murk above to stream another sleeve and to repeat three more cycles of target destruction. Altogether, four passes resulted in four destroyed sleeves dropped in front of the spectators and the Pilatus was out of targets. I think the RAF top brass now had a much better appreciation of what the 1 Squadron Harrier pilots had to fly though and the miracle that none of them was killed in action back in the Falklands in 1982. Indeed, the insanity of flying directly into heavy flak was taken aboard and the British were to follow the Americans towards the end of the Cold War in developing smart bombs with pinpoint laser accuracy that could be dropped from beyond the range of anti-aircraft guns and short-range missiles by the time of the First Gulf War, when Iraq invaded Kuwait.

If anyone had had doubts about the efficiency of this modern, up-to-date, leading-edge piece of anti-aircraft artillery development, it evaporated at the firing demonstration. Even Master Gunner Roe, who had lived a lifetime of Royal Artillery regimental level thirty-six simultaneous Bofors gun firings, positively glowed with delight that 'proper' guns were now back on 'his' range. At noon the air marshals flew off, leaving the rest of the MoD players with an opportunity to get right close-up and on board to play Star Wars with both the guns and the radar at passing seagulls. Many times over I was buttonholed to be told how they had not fully appreciated what a potent killing machine the Skyguard-Oerlikon weapon system was; this was to be a constant theme of conversation for the next decade that the equipment remained in service as the Cold War rolled to its end. As a final highpoint to the day, BMARCO had laid on a formal dinner for both the Swiss crew members and the MoD staffs, establishing a network of contacts for the future. As can be imagined, it was a very lively evening stimulated by the firepower just witnessed, as well as the culmination of nearly two years of preparatory paperwork and physical labour shared across a whole spectrum of individuals who would not normally come together in a social setting. I was very grateful to Spike and BMARCO for organizing it. I took the opportunity to remind all those in light blue that what they had witnessed this day was seriously expensive kit, in the ballpark equivalence in the cost-order of brand-new Harrier jets, only we did not have to spend it because the Argentine President, General Galtieri, had given it to us on a plate; we should not waste the opportunity and use it to our advantage. I think everyone present was fully on board. All that remained was for the Air Force Board to agree with us lesser mortals and sign the project off.

Chapter 19

Air Force Board Approval

Following the live firing demonstration, the Feasibility Study was over. The Skyguard-Oerlikon combination worked as fearsomely as it had in the Falklands. The bulk of the expense to launch a new unit in the RAF had been met by an effective and worthwhile 1983–84 financial year underspend and future small spending was now locked into the Air Force's main equipment programme. The way ahead seemed clear. Thanks to the Two Star witnessing of the proof firings, the Two Star level circulation of the proposal became the first draft of the four-page Air Force Board paper and was agreed to very quickly. Before anything could be put to the Board, however, the remaining major difficulty was now to identify where the manpower offsets for the fourteen Regular personnel required to be the command, maintenance and training core of the squadron were to be taken from. This might not sound like a great number of people, but with the Air Force already exceeding its manpower ceiling as authorized by Parliament, we could not hide this number in the adjustments of slack between new recruits and retirees on their last days of terminal leave. In order to close the over-manning gap, the Air Board Member for Personnel, Air Marshal Sir Peter Kennedy, himself a former RAF Regiment officer, had directed that no new tasks were to be created without showing exactly which current appointments had been cancelled in order to balance the manpower books. Thanks to the Falklands Campaign and the need to field an extra Rapier squadron on permanent station in the Islands, new manpower and equipment to fill the requirement had been authorized. However, due to the Falkland Islands garrison having only a few long-term, two-year appointments on the Islands, most of the manning there was achieved by the rotation of complete, ready trained and operationally worked-up manpower of whole units from the NATO front line. This was so much easier to execute since the RAF Regiment Rapier Force had been expanded by another four RAF Regiment Rapier squadrons formed to provide air defence of American airbases in the UK in accordance with NATO force goals. Indeed, as the RAF Rapier Force was now larger than the Army one, the RAF took over Rapier training from the Army as a cost-saving measure which, I am sure, increased inter-Service rivalry at the highest levels.[25] We were therefore able to use this 'ghost' Rapier squadron paper manpower as the offset for the new Skyguard squadron and could show this in the Air Force Board paper. However, because of the unusual nature of the formation of the Skyguard squadron, the Commandant General decided that the Air Force Board member who represented the RAF Regiment at Board level, Air Member for Supply and Organization Air Marshal Sir Mike Knight, should be briefed in person ahead of the deciding formal Board meeting. Sir Mike had been my former station commander at RAF Laarbruch in Germany at the height of the Cold War, sharply remembered for his short greeting words to our newly arrived Rapier squadron convoy paraded in front of him to take over air defence from the retiring Bofors gun squadron: 'Welcome to RAF Laarbruch, gentlemen. I have only one thing to say: if at first you don't succeed, you're sacked!' Bearing the air marshal's work ethic in mind, this presentation had to be a 110 per cent perfect and it fell to me to prepare it.

Obviously, with this extra load on top of my ongoing Rapier duties and all else that was going-on, I was under considerably more pressure than the rest of my peers and there was no way I could offload any of it to other officers as the project still carried its 'own time directive' and this was becoming a bit all-consuming. One day, while discussing Ordnance Board clearance of British-made Argentine ammunition not yet formally cleared for British use operationally[26] with the MoD(PE) civil servant armament specialist Brian Roberts, he introduced me to his attached service specialist, Armourer Sergeant Bernie Hughes, conveniently surplus to the RAF establishment due to the run-down of the Vulcan force at RAF Waddington. I asked him how this appointment had come about and he told me it was quite common; MoD(PE) would simply ring up the RAF personnel management centre and ask for the loan of specialists in particular fields for six-month or shorter-term tasks whenever something new and unknown to them came along. A light bulb immediately popped on in my head: I wondered if the personnel management centre would play this one for me and called them to ask if they had any ground radar specialists surplus that I could have in MoDUK(Air) to help me introduce the Skyguard radar into operational service. And so, in short order Chief Technician John Collins, a specialist in ground-based radars, turned up as available, pending promotion to flight sergeant. He was conveniently currently based at the RAF radar centre at West Drayton in London and quartered with his family at RAF Uxbridge nearby. As a further bonus, the Skyguard squadron radar technician establishment called for a flight sergeant, so Collins could, in theory, help me bring the radar into service and then be neatly put in charge of all the engineers on the squadron upon his promotion to the newly established post.

Coincidentally, many years before, John Collins and I had served together at RAF Khormaksar in Aden, but without ever meeting. We had in common the awful day when Aden's federal regular army, barracked on the airfield, had mutinied and were machine-gunning everything British in sight. It was my first day in Aden and as I emerged from the VC-10 to take over from Pilot Officer John Gatiss, I was greeted by a limping Gatiss, the heel of his boot having been shot off in the lively action that morning. More excitingly impressive than that, however, was his Land Rover, soon to be mine, sporting a fresh line of bullet holes beautifully stitched across the windscreen like a limo in a Chicago gangster movie. Some twenty-six soldiers had been killed coming off the RAF's on-base, 600m range that morning and Collins had been cowering on the floor of the Khormaksar air traffic control radar as mutinous bullets stitched the radar cabin in the same action. I was quite upset when the RAF vehicle mechanics insisted on replacing the windscreen on road safety grounds (in the middle of a shooting war?) and threw away the perforated one.

With that common experience, John Collins and I bonded quickly. He turned out to be a man of great initiative, who knew engineering in the Air Force inside out. To save generator running time, he acquired electric-to-electric generators which enabled the radars and guns to be plugged into the airbase's three-phase mains power network; this had the advantage of running guns and radars totally silently and much reduced jerrycan refuelling. It also reduced noise levels during maintenance in the workshop and for indoor training in our nuclear bomb bunker compound. Having seen the Oerlikon gun spares packaged in aluminium field containers, Collins found an Air Force department that manufactured similar cases for aircraft deployments and ordered bespoke sets of fly-away cases to be made for all the radar spares. Likewise, he was able to draw up lists of all the engineering tools, benches, cupboards and specialized extras that would make his workshop capable of undertaking even factory level repairs. Clearly, he was looking forward to being the engineering chief of brand-new, modern equipment on an independent unit. There was, however, one small downside to his 'assistant' status appointment in the MoD.

It had been assumed that it was only a matter of weeks before the new unit would be formed; as he was top of the promotion ladder, he would fill the next available appointment. When the weeks began to run into months over the man-power issue, it became clear that the Skyguard engineering vacancy would not be the first one to appear and he could be posted to the next available vacancy anywhere in the RAF. By now, he had his teeth well into Skyguard and had used the power of being in the MoD to fix and set up the engineering support with absolutely everything that he anticipated would be needed, well in advance of the as yet unknown formation date and was loath to swap this independent command for just another line engineer job in a large pool of 'techies' working a static rotation of narrow duties and responsibilities.

Luckily, he shared the morning train to work with our Director, who was able to square this problem away with the RAF personnel managers; the Catch-22 of the arrangement was that they could not promote and pay him in the higher rank until the new post existed and, therefore, at a personal level the delay was costing him a pay rise – but it was a gamble he agreed to take in order to land the plum job. I am pleased to say that three years later I was able to make it up to him after my command appointment, as in my next posting upon promotion, back in the MoD, I staffed the conversion of the single squadron into a wing of two squadrons by refurbishing more guns and buying two more radars to replace the radars wrecked at Goose Green. The new, expanded outfit would have a central-ized engineering set-up under a warrant officer, a unique post that John Collins was the only man in the entire Royal Air Force qualified to undertake. And so, without spending £100,000 on a Swiss-training for a replacement, a good man was to get early and just promotion to a warrant officer command appointment. The minus, of course, was that as 'Chief Penguin', he would continue to be surrounded by even more male and female 'Rock Apes' and would have to wear olive greens and boots for nearly a decade.

I was to be equally lucky with radios and transport. On the radio side, the Army was in the process of making a large Falklands-driven purchase of the then new Clansman radios to replace all those left in theatre by units which formed the initial garrison, as well as to replace those lost on the MV *Atlantic Conveyor*. I was able to include our full radio scale in this buy on the Falklands budget, which meant our new unit would start life with the latest brand new radios, adding high reliability and low maintenance as everything worked, fresh out of the manufac-turer's box, with a one-year warranty. None of my radios would be inherited, decade-old, tired, bashed-up and been-everywhere bits of kit.

On the transport side also, changing requirements in the Army had led to a sig-nificant number of brand new 8-ton trucks being stored in the war maintenance reserve and these were available for immediate delivery, so our entire transport fleet was also brand new. In my Bofors gun days we towed our guns with the 1950s standard 3-ton truck, the petrol-engined Bedford RL four-by-four, a rugged, simple and easy to maintain truck with a crash gearbox and no power steering. By the 1980s the RL would only be seen during firemen strikes in the guise of Green Goddess Civil Defence fire engines. The Bedford RL was replaced by a four-by-four version of the commercial Bedford MK, nominally rated at 4 tons, and so the four of these we got were earmarked for towing the 2-ton gun generators.

The 8-ton Bedford TM, by contrast, was designed from the wheels up as a go-anywhere, off-road artillery tractor with a mighty turbocharged diesel engine and a six-speed gearbox that could cruise the motorways with a gun or radar under tow, alongside all the articulated trucks, keeping up a steady 70mph up hill and down dale. With power steering and loads of reserve power, they were a joy to drive on and off-road, so much so that all the Regulars, including myself, would vie with each other to drive one. We had four cargo 8-tonners so that we could tow a complete fire unit of one Skyguard radar and three twin 35mm cannon into the field, the three smaller Bedford MK 4-tonners bringing-in the generators and their fuel, all in one convoy packet of seven trucks and trailers. We had two further 8-tonners: a flatbed with an on-board hydraulic crane for bulk delivery in the field of heavy 35mm ammunition and the other one fitted with a rescue towbar and a front and back winch with which to recover vehicles and trailers in the field. A shuttle run of all our trucks could then deploy the remaining fire units from our on-base storage bunkers and build up the air defence of RAF Wadding-ton in a matter of hours. For convoy deployments further afield, we planned to use the services of the go-anywhere RAF 2 Transport Squadron, supplemented by additional 8-tonners on loan from other units for a specific move.

With the future squadron armourer in MoD(PE) and the future radar engi-neering chief with me in the MoD, a lot of preparatory work was taken off my shoulders. Nevertheless, the days and weeks and then months dragged slowly because the manpower offset required the highest level formal decision not to raise another Rapier squadron to cover the Falkland Islands rotation on a trickle posting basis because, unlike other RAF branches, including aircrew, we rotated complete, operationally ready, formed units. At last, the decision was made not to man-up another Rapier squadron and so I was able to assign fourteen of the cancelled 121 Rapier squadron posts as a direct, *bona fide* manpower offset for the new unit and we could go ahead to deliver the final four-page Skyguard-Oerlikon paper to the Air Force Board.

We practised our Air Force Board level verbal briefing on the Deputy Director and the Director before presenting it, with a Ziegentahler or two of fine tuning, to the Commandant General. The Commandant General, the Director and myself were then summoned to give the briefing to the Chief of the Air Staff, Air Chief Marshal Sir Peter Harding, in person. The presentation went very well and we handed over the Air Force Board paper for formal Board approval. In the event we did not have to wait long as Sir Mike Knight circulated it to the other Board members and they all agreed to it out of committee and that was that: the Holy Grail was secured, not with a bang, but simply with a tiny slip of paper.

FORMATION OF ROYAL AUXILIARY AIR FORCE SQUADRON
TO OPERATE SKYGUARD

You will wish to note the Air Force Board has agreed to a formation of a Royal Auxiliary Air Force unit to operate Skyguard anti-aircraft artillery equipment. NATO will be informed on Tuesday 18 December and the Press release made on 19 December.

Signed
Personal Secretary to
Air Member for Supply and Organization

Fig. 18. The Holy Grail of December 1984.

With formation of the new squadron agreed, it was time to choose its number. Squadron numbers are to the RAF what regimental titles are to the British Army and ship's names are to the Royal Navy: identities that command loyalties and possibly demand the ultimate sacrifice in continuation of their forebears' sacrifices in bygone battles. These past achievements provide the ethos for the current unit members not to fail the benchmarks set by their predecessors. Maximum loyalty is most commonly given to one's very first squadron appointment as a junior officer and next as a squadron commander, most often an independent command on some challenging rotational operation somewhere troublesome in the world. As the new unit was to be part of the Royal Auxiliary Air Force Regiment, there was already a dichotomy as to who would have the lead in choosing the number: the RAF Regiment or the RAuxAF. As an additional consideration, all RAuxAF units, being founded in the civilian community as reserve units, had the place names of where they were raised associated with them.

There are other protocols associated with squadron numbers: after five years of service operational units are entitled to choose a heraldic squadron badge, to a design approved by the sovereign, and after a further twenty years of existence are also entitled to a squadron standard, equivalent to Army regimental Colours, upon which the squadron badge and any battle honours would be embroidered in silk by hand. Standards, like Colours, are consecrated devices, subject to special care in safekeeping and only handled with white gloves upon the orders of the squadron commander. They are paraded for Guards of Honour, formal parades and formal dinners by a guarded standard-bearer and only dipped in salute to royalty. Around this time I was informed by the Director that since the squadron was my brainchild, I would be awarded command of it. Not every squadron leader gets to command an operational RAF Regiment squadron twice in their career and to do so would be a very great honour indeed. It also motivated me to research and properly staff the choice of a number and name for the squadron.

Under RAuxAF Regiment precedents, the squadron would have taken the next number to follow on from the existing six squadrons and become 2628 (East Midlands) Squadron. I definitely could not see anyone wanting to die for the East Midlands and so instead I invoked RAF Waddington's very strong historical precedent of 1940, in that it had been home to the twenty-ninth newly formed RAF ground gunner squadron as 729 Squadron RAF, which then morphed into 2729 Squadron RAF Regiment on 1 February 1942, upon the formation of our Corps. With five years of Second World War service, 2729 would be immediately entitled to its own squadron badge and probably at least two battle honours. That left the unit title. An RAuxAF Regiment field squadron, 2503 (County of Lincoln) Squadron, already existed at RAF Waddington. With the city of Lincoln so closely associated with RAF Waddington, the cathedral being the central motif of the station badge, I asked the Inspector RAuxAF to approach the Mayor of Lincoln for a formal territorial association with the city. This was agreed and so the new, formal title of the captured ex-Argentine Skyguard radars and Oerlikon guns of GADA 601 became 2729 (City of Lincoln) Royal Auxiliary Air Force Regiment.

With 2729's official formation on 1 April 1985, my days in the MoD were rapidly galloping to a close and I finally escaped in the new year of 1985 to go to Waddington to set the unit up on the ground and have the Swiss conduct and complete our formal, contracted training before Formation Day. At RAF Waddington I was allocated a beautifully refurbished married quarter in the senior executives' quadrangle of the base, close to the officers' mess and opposite the main guardroom; this was the best married accommodation I had ever been given. It was wonderful to be a squadron commander again for a rare, second time and be in possession of all-new everything on the RAF's soon-to-be most important air defence airbase. And, as everything Oerlikon came in twos, my wife and I were to have two more children born in Lincoln during my time in command.

Chapter 20

The New Squadron Forms

The squadron was very lucky with its technical accommodation. RAF Wadding-ton had allocated the squadron the recently vacated and very secure former nuclear weapons storage site, which was conveniently just off-base, alongside the A15 main Lincoln to Sleaford road, just where the greatest number of aircraft enthusiasts would gather to watch aircraft coming and going at Waddington. The accommodation had enough room for us to share it with our sister Auxiliary infantry squadron, 2503, which moved in from RAF Scampton as that base was closing to be sold off. It consisted of a long line of super-hardened bunkers with a very high security fence enclosing the entire compound. Each gun or radar, together with its crew and all the associated accessories and field equipment, could be housed in an individual steel-fronted bunker. This made security, control and inspection of all equipment very easy and furthermore gave each Auxiliary junior commander full charge of his or her own individual secure space.

I wanted as much of the unit as possible to be prepared to function opera-tionally from day one. The personnel management centre organized the early arrival of all of my men, starting with my supplier, essentially the squadron store-man. Corporal Ralf Clements had already served on a Rapier squadron and was very practically orientated to field operations. He was also one of those rare storemen who believed that if the RAF stocked something and the squadron needed it, he would find a way to get it. What he did not know about the supply system was not worth knowing and he soon became 'Mr Fixit' as far as logistics was concerned. To him fell the task of ordering all the equipment for field opera-tions from combat clothing to picks and shovels, from tents, sleeping bags and field catering cookers to camouflage nets, from Best Blue uniforms right down to green underwear, green tea towels and green aprons for the chef, not to mention high value items such as binoculars, compasses, wrist watches, night-vision goggles and infrared weapon sights, plus combat webbing for a hundred soon-to-be auxiliary part-time volunteers. Unlike the Argentinians, we had full cold weather kit right from the start, to reflect the outside weather aspects of sitting on a 6-ton iron heat-sink of a cannon day and night in a Lincolnshire winter.

About this time I was to order myself an extra production-run of the aircraft recognition training material I had invented at the Royal School of Artillery. Along came 4,000 35mm colour slides and several hundred A1-sized aircraft recognition training posters, all sporting little bald eagle heads. It was, however, disappointing to find that there were no pin-up pictures included free with this lot. Perhaps the Soho photo-lab had heard we were recruiting females and that such material would now be most inappropriate. The station education officer also came over to assess our training support needs and agreed to furnish us with four excellent portable videotape recorders and cameras that we could fit, one to a Skyguard and one each on its three guns, and thus do real-time analysis of the training effectiveness of each crew element working together over a widely dispersed fire unit area. It was also good for operational feedback when debriefing aircrew, to show them that weaving about did not put a gunner off his aim and that it was more effective to fly routes so low that they could take advantage of visual screening by rising ground, trees and buildings. However, actually doing all this was still some way off, so we used the video kit to record the build-up of recruit selection and training first.

Just as the remainder of the squadron's Regular personnel were starting to arrive at RAF Waddington, the RAF's in-house newspaper, the *Royal Air Force News*, ran a front-page article about the formation of the new unit. 'Great Guns!' boomed the headline. For the next few weeks every one of our fourteen Regulars going through the base arrival procedure had to sign into their respective messes, clothing stores, the RAF police, the education section, the physical fitness flight, the medical and dental centres, the padre and pay accounts and so on, to be greeted with 'Oh, we read all about you in the *RAF News*', which was definitely good for morale and we probably all got better attention as a result.

The start point of all our activity was to take over the empty, and formerly the most secret location on the entire base, which for security reasons had been totally swept clean of every single stick of furniture; not even a paper clip remained. There was also only one telephone in the entire complex and to get it to my future office we had to run a long illegal lead from office to office, until additional telephones could be installed several months later by British Telecom, who then still worked at a snail's pace of a nationalized service. Also, thanks to the *RAF News* article, we were to be inundated with 'official' visitors on an almost weekly basis. Compared to the activity now taking place in the squadron compound, the MoD was beginning to look like it had been a very relaxing place to be. Thankfully, into this mêlée of activity, my fourteen hand-picked men set to with a will. In addition to my chief technician, soon-to-be Flight Sergeant John Collins, my three RAF Regiment flight sergeants arrived together: 'Big John' Kavanagh, so-called because he bore a close resemblance to John Wayne, was a respected Bofors gun commander from my independent command days in Belize; 'JR' Alec Bolding, so named for his uncanny likeness to a certain oil magnate in the TV series 'Dallas', who had served with me in Germany as a Rapier commander and later as my 81mm mortar line commander; only Steve Coupe, 'Mr Fitness', was unknown to me. He had come to us as the hard man from our elite parachute squadron because his hearing had been affected by aircraft and small arms fire noise and he could no longer serve in the infantry; so, with the unfathomable wisdom of our personnel management centre and RAF medical services, he was posted to my anti-aircraft squadron, which had the biggest cannon and provided the loudest bangs in the Royal Air Force. Between these three 'Rocks' and the engineer John Collins, I had a really strong leadership, management and training team all rolled into one. Only in my Regular officer was I disappointed; I had hoped for an experienced senior flight lieutenant instructor-in-gunnery, who only needed this tour to be promoted to squadron leader and hopefully take over the squadron from me. Instead, I was given a very young, wild, red-headed Irishman, Flying Officer Davey Johnston, the excuse being that there was a shortage of instructors-in-gunnery due to the expansion of the Rapier Force and, as I was an IG already myself, I could cover that aspect. It was a bit like saying that a transport squadron could do without a heavy goods vehicle driver because the boss had an HGV licence. Luckily, Davey was exceptionally quick to learn, had that wonderful, intuitive Irish ability to get on well with everybody, and had boundless energy and initiative, rising to take on a huge span of duties and responsibilities that he would not have found as a second-in-command of an already established Regular Rapier or field squadron. I very quickly came to depend upon him totally.

Then came Sergeant Gerry Matthews, the quietest man on the squadron, to look after the maintenance of all our trucks, trailers and Land Rovers: a total of 172 wheels. Of all the men on the squadron, he was the borderline one, workloading wise. The strict scaling formula for the number of technicians needed to maintain a vehicle fleet of a certain size meant that the job really needed more than one but was not quite enough for two. What the formula did not take into account was the weight and size of our radar and gun trailers and the fact that they were all four-wheeled heavy trailers, rather than lightweight two-wheeled ones. As a result, we found Gerry was well overworked, not immediately I might say, because he worked so unassumingly every day-off and at the weekends, when he was not directly involved in part-time training. The reason for his work overload was periodic servicing. Irrespective of how many kilometres each truck or trailer did, on the heavy vehicles the schedule involved removing, degreasing and regreasing every single wheel bearing, all 172 of them, every six months.

At that time, the base transport maintenance flight had a very pushy factory-foreman, union-minded, fellow in charge, who was very keen to sweep up our vehicles into his maintenance workshop in the certain knowledge he could fatten his manpower establishment. However, I refused to give up my transport independence as I knew from experience how inflexible this lot were, demanding to take a vehicle away in the middle of an exercise, or not servicing it but keeping it off the road anyhow because another, higher priority, vehicle had just jumped the servicing queue. I solved Gerry's problem in the short term on the basis that while we still did not have Auxiliary crews to man all the guns and generators,

I would simply mothball six to eight guns and generators and that reduced Gerry's overload until I got an extra Regular technician established at the six-month review of our manning. There is no comparison between the quality and flexibility of delivery of service of a specialist on a squadron compared to a large, centralized, union-minded base workshop serving hundreds of vehicles. Gerry was the most uncomplaining, quietly meticulous motor engineer I knew and he was worth his weight in gold dust to maintain the full independence of my vehicle fleet, keeping it totally separate from those of our parent base.

Next in were my three Regular corporals. Wilson, my clerk, was responsible for all my files and documents in a registry and for all the attestation, pay and discharge administration, plus the typing-up all the orders, instruction, training analysis, course design, course material and training programmes and records. His start point was an empty office, devoid even of a blank sheet of paper; however, starting from scratch, he was to prove a very on-the-ball administrator and would have made an excellent detective. Indeed, that is exactly what he wanted to be. On being interviewed by a civilian police force as an 18 year old, he was told to go out and get some real-life experience, which he did by joining the RAF – and here he was. Well, I can certainly say we broadened his experience by becoming an Oerlikon gun commander and instructing Auxiliaries, as well as gaining a huge span of interpersonal skills and administration, recruiting and training skills, so that after two years he got his wish and became a policeman, which is why I always still call him Wilson. Besides all those positive traits, his typing was awful. Knowing that my initial administrative load would be very high at unit start-up, I had included a second airman clerk in my establishment, the only non-ranking person in my fourteen Regulars: John Duffy, our youngest and most junior member, arrived as a leading aircraftsman straight out of clerical training which, unbelievably, did not include keyboard typing skills. This was 1982; we still used typewriters for letters, maximum three carbon copies, plus a Gestetner duplicating machine and waxed paper masters for printing anything in more than three copies. The final whammy for me with young Duffy, however, was that having invested all that Oerlikon training in him, plus teaching him to type and teaching him to drive a Land Rover, he was posted from us after just one year upon promotion to senior aircraftsman, now being deemed sufficiently experienced enough by the 'system' to be appointed as a 'proper clerk' in a large registry. It seemed to me I was running a nursery school for would-be policemen and clerks. Not only that, young John took away one of our carefully recruited and well-trained part-time alpha female gunner-girls, Trish Ryan, and married her. Thus, at a stroke I lost two fully qualified, part-time Oerlikon gunners.

Back to the Regular corporals: lanky Ron Holmwood was John Collins' radar technician and a wily reader of human character, whose dry wit popped many an egotistic balloon, especially RAF Regiment ones, once he had become a qualified Oerlikon gun commander in his own right. Being the only other radar technician on the squadron apart from Collins, he was largely left to get on with the electronics, which necessitated him staying cleaner and drier than most people on the squadron, even though he had to wear boots and greens all the time. He was backed up by his semi-electronic co-worker, the easy-going Steve Hamilton, who looked after the generators: one side of the generator was a Porsche flat-four racing car engine, and on the other end was a massive electricity generator. Because Steve was so good at rebuilding the engines from complete strip-down, we got all our generator engine spare parts directly from the local Volkswagen dealership in Lincoln, rather than from Oerlikon. Sadly, none of us could afford a Porsche car at the time, as it would have been lovely to have a personal Porsche car mechanic in-house. And being an electrician as well meant that Steve could handle Collins' electric-to-electric generators, not to mention all the Land Rover, truck and trailer electrics and also fix up wonderful lighting for our squadron social events. Finally, there were the armourers: Sergeant Berni Hughes and Corporal Paul Knott. Berni was the Spike Milligan of the squadron; in terms of engineering, the pair probably had the most complicated mechanical, electrical and hydraulic machinery on the squadron to look after: the biggest cannon in the Air Force, the Oerlikon twin 35mm guns. I guess after being responsible for atomic bombs, Oerlikons were toys to Berni. However, the ease of operation of the Swiss cannon mount should not be mistaken for simplicity of engineering component complexity. Paul Knott was Hughes's right-hand armourer; as a true Liverpudlian, he spoke a dialect of English that I, as a colonial brought up in flat South African English, simply could not understand and I needed Berni as a translator to decode all our social and military conversations. Paul was also the most unmilitary of all our Regulars, who gradually, by osmotic exposure to highly enthusiastic Regulars and the Auxiliaries, absorbed and then radiated our ethos to became one of the most respected best. Thirty years later I was to receive a wonderfully heart-warming letter from him, thanking me for turning his life and career in the RAF around and informing me that he had just graduated from university. Thirty-five years later another ex-Auxiliary, Peter Lavelle junior, butcher's apprentice and son of a Parachute Regiment dad, Peter, who was also a squadron member, would meet me in Australia, where he was now Head of Training for Hitachi heavy earth-moving machinery for the Far East, and thank me for his technical, leadership and training skills acquired as an Oerlikon gunner that ultimately led to his position in Hitachi.

Probably one of the best decisions I made in my entire command was to treat the Regular manpower of the squadron as the crew of a warship, so that every man could do more than just his primary trade. In the contract with BMARCO I arranged for all fourteen Regulars to be trained as Oerlikon gunners and Skyguard radar operators, irrespective of their RAF formal trade specializations. Naturally, the RAF Regiment flight sergeants, whose core profession it was, would be trained to the next higher level as formally qualified instructors, as would the various engineers to maintain the guns and radars within their specializations, bearing in mind that they too would be required to train their own part-time support personnel. The effect of the common training was four-fold. First, it brought everybody together as a team. The mechanical transport sergeant, the corporal supplier, the corporal clerk and the corporal armourer could all crew, command and fire a fully manned Oerlikon gun between them, whilst the radar and generator technicians and the non-typing squadron typist could crew the Skyguard radar and fire three Oerlikons remotely. Second, whenever an equipment demonstration was required, it was easy for a skeleton crew to roll out a gun and radar at short notice and with minimum diversion. We were called upon to do so many displays that the airmen nicknamed the exercise 'Rent-a-Radar'. There were two levels of squadron visitor hosting: 'Coffee Mug Jobs' or 'Silver Coffee Pot Jobs', depending on the status of the visitors. Third, it demonstrated to us, and indeed, to all of the RAF Regiment, that if non-technical personnel such as clerks, storemen, medics and cooks could be trained to operate high technology weapons systems in a matter of weeks, then training civilians from every walk of life should be no difficulty either. Finally, fourthly, just as soon as the Swiss training contract was fulfilled, we could actually deploy a complete Skyguard-Oerlikon fire unit operationally and could rapidly expand training in parallel on the remaining fire units to reach NATO operational status as quickly as any Regular unit. We see this back-to-front kind of training in Ukraine, where it demonstrably outperforms Russian conscript training at every turn.

The major activity during these pre-formation months was the contracted Skyguard-Oerlikon training. All other activities had to be fitted in around it. The Swiss duly dispatched a troupe of young, fit instructors, all of whom were also part-time anti-aircraft gunners in the Swiss Army, and they were to teach us all there was to know about the equipment – which was quite a lot, to say the least. All the training was done outdoors. Waddington in January and February that year experienced one of its severest winters ever, so we did all our gun drills out in the snow, just to make the Swiss feel at home.

Humour lightened the training hugely with our exposure to Swinglish, the Swiss interpretation of English idiom. Our two side-splitters were 'You put the cable up the backside of the radar like this' and 'Feel the wind from the backside of the generator with your hand over there.' Other titbits of Swinglish were quite trying. One instructor was in the habit of saying 'You stupid' when a mistake was made, especially when addressing Davey Johnston or Steve Coupe, whereas we would say 'That's incorrect. Watch me and do it this way. Got it?' Being instructors, the Swiss loved to reel off critical dimensions for deployment. For example, the maximum cable length of the gun generator was 80m and this would be paced out meticulously; ditto, the maximum displacement of each gun from the radar was 500m and this too had to be paced out or identified clearly from a large-scale, detailed map. On our first day Lesson One began with the generator, since power made the deployment of the 6-ton gun a breeze. We duly measured out the 80m from the gun, unhooked the generator from its towing truck and rolled out the cable, to find ourselves 10m short, earning the first 'You stupid' of the day. We rolled the cable back in, hooked up the generator to the truck and swept round to repeat the drop-off, cable roll-out – and again ended up 10m short, for another 'You stupid' comment. Determined to show us fairly mature officers and senior NCOs were lacking up top, he then produced a tape measure to demonstrate why we were so dumb and sure enough, the measure told no lies: this generator cable was exactly 70m long. A check of all the other generators showed they all had 80m. It then came to light that during the refurbishment at Faldingworth, one of the generators had turned up with a frayed cable end; an engineer had run the cable out to check it for damage and, finding none, simply replaced the missing plug at the end and rolled it all back. That generator belonged to the Oerlikon gun that had been turned over by one of the random bombs dropped on Stanley from 20,000ft, ripping 10m off the cable. We got less 'You stupid' after that and, in fact, to be honest, the training was superbly done and we soaked it up like thirsty sponges.

Mid-course, we were to have some light relief. Under tri-Service rationalization, the issue of military registration number plates falls to the Army and all trailers receive their own unique registration plates, following the custom of the Germans, where most of the British Army had been garrisoned during the Cold War. British military number plates consist of two digits, two letters and two more digits. A crate of new number plates duly turned up for the radars, guns and generators and it was left to us to physically allocate them to the individual trailer-mounted equipment. Here, then, was a wonderful opportunity to line things up in a neat sequence. Gun 00CV01 could go with generator 00CV11, gun 00CV05 could go with generator 00CV15, and so on. 'But why CV?' I enquired of the Army. '"Captured Vehicles", old boy! Haven't issued any of these kind of number plates in years. Thank you General Galtieri' came the reply from the ecstatic elderly civil servant.

Parallel to our intense, team-enhancing training, which was going apace, we were discovering one of the disadvantages of being issued with bulk orders of equipment. For example, if one ordered a tent, one got a tent neatly packed in its travel bag, complete with poles and pegs and liners. Order twenty tents and you get a 2-ton crate of canvas, a 1-ton crate of 200 poles and another 1-ton crate of pegs, all of which have to be unpacked, laid out indoors in the dry and assembled into complete tents: just another job for all-hands-on-deck between training. Even worse was combat webbing. A hundred belts had to be hooked-up to 200 ammo pouches, 100 yokes and 100 sleeping bag holders. On the other hand, all-new kit provided the opportunity to number-stamp every bit of field equipment from shovels to cooking pots with the number of the gun or radar to which it belonged, and that made post-exercise cleaning-up and accounting for loose equipment so much easier; the same with clothing, towels and especially sleeping bags. I knew from experience how even officers could, unintentionally, in the field pick up another man's unmarked kit and thus undermine comradely trust more quickly than stealing money.

By February, as part of our publicity campaign building up to recruiting our first part-time Auxiliaries, we held a press day at Waddington and invited the local and national press and television to attend. Martin Frey had generously arranged for some break-up shot ammunition. This is a special sort of disintegrating blank ammunition where the live shell is replaced by a plug of compressed metal powder which disperses into a cloud of dust as soon as it emerges from the barrel. This generates just enough gas pressure in the gun to operate the automatic fire mechanism. To a gunner on the gun, and to spectators, the gunfire looks, sounds and smells just like the real thing. One day, when I was a student at the Royal School of Artillery, the staff carried out a firing demonstration of a pair of Bofors guns at Larkhill and the instructors accidentally loaded solid shot instead of break-up shot. The shells from a long and impressive burst flew over from Larkhill to come through the roof of a building at the sister garrison at Bulford Camp, 16km away, causing the infantry brigadier to call the artillery brigadier to say 'I surrender. What the hell is going on?' Since then, I have always been extra careful to check the correctness of every kind of ammunition before firing it.

For the press day, a Tornado was tasked to make a high-speed 'attack' at low level. Just as it appeared on the radar screen, the generator ran out of fuel (we were, after all, still trainees!). Luckily, we had deployed a second radar next to it in order to double our throughput of visitors wishing to look inside one, so our quick-thinking Swiss instructors switched cables to reconnect the guns to the other, working Skyguard just in time to fire at the Tornado as it burst into sight in front of the spectators. As with all our firings, the ferocity and noise of the twin guns firing and the vomit of empty shell cases caught out the inexperienced in jaw-dropping shock and awe. We got great television coverage on both TV channels that evening and all the local papers and some national ones carried good stories in the next day's issue. RAF Waddington also received its first noise complaint from the city of Lincoln since the retirement of the mighty Vulcans in 1982, the continuous roar of three cannons, each with two barrels, being clearly audible 10km away. The publicity paid off and a flood of phone enquiries to join the squadron poured in.

In the middle of our training course we learned that our planned live-firing slot at Manorbier had been subsumed by a British Army trial of the Marconi Marksman flak tank which, incidentally, sported a pair of 35mm Oerlikon cannons just like ours. The search was on, therefore, for an alternative artillery range. Eventually, the Royal Navy came to the rescue and allowed us to use Wembury naval gunnery range at HMS *Cambridge*, just outside Plymouth. The place looked like the film set for the movie 'The Guns of Navarone'. Set into the cliffs overlooking the entrance to Plymouth harbour was a row of naval gun turrets representing every type of warship in service, from the latest modern, crew-less cannon, to the oldest in service still sporting Second World War twin, 4.5in calibre gun turrets. This was where naval gunners came to complete the last stage of their gunnery training with live firing before they joined their ships. The Royal Navy welcomed us with their characteristic hospitality and considerable professional interest. Our two Oerlikons, dwarfed by the mighty twin gun naval gun turrets, were squeezed in on a steep access track running down the cliff-face under the Navy gun-mounts.

In the RAF Regiment we are very wary of taking heavy guns down steep, cliffside coastal paths ever since one young officer in Cyprus entered regimental legend by allowing a 3-ton Bofors cannon to slip off a cliffside track into the sea. Not wishing to add a 6-ton Oerlikon to the legend, this deployment required the greatest of care, hugely assisted by the horsepower and traction of our mighty 8-ton Bedford TM tow trucks slowly easing the guns down the slope on the front tow so the driver could see first hand where the gun was going. So steep was the track that to level the gun, the front jack was at maximum extension and the rear one at minimum. From ground level, the view of the gun perched on the cliff-edge was spectacular and the picture of it was to become one of Oerlikon's most iconic sales images. Further up the cliff-face, where we had to deploy the Sky-guard, the radar jacks ran out of extension and we had to put a couple of railway sleeper-sized baulks of timber under the lower-most jack in order to level the radar. Finally, when we came to align the guns and radar up, the angle of depression between the gun and radar was within one twentieth of a degree of the absolute limit of the equipment – literally a 'Ziegentahler'; it certainly was a tight fit but we were 'in', as they say, and that was all that mattered.

Having suffered some grievous losses at the hands of the Argentinians, the Royal Navy were delighted to see our captured equipment put to British use. They were, of course, familiar with the 35mm gun's little sisters, the 30mm Oerlikon and the tiny twin 20mm Oerlikon fitted, almost uselessly, to most ships, which would have been better armed with a host of shoulder-launched Blowpipes or Stingers to fight a Second World War-style, retro-battle with the Argentinians. Hindsight is a wonderful thing. The really significant difference between our Oerlikons and theirs was the radar-laid tracking and computerized prediction of the Skyguard. The Range Officer, Lieutenant Commander Stephen Bridges, asked if we required the miss-distance indicator, MDI, to be fitted to the sleeve target to be towed by their Royal Naval Air Service aircraft. Based on our previous experiences of shooting away the sleeve targets during our proof test-firings at Manorbier, I rather casually said not to bother as we usually hit the target and it would be a shame to waste MDIs. Stephen closed his eyes, took a deep breath and rocked back on his heels. I could see him thinking what braggarts these

'Crabs' were but, being a gentleman as well as an officer, he passed no comment. Eventually everything was ready, my clerks, storeman, truck technician, generator technician, armourers, radar technicians and RAF Regiment trainee instructors were all tense and alert, ammunition loaded and cannon cocked, ready, as the aircraft brought the target into range. True to form, the first burst sliced the target sleeve in two, the cut-off half fluttering satisfyingly into the sea below. On the next pass the tattered remains of the sleeve were shot off the end of the wire and another sleeve had to be streamed, only to be shot off the wire. Finally, a third sleeve was streamed and that survived its first pass, though blasted into a series of tattered streamers. Each of my RAF Regiment flight sergeant instructors had now had their turn to destroy their targets in a radar-controlled live-firing with 100 per cent success. Even the most die-hard matelot, the bushy-bearded fearsome Fleet Chief Petty Officer Range Master, was unabashedly impressed, while the clerks and technicians manning the guns stood ten feet tall in the reflected glory of the Skyguard's performance. Now it was the turn of the Oerlikon gunners to shoot without the radar. At this point, the miss-distance indicator would have been of some use, as the accuracy of manual visual prediction aim-off could never match that of the radar. Nevertheless, our tradesmen-gunners gave of their best and between them finally managed to down the last sleeve after everyone had had several attempts. It was a great way to end the day. Royal Navy Public Relations were also in top form. That evening a video of our guns firing appeared on the evening television news; the next morning pictures of the Oerlikons appeared in all the national newspapers, much to the surprise of our Swiss instructors, because no such publicity had ever accrued to any Oerlikon firing in the other forty-odd customer countries, includingt Argentina. There, the military Junta rode rough-shod over the civilian equivalent of Blackpool, set their guns up on the famous Mar del Plata public beach, plugged the firing safety box into a city street-lighting lamppost and fired away. After the Malvinas defeat, I do not think their army would dare to do that today. For us, however, the Falklands victory factor, now three years on, was still very much working in our favour. We would return to HMS *Cambridge* again and again. Many years later I was to hear from a naval purser that we 'Crabs' of 2729 Squadron had consumed an entire year's supply of the Royal Navy's global supply of naval target sleeves!

The Swiss, contractor-supplied training culminated with these live firings. To mark the occasion, BMARCO laid on a formal lunch at their Faldingworth Training Centre. The station commander of RAF Waddington, Group Captain Mike Bettell, and all fourteen of us squadron Regulars were invited. Spike Jones, Martin Frey and all the instructors also came and the whole was hosted by BMARCO's managing director, General Donald Isles. After short speeches came the certificate awards, more Swiss Army knives and, to everyone's pleasant surprise, a Swiss Swatch for every member of the squadron, the in-joke being that the Swiss could not bear to think about our fine Swiss-trained gunners relying on anything Japanese. And for the unit as a whole, the company presented us with a magnificent, glass-cased, table-top model of an Oerlikon gun. Later, I was to have this model silver-plated by a firm in Devon; they did us proud and it now comprises part of the RAF Regiment's officers' mess historical silver collection. Training now complete, telephones in all the right offices and with most of our equipment safely delivered and sorted in our workshops and stores, we were now ready to commence recruiting and training.

Chapter 21

Recruiting the First Auxiliaries

After a well-deserved spot of leave, we all returned, supercharged, ready to start recruiting and training. Although the unit establishment provided for part-time technicians as well as gunners and radar operators, I decided to treat training as if we were going to war the next day and therefore, before anyone learned anything, they had to be trained as Oerlikon gunners first and foremost, even before they learned to salute. This would also remove the traditional friction between RAF Regiment 'Rock Apes' and RAF 'Penguins'; on this squadron, everyone would be a real gunner first and foremost.

Upon my return, I was introduced to the local Territorial and Volunteer Training Reserve Association (TAVRA), a powerful, non-governmental body with its own budget that supported the raising of volunteers; it came forward to assist me by designing and paying for our recruiting campaign advertisements in the local newspapers and arranging interviews about the new squadron on Radio Lincoln, where we could let it be known we were recruiting part-time personnel. As an extra bonus, they also bought the squadron an Amstrad word processor, probably the second computer on the base. We built a rugged container to use the computer in the field and on deployments away from base. Lin Dynan, our superfast gunner-typist christened the computer 'Jack'. Jack-in-the-Box speeded up our administration hugely. That summer, when RAF Waddington was invited to exercise its Freedom of the City of Lincoln, that civic permission to march through the city 'with bayonets fixed and pipes and drums playing', we added our military 'Colours' to the rear of the station's marchers: a pair of ex-Argentine guns, with crews on board, towed by our 8-ton trucks, the commander of each standing up through the roof cupola of the truck cab to salute as he or she passed the mayor. It was a great visual spectacle and public relations hit. 'Argie Guns Steal the Show' proclaimed the local paper, which also carried the TAVRA recruiting advert inside.

In response to this, our very first advert, we had over 200 mailed-in enquiries. The clerical effort to deal with this first wave was so great that RAF Waddington's HMSO stationery store actually ran out of envelopes. We also primed the Lincoln RAF recruiting centre to suggest to would-be applicants wishing to join the RAF that they might like to consider joining the new RAuxAF Skyguard-Oerlikon squadron instead, as such a step would enhance their chances of success in applying to become a Regular later. In addition, we dropped recruiting leaflets in all the letter boxes of RAF married quarters at RAF Waddington, RAF Cranwell and RAF Digby nearby, inviting ex-WRAF female personnel to rejoin the Royal Air Force part-time. Indeed, the very first ex-WRAF person to come forward was Lin Dynan, wife of the Lincoln recruiting office sergeant and I attested her on the spot on 1 April, our official formation day, because she could type! The solution to my manpower problem was woman power and I put a sign up to that effect in my office.

Talking to our RAuxAF sister, 2503 Squadron and the Territorial Army airfield damage repair Royal Engineer squadron assigned to RAF Waddington, I realized that the paper response to our first advertising campaign had been extraordinary and was as much to do with the nature of the Skyguard-Oerlikon radar-gun combination as the Falklands factor that went with it. With a first-shot paper recruiting response that was greater than our part-time establishment, it was clear that we could pick and choose our volunteers and we had to get that just right. We listened carefully to how the other units carried out their recruiting and arranged to sit in as observers at the local RAF recruiting office in Lincoln that had already given us our first recruit. I also visited the officer and aircrew selection centre at the RAF College at Cranwell to see what changes had been made since I went there for selection myself twenty years previously, as a keen member of the Air Training Corps. The basic procedure was still the same: remove social trappings by dressing everyone in overalls, conduct interviews with two interviewers: Mr Nice to build up confidence and lower the guard and Mr Nasty to ask the hard, penetrating questions. (I remember Mr Nasty asking me if I would drop an atom bomb on my granny, then living in Berlin. It was a tough question for a 16 year old. After a long pause I said 'Yes, if that was the ordered mission.' Atomic warfare was what the RAF did, back in 1962.) The other part of the selection was to set practical team exercises involving poles, planks, drums and bits of rope to cross imaginary rivers to see who were the leaders, the thinkers, the team players and the bullies. As Flight Sergeant Kavanagh succinctly put it: 'Gosh, Sir, we had better get this right; this is the first time I've ever had the chance to choose my own officers and airmen.' Melding all we had learned, we developed 'the recruiting weekend' as an all-out effort by all fourteen of us Regulars to select only the best.

The recruiting weekend would be a two-day, live-in, overnight event. It would begin with an immediate change into anonymous overalls, a short briefing on the importance of RAF Waddington and the part it played in the defence of the UK, followed by a run-down of historic attacks against the airfield. In the First World War a Zeppelin airship raided RAF Waddington one night and an errant bomb fell through the roof of the village church without exploding; that Zeppelin was shot down and the base still has some trophies from the burned-out wreck. In the Second World War the base was attacked by Heinkels, Dorniers and Messerschmitts; and in the expectation of the Third World War we anticipated

Fencers, Backfires and Bears, plus Spetznaz Special Forces, the latter to be dealt with by 2503, our sister Auxiliary squadron. Briefings would be followed by a quick climb-aboard tour of a running gun and radar, the parallel activity being the individual interviews led by my officer and the flight sergeants, supplemented by the sergeants and corporals, so that all the Regulars were part of the process. There would also be a sample group lesson on how to bring the generator into action. (One great revelation of the latter was how few people knew what an engine oil dip-stick was and where it might likely be found.) Meals would be in the airmen's mess, and for the evening we planned a little barbecue in our squad-ron canteen bar, to see how people behaved in a close social setting – *in vino veritas*, so to speak. Overnight accommodation would be field conditions, a sleeping bag on a safari bed, males and females in separate bomb bunkers. The next day would be the practical exercises, for which we had the ammunition storage area emergency water supply tanks complete with resident goldfish to cross as real water obstacles, one-up on Cranwell, which only had 'pretend' rivers. In addition, we would conduct second interviews, all to be completed by mid-Sunday afternoon. We Regulars would then pool and analyse our findings, review and discuss each candidate in turn, and then rank them in order. The final decision was mine.

No differentiation was made between men and women. Recruiting women to operate the guns and radars was to prove rather a controversial exercise at first. I believe the significance of the single line in the Air Force Board paper dealing with female personnel had not really dawned on the staffs or my flight sergeants until we actually started recruiting and training. In general, the women who volunteered tended to be better educated, smarter, more mature and more likely to follow instructions to the letter than the men, especially the over-confident younger men. Also, the women showed more respect for equipment and I would never find one treating a Land Rover or 8-ton truck harshly or recklessly in the field or on the road. They were also fussy about hygiene in the field and would not tolerate men not shaving or not washing in the field on their crews.

Three selection weekends were held over the next six weeks. Before we saw any recruits, they had to have a medical examination by their own GP, whose reports were then vetted by the RAF medical officer at RAF Waddington. Medically fit candidates were then invited in batches of about thirty to forty to spend the weekend with the squadron. The arrival of the first recruits was awaited with eager anticipation on that first Saturday of the first weekend. We all turned up early to open up the compound an hour before start time and were pleasantly surprised to find a queue of recruits had already beaten us to the gate, waiting patiently outside for our arrival. That was definitely a good sign. Our lecture rooms had been prepared, films wound on projectors ready for showing, guns and radars laid out for demonstration and brand-new RAF overalls, safari beds and sleeping bags prepared for issue. We set straight to work.

The overnight stay helped to emphasize that joining the squadron would involve time away from family and also gave us an opportunity to show recruits something of the social side of Service life through the informal barbecue and a few drinks. As it turned out, this little social experiment was to prove almost as valuable a selection aid as the formal exercises and interviews; those who greedily guzzled the free beer, became the worse for wear through alcohol, or behaved inappropriately towards the opposite sex were all earmarked as unsuitable. With the aid of a drink or two, individuals often gave out some quite revealing facts about themselves which they might not have volunteered in a formal interview: smoking cannabis, being discharged from the Regular Armed Forces without explanation, having marital, job or financial problems, to name but a few.

The variety of applicants to join the squadron was amazing, ranging from the manageress of Moss Bros at RAF Cranwell to a sixth-form schoolboy, from a graduate sociologist to a butcher's apprentice. Equally interesting was the broad range of recreational activities that these people already took part in, from church bell-ringing to teaching local sea cadets to sail. All in all, recruits and staff alike enjoyed the weekend. Those who decided not to join the squadron admitted that they had under-estimated the professional demands, the level of commitment required and the reality of the job to be undertaken by Auxiliaries; if nothing else, they departed with a better understanding of what the Armed Forces Reserves were all about. We rejected about a third of the candidates as unsuitable for one reason or another, and offered places to the remaining twenty. At the next selection weekend we accepted half the candidates, and by the end of our third selection session sixty-nine people out of over 300 aspirants had been invited to join the squadron. Of the sixty-nine, a few were to fall by the wayside at follow-up medicals by our RAF doctors, mainly due to colour blindness and deafness, the latter by and large due to disco music and personal stereos turned up too loudly. Six weeks after its formal formation on 1 April 1985 the squadron was 50 per cent recruited. I was very glad that I had recruited Lin as our first Auxiliary to cope with the resulting administrative bow-wave of documentation.

To have recruited 50 per cent of our requirement within six weeks of official formation was very impressive, but of course not one recruit knew a thing about Oerlikon guns, Skyguard radars or air defence in general. In between the recruiting administration, interviewing, selection exercises and socializing, the squadron Regular personnel were busy drawing up plans for training and deciding, in the light of our own Service experiences and the training we had received from BMARCO, exactly what the Auxiliaries should be taught at the eleven different rank levels and eight different RAF trade groups within the squadron. This was the first undertaking by a Reserve Forces unit to train part-timers from scratch across such a wide range of trade specializations, and it was a huge task. The squadron end product, what we would call a training needs analysis, was a substantial tome in which was listed the job description and training objectives to meet each task on the unit. Normally in the RAF this would be carried out over a period of months by a full-time team in the education branch, with representatives from each trade group; we did it in weeks between the fourteen of us. With a clear idea of what we needed to achieve, the next task was to design the courses to train the Auxiliaries to the required standard.

Although reasonably well acquainted with 'wriggly amps' thanks to my three years at Cranwell and a further year of intense study at the Royal School of Artillery, I am a great believer in 'bottom-up training', where recruits are taught only the actual physical job they have to do in war first, leaving all other things like saluting, marching, service history and, particularly, what goes on inside black boxes till much later. In infantry terms, give a man his gun on the first day and teach him how to shoot. This is the philosophy of every underground resistance force, mujahideen and the Israeli Army; they may not be especially smart to look at, but nobody can question their motivation or ability to fight with their equipment. My favourite working example of this is the fact that there are over 40 million men and women efficiently and safely driving motor cars at up to 70mph on Britain's roads without the faintest idea of the Otto cycle, advanced or retarded ignition, epicyclic gears, torsion bar tensions or any of the thousands of technicalities which go into the design and construction of motor vehicles. I have always believed that such training is peripheral to the aim and leads to unnecessarily long courses and a sort of closed-shop, unionized attitude on the part of those instructors who graduate from such training, believing that as they did it 'this way', nobody else can possibly do their job without such a grounding. I accept there is a need for in-depth training, but I believe it should be regarded as a long-term investment and should not be confused with essentially simple operating skills needed to make a machine perform. On 2729 Squadron there was nobody else to tell me to do it differently, all the other staffs having had ample opportunity to volunteer to provide the above as services within their own fields during the MoD circulations of the Air Force Board paper at squadron leader, wing commander and group captain levels, so I made my own decision that every single recruit, male and female, should be taught to operate the Oerlikon twin 35mm cannon before any other element of their military training. Moreover, I decided that within nine weeks of evening and weekend-only training, these fifty or so recruits would carry out a radar-less live firing with operational ammunition against a sleeve target towed by an aircraft, as if war had been declared yesterday. The Regular instructors blanched a bit but we put together the necessary course and planned to start the first night of formal Auxiliary training on 11 June 1985.

Concurrent with all our recruiting, taking delivery of unit field equipment, training needs analysis, Auxiliary attestations, kitting-out and course design, the 'Rent-a-Radar' and 'Oerlikon Gun Show' of demonstrations was in full swing. Between 1 April and 10 June, starting-off from the top, we were visited by the Chief of the Air Staff of the Royal Air Force, the Commander-in-Chief Strike

Command, the Commanding General of the French Air Force, individual members of the Air Force Board and many others, to make a total of 152 visitors sufficiently important to name them all in the Squadron Operational Diary, the RAF form 540. I believe that a large part of this was due to the impending death knell of the ill-fated Nimrod AEW aircraft. Upon coming into RAF hands from the contractor Marconi, the radar part of the aircraft turned out to be such a bag of worms that it was less capable of detecting targets than the un-military local air traffic control radars of the bases the Nimrod was supposed to oversee. Killing-off such an expensive project would require the top-level officers of the Royal Air Force to see the depressing results for themselves and I guess a visit to the Skyguard-Oerlikon project, which happened to be going swimmingly well, was programmed in as a morale-booster to cheer them all up. They certainly cheered me up; on 10 June I was informed that I had been awarded an MoD booty prize of £1,200 for my work in rescuing and bringing the captured Argentine radars and guns into operational service; at 0.00005 per cent of £30 million, this was much lower percentage in prize money than was paid in Nelson's day, but then, I had only fought paper battles. Next, on the 12 June, the morning after we started our first night of Auxiliary training, the station commander, Mike Bettell, sprang the news at the daily commanders' operations briefing that I had been awarded the MBE in the Queen's Birthday Honours List. Life in the fast lane was certainly being kind to me.

Chapter 22

Training the First Auxiliary Recruits

Normally, Auxiliary units would train one evening a week and one weekend a month. To train one gun crew of six required one instructor for the full session; we had three RAF Regiment instructors, so that meant training three crews at a time. By doubling-up to two evenings a week and two weekends a month, we could increase this to six crews. Finally, by bringing in my clerks, armourers and storeman, plus myself and my young officer, we could increase this to eight gun crews training in parallel, taking care of all fifty of our recruits. The gun course was 80 hours long, equivalent in normal RAF 40-hour working weeks to a two-week course or, more realistically, to include administration, kit issue, orientation, sports afternoons and so on, a three-week RAF full-time course. We broke this down into evening packets of 3 hours, weekend packets of 24 hours and one week of full-time training immediately prior to firing camp, plus just over half a week at firing camp and a couple of days to clean and clear away equipment. At the beginning it seemed impossible: there was so much hands-on learning to do, especially when the manual dexterity and technical innocence of some recruits was staggeringly underdeveloped. The lesson for us instructors across the board was that absolutely nothing could be assumed as prior knowledge in our training.

Every morning, after an evening of training, we held a Chinese Parliament (where everyone got to speak, but only the boss makes decisions) where we pooled our experiences of teaching the night before and, if necessary, would rewrite some or all of the lesson plans in time for the repeat training to the next batch of recruits on the following evening. The Tuesday night crews would not meet the Thursday night crews until the pre-firing camp week of full-time training. It was hard work but we made lightning progress. It was a wonderful experience to see how the Auxiliaries gained in stature, confidence and handling of the heavy machinery that made up the twin cannon, and how the various Regular clerks, storeman and technicians morphed into trainers, gaining stature, status and a leap in interpersonal skills as they passed on their own newly acquired knowledge. Very early on we were also able to see potential leaders emerge amongst the recruits and through our Chinese Parliament we were able to guide these individuals to fill the commanders' appointments as training progressed. We also experienced our first voluntary withdrawal from training. One of our older Auxiliaries, an ex-Regular serviceman, was at sixes and sevens with the correct sequence of an important set of firing drills and took most unkindly to the helpful coaching by one of our female recruits already in charge of a gun. Sue Ford was an operating theatre staff nurse in her 'real' life and ran her trainee crew like a surgical team. She was quick and accurate and painstakingly patient to get everything 'just so'. The more she tried to help this poor chap, the more catastrophic his mistakes became. Suddenly he threw down his beret, stamped on it, declared in loud and no uncertain terms that he would never serve under a woman and stomped off home, back to the comfort of supplementary benefit. We sent our storeman to his home at the weekend to collect his military kit, handed over his outstanding pay and got him to sign his discharge form.

We were now at the end of the seven weeks of part-time training. The next two weeks would count as the mandatory fortnight of 'annual camp' which, at the end of the year, would qualify them for their first-ever Reserve Forces annual bonus, small in the first year but growing into a tidy sum by the end of a decade. One week of the camp was to be held at RAF Waddington, most of the other at Manorbier gunnery range in Wales.

The Oerlikon gun drills were really coming together well in this first week and reached the very high standard required for live firing. Even the school teacher in the recruit group appreciated that the pass mark had to be 100 per cent in our exams, a step-change in outlook for the university-attuned academic. The Tuesday and Thursday crews got to meet each other for the first time and a lively rivalry arose to be the first and best, accelerating progress further. We also introduced peripheral field training to ensure our gunners could erect tents and live under canvas, since all the wartime barrack accommodation at Manorbier had been cleared away in the run-down of the camp. Visits to the squadron continued apace, with our RAF Regiment Commandant General popping in for the first time to view the progress of the Auxiliary training. Mindful of the value of good press coverage on our future recruiting, we volunteered our guns and radars for display at the public air days at RAF College Cranwell and at RAF Marham. These events were popular with the Auxiliaries as they put themselves and their equipment very much in the public eye. Naturally the 'Falklands factor' drew considerable interest from serving RAF personnel, who attended these shows with their families and friends, only to be blown away by being knowledgeably shown over the high-tech equipment by men and women who had less than two months' part-time military service experience under their belts. These outings were excellent for Auxiliary morale, stature and confidence; they came away ten feet tall, were able to reel off facts and figures about the guns and radars like cathedral guides and, when they knew somebody was watching, always performed their drills with extra panache. Indirectly, as they walked around the other displays and equipment exhibitions around the air days, without knowing it, the Auxiliaries were soaking up general service training, gaining an awareness of the different types of aircraft and RAF equipment on display, especially an

invaluable dose of my favourite air defence medicine: aircraft recognition prac-
ticed on real aircraft in the air.

Forty-seven of the fifty Auxiliaries on strength were able to attend the first
week of annual camp on base at RAF Waddington. For their return from firing
camp, I planned to make something of a public relations exercise of their achievement and hold a families day on the weekend of their return. Quite by coincidence, our sister squadron, the County of Lincoln Squadron, was to run a
cocktail party in the officers' mess and had invited all the local dignitaries in the
county to attend. It seemed a golden opportunity to show a united Auxiliary Air
Force front between the County and the City squadrons, so I had their invitations
extended to include taking afternoon tea with the families of their other Lincolnshire squadron, 2729 (City of Lincoln) Squadron as well. In the event, 2503's
invitation list read like something of a county coming-out party: the Lord
Lieutenant, the Chief Constable, the Mayor, the Sheriff, the chief executive of
the county council, the local Members of Parliament, numerous retired air
marshals and generals, the local Territorial Army brigade commander, the Commandant of the RAF College, and so the list went on. Not being much into
poodle-faking myself, I decided to make 2503's cocktail party a whole lot more
interesting by exposing all these people to my girl and boy gunners, their families
and our photogenic 'Wow! Kit', the Skyguard-Oerlikon combination, in the sure
knowledge of which part of our now-extended joint Royal Auxiliary Air Force
event would most stick in their memories, the officers' mess do or the Oerlikon
gun do, with its citizen-gunner crews, freshly blooded by live firing. So, having
fixed the arrangements for a super end-of-camp homecoming, it was time to get
back to the preparations for the firing camp itself.

The first lesson on the first day of the Waddington week of annual camp was
the next step in operational preparation of the gun crews: physical integration
with the Skyguard radar to take control of their guns. There are a number of very
important calibration steps to be taken in this exercise, where each gun can be up
to 500m away from the radar in order to point the gun with an accuracy of 1m at
a target 4km away. To achieve this level of precision, the Auxiliary gunners have
to align the gun and radars to within a twentieth of a degree in vertical and
horizontal angle and to the nearest 30cm in distance over a range of 500m. For
this specific task, normally conducted by the officer-level radar commander, we
specially trained our squadron non-typist, the most junior Regular airman of the
squadron, Leading Aircraftsman John Duffy, as the radar crewman to perform
this one task to Ziegentahler precision.

By the next day the Auxiliaries were doing the gun-radar integration against
the clock. They were also now introduced to the next critical step in their training: cleaning the gun after live firing. I used to get very cross with any Rapier
operators dismissing our guns as 'something simple', especially as they were not

allowed to change, let alone even open up, a black box on their Rapiers. Stripping down each 35mm cannon to clean it after rain during training, after live firing or just periodically (in our case at least once per month) was a mechanical exercise equivalent in complexity, in sheer numbers of parts and of handling heavy weights to taking out and putting back both the engine and the gearbox of a large SUV. And, again, there was only one pass-mark: 100 per cent. Slipping in other essential field training for the Oerlikon guns, I introduced them to Auxiliary Aircraftsman Ian Garrick, a former corporal-instructor at the Army School of Infantry, who in turn introduced them to personal camouflage with the assistance of Elizabeth Arden and soon their faces were zigzagged with chocolate brown and green lightning bolts of Arden's best camouflage cream. Meanwhile, Flight Sergeant Coupe had departed for Manorbier range with all the tents, the cook-house and one gun and generator in tow.

Conveniently, with the Nimrod in disgrace, flying at RAF Waddington was limited to a University Air Squadron summer camp, with a host of Chipmunk light training aircraft doing continuous circuits-and-bumps, while advanced students practised aerobatics, thus providing both the gun and radar crews with plenty of interesting targets milling about in the sky to track and 'engage', all recorded on our newly acquired TV tape recorders. Finally, the big day came to convoy all the equipment down to Manorbier, with more osmotic training along the way, learning a vocabulary of very specific military meanings to specific words: vehicle loads, personnel allocation to vehicles, ammunition handling, ammunition guards, orders for ammunition live-armed guards; this was all getting seriously military and quite warlike, once everything had been typed out. Then came forming-up point, start line, route card, signal instructions, order of march, convoy speed, packet spacing, lost rendezvous, breakdown orders, crash orders, laying-up points, identity flags and so on, all helping to pass the quiet overnight evenings in the bunkers. The Regulars and Auxiliaries were also to see their guns and radars wearing their new 'Captured Vehicle' number plates. We had also now enhanced the status of each cannon and radar by naming each major piece of equipment after a battlefield site in the Falklands Campaign, a practice the RAF inherited from the Royal Naval Air Service, which named its early airships and air station defence Rolls-Royce armoured cars after battles in the First World War. Each bunker now sported an Argentine flag with the central sun motif replaced by the name of the gun or radar inside, making a walk around 2729 Squadron a reminder of all the critical battlefield locations of the Falklands Campaign, emphasizing the links to the origin of the squadron equipment and the units that fought at these locations. Thus, the Oerlikon gun Goose Green carried the Para badge, the gun Pebble Island an SAS badge, and so on. Each Skyguard Radar was a junior officer's command of a radar and three guns, making it a flight, so A Flight radar became Ajax Bay, B Flight Bluff Cove, C Flight Camilla Creek and

D Flight Darwin. We set the Auxiliaries off to learning them off pat so everyone could recognize what belonged to whom at a glance; another quiz-cum-learning game to play in the bunker, as per the allocation list of names below:

	A Flight	B Flight	C Flight	D Flight
Radars:	Ajax Bay	Bluff Cove	Camilla Creek	Darwin
Guns:	Goose Green	Mt Kent	San Carlos	Two Sisters
	Fitzroy Mount	Longdon	Stanley Airport	Mt William
	Mt Harriet	Pebble Island	Mt Tumbledown	Wireless Ridge

In addition, we were to introduce them to the first batch of squadron radio callsigns, together with instructions on the all callsigns answering sequence, making a call, answering a call, answering a multi-callsign call, the NATO phonetic alphabet, NATO pronunciation of numbers 0–10, breaking up long messages and ending calls. Our radio callsigns were:

The Boss:	9			
Control:	Zero			
Radars:	11	21	31	41
Guns:	11A	21A	31A	41A
	11B	21B	31B	41B
	11C	21C	31C	41C

The trip to Manorbier began with an early morning parade at the airmen's mess, my squadron commander's guarantee that everyone would have a 'full Monty' pre-deployment breakfast of eggs, bacon, beans, sausages, toast and lashings of tea as motivation for getting up promptly.[27] The troops then collected their 'nosebags' (packed lunches) and paraded in full kit to make sure nothing was left behind, followed by the order to load-up, radio check, start engines, move to the FUP and cross the start line at the H-Hour of 0800hrs.

The convoy was a mix of 8-ton trucks towing radars and guns and 4-ton trucks towing generators, with the ammunition truck sandwiched between live-armed guards, one Land Rover in front and one behind. Each 'packet' had a different coloured identifying flag and every vehicle carried a red breakdown warning flag. At the very end of the convoy was the winch-fitted recovery 8-tonner. The drive to Manorbier was a two-day exercise since the UK was now following European Union driving laws, limiting military drivers to the same restrictions as civilian ones, at least in peacetime. The 4-tonners failed miserably to maintain convoy station with their more powerful 8-ton cousins, causing gaps to appear in the packets and allowing unpredictable civilian cars to get mixed in with the convoy; worse still, the 4-tonners nearly ran out of fuel in their efforts to keep up, requiring an unplanned diversion to refuel before they ran dry. The other notable event was that one or two of the more enterprising girls used their initiative to forsake their safari beds in the great squadron gymnasium doss-down, which included the officers. Instead, they sneaked off for a night of comfort in individual rooms with pink teddies in the all-female WRAF barrack block. In the morning, when it was discovered, they got a deserved roasting about field living for one being field living for all. Then, driving the lead 8-tonner in the headquarters packet myself, I took a wrong turn off a slip road on the spaghetti junction nightmare that is the M4-M5 interchange just outside Bristol, confusing the packet leaders behind me and forcing them to make the decision to follow my mistake or follow their orders. Not everybody got it right. My punishment was to see Oerlikons and 8-tonners on just about every level of the flyovers, all going off in totally different directions, a Monty Python moment if ever there was one. I guess it stretched the fuel margin of one 4-tonner just a touch too far and tested the breakdown plan to the full. The perk of this diversion was that Flight Sergeant Kavanagh, never one to miss an opportunity, negotiated that the refuelling of the entire convoy entitled it to the forecourt-advertised, pro-rata reward of a free Shell glass for every 4 gallons of fuel and cleaned out their entire stock of freebies. The convoy experience gave grounds for a change in vehicle establishment on the basis that the slower 4-tonners were a motorway safety liability and a security risk that could compromise the transport of live ammunition by not being able to keep station; they were duly replaced by 8-tonners in time for the next live firing camp.

At Manorbier the squadron's arrival was greeted by torrential rain. The advanced party had used their initiative and set up tented lines inside the old Army REME workshop hangar. The roof leaked and the building was scheduled for demolition but at least it provided shelter from the misery of horizontal, wind-driven rain, so that we were able to keep most of the field equipment dry, which saved a monumental canvas-drying operation upon our return. This time the Auxiliaries were billeted by crews, rather than by gender – another first. Just as at HMS *Cambridge*, the press and local VIPs were invited to view the live firing, only this time the Oerlikons were to be crewed entirely by part-timers with a grand total of nine weeks of part-time training. But that would come later. First they had to be briefed on range orders and safety procedures; the two Skyguards, each with two Oerlikons attached, were deployed to the firing line, the gun-radar alignment checked and range safety measures rehearsed and tested. Then the weather worsened and the 100 Squadron Canberra target tug was grounded for the moment. However, we had one more card up our sleeves: fictional target firing. A fictional target location was fixed into the predicting memory of the Skyguard computer, which locked the tracking radar up to point at this fictional spot in space. If all the gun-radar alignments were correct, then the shells fired by the guns should be seen to cross over in the centre of the TV tracking crosswires. We fired, and the pyramid of shells came to a point in the TV crosswires. The weapon alignment with the radar was perfect.

At last the weather cleared and the Canberra came on-range for the last 45 minutes of the notified range firing day. With such a short time of Canberra availability left, there was no need to ram the superiority of Skyguard-directed radar firing over manual firing down the throats of the Auxiliaries; after all, the aim of this firing camp was to give them the experience and qualification of aiming and firing the cannon over open reflector gunsights at the target under their own joystick control.

We had two guns set up with safety stops for this exercise and planned to cycle firers through the 'hot seat' at each target pass in order to get the most out of the aircraft availability. First off were our two potential gun commanders, Sue Ford and Bob Stafford. They each fired an anxious short burst at the target pass. We could not see the low-light Argentine tracer through the dark, scudding clouds and the target sleeve passed intact overhead. We changed each firer over after each firing run, the next pair having spent the previous run dry tracking on the other two ammunition-less training cannon further along, down range. This is how we conducted Rapier operator firings but it was not working well for us. Each firer was hurried along from the dry tracking guns to the live firing guns, arrived breathless and anxious, and had to leap aboard and fire at the next incoming target. The shooting became very erratic as firers had difficulty in seeing the target sleeve and the careful training of the last nine weeks evaporated into panic shooting. One or two gunners of both genders even burst into tears at the stress of it all. By the end of 45 minutes everybody had fired something at the target that they may or may not have seen. A total of 230 rounds had been expended, which meant four to five shells each, a quarter of a second's firing per person. While Auxiliary morale was quite high because they had each actually fired the real thing, we Regulars were less than happy with the training value of the outcome. The gunners needed to have confidence in their skills and this was not the case.

While the troops relaxed over a beer, we Regulars held another Chinese Parliament. On the morrow we decided to deploy all our Regulars to provide safety control and load all four guns with live ammunition. Each gun was to be crewed by its own Auxiliary crew and commander, and each aimer was to have as many dry runs as they wished, until they were ready to fire. Opening fire was their decision entirely, when they were ready for it, just as it would be in war. The function of the rest of the crew was to point out the target and keep the gun fed with ammunition, while the commander was responsible for correctness of drills and the range safety staff were there to cut off the power to the gun if it strayed towards the limits of the allocated firing arc.

The following day began with a complete rebrief on the revised firing procedure. It was made clear to the Auxiliaries that the entire squadron and range staff were subordinated to supporting the gunner-aimer in the hot seat to get a good kill on the target and that they should only fire when they were calm and confident and had a good steady bead on the target. The final decision to fire was theirs alone, just as it was for a single-seat fighter pilot. Cool and calm was the order of the day. Their change in facial expressions said everything as they digested the new emphasis. I believe they now really understood, for the first time in their brief military careers, that they personally were in control of the killing end of the whole weapon system. Both the weather and 100 Squadron atoned for the poor showing of the previous day: we had clear skies, calm winds and two Canberras on task to cover the whole day. As Corporal Bob Stafford's employers, British Telecom, had given him four straight paid weeks off work to complete the Regulars radar course, we decided to qualify him as a Skyguard radar commander by having him conduct a radar-directed firing with two guns under radar control first off. This would achieve two things: he would be our first Auxiliary, live-firing, fully qualified Skyguard commander and, in all probability, he would bring down the first target on the first pass, always a good start to the day. As expected, at the first pass, with full target lock on both the tracking radar and the coaxial TV tracker, Stafford rather fearfully dabbed the red fire button and about three rounds went off, criss-crossing the sleeve. On the next pass Stafford was more confident; he pressed and held down the fire button for a full operational burst and the sleeve disintegrated in the hail of direct hits, which everybody cheered. We disconnected the radar, congratulated Stafford and set all four guns up for independent firing at the next nineteen passes of the new sleeve streamed by the Canberra. A total of twenty-nine aimers fired over the open reflector gunsights. Sometimes only one gun fired; at other times they all fired together. The standard of shooting went up rapidly as the gunners, male and female, built up their confidence and fired longer and more accurate bursts. They were now enjoying it and began to get quite competitive. Indeed, by the end of the first Canberra's sortie, Sergeant Bernie Hughes, who was responsible for unboxing and clipping up the ammunition, warned that he was having trouble keeping up with the rate of ammunition consumption. It was clearly time to emulate the Swiss Army training routine and only fire out of one barrel on each mount at each pass. This halved the rate of fire, giving the gunners more firing runs. The shooting paused abruptly when recruits Goddard and Gaylard between them shot down the target sleeve with just one barrel each. In the afternoon the Canberra advised us that, while they could stream another target, they now only had enough fuel remaining for four more passes. I decided to follow General Mont-gomery's training dictum always to end an exercise on a high point and so sent the Canberra home to an early tea, while we reviewed the day's excellent achievements.

We had fired 995 rounds, a quarter of the grand total that the Argentinians had fired in their entire fifty-three day *Malvinas* war. All the recruits were now quali-fied as safe ammunition handlers and reloaders, and 80 per cent had qualified as confident, competent aimers, which was a prerequisite for promotion from the rank of AC Plonk to leading aircraftsman, provided they could march, salute, recognize all the RAF ranks, reel off the names of all the RAF's aircraft and draw an organization diagram of the RAF commands at home and abroad, as well as operate a radio, put up a tent, dig a slit trench and fire a personal weapon accurately and safely. Needless to say, all previous signs of stress had evaporated and morale was sky high as the crews settled down to the 2-hour task of cleaning the guns in the late afternoon sun after firing. With only a few personnel left to qualify, there would be plenty of time the next morning, before breakfast, to introduce the Auxiliaries to a bit of serious marching and drill rehearsal for the parade to impress their families at our families day. The tent lines were inspected to ensure all beds were made up neatly, sleeping bags aired inside out and personal kit all neat and tidy. It was just as well we had done this because Spike Jones unexpectedly arrived devilishly early with our Swiss VIP guests, Herr Burghi, Herr Ziegentahler and Martin Frey, who commented on how very impressed they were at the newness and tip-top quality of our military kit and the neatness and tidiness of our troops living in field conditions. By lunchtime, the Canberra had been and gone, leaving us a tattered sleeve as a souvenir of the day's shooting. After gun cleaning, we could turn our attention to the press day scheduled for the following morning.

This began with a calibration firing conducted only by the Auxiliaries; similarly, they too would carry out the actual live firing demonstrations. The fictional target firing went faultlessly and so the Canberra was ordered onto the range. To conserve ammunition, only one cannon on each twin mount would be loaded. Corporal Stafford was the Skyguard radar operator and destroyed the target with the first burst. The Canberra retired to stream another sleeve. On this run the aircraft allowed the sleeve to drift very close to the left-hand safety arc and only one of the two connected guns was inside the arc. This single gun, with only one barrel firing, destroyed the new sleeve at first pass, thereby completing a very satisfactory rehearsal.

The firing demonstration proper, which doubled-up as confirmatory training for the now qualified Auxiliaries, began in the afternoon with a briefing for about fifty visitors, who included the Swiss team, local reporters from Lincolnshire and reporters from BBC TV, BBC Radio and TV AM. The scoop of the day was for TV AM's Michael Voss to produce Squadron Leader Bob Iveson, the Harrier pilot who had been shot down by these self-same Oerlikons at Goose Green. With all eyes and cameras on the target, the Canberra came on range. The Auxiliaries and the equipment did me proud. The sleeve was blown to pieces; as the larger two pieces of sleeve fell away, they too were hit and blasted into even smaller pieces. A new sleeve was streamed and that was destroyed on its second pass. TV AM then invited Bob to say a few words. He praised the skill of the Auxiliaries, which was really down to the Skyguard radar, and went on to say that having seen the guns so close up, he considered himself very, very lucky indeed to be alive. The TV crews then homed-in on our very photogenic gunner-cum-8-ton truck driver, Louise Bromley, who gave a very good account of how the men and women carried out identical operational jobs on the squadron. That evening video of the Skyguard-Oerlikon firings, Bob Iveson and a very glamorous Louise Bromley appeared on both TV channels, which no doubt provided the Swiss with some very good PR with which to impress their customers; for us, it did a whole lot of good for our recruiting.

The next morning my wife rang to say that she had nearly dropped her breakfast into her lap when her husband appeared with Michael Voss on early morning national TV. It was another excellent, free, public relations exercise. We used recorded replays of the Canberra, the sleeve and the guns firing for recruiting, showing the Skyguard-Oerlikon as a great piece of Star Wars kit that spectacularly blew things up for real. That evening we threw a party for the squadron and invited the Swiss as our principal guests and to thank Spike and Martin for fronting up the refurbishment of the Skyguards and Oerlikon guns. Even though the Swiss Army is virtually all manned by part-time militia, who serve only three weeks a year, the Project Angel instructors kept asking the Auxiliaries if they truthfully had only just had nine weeks of part-time training to get to the standard they now demonstrated. And as for girl-gunners, well that was just too revolutionary for them.

John Kavanagh, our arch-organizer, went to town on the barbecue and produced a huge feast. Spike kindly produced a barrel of beer out of thin air and the party, which was held in the old Bofors gun training dome, took off. The dome probably matched the size of the St Paul's Cathedral dome in London; it also had the same acoustics, whereby one could whisper a message to someone on the other side of the dome. It was a lot of fun to butt in, unseen, on other people's lively conversation on the far side of the dome or conversely to eavesdrop on other conversations at long range.

Towards the end of the evening the girls all came on together as a dance troupe wearing new T-shirts showing an Oerlikon gun emblazoned with the caption '2729 Girls like to do it with a Bang!' I was then summoned to the chorus line and blindfolded, not without some anxiety, I might say, as an image of myself being ticked-off by the Air Officer Commanding 11 Group, not known for frivolity, poodle-faking as he called it, flitted through my brain. The AOC's image sharpened considerably when the tittering girls started to unbutton my shirt. However, gun commander Sue Ford whispered in my ear 'It's OK, Sir, really. Trust me!' She then slipped a T-shirt on me to uproarious cheering. When I looked down, it simply said in bold black letters 'And so do I'. It took me a long time to explain to my then very expectant wife Christina what the curious T-shirt message actually meant. To end the evening, Lin produced the first of her many talented odes and had the squadron sing my favourite song, 'Don't Cry for me, Argentina', to a new set of lyrics that went as follows:

Don't cry for me Argentina
Mike Fonfé has got your guns
We wish you had spiked them
So we don't have to clean them
Mike and Martin got them together
Mike Fonfé hired some civilians
And gave them some gun training
They worked real hard now
So they deserve a bow
Mike's civvies are called Auggies
And he took them to Manorbier
They fired the guns there
And some, they showed some fear
But when they hit, boy did they cheer ...

After a two-day return trip to Waddington in the back of the 8-tonners, the Auxiliaries, singing lustily all the way, arrived back home. Wives, husbands and children waited patiently in the squadron car park to reclaim their loved ones. Anyone watching might have thought they had just come back from the Falklands, not Manorbier. As soon as the equipment was safely tucked away back in the nuclear bunkers, the squadron was paraded and dismissed. For the Regulars there was little respite. Loaned vehicles had to be checked and returned clean to distant RAF stations and of course, with access to our own proper workshop, Sergeant Matthews worked all-out to get the vehicles and trailers fully serviced. The following Saturday was the families day. The 'Best Blues' had come back from the tailors on the Friday morning; they must have been left in a huge pile while we were away because they were so badly crumpled they were unwearable. Corporal Clements refused to take them on charge until they had been dry-cleaned and steam pressed, which took all day. Thus, the first chance for the Auxiliaries to wear their new uniform since tailoring was on the Saturday morning; thankfully, they looked smart as new pins in them. In the afternoon the VIPs for 2503's cocktail party arrived. A line of joined-together and now dry tents constituted the guest area for VIPs and families to take their places. The sun came out to greet the bagpipes and drums of RAF Waddington's voluntary band leading the Auxiliaries resplendent in their hours-old, brand-new best blues. According to the Squadron operational diary those present were Air Vice Marshal Hughes, a famous Battle of Britain pilot, former Commandant of the RAF College and now Honorary Air Commodore of Lincoln County; General Toler of the Territorial, Auxiliary and Volunteer Association, with his secretary, Colonel Clark; General Isles of BMARCO; Martin Frey from Switzerland; Air Commodore Anderson,

Director of the RAF Regiment; Group Captain Batt, Commandant of the RAF Regiment Depot; and Group Captain Gibson, my previous boss, now retired also. Air Commodore Anderson inspected the parade, speaking to and congratulating every Auxiliary with his usual warmth and charm. However, instead of risking a march past, we had substituted far more important skills. To a clarion call of 'Action Stations!', the Auxiliaries disappeared into their gun bunkers behind the parade, making a lightning change out of best blues into green working dress. At another given signal, six Oerlikon guns were wheeled out of the bunkers and went into action station positions, barrels all facing left at the same angle, to greet the last remaining flying Vulcan in the Royal Air Force with a burst of fire crackers on the ends of their barrels. The Vulcan responded by opening its bomb-bay doors and firing signal pistol flares back down through its cockpit floor, before treating everyone to a thrilling flying display. Families and friends were then shown over their respective guns and radars by their proud Auxiliary crews. One small boy brought a lump to my throat when I overheard him say in an eyes-wide, awed voice, 'Mummy, did you really fire this great big gun yourself?'

After the VIPs conveniently left for 2503's cocktails, the squadron barbecue was lit. Auxiliaries and Regulars, together with their two hundred or so friends and guests, settled down in the late summer sun to enjoy the best party yet. Special praise must be given to the three flight sergeants, Mr Fitness, John Wayne and JR, who organized the parade, gun demonstration and barbecue between them. Just to round the month off, the squadron was visited by the Chief Engineer of the Royal Air Force, Sir Eric Dunn, and then Christina went into hospital and, in the presence of myself and our two teenage daughters (whom we jokingly refer to as Batch One), watched their little sister, Baby Alix, the first of our two RAF Waddington Batch Two babies, being born. After such a busy six months, it was now time to shut up shop and send the whole squadron off on three weeks' well deserved block leave.

Chapter 23

Even More Excitement

With the publicity of our national TV appearance still fresh, we took in another batch of thirty recruits in the autumn. The selection weekend was the biggest we had run thus far, and also the most highly educated. The fifty-five applicants had, between them, three degrees, twelve A levels and ninety-two O levels. (This was in the days before easy-as-pie GCSEs). The squadron also took part in a major UK home defence exercise which promised Spetznaz-type Special Forces attacks and half of NATO to come and 'bomb the hell out of us' at RAF Waddington, still the home of the useless Nimrod AEW. Naturally, we deployed on and off base for this exercise. In our explorations of the less-visited parts of the airfield, we discovered some underground bunkers which must have served some wartime bomber dispersal area and made for a very safe, secure, cosy and concealed deployment location for the crews of one of our Skyguards and its three Oerlikon guns. We fortified the area around with lashings of barbed wire and traps, making it very difficult to attack. In fact, because it was so good, we left everything in place and used it for demonstrations, as all we had to do was drive into position and throw up a few camouflage nets. The underground bunker was always a great surprise for visitors, especially if we had laid on a very British candle-lit, silver service tea or dinner underground for our unsuspecting visitors.

Bad weather totally grounded most of mainland Europe so our hoped-for mass air raids never materialized. To ginger things up for us, an over-zealous exercise umpire called a 'paper' Air Raid Red. The base air raid sirens duly howled and our enthusiastic gunners 'shot down' the only aircraft in sight, an Air Training Corps Chipmunk giving cadets air experience rides. It was to be the only air action for the squadron in the whole exercise. The ground activity, however, proved to be quite exciting. An SAS patrol ambushed me in my Land Rover as I was doing the rounds, checking an off-base Skyguard position. Given the option of parole to play dead or being tied up for real, I chose parole. The SAS used my Land Rover to gain access to the heart of the base and attacked the station operations bunker with blank ammunition and 'Thunderflash' simulated grenades. Not surprisingly, the command staff inside declined to open the door, so the SAS produced a chainsaw, cut themselves a large hole and poured in. If that was not frightening enough, they upped the terror level by cutting the duty controller's desk in half and waving the still snarling saw about menacingly. Not surprisingly, surprise turned to shock, then fear, as the odd table leg was amputated and the totally terrified occupants were lined up against a wall, to be 'shot' by the black-hooded and black-suited ersatz-Spetznaz. At this point the umpire decided to call it quits just as I wandered in. The senior operations room officer was apoplectic and turned to me for support, pointing to the dramatic damage and the still phut-phutting chainsaw. 'What do think of that?' he demanded. Looking around at the still pale and shocked operations room staff, I said that I thought the experience, as an exercise in the mastery of fear and the need for bravery in leadership under extreme duress, instead of mealy-mouthed management, it was a wonderful exercise, well worth the few hundred pounds it would cost to replace the furniture and the door. I got a very old-fashioned face-pull for that observation, then I congratulated the SAS and asked for my Land Rover back. Next time I saw the door, it was a double thick sandwich of steel.

With two recruit courses to run and those already trained as airmen, training was getting more complicated. In a Regular unit, if one needed a corporal, the RAF would put forward a man with about five years of experience; for a sergeant ten and for a flight sergeant about fifteen. Of course, a Regular of such long service could be posted to do any job of his rank and, if the new job was in an area he had not worked in before, he would be sent on the appropriate course, which could be anything from a week to a year. In our case our Auxiliaries would only ever work on the Skyguard-Oerlikon weapon system. We needed officers to know as much about the gun and radar as the men did to command a whole fire unit of twenty-eight troops; we needed flight sergeants to support the deployed men in the field administratively, logistically and operationally; we needed sergeants to command each gun and radar crew, and equally well-trained corporals and air-men to sustain operations on each weapon 24/7, with anybody capable of being used to replace a senior or junior casualty immediately in combat. We certainly could not wait fifteen years for people to percolate up the promotion chain. Having recruited enough gunners to fill all the positions with airmen of the lowest rank, we needed to start training individuals to fill more senior positions: corporal, sergeant, flight sergeant and junior officer. That meant four more courses, plus the need to recruit and train replacements to fill the vacancies arising from promotion, both from Auxiliaries joining the Regular Air Force and from retirements due to personal circumstances. As a minimum, we were looking at simultaneous, parallel training at five different rank levels and two specializa-tions, the Oerlikon gun and the Skyguard radar. Following my 'back-to-front' philosophy of making sure that every single recruit was a competent Oerlikon gunner first and foremost meant that every promotee had to be totally competent to do the job of any junior below them, as well as understand the job above them. What we needed to do now was solve how we could speedily accelerate the train-ing of non-commissioned officers and junior officers, using the same principle as for the recruits by reviewing the training required in the light of the question: 'We are going to war tomorrow. What do we really need to know in order to fight and win?' And the answer was everything to do with fighting the gun and radar. Once we had that, we could get NATO operational declaration. One does not achieve this for knowing the unit history, bulling boots, polishing floors, sports afternoons and endless standing around the hangar waiting for training to begin. One gets NATO declaration for showing that the unit, and every man on it, knows how to fight their weapon through every imaginable simulated set-back, to the last man, to the last bullet, so to speak. That was to be our next Holy Grail. Filling in the rest would be nice light relief for dark winter evenings.

We put this need to accelerate promotion, in not quite the same words, to all of the Auxiliaries we had trained thus far who had shown leadership and instructional qualities. We offered speedy promotion for a one-off increase in training hours commitment, salaries to be paid at the current hourly and daily rates, along with travel and subsistence allowances, the biggest carrot being increased responsibility status in rank and near exponential rises in the pay that went with promotion. The difference between us and the Regulars was that the Auxiliaries would be absolute masters of just one single weapon system for their entire careers, unlike the Regulars, who would weave their way upwards, in and out of various sub-specializations, as they rose in rank. We nicknamed this volunteer-within-volunteers group the 'fast squad'. They were all alpha people, mature, better educated and more worldly-wise than your average Joe Citizen. We doubled their training evenings from once a week to twice a week and doubled the weekends to twice a month for a promised six months, with the target of making promotions in time for the next annual camp. With their agreement, I pressed the 'Go' button and unleashed my young officer, Davey Johnston, and the three flight sergeants, Bolding, Coupe and Kavanagh on them.

There was one other problem I had to address and that was relatively senior ex-servicemen wishing to join the squadron: experienced captains, flight lieutenants, warrant officers, senior sergeants and even what we called 22-year soldiers and airmen, as well as others from other Services. Most, I found, were looking for social military company or a minimum boost to their pensions. This might work in the average infantry field squadron; however, I had seen Reserve Forces units run downhill very quickly, to become social organizations of little military value: poodle fakers, as AOC 11 Group, Air Vice Marshal Ken Hayr called them. But my outfit was Star Wars modern, fearsomely powerful, heavy artillery. I did not want or need corpulent and bureaucratic middle managers; I wanted a Para, a Royal Marine, an RAF Regiment or an SAS-like meritocracy. If I thought they would fulfil the requirement, I would offer the individual an appointment on the condition they started with the lowest rank and position on the gun and mastered every crew duty, each stage confirmed by live firing, with accelerated promotion up through the ranks as fast as we could train them. When they had worked their way through all the gun and radar crew positions, I would consider them for commissioning as junior officers, not in their old ranks.

Consequently, I only recruited the best ex-servicemen. My benchmark in this direction was to take on the former college warrant officer of the Royal Air Force College Cranwell, Warrant Officer Andy Robertson; they didn't come much better than him. Above all, I myself wanted to be replaced by an officer with 110 per cent knowledge and 200 per cent commitment and in that I was lucky enough to be followed by Squadron Leader Bob Kemp, one of the RAF Regiment's great up and coming young officers.

In the meantime, visits by high-ranking officers continued and it was especially enjoyable to welcome my old station commander from RAF Laarbruch in Germany (he of 'If at first you don't succeed, you're sacked' fame), now Air Chief Marshal Sir Michael Knight, UK Military Representative to NATO, who had, as a member of the Air Force Board, been the sponsor for the Skyguard-Oerlikon project. By November 1985 the second intake of recruits were starting their initial Oerlikon training, with the aim of live-firing at HMS *Cambridge* early in the New Year. The first intake, having reached Oerlikon operational capability, were now busy with 'backwards' catch-up training and were into such exciting things as throwing live hand grenades and close-quarter battle shooting, a kind of hunt-the-enemy, as in a paintball shoot, except with pop-up targets and real bullets. The squadron diary recorded that with the visit of Air Chief Marshal Sir Thomas Kennedy, Air Member for Personnel, the squadron had now been visited by every single member of the Air Force Board, so my Auxiliaries had personally met more of the top ranks of the Royal Air Force in a year than most mid-ranking Regular officers did in their entire careers. The highlight of the year, however, was far more basic than that.

The enterprising Kavanagh organized a duty-free shopping trip to RAF Laarbruch, a place that seemed to crop up often in 2729's life. Learning that HM Customs allowed individuals to import 50 litres of duty-free beer each, he hired a fifty-seat luxury coach for a weekend and when the driver, not un-naturally, enquired how come everyone was only travelling with hand luggage, he was told they were 'saving room for the beer'. He must have thought he was about to take a bunch of football hooligans on a holiday but when the troops turned up for the trip, Kavanagh had ready a coach-hold of empty German, Dutch and Danish beer crates full of empty bottles. The enterprising fellow had been around all the bases in Lincolnshire, rounding up empties from married quarter garages, officers' and sergeants' messes and base social clubs who were happy to get rid of these foreign beer cases and bottles that could not be returned in the UK. The troops camped on safari beds in the Laarbruch gymnasium, went sightseeing at Arnhem and then came home, each with 50 litres of bulk-bought, crated Grolsch beer, 2½ tons of it, bought through the sergeants' mess, whose duty-free beer bulk-buy price undercut that of all other suppliers by a wide margin. The bus home very nearly did not make it up Lincoln Hill but at least now the driver knew why it was so important for his passengers only to travel with hand luggage. The Auxiliaries gained an adventurous weekend abroad, a military-historical educational day pertinent to the Parachute Regiment and a cellar full of the finest German beer for Xmas at a knock-down, truly duty-free price. For my part, I suspected that Kavanagh might take another thousand or two Grolsch empties scattered around Lincolnshire back to Germany some time again in the future.

The 'fast squad' were now being hardened by taking their extra training outside, overnight, in the winter. The squadron also came into possession of a historically significant new war trophy: an original Second World War RAF ground gunner Oerlikon 20mm gun mount, with half an Oerlikon gun still attached, predating even the formation of the RAF Regiment. The circumstances of the find were this. My step father-in-law was staying with us. As an airman armourer in the Second World War on Halifax bombers, he had had his leg crushed by an unreleased 'hung-up' bomb from the previous night's raid. When the aircraft bomb doors were opened for rearming, the bomb rolled out on top of his leg, crushing its bones and he thus became an early McIndoe reconstructive surgical guinea pig. I offered to take him on a trip down memory lane to visit his wartime airfield at Pocklington, not too far away. The airfield was, by then, in almost total ruin: grass growing out of the cracked runways, the air traffic control tower a windowless shell sprouting trees, almost the filmset of that classic war movie, 'Twelve O'Clock High'. Frank described the nightly line up of thirty or more Halifax heavy bombers revving up in the dusk, waiting for the coded flare order to take off. And in the morning, counting smaller numbers of aircraft coming home, with stragglers crashing and burning and flesh being pulled off hands as they tried to extract dead and dying aircrews from burning wrecks. Worst was the sound of burning corpses sizzling in their own body fat, like sausages on a barbecue spit. Then, by mid-morning, Auxiliary Transport Service female pilots would bring in brand new replacement bombers. And here, we found the gap in the hedge where, as young airmen, they would elude the RAF Regiment guards and sneak into town, to a pub with a large Toby jug in the bar, its face turned to the wall if there was to be a mission that night. The Toby jug was still there. Then Frank mentioned a house nearby he used to play the piano for a family that hosted lonely airmen for a break away from war for a few hours during these dark days. I pressed him to show me the house and when we got there, I pressed him again to ring the doorbell. A woman of about 50 opened the door, and blinked and blinked and finally said 'I remember you. You are Frank who played the piano. I was only a child, but I always wondered if you had been killed when you didn't come back. And now you have!' And with that she burst into tears. It was a very emotional reunion that brought home to me, at a very personal level, the huge sacrifices that Bomber Command made to carry the war back to the heart of Nazi Germany alone, night after night, for five years. On the way back through the hole in the hedge, I noticed an Oerlikon mount grown into the hedgerow, so made an effort to find the current owner of the airfield. I asked if I could recover it for my squadron, a permission he duly granted. We cleaned it up, put an explanatory plaque on it and stood it outside the squadron headquarters, proudly alongside its newer sisters.

Another unusual possession was also to come into my hands at this time. It was an 8mm colour movie film of GADA 601's first firing of their Oerlikons, now mine, literally on the principal tourist beach of Buenos Aires, Mar del Plata. To power up the range safety firing circuits breaker, an Argentine gunner could be seen going up to a nearby traffic light, breaking into its wiring box and tapping into the electricity supply. When the guns actually fired, the civilian traffic continued, non-plussed, about their daily business. Two military personnel sat at a fold-flat table, one clearly an officer, the other a conscript. On the table was a field telephone. When it rang, the conscript picked it up and handed it to the officer, who spoke a few words; then the procedure was reversed. That was an army that treated its conscripts and civilians with such disdain that it was no wonder they lost. The final highlight of the year was to go to Buckingham Palace for my investiture. One is not allowed to report private conversations that take place with Her Majesty, so I can only say that, when I explained I was there because of the captured Argentine Oerlikon guns, those intensely blue royal eyes sparkled ever so much more. Afterwards, we did all the poses with the medal in front of Buckingham Palace Gates and blew my entire MoD award on a super 5-hour lunch in the Horse Guards Hotel for a deserving crowd of family, friends, military colleagues and, of course Spike Jones and Martin Frey. 1985 had been quite a year.

After Christmas leave, everybody came back to work refreshed and energetic; they needed to be, as the breakneck speed of formation of the squadron continued. There was now a small number of high quality ex-Service and civilian applicants who had been in touch with the squadron since our last recruit evaluation weekend. We ran a mini recruit selection weekend and accepted a further ten Auxiliaries, mainly to top-up losses from the fast squad. Unfortunately for me, but not for the Armed Forces as a whole, three of my best trained Auxiliaries had decided to join the Royal Air Force as full-time Regulars. My only grump was that the unit got no financial kickback for doing the job of the Directorate of RAF recruiting. For the Regular squadron instructors, life was becoming more interesting as more parallel training courses came on line as we trained smaller numbers at higher rank and responsibilities on the radar and gun. We now had three corporals nearly fully qualified to command both the gun and the radar and they needed a live-firing experience to be signed-off at this level. We also had a couple of gun crew aimers who needed to do their radar-less, reversionary live-firing over the open Ferranti gyro gunsight. One of the soon-to-be corporals was Betty Stacey, a founder recruit from Intake 1, whose young son joined at the same time. Her other two sons were at Cambridge University. Betty was not your average Service wife; she was tiny, grey haired and wore thick glasses but she surprised us with her agility, fitness, strength and phenomenal ability to absorb training. We realized we had a potential winner here, but Betty was so modest that it took some time for all her talents to emerge. It turned out that she was a trained archivist, an official guide at Lincoln Cathedral, a bell-ringer at the local church and read novels in Norwegian for relaxation. As a side task, she went through the hundreds of Argentine captured documents that came with the guns and sorted the lot out into catalogued, subject and date order, which is how we came to possess the entire set of GADA 601's daily orders and the priest-produced *Gaçeta Argentina*.

We were now starting to enjoy using part-timers to train recruits directly under the looser supervision of our Regulars, as they gained confidence and our trust. Twenty-eight of our Auxiliaries learned to drive, passing their DVLC tests on a Land Rover at great saving to themselves and increasing our flexibility of deployment as a unit, freeing up more Regular instructional time for us to further advance training. We also sent male and female gunners down to the RAF driving school in Wales to come back as fully licensed 8-tonner drivers. The squadron fielded a team to enter the Dutch 'Nijmwegen Marches', a 40km-a-day, four-day competition held over 160km of marching in full military kit. A Regular RAF Regiment team from Germany was surprised to find itself in a stiff race against 'Auggies', who were giving as good as they got. The Marches that year were carried out in absolutely atrociously cold weather conditions, with water in water-bottles freezing up overnight. Our winter outdoor training was obviously paying off, earning one team member, Leading Aircraftsman Tony Lee, the epithet 'Duracell' because he just kept going and going and never faded out. The medals the team brought back laid the motivational foundations for participation in subsequent Marches in greater numbers in years following.

Soon it was time to visit HMS *Cambridge* again, to qualify the small number of gunners and radar operators at the next rank level and sign off new gun aimers. The great advantage of the naval station ashore was that it provided proper, decent, peacetime, normal accommodation and messing for our troops in buildings that overlooked the firing gun line down the front of the cliffs, only a short walk away. Also, it was already a physically secure base in counter-IRA terms, so we as a small unit did not have to guard our weapons or ammunition overnight. Finally, there was the generous naval hospitality and interest, especially towards our girls fulfilling the combat roles, something to which the many Wrens aspired to but were not yet allowed to undertake. And as usual, the Skyguard radar firings slaughtered all the target sleeves.

While we were there, we learned that news of our unique existence had percolated into NATO and the unit was invited to take its annual summer camp in Denmark to participate in the Danish tactical weapon fighter meet at the Oksbol aircraft gunnery and bombing range. This was a live shooting and bombing competition for all the ground-attack aircraft in NATO. Pilots from as far apart as Norway and Turkey would come to fire and drop weapons in realistic flight paths to hit real targets in stiff competition: quite a different exercise from lightly laden Canberras parting the wheat fields of Lincolnshire with their jet flux to beat-up and terrorize us. To make the fighter meet more challenging, the Danes also invited air defence units from throughout NATO to provide the flak to defend the range. The fields and sand dunes all around were carpeted by examples of just about every kind of anti-aircraft weapon in NATO, from the long-range Patriot missile to the hand-held Stingers and Blowpipes, with every calibre of gun in between, it was a professional educational feast of the first order, with the bonus of a sea voyage and an exciting new country thrown in. We were not going to waste this opportunity and planned to go with 100 per cent of our manpower and equipment. As a deployment task, it would emulate GADA 601's journey to the Falklands, except in our case we would be coming back in good order afterwards. So, back to recruiting, the aim was to reach 110 per cent Auxiliary manning, to cover for personnel losses in training. We acknowledged that not everybody could be free from their real-world jobs to go to camp, given the marathon commitment in time that some individuals had already made.

For a change of venue and recruiting style, we hired a pitch in Lincoln Market Square at twenty five pounds for the day; no concession being given just because we called ourselves the City of Lincoln Squadron. We put up a radar and gun and had a continuous loop of our various live firings and deployments running on video. Oerlikon had very kindly sponsored a full-colour recruiting booklet, which we were able to hand out to people who were interested enough to climb on board the gun and take a bead on passing pigeons, or climb inside the radar and have a Star Wars go at tracking a Red Arrow or two. The market deployment was also reported in the local press, which saved us the cost of placing formal advertisements. Best of all, for this type of high-profile display, we only needed one Regular to be present (to guard my six o'clock); the rest of the show was manned by Auxiliaries, who thrived on the publicity. With lots of RAF bases around Lincolnshire, many Regular RAF personnel shopping in the city were surprised to see part-timers manning such high-tech equipment; their respect and admiration was a great boost to the Auxiliaries. We also ran a letter-box campaign, giving every Auxiliary 200 leaflets to post up and down the streets where they lived. These efforts were reinforced by yet another Freedom of the City parade and gave us the opportunity to roll down the High Street with our twin cannon barrels ferociously bared to steal the show. The recruiting that followed exceeded expectations yet again and we reached our pre-annual camp target of 110 per cent. On paper, at least, we were a fully manned Reserve Forces unit within a year of formation, with 70 per cent of the unit now able to deploy and fully man all four Skyguard radars and twelve Oerlikon twin 35mm AA guns.

By May 1986 we had another gun course ready for live firing and made our way down to HMS *Cambridge*. This time, the live firing was witnessed by the new Commandant General of the RAF Regiment, jet pilot Air Vice Marshal David Leech. The Inspector General of the Royal Auxiliary Air Force, the charismatic and immensely popular Air Chief Marshal Sir John Barraclough, and the modest Inspector Royal Auxiliary Air Force, Group Captain Lord Peter Harris, also looked in, while the Captain of HMS *Cambridge* enquired ever so softly under his breath how was it possible for such a little unit to pull in so much brass every time it came to fire from his ship. It must have been a great inconvenience to have to spruce up everything for all these VIP visits and I really appreciated his great support. One of our female gunners was Paige Lattimer, the daughter of Warrant Officer Terry Lattimer, now holder of an MBE, who did so much for the project in its greatly uncertain early days; Paige achieved what her Dad never managed and that was to fire the Oerlikon guns for real. We also beat the Royal Navy at football and fielded a nearly all-girl hockey team against the matelots. To end our stay, the captain had to endure just one more VIP for an hour, a Harrier pilot and former Harrier Force commander, the new Air Officer Commanding 11 Group, Air Vice Marshal Mike Steer, who dropped in and out by helicopter just in time to witness Corporal Betty Stacey destroy the last sleeve of the firing camp with a 1 second Skyguard radar-controlled burst. In my other life, I had been commander of 15 Squadron RAF Regiment, protecting Steer's thirty-six Harriers in the field on NATO's biggest-ever peacetime mobilization exercise of the Cold War. During the exercise I was lucky enough to be given a flight in one of his magic Harriers and to feel for myself the thrill of fast jet low-level flying, followed by the amazing sensation of slowing to a complete stop in the middle of the air for a vertical landing. The squadron was now being invited to take part in more and more exercises. I was beginning to wonder if the requesting Headquarters Strike Command staffs appreciated that we were a part-time Reserve Forces unit, as most of these requests asked for deployments during the working week, difficult when the RAuxAF volunteers were at their civilian jobs. However, there were always enough part-time volunteers and flexible employers for us to deploy at least one radar and a gun on skeleton manning for a day. Our favourite exercise was to go to the nearby RAF gunnery and bombing ranges at Donna Nook on the Lincolnshire coast or Wainfleet on the Norfolk coast. On these days at the seaside, we would be rewarded with Tornados flashing past at high speed and low level, to drop puny 25lb practice bombs through the middle of an oversized archery target, out on the mudflats. Seen from the Skyguard, the Tornado was a dead duck. For real, however, the Tornado was equipped with a huge submunitions dispenser, equivalent to many, many, small BL755 cluster bombs. One such dispenser could wipe out a Skyguard and all its three guns spread out over an entire 1km map square at a single pass. Sadly, we were never to see a live-drop of that particular weapon. What we did get to see more of, however, were the

American A-10 Thunderbolt tank-busters, single-seat jet aircraft that could nearly carry the entire bomb-load of a Second World War four-engined Halifax heavy bomber; in addition, they were armed with a truly ferocious 20mm Gatling gun that could vomit shells faster than three of our twin 35s put together. Luckily, our Oerlikons outranged the Gatlings by a full 2km. These two aerial gunnery ranges provided magnificent, close-up, live training for our men and women and many a time Tornados, Thunderbolts and many other NATO aircraft types would have been aware we had them 'Dead Turkey' in our sights from the grating sound of our radar lock-on in their radar warning receivers. It was a tremendously valuable training exercise for both parties and I always wondered why we never garrisoned anti-aircraft units right alongside such ranges in peacetime: it was the first thing I would done had anyone asked me to become an air marshal or a general of anti-aircraft artillery.

The fourth anniversary of the Falklands Campaign in June 1986 was also galloping towards us. I thought this would be a most appropriate time to award our Auxiliaries with the coveted RAF Regiment flash to wear on the shoulders of their uniform. Our gunners had by now sufficiently demonstrated their prowess and skill in operating our front-line equipment to wear the flash. I cleared it with the Commandant General, David Leech, who conveniently lived nearby. However, he was not in my operational chain of command; that fell to the AOC, Air Vice Marshal Mike Steer of 11 Group, who commanded all the air defence bases, including RAF Waddington. Having sorted out the protocol, the Commandant General would be the AOC's guest and the AOC himself would pin the RAF Regiment flashes on 'his' men. By coincidence, the Commandant General asked if he could bring, as his personal guest, Brigadier General Neal Scheidel, the Commanding General of the 80,000-strong United States Air Force Security Police Force, the USAF's opposite number to the RAF Regiment, which opened the door just a tiny crack for me to land a later posting to their staff in Albuquerque, New Mexico and initiate an exchange visit programme with the New Mexico National Guard . But that was far, far in the future.

Back in Waddington, we planned to repeat the format of the families day, only this time, thanks to fill-in training, plus a huge dose of motivation, our Auxiliaries were now crack Best Blue marchers with rifles and as smart as any RAF Regiment unit. We had the advantage of our own RAF Waddington pipes and drums band and it was an opportunity for the AOC to hand out unannounced corporal and sergeant stripes in a rare act of promotion-in-the field to our part-time gun and radar commanders who had made so much outstanding progress in the fast squad. The summer sun did its bit, the band played, the AOC praised, and the guns and radars rolled out; even the Vulcan popped in for a chest-reverberating beat-up of our gun-line; families smiled and little boys and girls ooh-ed and aaah-ed in the radars and on the guns, before the barbecue for 500 people was lit.

There was, however, no time to rest and lie back on our laurels. The Royal School of Artillery was about to hold its premier event for the public and for the world's assembled defence attachés stationed in London: Artillery Day. As the commander of the only anti-aircraft artillery cannon in British land service, this was not an event I was going to miss. While my young officer David Johnston was carrying out a recce of the ground ready for our summer camp in Denmark, I went off to Larkhill to negotiate our participation. In between the two, we had a Royal College of Defence Studies demonstration of all British land-based artillery to prepare for, plus an invitation for the Skyguard and Oerlikons to appear at the Royal Tournament. Finally, we heard that the Royal Canadian Artillery was to be equipped with the Skyguard-Oerlikon combination for the defence of their two NATO airfields in Germany; their future commander was an officer with whom I had worked closely a decade previously on the Rapier cold trials in Canada. Not waiting for me to look up an old acquaintance, Spike Jones of BMARCO turned up at RAF Waddington with Major (soon-to-be Lieutenant Colonel) Randy Stowell, future commander of the Canadian Oerlikons. On that surprise reunion visit, I 'sold' the Canadians my aircraft recognition training system, which earned me another small MoD royalty payment. More importantly, I volunteered the squadron for a summer camp at RCAF Baden-Sollingen airbase in Germany in 1987 by suggesting that they invite us to participate in their biennial NATO tactical evaluation. We would provide our Skyguard-Oerlikons to work with their 40mm Bofors gun units by way of early exposure to their future equipment scheduled for delivery the following year. In return, Randy asked if he could bring his officers over to RAF Waddington in the new year to see how we did things and would I mind coming over to Toronto, all expenses paid, to brief them on our aircraft recognition system, this side of Christmas. It was quite remarkable to see how the free association of sovereign nations in NATO worked so well together, way down at the personal level, even between small units.

Artillery Day was a major British Army event. At stake were billions of pounds of potential future armament sales to nations friendly towards us, putting a lot of bread on the tables of British workers and helping to keep the Soviet Union and its coerced 'allies' of the Warsaw Pact at bay. Every single calibre of artillery in service with the British Army was brought into set-piece action, building-up into ever-larger fire missions in response to requests for artillery fire support to other arms and Services. It was also a great professional development experience, as not many soldiers or airmen get to see and feel the effects of large-scale artillery bombardment close-up, for real. The cure for fear in battle is, of course, experience, even if it is only 'been there, seen that'. About 200,000 military personnel attend the day for this reason. Even the famous Second World War 25-pounder, nearly a thousand of which were fired together at the start of Monty's set-piece dismemberment of Rommel's Afrika Corps at El Alamein, was rolled out and fired for the benefit of nostalgic veterans. What I most liked about Artillery Day, however, was that as the concentration of artillery drew to its peak with the thunderous bombardment of a divisional fire mission (i.e. every gun on the battle-field focused on just one target), the grand finale of the day was for a single Harrier jet to drop a real, live 1,000lb bomb, which totally obliterated the target at a single pass, to leave an unmistakable message about the superiority of air power.

The event was staged in a gigantic natural amphitheatre on Larkhill Ranges, on Salisbury Plain. Some weapons were towed into firing positions, some arrived by helicopter; more arrived in a very impressive demonstration of a dirt-landing by a C-130 Hercules; and self-propelled guns on tracks raised impressive columns of dust as they manoeuvred into position. Next to a 105mm self-propelled Abbot, our long thin 35mm barrels with their wire cages at the end looked pretty puny. Beefy Royal Artillery gunners looked down from their lofty Abbot perches and enquired, jokingly, if we intended to fire our 35mm gun commander, the slim Sue Ford, out of the barrel; we said nothing. A line of six Abbots were on show in the event before ours. They had, as targets, six tank hulks in the middle distance. Each had been primed with a liberal splash of petrol to ensure a good brew-up when they were hit. The intention was for the first Abbot to kill the first tank, the second Abbot the second tank, and so on, all the way to the end. The first Abbot fired. Close, but no hit; ditto the second and third and fourth. Plenty of shrapnel dust was raised; also, had any personnel been around the tanks as covering infantry, they would have been killed. However, in the context of the demon-stration, the spectators' expectation was that all six tanks would brew up spec-tacularly and that just did not happen.

Next up were 2729's Oerlikon twin 35mm cannon firing in the ground-to-ground role at a row of petrol-filled, cardboard helicopters about 200m further out from the tanks. Our shells travelled at 1,100m/s, against the 300m/s of the Abbot shells. Over the 2,000m range, our trajectory was virtually flat. Our 8-tonner truck towed the Oerlikon into position; in earlier preparation, the generator cable had been laid out and buried and the generator itself was out of sight. With power operation, the gun was off its wheels and down, ready to fire in seconds. The single sighting shot exploded the first 'helicopter' and the following long burst of 2 seconds walked down the row, exploding all the helicopters as the Oerlikon vomited out empty shell cases in a long, continuous roll of thunder. By the end of the day, we were having Royal Artillery instructors-in-gunnery discreetly enquiring how they might wrangle a posting to our unit. They were even more taken aback to discover that half our crews were female; it was a great day for Auxiliary morale. I wondered idly how many Regular RAF Regiment personnel had witnessed a divisional fire mission; I would guess fewer than a handful.

Another discovery arose out of our Artillery Day attendance. Every time the Royal Artillery fired, we were able to pick out their shells in-flight on the Skyguard radar and track them all the way out to the target, both by radar and visually on the TV tracker. That was how we came to know how fast the artillery shells were flying, because the radar gave us a numerical read-out of target speed on the TV tracker screen: 300m/s. When I mentioned this 'discovery' of mine to Martin Frey, he laughed. The Swiss Army used the Skyguard for artillery prediction and, against incoming fire, for firing-point detection of enemy artillery for counter-battery fire; in this role they called it Landguard. Ever mindful of Oerlikon sales, Martin went on to ask if the British Army might perhaps like to look at one? I suggested that as Artillery Day was a British sales pitch, he might like to try some other venue, while we put the squadron down for another Artillery Day appearance two years hence, signing-off a few more aimers as live-firing qualified to complete the day.

Meanwhile, at Earl's Court preparations for our participation in the Royal Tournament were under way. Flight Sergeant Steve Coupe had taken a small team of Auxiliaries, together with our Oerlikon gun, Goose Green, and our Skyguard radar, Ajax Bay, down to RAF Uxbridge to work out the initial display routine. Coupe, equally as enterprising as Kavanagh, took with him a thousand of our fired ex-Argentine 35mm shell cases and, with Corporal Jo Marsh's Moss Bros marketing skills, set up a little stall to sell 'Genuine Captured Argentine Anti-Aircraft Shell Cases from the Falklands War' in aid of our squadron fund. Returning to the more serious business of the display itself, we learnt that the arena was actually a covered-over Olympic swimming pool and that the cover would not bear the 5-ton weight of the Skyguard. After Bofors guns falling into the sea in Cyprus and our nail-biting cliff-side Oerlikon deployments at HMS *Cambridge*, we had no wish to drop a Skyguard into a swimming pool, no matter how Olympic it might be. So, both gun and radar were confined to the solid poolside edges.

The bulk of the RAF routine for this year was to be carried out by the RAF Regiment, between the ceremonial Queen's Colour Squadron (QCS), a light armoured squadron, a Rapier squadron, a sister Auxiliary field squadron and ourselves. While the number of units participating looked large, no more than a dozen soldiers, sailors or airmen from each unit were actually committed to the Tournament, the purpose of which was to show off the Armed Forces to the public and raise money through the proceeds of entry tickets for Service charities. In a parody of the RAF Regiment's miniscule participation in the Falklands Campaign, the setting was the capture of an enemy airfield. The QCS would fall from the roof of the arena by parachute, and an enemy would counter-attack these light para forces; then Auxiliaries from the field squadron would blaze in, SAS-like, with their machine-gun-armed, stripped-down Land Rovers, followed by the big guns of 58 Squadron's Scorpion light tanks and their armoured personnel carriers; the ensuing enemy air raid would be foiled by the whoosh of Rapier missiles simulated by Brocks-supplied rockets running up invisible wires to the arena roof and the ripping-roar of Oerlikon guns firing for all they were worth, also using Brocks special effects, giant firecrackers on the ends of our barrels. In the half-dark of the arena, with the crackle of rifle fire, rockets, cannon, sound effects and gunpowder smoke, it could have been Arnhem or Goose Green all over again. Had Kavanagh been there, I am sure, he would have played John Wayne. As a public relations hit for the RAF Regiment and its part-time sister, the RAuxAF Regiment, it was a great success. It was also three weeks of training in organization and split-second timing in the deployment of the equipment, as well as harsh living, to earn the adoration of the public, put a thousand pounds in the squadron fund kitty and raise hundreds of thousands of pounds for Armed Forces charities.

As every professional actor knows, backstage things were somewhat different. The troops, men and women of the RAF, British Army and Royal Navy lived in field conditions, sleeping on the floors of the outer reaches of the arena (we had safari beds), sharing space with horses, dogs, guns, vehicles and tanks. After every show, the dust, grime and horseshit of the previous displays had to be removed, and all the kit polished up and prepared for the next performance. Accommodation between units was screened-off by hessian enclosures. No personal kit could be left out in-sight or off-stage. Our £3 million radar and gun had to be guarded 24/7, so there was plenty of military training going on to be absorbed by osmosis. Over the three weeks of the Royal Tournament, we rotated personnel weekly to give everyone the experience, the quid-pro-quo being that they could watch all the fabulous displays for free and meet all the interesting foreign participants who came from far and wide. How many Auxiliaries get to meet, at a personal level, real Maori warriors from the New Zealand Army, or discover that India has twenty times more Gurkha Regiments than Britain does, or meet real Canadian Mounties, splendid in red on horseback, out to get their man. I always thought that using the supposed diversionary cost of troop participation was a mean, bean-counter excuse to cut out the Royal Tournament from public display. As usual, broadened experience, panache, morale and working with allies, not - to mention training in field administration, logistic nightmares, harsh living, hard work, liaison, tolerance, can-do and cooperation a battle-winning armed force cannot be easily calibrated in money: a pox on bean-counters. The final gilding of the Tournament lily came when two of my airmen, Sandra Brooks and Alex Goddard, were presented to Prince Edward. It was after, all the Royal Tournament.

While on my official visits down to London to check on the welfare of my troops and the security of my valuable Skyguard equipment, Sandra Brooks was to come into royal orbit again, this time more indirectly, but tangibly royal, nevertheless. The mission was to design the heraldic device that was to be the official badge of the squadron, a small piece of Britain's heritage personally signed off by the monarch. Thanks to its wartime service, 2729 was immediately entitled to a squadron badge with a heraldic device of its own. The opportunity to be the author and designer of such a badge does not come round to individuals very often; I say author because it needs a motto and designer because it needs a completely unique heraldic device. As the RAF's founder, Lord Trenchard, had chosen a double circle of laurel leaves with a crown above and a scroll for a motto below as the standard base design of all the badges of all RAF squadrons, stations, groups and commands, leaving the central space for any heraldic device. All I had to do was create a central heraldic device that had not been used before in the thousand years or so of device allocation by the Royal College of Arms. The initiative to commission an official badge rests wholly with the unit commanding officer, so it is a very personal opportunity. I went to see the man in charge of this august exercise, the Norroy and Ulster King of Arms, Sir Walter Verco himself. He was a delightfully enthusiastic man in his 80s, with an encyclopedic memory of all the devices stored on vellum, literally going back centuries. The main criteria, he advised, was that the design had to be absolutely unique. He then went on to say that it was very important to keep it bold and simple, so that when it was shrunk down to an inch or so, as for use in modern correspondence letterheads, for example, it should still be clear what the device represented. Too many units fell for complicated designs which looked like an indecipherable mess when viewed from a distance or shrunk down to a letterhead. There was also a significance in which way a device faced: looking left was bold and challenging; facing right was timid and retreating. I definitely needed to get that right. Choosing a heraldic link with the Falkland Islands would not be smart as their central device was a sheep. Better was an Andean condor, a device clearly linked to South America but not solely directly attributable to Argentina. Sir Verco thought that was a good choice and it would certainly be unique in British heraldry, where eagles, falcons, hawks, owls and other birds of prey abounded. He also mused that a condor, being a genus of the vulture family, would be very appropriate for a unit that had scrounged its weapons off a battlefield from a defeated enemy. All I had to do was find a suitable image of an Andean condor.

I was to become something of an avian expert on condors at a time when the universal internet did not yet exist. I discovered that the most common condor, the Californian one, was not common at all; indeed, it was in immediate danger of becoming extinct and a desperate survival breeding programme was under way in California to save it. I started my search in Foyles bookshop and did the whole '85 Charing Cross Road' antiquarian bookshop thing, which only yielded more common Californian condors; Andean condors were rather rarer, given that their hunting grounds were the sparsely populated and high, isolated ranges of the Andes. Even an encyclopaedic search through the Natural History Museum did not yield anything heraldically interesting. Antique painting and manuscript dealers offered beautifully rare, hand-painted works of art that I was now sufficiently expert in to reject as common Californian condors; what I was looking for, I would say loftily, was 'Vulture Gryphus', the Andean condor. Even the BBC's wonderful natural history documentary, 'Flight of the Condor', with its spell-binding photography, failed to yield a heraldic candidate image.

What came to my rescue was my parents' lifelong subscription to the American *National Geographic* magazine, going back to 1944. In our remote farm in Zulu-land, in the valley of King Shaka's royal hunting ground, there was no electricity, no running water and no neighbour for 16km in any direction; my growing-up window on the world from about age 3 was thus the monthly *National Geographic*. It was, in effect, the family encyclopedia and so I visited my mum to search through forty years of carefully collected family back-issues; in one of them I found a definitive and lavishly illustrated article about Andean condors. I became even more expert. The male condor was a definite no-no: it has a well-developed, red cock's comb on its head and it looks just like a turkey cock. I had no wish to command a turkey squadron, so we searched on and found a splendid head-shot of a totally bald and sharp-beaked female Andean condor, with a mean red eye and a wonderful snow-white ruff of soft feathers around her neck. I showed the picture to Sandra; she turned it into a hand-painted watercolour and I sent that to Sir Walter. It was perfect; it even faced the correct direction.

All we needed now was a motto. In those pre-internet days of the 1980s, it took me another half-day out from checking the troops at the Royal Tournament, back into the bookshops. I was directed to a *Dictionary of Mottos, Foreign and Domestic* – a first edition from 1790-something, price way above my pay grade. Not for buying then, but a quick thumb through took me to 'Death to the Enemy who Flies', with its original version in Spanish alongside. I quickly copied it down in my notebook and showed it to my former squadron commander and Spanish-speaker, now the late Group Captain David Salusbury. It turned out that the word 'flies' in Spanish as quoted correctly translated meant 'fly' as in to flee in defeat, which was not quite what I wanted. In less than a nanosecond David had the right Spanish word for 'flies', in the sense of birds and aircraft. That would do very nicely indeed for a motto: *Muerte al Enimigo que Vuela*. The draft drawing went up the chain of command from Station Commander, AOC 11 Group, Commander-in-Chief Strike Command, Commandant General RAF Regiment, Air Force Board and, finally, through Sir Walter Verco to Her Majesty, for that magic 'Approved. Elizabeth II' signature on vellum. The lovely thing about the condor in the badge was that it resembled me even more than the Baldeagle caricature that I had inherited from the Royal School of Artillery. I would love to have been known as 'El Condor' but it was too late. To too many of my com-rades I am still Baldeagle, and that is that. Forty years on my now ex-officers and I raised the £700 necessary for the College of Arms to paint an exact copy on vellum of our badge and that copy has now joined the Wall of Honour of more than 700 Royal Air Force squadron badges in the Royal Air Force Club. It was considerably cheaper to have the same carved into stone on the floor of the Royal Air Force Church, St Clement Danes, in London's Strand. And so, between the Queen, the Church and the Club, I think I have immortalized 2729 Squadron sufficiently, my small personal contribution to its posterity.

Fig. 19. Draft line drawing of the 2729 Squadron badge by Sandra Brooks. Appropriately, the female condor defends its nest of chicks with fury.

Chapter 24

Summer Camp in Denmark

The big highlight of the year was the two-week summer camp at the Danish aircraft bombing range at Oksbol in Denmark. This was to be the first time since the Argentine misadventure to the *Malvinas* that all the guns were to take a sea voyage together. Our journey, however, was considerably less stressful, thanks to the RAF Movers and the RAF's 2 Mechanical Transport Squadron slickly swinging into action. Six 40ft Seddon & Atkinson articulated trucks turned up at Waddington and swept up the six guns and generators piggy-back and transported them to our ship, DFDS *Danna Anglia*. The remaining guns, generators and radars were towed by our own 8-tonners, following in a second convoy. As we were going to share a commercial ferry with holiday-makers in peak season, we sent this convoy down a day ahead and pre-positioned our vehicles in convenient loading order on the dockside so that they would not get mixed in with cars and inconvenience the public. A mixed guard of Auxiliaries watched over the equipment overnight and were rewarded for their extra duties by a decent bed in a hotel. The rest of the squadron bussed down the next day and everything was quickly and safely stowed aboard for the 24 hour crossing. The DFDS Line is probably the best of all cross-channel ferry services; the ship was immaculate, with a superb Scandinavian smorgasbord restaurant, cabaret and disco on board, creating a slight sense of disbelief that this was a military deployment. DFDS even produced a birthday cake for one of our gunners. The whole slightly surreal experience would probably ring a bell with those who went down to the Falklands on the *QEII* in 1982. In the morning we arrived in Esbjerg and all the trucks and trailers were offloaded swiftly onto the dockside. Using only our organic 8-tonners, it took us half a day to shuttle all the guns, generators and radar trailers the last 40km from Esbjerg to the Oksbol Danish barracks, where we would stay when not deployed in the field. The reception arrangements were excellent and it came as a pleasant surprise to see the high standard of Danish military accommodation.

Just about every NATO country had sent a representative anti-aircraft unit to participate in the Fighter Meet; there were units of Danish Red Eye, German tracked Rolands, British Army Rapiers, Dutch Hawks, Norwegian Bofors guns, German Rheinmetall twin 20mm guns and even some quad .50 calibre truck-mounted gun turrets of Second World War vintage present. There was also a German Navy 40mm Bofors battery responsible for defence of a Baltic airfield of

German Navy Tornados. All these diverse but related units were crowded, cheek-by-jowl, into the fairly small dry training area alongside the bombing range on the Jutland peninsula. It was a great opportunity for units to visit each other and compare notes and technical innovations for dealing with the common problem of how to shoot down aeroplanes. Whenever an air raid was announced, one only had to glance outside to see who was first to find the targets by observing which way the various guns and missiles were pointing. All the units were linked together by radio and naturally everybody claimed to have shot down everything.

The excellent domestic facilities enabled us to run three separate levels of training at the same time. The newest recruits did a concentrated Oerlikon gun course in barracks on a neatly laid-out gun-line on the sports field from 8.00am to 8.00pm. It was such a scene of activity that casual groups of off-duty Danes, Germans, Dutch and even Brits would come along to watch the into and out-of-action drills and, I suspect, look at the unusual sight of girl gunners. This outside interest, of course, sharpened up performance and competitiveness between the crews and they quickly reached the highest standards we demanded. So seriously were they taking their training that one day, seeing a row of them unwinding on the swimming poolside nearby, I noticed that they all had their gun drill books in their hands and were quizzing each other whilst enjoying the late evening sun, feet in the water.

There were, of course, some lighter moments. The troops on early morning parade doubled up when the squadron Warrant Officer Andy Robertson's clarion voice demanded to know which slack, idle, slovenly gunner had left her smalls in a communal washroom basin for his embarrassment. There were other good reasons for high morale. The Danes ran a pay-as-you-dine messing service, so the RAF had advanced us cash-in-lieu-of-rations. With typical British thoroughness, our command catering staff had based the allowance on the assumption that every airman would eat a full English breakfast as provided in our home messes, namely fruit juice, cereal with milk, egg, bacon, beans, sausages, toast and marmalade, all washed down with at least a pint of tea, all of which was nothing like what the health-conscious, dainty Danes were actually eating. Notwithstanding the excellent food available, there were one or two Regulars with mortgages to pay who saw this allowance as an opportunity to save a sizeable sum of money from the arrangement and had brought suitcases of food from home to eat over the fortnight. Each to their own.

Concurrent with the gun course in barracks, the radar course was taking advantage of a week's continuity to work everybody up to the next rank level of responsibility. Alongside us was a Regular RAF Regiment Rapier squadron and it was very welcome to be complimented on the high state of training and efficiency of our Auxiliary crews on the radars and guns. They were certainly impressed with the modern features of our equipment, especially the ease and speed with which we could deploy from our road-travelling positions. On the other hand,

I liked to point out that even quite small helicopters could easily and quickly lift the lightweight Rapier trailers into position, whereas our heavy equipment required a Chinook. It was horses for courses, but in terms of long-term crew comfort, ease of operation and reliability, our Skyguards won hands down. For those members of the squadron who were now fully gun and radar qualified, we ran a 'Backfill' training course on the small unit infantry skills that we would need to have in order to protect our equipment in the field: advanced map reading, site recce, ground clearance patrols, standing patrols, anti-ambush drills, defensive trenches, GPMG machine-gun drills, and so on. While these drills were important, they were a secondary part of the operation of our main equipment.

In fact, the deployment problems we faced in Denmark pretty well matched those the Argentinians experienced amidst the sand dunes and marshes around Stanley. Despite the most thorough route recces through the tussock grass, we found that when the surface gave way, we could be up to our axles in no time at all. Prior to our full squadron deployment in the second week, we had planned to set up a demonstration site deployment for the arrival of the Four Star Inspector General of the RAuxAF, Air Chief Marshal Sir John Barraclough. It was as well for us that he flew in on a late Sunday afternoon. Although the civilian airport was nominally closed, the Danes accepted his military jet and, out of respect for his very senior rank, the airport manager opened up the duty free shop for his personal convenience, which was an extremely thoughtful gesture and, luckily for us, kept him away from the squadron while we played out our own overnight crisis.

We had got a Skyguard radar and 8-tonner stuck when the wheels broke through the tussock grass into the slippery, soft sub-soil beneath. Attaching a rigid tow to our recovery truck only added to the rescue problem: we now had two 8-ton trucks and a 5-ton trailer stuck. Our nearest neighbours, the German naval battery, were delighted to turn-out their 'superior' 10-ton six-by-six truck and promptly bogged that in up to the axles. As it got dark, it started to rain and rain, turning the ground into a quagmire. In fact, out in the North Sea a full-on howling gale was blowing and I worried about my eldest daughter on the sail training ship *Sir Winston Churchill* tearing its way before the storm all the way up to Scotland. Back in Denmark, the slashing rain glowed in the lighthouse-like beams of the truck headlights and ghostly forms of gunners hunched over in the wet, grunting in the mud. Two British Army Scammell field recovery tractors joined the fray and soon joined the immobility of the earlier, failed, would-be rescuers. By now, the swearing had become pretty international. Final rescue came in the wee small hours, thanks to the incentive of a bottle of whisky from our engineering chief, John Collins, to waken the crew of a 60-ton Danish Centurion recovery tank. One by one, it pulled the vehicles out of the morass. My only regret was that iPhones had not yet been invented as the scene would have made for some spectacular photography. The experience made us more careful.

Every radar and gun would henceforth only be deployed by a double-header of two 8-tonners linked together with a rigid tow. Next day, we took Sir John on a tour of the squadron but what he most wanted to do, he said, was to drive one of the 8-ton trucks himself, so John Collins took him out for a long driving lesson in the dunes, judicially avoiding the churned-up area of our previous night's excursion.

We now brought all elements of training together to work as a whole squadron might in war. Each day would begin in barracks. The commanders and guides would recce their new positions for the following day at last light the day before and leave marker stakes which the guides would use to direct their equipment to their exact positions; this was not a place to find out that one had got a cable-length wrong after the double-headed towing trucks had departed. At dawn each fire unit of radar, three guns and three generators would be towed to a harbour area which an Auxiliary foot patrol had cleared earlier. Further foot patrols, made up of the gun and radar crews, then fanned out to clear the actual deployment locations and, when ready, to call up the first gun and generator. Once the gun was operational and running under power, the radar would be brought up under the protection of that gun, which would then be integrated with the radar. Then, under the cover of a now radar-directed cannon, the second and third guns would in turn be deployed and integrated with the radar, bringing the fire unit up to its maximum all-weather killing capability, all the while in full communications with the command post. Defensive fighting positions were then constructed by digging-in, tents pitched in the minimum low-profile mode in hollows in the dunes, and the whole lot camouflaged. A competition was held for the most tactical site and the most flavourful meal cooked out of British field rations, the judges being the crews of the other fire units, so that everybody got to see everybody else's deployment positions. The standards were very high indeed and I was confident the squadron was within a few percentage points of being ready for full declaration to NATO, the missing percentage being that this field deployment was not in defence of an airfield where, to ensure the safe passage in and out of friendly aircraft, an additional level of command and control of the battlespace would have to be put in place and practised. During the exercise we 'engaged' a total of 103 aircraft, all shot down of course. There had not been a single vehicle, gun, generator or radar failure, accident or disciplinary case of any kind. And of the squadron outing to Legoland, Lin Dynan recorded in the spoof Squadron diary that the pixies, gnomes and fairies had such a disappointing day not being allowed to wear their wet uniforms or sodden webbing. They also missed the morning swearing lessons from the second-in-command and were anxious to know who had the maggotiest mess tin. In fact, they were all so depressed that even buying funny Viking hats with horns on them did not cheer them up until they discovered that Dim and Glim had missed the bus home. The reason they missed the bus was they must have thought they were in a new deployment area and were later found building a Lego gun position complete with Lego admin area, Lego slit trenches and Lego shell scrapes. Actually, the pair took a 40km taxi trip back to camp that night, no doubt paid for out of their generous meal allowance, in time for a sheepish breakfast the next morning.

At the end of the ten-day camp we were very grateful that the Danish barracks had a tank-washing facility for a massive clean-up of trucks, radars, generators and guns for the journey back to England. With the convoy drivers all wearing horned Viking helmets, everything was soon delivered to the dockside and in the space of 15 minutes all vehicles were safely aboard. From the stern deck, the troops sang the HMS *Ark Royal* song 'We are sailing' in farewell to the Danes, modified to include references to excesses of Carlsberg, the latest squadron bulk-bought, NATO duty-free brew.

On our return to Waddington, things went rather quickly. First of all, I had the pleasure of commissioning our first two young RAuxAF officers, Pilot Officer Steven Howard (affectionately abbreviated by the troops to POSH) and Pilot Officer Trevor Wright. The next young officer after that was Pilot Officer Lance Saxby, whose nickname became POLS. Then the hugely popular Sir Rex Hunt, who had retired from his position as Governor of the Falkland Islands, accepted our invitation to become the squadron's Honorary Air Commodore; as a Second World War veteran RAF Typhoon tank-buster pilot, he understood flak. Next came the Royal Canadian Artillery for a mutual Skyguard-Oerlikon brainstorming session, which included us treating them to a surprise underground bunker silver service curry lunch at our favourite demonstration deployment site in the snow. The outcome of this fine lunch was a formal invitation for the squadron to hold its next summer camp at the Canadian Air Force base at Baden-Sollingen in Germany and help them introduce their Skyguards into service by taking part in their NATO tactical evaluation. This proved such a success that the squadron went to the Canadian bases two consecutive years running.

Finally, the station commander called me in, shook my hand and gave me a new set of orders. I was to report to RAF West Raynham wearing the badges of rank of wing commander, undertake the two month-long Bloodhound surface-to-air missile course and then report to MoDUK(Air) in the rank of substantive wing commander, to be the principal officer responsible for all RAF ground-based air defence in the Directorate of Air Defence, the first RAF Regiment officer to fill this post. And, in a nice twist of fate, my group captain boss was to be John May, the air planner who had had the vision to support my initial initiative back in 1985. I had come full circle.

My replacement was my very much respected long time friend Squadron Leader Bob Kemp. In the blink of an eye, or so it seemed, I was formally dined out of 2729 Squadron at a splendid all-ranks, formal dinner night in RAF Waddington's airmen's mess. It was a truly special event for me because I had, as my personal guest, one Squadron Leader Ron Snashall MC, RAF Retd, who had been a founder member of 2729 Squadron in the dark days of 1942 and had served with the squadron all the way across war-torn Europe from the beaches of Normandy, finally to march through Berlin's triumphal arches, *Unter den Linden*, as a participant of the massive Allied victory parade that marked the final defeat of Nazi Germany in 1945. In place of the usual speeches, the squadron poetess Lin Dynan had the last word, delivered by Bimbo, my second-in-command, now a mature Flight Lieutenant Davy Johnston.

And that was it. I hung up my greens and boots; shook the mothballs out of my MoD suit and became, once more, a military man in civvy disguise in that famous building that made bigger boobs inside.[28]

Chapter 25

Postscript

As is proper in military circles, an ex-squadron commander never visits his old command for at least five years after he has left, something the current crop of Parliamentarians might like to consider. Further overseas postings then ensured I never managed to formally visit either the squadron or the wing that it had grown into ever again, except as a guest of honour at its formal disbandment parade and final lunch. Many of my military friends subsequently commanded 2729 and 2890 Squadrons and its parent 1339 Wing and, as their commands were to cover another seven years of fine performance, I leave it to them to pull up a sandbag to recount more tales of derring-do covering a period three times as long as the one I have recorded of my short time in command.

There are three special former members of the Oerlikon squadrons and wing that I would like to mention. The first is Steve Coupe, who has never ceased to use his extraordinary II Squadron RAF Regiment (the Parachute Squadron) fitness to raise both money and the profile of issues for Service charities, particularly the Gurkhas, in all these intervening years; he was awarded the MBE in 2021 for his services to the military community. Next is George Batterbee, the person in our RAF personnel management centre responsible for posting Regulars to 2729 Squadron and then 1339 Wing, who decided the Oerlikon life appeared so interesting and exciting that he posted himself there. When the time came for him to eventually retire from the Royal Air Force, George founded a boutique brewery in nearby North Hykeham, close to RAF Waddington. Not many RAF squadron associations can boast of having their own private brewery with adjoining pub within their alumni. The pub is appropriately called the Poacher's Den and happens to serve a fine brew called Rock Ape Ale in a wonderful venue for regimental reunions which I personally can highly recommend. The last person I wish to commend to all is Flying Officer Louise Boulton BSc RAuxAF Regt retd, who was the first female commissioned officer to earn her RAF Regiment flashes as an operational Oerlikon gun commander; a Skyguard-Oerlikon flight commander with a finger on the NATO fire button of her fire unit of a radar and three guns with the simultaneous firepower of an entire, earlier generation RAF Regiment Bofors 40mm gun squadron; and, on her final tour of duty, as the first female Rapier flight commander on the Auxiliary-manned 27/48 Squadron Rapier Cadre nearly four decades before the place of women in combat was enshrined as an equal opportunity in the Regular RAF Regiment as it is today.

On reflection, my five years of Skyguard-Oerlikon was luck indeed. Three years of Cranwell and a year of Larkhill training gave me, an infantryman, the depth and breadth of radar, artillery and missile knowledge to seize an opportunity rarer than hen's teeth. It provided the chance to execute the entire introduction-into-service of a much-feared sophisticated weapons system fresh-off a victorious battlefield in a far-away land and then raise, train and command virtually every detail of the new unit thus created. The outcome was a *Boy's Own* dream, and I sometimes have to pinch myself to believe that it was possible to pull off such an unusual feat.

My promotion and next posting was to the Directorate of Air Defence, a first for an RAF Regiment officer. The specialist responsibility for the policy of all the Air Force's ground-based air defence assets required me to review the elderly Bloodhound, whose missiles had stood sentinel outside in the elements for more than two decades. Despite buying back extra missiles from the Swiss, who kept theirs dry and warm inside mountain caves, the system was doing more to prop up its manufacterers, Ferranti and British Aerospce, than it was to cover a swathe of valuable airfields with a thin skein of elderly low-level missile cover. The system required a huge number of engineers, over 600 of them, whilst the missiles waited in the rain to be launched by grounded aircrew who had not fired a single rocket between them in a decade. Moreover, the aircrew/engineer mix had resulted in what was originally conceived as a mobile system (as used by the Army) morphing into a concreted-in static target. In the face of developing Soviet Fencers and Backfire bombers, it was not a very hard calculation to show that replacing fixed Bloodhound with mobile Patriot, using one-sixth of the man-power and one-sixtieth of the engineers, would give the Service a brand-new weapon that could move about and hide until required and then fire ripples of missiles against targets in multiple directions simultaneously, without having to lock one ground radar to one target at a time. In addition, Patriot could intercept ballistic missiles like the Scud, prolific in Soviet client states like Iraq and Syria. Over a ten-year period, its introduction into service promised to save hundreds of millions of pounds. Naturally, whispers of the possible demise of Bloodhound made a certain Rock Ape outsider in the grounded aircrew air defence world very unpopular, especially as Patriot was slated to be manned by the RAF Regiment.

The two projects I flew with the Deputy Director Air Defence, Group Captain John May, and subsequently Rick Peacock-Edwards, together with fellow RAF Regiment officer Wing Commander Ron Smith, who now filled John May's old job in Air Plans, were to do with Skyguard, Patriot, Starstreak and Rapier. The first was to buy two more Skyguards and make two squadrons out of one, under the command of a wing commander, to defend two airfields instead of just one. Then, in a further brainstorm, to use our three excess Oerlikon guns, buy five more and marry them up with four gun-less Skyguards of the German Air Force, which were being solely used to police NATO aircraft breaking low-flying rules over Germany, and to form a joint Anglo-German unit, effectively a third reserve-manned squadron, to use on our two most important forward airfields in Germany. This latter plan specifically was endorsed in a personal heads of government meeting between Margaret Thatcher and Herman Kohl. The second was to buy Patriot, supplemented with this bigger Skyguard force and a host of low-cost, Mach-3 shoulder-launched missiles, the Shorts Starstreak, to be manned by Auxiliaries, along with a more spread-out Rapier, that together would create a layered, in-depth, multi-system, ground-based air defence covering all of our top priority airfields as a large, overall, cost-saving measure brought about by retiring the past-its-sell-by date Bloodhound.

The first and easiest of all these steps to take was the purchase of two new Skyguards, which enabled the single squadron at RAF Waddington to be expanded and split into two squadrons: 2729 continued to protect its home base, the other, 2890, protected the nearby fighter base of RAF Coningsby. Maintenance and training was centralized at wing level, making 1339 Wing a wing commander command appointment to mirror the wing headquarters of the Regular RAF Regiment Rapier and light armoured squadrons, and John Collins was to be its warrant officer engineer. That much all happened under my direction.

Bloodhound was finally consigned to history by means of a budgetary savings measure agreed between the directors of Air Plans and Air Defence, to be replaced by Patriot, which Ron, in his last act before leaving the RAF, pushed to the top of the Air Force's acquisition list. However, by the time it was due to be executed, the Berlin Wall had crumbled, the Soviet Union's iron grip on Eastern Europe had disintegrated and the need for the new weapons evaporated. Indeed, such was the speed of strategic change that Buccaneers, Jaguars and even brand-new Harrier jets vanished and the Royal Navy's aircraft carriers were sold off. Thus, the only tangible, physical evidence of my second trajectory through the MoD was the formation of that extra Skyguard squadron; it was time to take up the offer of an exchange posting with the United States Air Force Security Police in Abuquerque, New Mexico, experience two years of the American Dream and constitutional right to the pursuit of happiness under a General Frank Martin, who was to become a lifelong friend and mentor.

The Skyguard-Oerlikon Wing continued up to 1993, by which time East and West Germany were being reunited and 1339 Wing was disbanded. A rump of its trained anti-aircraft personnel were converted to man the retiring Rapier B1 models under the command of our first female RAuxAF Regiment officer, Flying Officer Louise Boulton, to provide NATO declaration continuity whilst the Regular Rapier squadrons undertook delivery and trained up on the new, third generation of Rapier Field Standard C, a completely new weapon system. With the final retirement of Rapier Field Standard B, the rump of the Auxiliary air defence force disbanded.

In a further contraction of the Armed Forces, the RAF Regiment lost all its third generation Rapiers to the British Army and came out of ground-based air defence altogether for the first time since 1940. In 2020 Rapier itself was retired after around fifty years of service. In the meteoric further shrinking of all three Services, Sky Sabre entered service in the British Army to replace Rapier. It is a land-based version of the Royal Navy's new anti-aircraft, anti-ballistic missile and anti-drone missile system, itself sharing a core of commonality with a new RAF advanced medium range air-to-air missile. Vertical launching out of a sealed box should keep the missiles nice and clean and dry for years. Its current deployment includes the Falkland Islands and Ukraine. Hopefully, our three Services are now more effectively integrated in ground-based anti-aircraft defence than they were in the 1982 campaign. At least as a nation we also once again own two powerful, brand new super-aircraft carriers with the absolutely latest jump jet, the F-35, but even those ships cannot move forward as quickly as the Royal Air Force in establishing a well-defended expeditionary airfield in a far-off land, a Joint Service concept the RAF Regiment should be locked into.

If the Armed Forces shrink any further, in the inter-Service rice bowl battles that are sure to follow, the challenge will be for the Royal Air Force to retain its RAF Regiment integrated infantry force if it is to avoid once again becoming a collection of uniformed technicians in the prime of life guarded by detachments of British Army soldiers who are quite without any understanding of fighting on the ground in a highly technical, aeronautical working environment.

The actual ex-Argentine Skyguard radars, however, still have the last word. The Skyguard-Oerlikon weapon combination has been purchased by more than forty countries, some of which are potentially hostile to the West, including China, which purchased a few fire units and then cloned entire regiments of Oerlikon twin 35mm cannon and Skyguard radars into service, reminiscent of the way that the Russians in the 1950s bought a sample of British Whittle jet engines and cloned them for their MiG15 jet fighters. For this reason the now ex-RAuxAF Regiment Skyguard radars remain in RAF service forty years on from the Falklands Campaign and will continue to provide NATO aircrews with training in flak radar avoidance and electronic counter-measures for as long as those countries continue to possess Skyguard-Oerlikon air defences. All in all, not a bad outcome for a battlefield gun-grab of half a lifetime ago.

What has surprised, pleased and humbled me most, however, has been the follow-up four decades of camaraderie and friendship of this amazingly diverse group of male and female gunners-cum-civilians across all ranks, Auxiliary and Regular, into whose laps the war booty of the Falklands Campaign fell. Indeed, so much time has now passed that some of these never-to-grow-old boy and girl gunners have passed away. Yet they still keep together in perpetuity, in an

Oerlikon cluster of individual memorial stones in our RAF Regiment Corps Memorial Garden at the National Memorial Arboretum. The first female operational Oerlikon gunner to pass away, Karen Sargent, already has her name set in stone there. She is joined by several others, sadly added to each year, who include our prematurely deceased young officer 'POLS' Lance Saxby, Warrant Officer Andy Robertson, Flight Sergeant John Kavanagh, and gunners Fred Abbott, Peter Lavelle Senior, Sid Robinson and founder Second World War 2729 Squadron members Squadron Leader Ron Snashall MC and Leading Aircraftsman David Lumpkin, while the memorial to our sister squadron commander, OC 2890, Squadron Leader John Gollins, rests on one side of our Honorary Air Commodore, Sir Rex Hunt; I personally have already reserved my OC 2729 memorial place on Sir Rex's other side. A distant Argentine military misadventure drew us all into one fiercely good fighting formation and here our names will lie together in military comradeship for eternity.

Muerte Al Enemigo Que Vuela
Per Ardua

The Malvinas March and the Sonnet of Morgan and Drake

Nuestras Malvinas Marcha
(Letra y Música de Prudencio Lacámara)

Los Ingleses pretendian
el quitarnos Las Malvinas
Dios y la jente ha querido
que eran y son Argentinas

Y sgamos el camino
que nos abrios San Martin
con amor y Patriotismo
los que vivimos aquy

Hace 150 anos
los Inglerses invadian
ese lugar tan hermoso
nuestras queridas Malvinas

Archipiélago Argentino
que siemre te hemos nombrado
el 2 de Abril muy contentos
por haberte rescatado.

[*Dedico al Batallón 121 de Rosario 2 de Abril del anno 1982*]

The Malvinas March

The English wanted to take away the Malvinas [that] God and the people have wanted, who were and are Argentinian

And let's go the way that San Martin opened for us, with love and patriotism [of] those of us who live here

150 years ago the British invaded such a beautiful place, our beloved Malvinas

Argentine Archipelago [is what] we have always named you, for having rescued you very happily, on April Secondo.

[With thanks to the late Flight Lieutenant Guy Bransby RAF Regiment, Her Majesty's Interrogator, for the translation.]

* * *

Soneto de los Morgan y los Drake

Allá va Margarita 'LA ARROGANTA'
La heredera del caco, del pirate,
Del cerdo, del gusano y de la rata
Pretendiendio llevarnos por delante.

Menopáusica ruin y petulante,
Ninforma caliente como gata
Te vamos a tocar la serenata
Que splaque tu furor ten desbordante

Álla va, con su trompa de elefante,
Agrediendo con toda su bravata
Creyéndose 'DE HIERRO', es de hojalata,

Prototipo de 'neura' delirante
BAJATA LA BOMBACHA MARGARITA
QUE EN BOLAS BAILARAS 'LA CUMPARSITA'.

Sonnet of Morgan and Drake

There goes Margaret 'The Snob',
The descendant of shit, pirates,
Pigs, worms and rats,
Pretending to be one of us.

Menopaused ruin and petulant one,
Nymphomaniacally hot like a cat,
We are going to play you a serenade
To placate your overflowing fury.

There she goes with her elephant's trunk,
Aggressive with all her bravado,
Believing herself 'Of Iron', instead of tin,
An example of a neurotic delirious one.

PULL DOWN YOUR KNICKERS MARGARET
SO THAT WITHOUT YOUR CLOTHES YOU
WILL DANCE 'LA CUMPARISTA' [A very rude dance]

Appendix II

Letters from Argentine Children

These letters, literally picked up off the ground around abandoned Argentine positions, came franked with the handstamps of the different primary schools that sent them, indicating some kind of national official direction of class activity. Postage to the military in *Las Malvinas* was, of course, free, just as it is to our own armed forces in the field. They were either addressed to *El Gobernador* or to *Soldedos Argentinos en las Malvinas*; a sample of each is below.

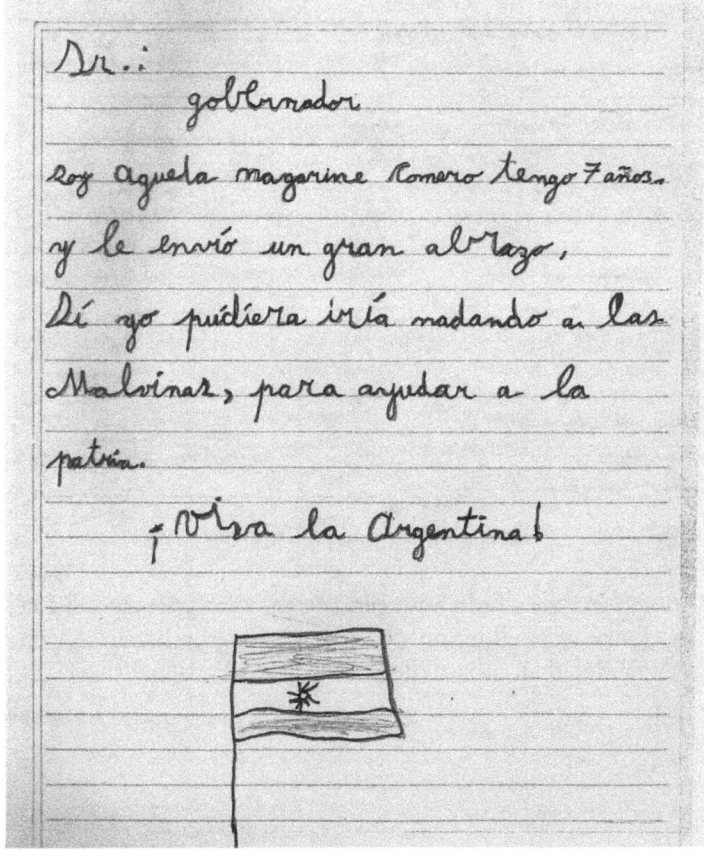

A letter to the Governor.

A letter to an Argentine soldier.

There was something very sad about picking up such correspondence, reminding one of the Duke of Wellington's comment after the Battle of Waterloo that the only thing sadder than a battlefield won was a battlefield lost.

Inventory of Argentine Anti-Aircraft Weapons Captured in the Falklands

Armada

- 3 × British Short Brothers Tigercat missile launchers
- 12 × Hispano HS 831 30mm one-man guns
- 1 × Israeli Rasit short-range local alerting radar

Fuerza Aerea

- 1 × Westinghouse TPS-43 mobile long-range surveillance radar
- 3 × British Short Brothers Tigercat missile launchers
- 1 × Oerlikon-Contraves *Superfledermaus* gun fire-control radar
- 3 × Oerlikon GDF 001 twin 35mm guns
- 1 × Israeli Elta short-range local alerting radar
- 6 × Rheinmetall twin 20mm one-man guns
- An indeterminate number of Soviet Strela shoulder-launched missiles

Ejercito

- 6 × Oerlikon-Contraves Skyguard fire-control radars
- 12 × Oerlikon GDF 002 twin 35mm guns
- 1 × Franco-German Roland road trailer containerized missile launcher
- 8 × Hispano HS 831 30mm one-man guns
- 3 × Rheinmetall twin 20mm one-man guns

La Gaçeta Argentina, Anno 1, Nro 1

"LA GACETA ARGENTINA"

EJERCITO ARGENTINO, 08 de mayo de 1982   AÑO 1-Nro 1

CREACION. Puerto Argentino - Por orden del señor Comandante Militar Conjunto de las Islas Malvinas, Grl Br D MARIO BENJAMIN MENENDEZ, se creó en esta capital "LA GACETA ARGENTINA", designándose como Director de la misma al Capellán Castrense FRAY SALVADOR SANTORE OP y como Subdirector al Capitán D FERNANDO ORLANDO RODRIGUEZ MAYO, Oficial de Prensa de la Gobernación Militar.

EDITORIAL: LA GACETA ARGENTINA tiene un por que: cubrir una necesidad de tipo informativo entre los miembros de las Fuerzas Armadas. Por consiguiente nuestro primer objetivo será informar la verdad, que viene de lo real y da un nuevo sentido histórico y social a estas tierras malvinenses.

La falsedad en las informaciones crea ilusiones absurdas o imaginarias, por el contrario la misión informativa limpia, muestra horizontes y mantiene en nosotros el alerta viril de la lucha justa y noble que hemos emprendido y que no debe cesar.

RESEÑA DE LOS HECHOS OCURRIDOS ENTRE EL 01 AL 07 DE MAYO DE 1982.

1. 01 MAY 82

0440 Hs. Un avión enemigo no identificado ataca el aeropuerto de PUERTO ARGENTINO, arrojando dos bombas de 450 Kgs cada una.

0734 Hs. Explota en aeropuerto PUERTO ARGENTINO una bomba con retardo arrojada durante la primera incursión del enemigo.

0740. Hs. Se produce un segundo ataque del enemigo con cuatro aviones SEA-HARRIER sobre el aeropuerto de PUERTO ARGENTINO y posiciones del BIM 5, con cohetes y cañones.

0825 Hs. Tercera incursión aérea del enemigo con 4 aviones SEA-HARRIER que arrojaron bombas sobre el aeropuerto de PUERTO ARGENTINO, produciendo destrozos e incendios en las instalaciones del mismo. Un avión SEA-HARRIER es derribado con el disparo de un misil superficie-aire ROLAND y otro SEA-HARRIER es derribado por los cañones bitubo de 35 mm y/o un disparo de un misil superficie-aire TIGER CAT.

0815 Hs. El enemigo ataca el aeropuerto de DARWIN con cuatro aviones SEA-HARRIER con bombas y cañones. Resultado del ataque son destruidos en tierra dos aviones propios PUCARA.

1520 Hs. Un helicóptero enemigo ataca a una de las lanchas patrulleras de la PREFECTURA NAVAL ARGENTINA, sin éxito.

1600 Hs. Tres naves de guerra enemigas bombardean con fuego naval a la posición del RI 25 sin causar bajas de importancia.

1620 Hs. La FUERZA AEREA ARGENTINA ataca con aviones DOUGLAS A-4 a buques de guerra enemigos en la zona del canal CHOISEUL, produciendo daños mayores en un buque y daños menores (sin poder precisar el grado de destrucción) en las otras dos naves. El enemigo se dió a la fuga.

En estas acciones de combate el enemigo abatió 2 aviones propios (un A-4 y un CAMBERRA), salvándose los dos tripulantes del avión CAMBERRA.

1700 Hs. En un combate aéreo se produjo un choque en vuelo entre un MIRAGE III (propio) y un SEA HARRIER (enemigo), destruyéndose en el impacto ambos aviones. Se recuperó con vida el piloto argentino, se desconoce el paradero del piloto enemigo.

1730 Hs. La lancha pesquera FORREST tripulada por personal de la Marina de Guerra, rechaza un ataque de un helicóptero enemigo artillado SEA LYNX y lo persigue hasta que el mismo huye, La lancha rechaza el ataque haciendo fuego con los fusiles y las pistolas de su tripulación.

2100 a 2145 Hs. El enemigo hace fuego naval (cañoneo) sobre la zona de SUPPER HILL produciendo un muerto y cinco heridos.

2300 Hs. El enemigo repite el fuego naval sobre SUPPER HILL.

2. 03 MAY 82.

0130 Hs. Cuando el aviso ARA SOBRAL se dirige al rescate de los pilotos de un avión propio CAMBERRA abatido, es atacado por tres helicópteros enemigos (un SEA KING y dos SEA LINK). El enemigo es rechazado y en la acción mueren el comandante de la nave y 7 tripulantes. La nave logra alcanzar un puerto continental argentino.

1530 Hs. Un avión propio, AEROMACCHI 339, de la Marina de Guerra (ARA) se pierde en acción, falleciendo su piloto.

1600 Hs. El crucero ARA BELGRANO es hundido por un submarino enemigo, el cual le disparó dos torpedos. Se logran rescatar más de 800 hombres de una tripulación de 1.000. Se continúan las acciones de rescate.

3. 04 MAY 82.

0530 Hs. Un avión enemigo no identificado bombardea el aeropuerto de PUERTO ARGENTINO.

1130 Hs. Dos aviones de ataque de la Marina de Guerra SUPER ETENDART atacaron la escuadra enemiga con misiles aire-mar EXOCET, disparados desde una distancia de 32 Kms del blanco, hundiendo al destructor misilístico SHEFFIELD por impacto directo en el centro de la nave, falleciendo 97 hombres de sus 300 tripulantes. En la misma acción otro misil EXOCET produjo daños en otra nave no identificada.

1310 Hs. Tres aviones enemigos SEA HARRIER atacan a la Fuerza de Tarea Conjunta "CAPITAN GIACHINO" (DARWIN), siendo en el primer pasaje de los mismos derribados dos de ellos por el fuego de las piezas de artillería de defensa aérea. El Teniente Inglés NICHOLAS TAYLOR, piloto de uno de los aviones derribados, es enterrado con los honores militares reglamentarios en el cementerio de DARWIN.

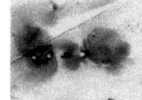

4. **06/07 MAY 82.**

Entre los días 06 y 07 de mayo han sido evacuados a COMODORO RIVADAVIA, todos los heridos durante las acciones de combate.

5. RESUMEN DE BAJAS DE PERSONAL HASTA LA FECHA:

	HERIDOS	MUERTOS
EJERCITO	8	---
MARINA	8	2
FUERZA AEREA	20	10
PREFECTURA NAVAL	1	---
TOTAL DE BAJAS:	37	12

6. NUESTRO BAUTISMO DE FUEGO

Los argentinos de ayer fueron capaces de cruzar los Andes y surcar los mares para dar la libertad a medio continente.

Los argentinos de hoy tenemos la tarea de reintegrar la parte de nuestro territorio arrebatado hace 149 años por Inglaterra.

En los corazones de nuestros hombres laten los mismos ideales de antaño. Nadie abandonó su puesto, Bajo las bombas o el fuego de los cañones cada uno cumplió con honor su deber.

Ahora el enemigo sabe de la precisión de nuestros fuegos, de la capacidad de nuestras armas, sabe que el juramento que hemos hecho no es palabra vana.

Cada hombre debe sentirse satisfecho, en la hora de la prueba ha triunfado.

Appendix V

Analysis of Aircraft Kill Claims by Argentina

Claims by military Junta official communiqué	Claims by Argentine Army and Air Force	Acknowledged losses by either side
[1 May] Communiqué 1 3 × Sea Harriers. 2 × Helicopters.	[1 May] 1 × Sea Harrier to 35mm.	[1 May] Sea Harrier ZA192 hit on return to carrier. 1 × Mirage I-019 own goal. 1 × Sea Harrier to Roland.
[2 May] Communiqué 23 2 × Sea Harriers. 6 × Sea Harriers damaged and probably fell into the sea.	[2 May] None.	[2 May] None.
[4 May] Communiqué 40 2 × Sea Harriers.	[4 May] 1 × Sea Harrier to 35mm Skyguard 3B GADA 601 at Ganso Verde.	[4 May] Sea Harrier XZ450 destroyed at Goose Green; pilot Lt Taylor RN killed.
[12 May] Communiqué 44 1 × Sea King Helicopter.	[12 May] 1 × Skyhawk C-248 own goal shot down by 35mm at Ganso Verde; pilot Lt Gavazzi killed.	[12 May] None.
[21 May] Communiqué 74 3 × Sea Harriers. 2 × Helicopters.	[21 May] 1 × Harrier GR3 to Blowpipe Patrulla de Commandos. 2 × Gazelle Helicopters to Small Arms.	[21 May] Harrier GR3 XZ972 destroyed; pilot Lt Glover captured. Gazelles XX441 and XX402 destroyed and crew killed. Skyhawk 665 destroyed by 35mm at Stanley after pilot ejected.
[22 May] Communiqué 78 1 × Sea Harrier.	[22 May] None.	[22 May] None.

Claims by military Junta official communiqué	Claims by Argentine Army and Air Force	Acknowledged losses by either side
[24 May] Communiqué 86 1 × Sea Harrier.	[24 May] None.	[24 May] None.
[25 May] Communiqué 87 3 × Sea Harriers.	[25 May] None.	[25 May] None.
[26 May] Communiqué 90 1 × Sea Harrier shot down by Coastguard *Rio Iguazá*. 2 × Sea King Helicopters shot down.	[26 May] None.	[26 May] None.
[27 May] Communiqué 91 1 × Sea Harrier shot down near Darwin.	[27 May] 1 × Harrier GR3 to 35mm Skyguard 3B GADA 601 at Ganso Verde.	[27 May] Harrier GR3 XZ988 destroyed at Goose Green; pilot Sqn Ldr Iveson ejects and evades capture.
[28 May] Communiqué 103 2 × Helicopters shot down.	[28 May] FAA Pucara shoots down 1 × Scout Helicopter.	[28 May] Scout XT629 shot down by Pucara; pilot Lt Nunn killed.
[29 May] No Communiqué None.	[29 May] 1 × Sea Harrier to 35mm Skyguard 2A GADA 601 at Stanley.	[29 May] None.
[30 May] Communiqué 110 2 × Harriers shot down. 1 × Harrier damaged.	[30 May] 1 × Harrier GR3 to 35mm Skyguard 2A GADA 601 at Stanley town.	[30 May] Harrier GR3 XZ963 hit by inert shell causing fuel leak; Pook ejects and rescued from sea.
[1 June] Communiqué 191 1 × Harrier shot down by AA guns.	[1 June] 1 × Sea Harrier shot down. 1 × Sea Harrier shot down at Stanley.	[1 June] Sea Harrier XZ456 destroyed; Flt Lt Mortimer ejects and rescued.
[6 June] No Communiqué None.	[6 June] None.	[6 June] Gazelle XX377 own goal by HMS *Cardiff*; Maj. Forge, SSgts Baker and Griffin and LCpl Cockton all killed by ship missile.
Totals: 29 Harriers, 9 Helicopters.	**Totals: 8 Harriers, 1 Scout Helicopter, 3 Argentine own goals.**	**Totals: 5 Harriers destroyed, 2 Harriers damaged, 1 Gazelle own goal.**

Notes

1. U-570 was caught on the surface on 27 August 1941 by an RAF Coastal Command Hudson of 269 Squadron flown by Squadron Leader James Thompson, who dropped four 250lb (110kg) depth charges on the submarine as it attempted to crash-dive. One detonated just 9m from the boat. Thompson then machine-gunned the submarine until it ran up a white flag of surrender. He remained on station over the U-boat until it could be secured by a Royal Navy prize crew. Its capture yielded a wealth of intelligence, most importantly an intact Enigma code machine. The British also discovered that the U-boat could dive to almost twice the depth of British submarines; this resulted in the resetting of British depth-charge fuses to greater depths. The submarine served as HMS Graph until 1944. [From Wikipedia]
2. Argentine Junta Official Communiqués 18, 24, 26 and 29.
3. Annexo 66, Conflicto Malvinas, Tomo II, Abreviaturas, Annexos y Fuentes Biblograficas [Annex 66, The Malvinas Conflict, Vol. 2: Abbreviations, Annexes and Bibliography].
4. Pook, Sqn Ldr J., MBE DFC, *RAF Harrier Ground Attack Falklands* (Pen & Sword Books, 2007), p. 161: 'on talking to Scots Guards, "Oh yes, we all fired at you, Sir – both times round!"'
5. One of two Argentine Coastguard vessels, its sister ship being the *Islas Malvinas*.
6. Pook, *RAF Harrier Ground Attack Falklands*, p. 70.
7. Murphy's First Law: If it can possibly go wrong, it will, eventually. Murphy's Second Law: When it does go wrong, it will be at such a time as to maximize the inconvenience.
8. Pook, *RAF Harrier Ground Attack Falklands*, p. 87.
9. Author's Note. For a comparative perspective, the Paras suffered just two more fatalities at Goose Green than the IRA had killed in the Warren Point ambush in Northern Ireland on 27 August 1979.
10. Bicheno, H. *Razor's Edge The Unofficial History of the Falklands War* (Orion Publishing, 2006).
11. *Schwerpunkt*. Literally translated as the 'bad point'. The term was coined by the 19th Century philosopher, Clauswitz, in his famous work declaring that war was simply an extension of politics by another means. In English we would say lynch pin or turning point: a point in a battle from which there was little chance of recovery.
12. In a final postscript about Piaggi's fine command, a few days later an Argentine conscript was enveloped in napalm when he set off a booby-trapped container and was shot dead in a mercy killing by a British Medical Corps staff sergeant. Then, nearly a month later Lance Corporal Limbu, the only Falklands casualty sustained by the Gurkhas, was killed by a grenade booby-trap, one of many such booby-traps left in soft drinks cans by the Argentinians under Piaggi's command. Later, as a POW in Ajax Bay, Piaggi complained about being accommodated in a sheep pen and was told by the Red Cross not to expect too much sympathy since it was the Argentinians who had sent tents for 4,500 men to the bottom of the Atlantic Ocean when they sank the MV *Atlantic Conveyor*.
13. Even the new replacement Harrier GR9 of the 1990s could not laser designate from the air. In Afghanistan the Harriers had to be paired up with 30-year-old ex-Royal Navy Buccaneers which carried a target-imaging TV camera with laser designator in an under-wing pod so that laser-guided bombs could be launched from well above flak height. It was this clumsy arrangement

which led to the sudden demise of both types in order to afford the latest American F-35 stealth aircraft for both the RAF and the RN for land and carrier use. Jointly manned F-35s are now embarked on HMS *Queen Elizabeth*.

14. Informe Ejercito Argentino Conflicto Malvinas Tomo II Abbreviaturas Annexos y Fuentes Biblliograficas: Annexo 69 Effects of Anti-Aircraft Fire Against Enemy Aviation.

15. Pook, *RAF Harrier Ground Attack*, p. 126.

16. In fact, these were two wrecked and much smaller Aermacchi fighters that were known about for some two weeks by 1 Squadron on board HMS *Hermes*. The Argentinians had cleverly placed sheet metal underneath their wings to create the impression from above that they were much larger aircraft; the Admiral, however, would take no risks and ordered the task to go ahead.

17. Wing Commander Loughborough's War Diary forms part of his book about 63 Squadron.

18. This counters the belief in other post-action writing that the Oerlikon guns were silenced by Harrier attack. The fire-control Skyguard, when it came into my hands, was absolutely riddled with so many small arms bullet holes that it was considered, upon recovery to the UK, to be beyond economical repair; these holes must be attributed to 2 Para and it follows that the Oerlikon gun crews had probably already abandoned their cannon under Para small arms fire, possibly having already run out of ready-use 35mm ammunition by the time the final three Harriers, which reported no radar detection or return fire, delivered their *coup de grâce* to the Goose Green garrison, precipitating its surrender the next day.

19. The differences between the 001 and 002 cannon were miniscule, the later model having a cage of wire sensors on the muzzle brakes so that accurate muzzle velocities of individual shells could be measured to update aim-off prediction as the barrels warmed up and shells slowed slightly down with firing, thus adding even more lethality and accuracy to the weapon in the radar-controlled firing mode. The later 005 model, then beyond the current RAF budget, reduced the gun crew to just one man, with a silent, on-board diesel generator, a laser range-finder and a digital computer which together made it independently as accurate as a radar-directed cannon, effectively tripling the number of targets a three-gun Skyguard fire unit layout could handle simultaneously.

20. One Oerlikon arrived at RAF Waddington with two seriously bent barrels looking very sorry indeed. I had the bent barrels taken off and welded together in the form of an X, a parody of the RAF Regiment's crossed rifles badge, and mounted them on the outside wall of my bunker office. That gun, and the other referred to by Kaye, I held at Waddington until I could staff a second wave of refurbishment and purchase two additional radars to split all the assets and form two squadrons to defend two airfields. Clearly some of the British toss-bombing achieved some useful random destruction of enemy assets: only a 1,000lb bomb could turn over a 6-ton cannon.

21. In operational use under radar control, the guns would typically have been fired for no longer than a one-second burst, which would put about ninety-six shells from three linked cannon, i.e. six barrels, in a box around the target, so Kaye's firing of 180 rounds from a single mount was actually a little over-enthusiastic and he sensibly stopped in time to prevent a 'cook-off', where a round explodes in the breech before it is safely locked shut, an event that is seriously dangerous to the crew.

22. Not the actual figure, as prices are commercially-in-confidence.

23. Again, an illustrative ball-park figure.

24. When I served at RAF Abingdon, a radio mast was needed in Singapore that was longer than the cargo hold of our then largest transport aircraft ever, the Belfast. In the end the movers removed the pilot's windshield, threaded the mast through, all the way back into the deepest recess of the tail, replaced the windscreen, sent the plane on its way and waited. After two days a signal message arrived back on base: 'OK, we surrender. How did you get the fucking thing in?' A very competitive lot, the movers!

25. In the so-called peace dividend of savage defence cuts and inter-Service battles of who does what, the Army were to claim back all Rapiers from the RAF Regiment when the need for Rapier

defence of airfields in Europe and the UK evaporated with the end of the Cold War, the same event that retired the Oerlikons in the early 1990s. As a nation, we no longer mothball and store long procurement time equipment against a rainy day as we did earlier.

26. The Ordnance Board is tasked with ensuring that British ammunition design is absolutely safe to use, does not go off when dropped or explode prematurely on firing, and functions everywhere from Arctic to jungle to desert without fail. The Argentinians ordered their ammunition to their own specification, hence the task of bringing British-made 'foreign' ammunition into the British regulatory sphere.

27. Full Monty. No, not the popular film! Those who have read Field Marshal Montgomery's memoirs will recall that Monty would give his orders to his staff and commanders at tea time, go to bed early at 6pm, rise at 2am and have a full English breakfast with all the trimmings, known to his officers as 'the full Monty', before he went out to the front line to lead and inspire his troops and keep Rommel on the run.

28. The MoD so-called Main Building is actually originally the Air Ministry Building, constructed with great foresight to be capable of managing a million-strong Air Force in the forthcoming Second World War. It had a weather station on the top floor from which originated the BBC's line 'and the temperature in London on the Air Ministry roof is ...'.

Index